Drama and Delight

The Life of
Verity Lambert

Drama and Delight
The Life of Verity Lambert

Richard Marson

Drama and Delight – The Life of Verity Lambert

This edition first published April 2015 by Miwk Publishing Ltd.
Miwk Publishing, 12 Marbles Way, Tadworth, Surrey KT20 5LW.

ISBN 978-1-908630-33-9

Copyright © Richard Marson 2015.

The rights of Richard Marson to be identified as the author of this work has been asserted in accordance with the Copyright, Designs and Patents Act 1988.

All rights reserved. No part of this publication may be reproduced, stored in or introduced into a retrieval system, or transmitted, in any form, or by any means (electronic, mechanical, photocopying, recording or otherwise) without the prior written permission of the publisher. Any person who does any unauthorised act in relation to this publication may be liable to criminal prosecution and civil claim for damages.

All photographs in this volume are subject to copyright and may not be reproduced without permission. A large number of these images were sourced from the University of Strathclyde Archive and from Verity Lambert's own collection. Other pictures supplied by: Linda Agran, Maggie Allen, BAFTA, Graham Benson, Rea Francis, Waris Hussein, Anthony Joseph, Kate Kagan, Ted Kotcheff, Lynda La Plante, Brenda Loader, June Mendoza, Mirrorpix, Robin Prichard, David Renwick, Rex Features, SFX Magazine/Future Publishing and Cinema Verity. We thank them all for digging out their albums and in some cases letting us undo no doubt very expensive framing.

A CIP catalogue record for this book is available from the British Library.

Cover and book design by Robert Hammond.

Typeset in Utopia and Trajan.

Printed in Great Britain by TJ International, Padstow, Cornwall.

This book is sold subject to the condition that it shall not, by way of trade or otherwise, be lent, re-sold, hired out, or otherwise circulated without the publisher's prior consent in any form of binding or cover other than that in which it is published and without a similar condition including this condition being imposed on the subsequent purchaser.

www.miwkpublishing.com
This product was lovingly Miwk made.

CONTENTS

Acknowledgements ... *9*

Introduction ... *13*

An Only Child ... *19*

Piss and Vinegar ... *35*

Adventures in Time and Space ... *55*

Do You Dig Me? ... *83*

The Door of Opportunity ... *103*

Bucksey's Bird ... *123*

Votes for Verity ... *145*

She Who Must Be Obeyed ... *173*

I Could Be So Good For You ... *199*

On the Rocks ... *221*

Leading Lady ... *241*

She's Out ... *263*

Sunburnt ... *287*

Onwards and Sideways ... *313*

Plentysomething ... *337*

Epilogue ... *363*

Appendix ... *373*

Bibliography ... *378*

To my sister Deborah

who has given me a lifetime of unconditional love

ACKNOWLEDGEMENTS

The following spoke to me about their memories of Verity and many were extraordinarily generous, accommodating my follow-up questions and, in several cases, reading drafts of the various chapters as I sought to refine them:

Maggie Allen, Linda Agran, Michael Aitkens, Jack Andrews, Peter Ansorge, Moira Armstrong, Dame Joan Bakewell, Robert Banks Stewart, the late Christopher Barry, Graham Benson, Dr Laurence Blonstein, Sharon Bloom, Peter Bowles, Lord Melvyn Bragg, Patricia Brake, Sheila Brennan (Savory), Susie Bruffin, Colin Bucksey, Chris Burt, Jeremy Bulloch, Anna Callaghan, Ruth Caleb, Jenne Casarotto, James Cellan Jones, Esta Charkham, Emma Cherry (Rolf), Ted Childs, Judy Cornwell, Peter Cregeen, Rosemary Crowson (Skinner), Robin Dalton, John Dark, Alan Davies, Russell T Davies, Jacqueline Davis, Eileen Diss, Clive Doig, Nancy Dowd, Graham Easton, Russell Enoch, Geoff Feld, Michael Ferguson, the late Rex Firkin, John Flanagan, Carole Ann Ford, Henry Foster, Sir Paul Fox, Rea Francis, John Frankau, Donald Fraser, Stephen Frears, Christine Gernon, Guy Gilks, Jack Gold, the late Johnny Goodman, John Gorrie, Sir Michael Grade, Tamsin Greig, Trevor Griffiths, Tanika Gupta, Gareth Gwenlan, Piers Haggard, Sheila Hancock, Freddie Ross Hancock, Barry Hanson, Valerie Hardy, Juliet Harmer, Gerald Harper, the late Michael Hayes, Sally Head, Marilyn Heller (Gross), Jill Horwood (Sampson), Waris Hussein, Sir Jeremy Isaacs, Tina Jamieson, Marilyn Johnson, Sandy Johnson, Anthony Jones, Tony Jordan, Dr Anthony Joseph, Kate Kagan, Jenny King, Paul Knight, Ted Kotcheff, Suri Krishnamma, Lynda La Plante, Annabel Leventon, Michael Lindsay-Hogg, Maureen Lipman, Douglas Livingstone, John Lloyd, Brenda Loader, Pamela Lonsdale, Sydney Lotterby, Joanna Lumley, Colin MacCabe, Emma Mager, Felicity Marshall, Richard Martin, Val McCrimmon, Andrew McCulloch, David Medway, Paul Mendelson, Ann Mitchell, Christopher Morahan, Judy Morris, Reggie Nadelson, Jean Naggar, Maureen O'Brien, Michael Palin, Adele Paul (Winston), Viviane Phillips, Peter Purves, Lord David Puttnam, Alvin Rakoff, Peter Ransley, David Renwick, June Roberts, Philip Saville, Fred Schepisi, Howard Schuman, Anne Summerton (Mills), George Taylor, Brian Tesler, Pam Tinero, Garth Tucker, Margaret Turner (Toley), Kenith Trodd, Beryl Vertue, Fay Weldon, Joy Whitby, Katharine Whitehorn, Hugh Whitemore, Kath Williams, Betty Willingale, Herbert Wise, Jean-Pierre Worms and Robert Young

I received invaluable email and written contributions from: Jonathan Alwyn, Sir David Attenborough, Daniel Barry, Susan Belbin, John Finch, Jeremy Fox, Jonathon Green, Lesley Judd, Raymond Menmuir, Linda and Vernon Layton (who were unfailingly generous with their time and effort), Jonathan Llewellyn, Jonathan Powell, Peter Prince, James Purefoy, David Reid, Martin Shubik, Jeremy Swan, Jacqueline Tong and John Walbeoffe.

Special mention must go to several individuals for their particular kindness and help. Anna Callaghan dealt with all my numerous questions and requests with incredible efficiency, speed and good humour. Kate Kagan made a multitude of excellent suggestions over many months and was always wonderful company. Howard Schuman was both thoughtful and amusing and put me in touch with his Stateside friends June Roberts and Verity's ex-husband, Colin Bucksey. I'm especially grateful to both Colin and Ted Kotcheff for granting me frank and compassionate interviews about their relationship with Verity.

I'm indebted to the helpful agents and individuals who put me in contact with key contributors or who made the vital arrangements for interviews: Stanley Appel, Louis Barfe, Paul Bird at Mayday Management, Jenne Casarotto, Lesley Caton, Chris Chapman, Laifan Chung, Matt Clinch, Michael Cox, Natasha Cox (who has been an amazing ally throughout), Rob Craine, Vena Dacent and Liz Nelson at Conway van Gelder Grant Ltd, Liane Dalley, Andy Davidson, Linda Drew, Barnaby Eaton-Jones, Lucy Fairney at PBJ Management, Rea Francis, Ian Greaves, Toby Hadoke, Ruth-Maria Hammond, Barrie Heads, Christopher Hodson, Sally Hope, Nicholas Horne at Casarotto Ramsay and Associates Ltd, Tory Macdonald, Cheryl Miles of *Prospero* magazine, Keith Musselwhite, Andrew Orton, Gareth Owen at Infinite Artists, Carol Ormerod, Norah Perkins at Curtis Brown, Tracy Rashleigh, Alyson Ritchie, Douglas Schofield, Ros Sloboda, Nigel Stoneman, John Thompson, Richard Turley, Garry Tyler at Red Planet Pictures, Susan Vinnicombe, Jim Vogiatzis, Giles Smart and Danielle Walker at United Agents, Marcia Wheeler, Ralph Wilton and Gabriel Woolf.

Over the months that I was researching the book, I was lucky enough to be given access to a vast range of important archive material and my thanks go to the following: Rachel Pike from the University of Strathclyde Archives, custodians of the Verity Lambert collection, was both helpful and enthusiastic. Andrew Martin of BBC Information and Archives was meticulous in tracing Verity's surviving BBC television and radio appearances, as well as several rare examples of her work. Rory Clark sent me a copy of Verity's LWT play, *A.D.A.M.* and assorted editions of *TV Times* relating to her career, while Dominic May lent the glossy *Eldorado* press pack. Jessica Hogg at the BBC Written Archive Centre retrieved many production files from Verity's BBC programmes and the drama department in general. Jonathan Bignell from the University of Reading, Cultures of TV Drama research projects sent me a transcript of an interview that Verity gave at the faculty in 2004. Similarly, Simon Coward provided a recording of an extensive career-wide interview with Verity conducted less than a year before her death. Both Kevin Jon Davies and Ed Stradling located the rushes of interviews they shot with Verity for various documentaries and Jaz Wiseman sent me the commentaries Verity recorded for the Australian DVD releases of *Minder*. Andy Owen sent me both the transcript of the interview he conducted with Verity for his biography of Nigel Kneale, *Into the Unknown*, and the relevant chapters of the book itself. Oliver Wake contacted me with his exhaustive research into *Underground*, the fateful *Armchair Theatre* edition on which Verity worked. The ever-diligent Andrew Pixley unearthed scores of vintage newspaper items relating to Verity, while Richard Bignell was on the genealogical case with details of births, marriages and deaths. From Roedean School, Alison Gardiner, Editor of the *ORA Magazine*, Lois Johnson, the ORA Membership Secretary and Jackie Sullivan, the Archivist, did all they could to assist my research. Sharon Bloom produced two huge boxes with Verity's own press cuttings files from the 1960s and much Cinema Verity material besides. Further precious photographs and personal documents were lent or located by Maggie Allen, Mark Ayres, Graham Benson, Sharon Bloom, Anna Callaghan, Judy Cornwell, Robin Dalton, Waris Hussein, Dr Anthony Joseph, Kate Kagan and Brenda Loader. The artist June Mendoza went to a lot of trouble to facilitate my desire to reproduce her striking portrait of Verity in the book and to explain the work that went into it.

Marcus Prince and Dick Fiddy of the British Film Institute curated the Verity Lambert season tied into the launch of this book and were both enthusiastic supporters.

Patrick Mulkern, *Radio Times* writer and my best friend, very kindly found the time to proofread the manuscript, as did my mother, whose life's work was spent in journalism and publishing. Phil Ware also cast an eagle eye over everything written. The talented Robert Hammond did a fabulous job with the design. Ollie Marchon helped me stay in shape through the many weeks of sedentary typing.

It was my publisher Matt West who first asked me to write the book and all the way through he was ceaselessly encouraging and practical even when the pressure of the workload threatened to overwhelm me. His professionalism and brilliant sense of humour make him a pleasure to work with.

My children Rosy and Rupert are always in my head and my heart. They help to sustain me in everything I do. But I could not possibly have accomplished this task without the love and support of my wonderful wife, Mandy. Her tolerance, understanding and belief in me have never wavered and I'm lucky to have her.

INTRODUCTION

'I have been extremely lucky about being in the right place at the right time. That's luck. What you do with it afterwards isn't.'

Verity quoted in *The Daily Express*, 1982

When you consider her remarkable five decades as one of the major talents in British television drama, it is not surprising that soon after she died the BBC gave Verity Lambert the honour of an hour-long obituary, with the corny but appropriate title *Drama Queen*.[1] What is more curious is that it has taken so long for a biography to appear. Verity is referenced and talked about in many books and the memoirs of a gallery of famous names. She has been the subject of a play, given her name to a podcast and had a plaque unveiled in her memory at Riverside Studios. There is even a meeting room at the BBC named in her honour. In 1983, she was both the *Woman's Own* Woman of Achievement and the Veuve Clicquot Businesswoman of the Year[2]. She received the Alan Clarke BAFTA Award for Outstanding Contribution to Television, was admitted to the Royal Television Society Hall of Fame, granted an OBE and awarded a posthumous lifetime achievement award from Women in Film and Television. The television programmes and films for which she was responsible won her many further awards, both at home and internationally. In the ephemeral media landscape, much of her popular and prestigious output has achieved lasting significance and acclaim. Even her most notorious failure has a certain cult status.

One of the stand-out figures of her time, she deserves to be lauded, and her spectacular career analysed and acknowledged. Among the many friends who have contributed to

---

[1] Transmitted on BBC4 on 05.04.08. This was shown alongside a short selection of Verity's most celebrated programmes including *The Naked Civil Servant*, *Minder* and *Doctor Who*. The documentary was narrated by Sam Neill, one of Verity's favourite actors

[2] Awarded for her work at Euston Films throughout 1982

this book is the writer and broadcaster, Melvyn Bragg. 'I was looking through her formidable track record,' he says. 'It just goes on and on and it is astonishing. Up among the best in British television – innovative, varied and very bold. It was combustible creativity. I couldn't believe that she had done so much.'

'There was never anything second-rate, second-hand or derivative about anything she did,' says former controller of BBC1, Jonathan Powell. 'Verity paid instinctive and unerring attention to the needs of the audience but the results always came to the screen freshly minted and convincingly realised. She had an eye for the provocative and the innovative, she championed originality, but she was always accessible and entertaining.'

'She just had a magic touch,' adds television executive Michael Grade. 'She spoke up, she spoke her mind and guess what? She was usually right.'

'Hurricane Verity', as some nicknamed her, invariably held strong convictions, and was fearless in expressing them. In an era of deep inequality, her example to other women is striking and noteworthy. Once she earned her opportunity to prove her abilities, there was no hesitation. She always believed passionately in her projects, devoting herself utterly to them and channelling her powerful intellect to achieve a rare synthesis of commercial and critical success. Adept at spotting talent on both sides of the camera, she was willing to take creative risks and put her faith in the alchemy of the script. But she never lost her identity in her work, and her personality, joyful, generous, sybaritic, questioning, occasionally capricious, frequently volatile, continues to illuminate the memories of her friends. Friendship was another of her great gifts and she was eclectic in her choices. Once in her circle, such was her unusual loyalty and energy, usually it was only death that intervened.

While she was comfortable with what might be termed her public life, and rarely refused invitations to step into the professional limelight, she belonged to a generation that did not freely discuss their emotions. Even close friends have testified to the fact that she could be reserved and unwilling to talk about herself. But when she did, she never dissembled or found refuge in self-pity. Happily for any biographer, she was seldom elusive when it came to granting interviews and sharing her memories and opinions in print, on television or DVD commentaries. Like most of the great players on the British show business scene, she had a considerable ego and enjoyed recognition and acclaim. She also knew the value of such things for giving her continued relevance and currency. Sadly, she did not live to witness the unusual accolade of being herself transformed into a character in a major screenplay or to judge the results.

The film was *An Adventure in Space and Time*,[3] Mark Gatiss' affectionate and lovingly made story about the origins of Verity's first and defining success, *Doctor Who*. The actress given the task of playing Verity, Jessica Raine, told Patrick Mulkern of *Radio Times*: 'She was very strong-willed, very compassionate and very warm....a really classy woman.

---

[3] Transmitted on BBC2 on 21.11.13

When you first hear the name and hear what she did, you think, "Wow, she must have been a real ball-buster." But actually that would have been a boring way to play her because there's so much more with the warmth and vulnerability that comes with that. Walking into a building where everyone is saying she probably slept her way to get there.'

The drama was generally well received but, as well as the millions of viewers intrigued to immerse themselves in Gatiss' fairy tale, many of Verity's friends and *Doctor Who* colleagues were watching too. Perhaps inevitably, they watched with a critical eye, struggling to recognise the Verity they had known as the woman portrayed on screen.[4]

'I don't think he got the measure of Verity,' says her long-term creative collaborator, the director Moira Armstrong. 'I think if she had seen it, she would have been very irritated. She had a highly developed sense of humour and could be quite witty. The thing about Verity was that she could be as chummy and flirty as you like but underneath all that she was always in control. The wardrobe department didn't do her justice either. They dressed her in such a demure fashion whereas Verity had money and dressed with style and flair. She was not beautiful but she was striking, unlike pretty-pretty Jessica Raine, who didn't have the star quality necessary.'

'I wasn't too convinced by Jessica Raine as Verity,' agrees actor Russell Enoch, who remained in touch with Verity years after they had worked together on *Doctor Who*.

'She had no presence at all,' sniffs Maggie Allen, who was one of the secretaries on that first *Doctor Who* series. 'I didn't recognise Verity in that performance. She never looked scared and nervous like that.'

'Too nice, too soft,' observes actress Carole Ann Ford, who was another of the regular cast in *Doctor Who*.

'Pretty and prim and rather soft,' echoes director and good friend, Waris Hussein. 'Verity was very strong. She really disliked inefficiency and absolutely demanded certain things be done. That's what made her into who she was.'

'It was all too *serious*,' feels actress Maureen O'Brien, another whose career Verity launched when she cast her in *Doctor Who*. 'Verity was having fun and was much more gutsy and positive. One of the things you remember about her is her laughter – she laughed a lot.'

'If Verity had been around to see that, I think she would have wept with laughter,' says television executive Linda Agran, who, with Verity, turned Euston Films into a creative

---

[4] Although Gatiss undertook extensive research before writing the screenplay, he could not possibly have done justice to every character involved; some were even amalgamated into one. First and foremost, his version of Verity had to perform a dramatic function

powerhouse in the late 1970s and early 80s. 'Extraordinary. I mean, they cast one of those little nice midwives, a very coy little girl with Sydney Newman? It was just a riot.'

'I think she would have been flattered,' says director Alvin Rakoff, who knew Verity professionally and personally for 50 years. 'But she would have criticised it and made it more involving.'

Meeting and talking to so many of Verity's close friends and colleagues has been one of the great pleasures of writing this book. Their anecdotes were often hilarious, sometimes farcical, occasionally poignant but never pedestrian. Often, the memory of her and the reminder of her absence triggered tears. Sometimes there was anger, irritation or bitterness, usually on Verity's behalf. As I heard their stories, I began to understand that she clearly had a magpie approach to friendship, filling her life with clever, talented, sexy, funny and fascinating people. Their willingness to share some of their memories and emotions paid vivid tribute to the fun they enjoyed and the love that has survived her death.

I only met Verity Lambert once, by chance, in the bleak surroundings of the BBC's multi-storey car park at Television Centre, during the autumn of 2001.[5] Even with a ticket, places in the car park were precious and latecomers had to take their chances. On this particular morning, which was cold and wet, the only spaces were right at the very top, open to the elements. Once I'd parked, I resolved to make a dash for the lifts. But something stopped me. Out of the corner of my eye, I noticed a woman briskly locking her car door and when I looked closer, I immediately recognised her as Verity. She was laden with bags and looked a bit cross so I carried on my way. I was still waiting when she joined me and now she smiled and I thought, 'What the hell?' and introduced myself.

I wanted to commiserate with her because I, like many others, was annoyed that the BBC had just decided to renege on their agreement with Cinema Verity to dramatise Elizabeth Jane Howard's *Cazalet Chronicles* in their entirety. I explained that my wife and I had hugely enjoyed the books and thought the first series a really superb piece of work. We were very disappointed that there would be no more. The official line was that the series was expensive and had struggled to find an audience to justify this. Not too surprising when it had been held back and shown on Friday nights during the summer. Everyone in the BBC knew it actually had much more to do with a change of BBC1 controllers, Peter Salmon having given way to Lorraine Heggessey. New brooms rarely want the material they inherit, not least because, if successful, they can't claim the credit for it.

I thought that Verity would listen to my commiserations, acknowledge them politely and bustle off. Not a bit of it. Ten minutes later she was still in full flow, berating the way

---

[5] I was then the series producer of *Blue Peter*

that management didn't want to pay for serious drama, were no longer people of their word and that 'the women are often the worst'. She was really venting and I felt guilty for having so clearly touched a nerve. But I was glad, too, that I had had the opportunity to tell her how brilliant I thought the series had been. I might have added that, like so many millions of others, I had watched, enjoyed and admired much of her astonishing body of work.

Throughout the many months that I have worked on this biography, I've felt most the pressure, not of any deadline, but of the abstract thought that if Verity herself were to pick up the manuscript and give it her scrutiny, in which aspects would she find it wanting? What would the rewrites be and the cuts consist of? Now that I have finished trying to distil the essence of her life and work, to conjure up something of her personality and passions, I find it oddly reassuring that her own search for truthful and sensitive ways of reflecting the human condition continually inspired the man who sought to tell her story.

Richard Marson,
St Albans
2015

CHAPTER ONE
AN ONLY CHILD
1935–1955

'In some ways, I'm very competitive. I want to be good. But I never had any idea of what I was going to do at school, and after that I never had any thought or outline of what I was going to do.'

Verity to Sophia Watson, *Winning Women*, 1989

In the Europe of the 1930s, being Jewish very often meant a life of exclusion and a future without certainty. Anti-Semitism was a toxic lubricant in the engine firing both communism and fascism, the opposing forces that were steadily dominating East and West. British Jews may have been better off than most but they were not immune from the same unreasoning prejudice that made their race the scapegoat of nations. Throughout Britain, it was not hard to find those who believed the Jews to be a common enemy and so openly approved of the vicious State-sponsored racism being embraced on the continent.

In a world still scarred and sickened by the legacy of the first war, nothing seemed worse than that there should be another. 'The war to end all wars' was the phrase coined and quoted with fervour. Yet, increasingly, many believed that civilisation was again on the precipice of just such a calamity.

It was into this climate of mounting prejudice, international aggression and a deep concern for the fragility of peace that on 27 November 1935, a baby girl was born in 63 Fitzjohn's Avenue, the Hampstead home of an affluent Jewish couple, Stanley and Ella Lambert. Whatever misgivings her parents may have felt about the world into which they had brought her, their daughter, whom they named Verity Ann, was adored from the moment she arrived. As with all babies who are longed for, she represented hope for the future and was all the more precious because the Lamberts had already suffered the agony of losing their first child, a stillborn daughter. The tragedy necessarily cast a long shadow over the months leading up to Verity's birth and her parents' relief at her robust good health can only be imagined.

Verity is an old French name, meaning truth, and this turned out to be an apt choice as two of Verity's defining characteristics were her honesty and directness. On the few occasions when she allowed herself to deviate from the literal truth there were generally good reasons, as we shall see.

Materially, she wanted for nothing, but neither was she spoilt or over-indulged. Both of her parents could be strict if necessary and, keen that their daughter should be a lady, they insisted on good manners and behaviour. Yet allied to their rules and expectations was the constancy of their love and affection, which Verity instinctively reciprocated. This gave her the solid foundations for a lifetime of confidence, self-belief and security. In the often tortured, and torturing, world of show business, this was to give her a powerful and unusual advantage over many of her colleagues.

Stanley Lambert was a laudable role model for his daughter. A successful chartered accountant, he was a tall, hard-working man with natural high spirits and plenty of easy charm. He loved travelling, opera and golf and had done well for himself. He was born in 1909, to a working-class family (on Stanley's birth certificate, his father's occupation is listed as a dock labourer). Professionally and socially, he propelled himself upwards with his intelligence and work ethic. His wife, Ella Lambert, seven years older, was known as Corrie (derived from her unusual middle name, Corona). Corrie was much the quieter of the couple and lived rather in her imposing husband's shadow, sometimes offering him secretarial assistance but otherwise devoting herself to the unremitting labours of housewife and now mother. Verity loved her mother deeply but was undoubtedly, and perhaps predictably, a daddy's girl. She inherited Stanley's exuberance and sense of fun, which mirrored his own, and he was delighted with her obvious natural intelligence.

Unfortunately, as with many bright children, there was a tendency towards a certain indolence, especially when it came to those lessons in which she was less interested. However, no persuasion was needed to get the young Verity to read and by the time she was four, she was fluent. She later said that the fact that she was a 'fanatical' reader as a child was a side-effect of being an only child.[1] About this, she never expressed any sense of regret. One of her lifelong qualities was a lack of sentiment about herself. It is interesting to speculate what the impact of siblings might have been; other children for her to be compared with and to compete against.

No matter how much he loved his daughter, Stanley always made it perfectly clear that

---

[1] Quoted in *Women with Attitude* (see bibliography)

he had hoped to have a son. It would be unlikely for a man of his generation for that ambition to have simply melted away. Perhaps after the dreadful experience of losing their first baby, the Lamberts decided not to tempt fate again. Perhaps they did try but it was not possible. Just as credibly, many parents at this time avoided having children while the international situation remained so bleak and threatening. After the war, Corrie would have been too old.

The relative solitude of Verity's early years was mitigated by a thriving extended family on both sides. Eccentric characters abounded, gatherings of the clan were frequent, and these provided steady intervals of drama, fun and interest. There was the redoubtable Great-Aunt Sheba, who lost her husband in the devastating flu epidemic that spread throughout Europe at the end of the first war. Sheba had better luck in 1928, when she bet on a horse in the Stock Exchange Derby, won and overnight became a very wealthy woman. A whole slew of relations lived over in France. A certain glamour was attached to the memory of Verity's great-grandfather, Alphonse Lambert, who died in his hundredth year, and had at one time been chief designer at the famous Gobelins tapestry works, before settling in England. At the age of 16, Stanley had been sent to France to stay with relatives and learn the language and, with typical application, he returned fluent.

Stanley had an older brother, Baron, with whom he never enjoyed an easy relationship, perhaps in part because Stanley was the more successful of the two. He was closer to his first cousin Arthur Joseph (Arthur and Stanley's mothers being sisters) and one consequence of this was that Arthur's children, Anthony and Richard, though both younger, were occasional playmates for Verity when the families visited each other or shared holidays. 'Verity and I quarrelled incessantly,' remembers Anthony, who grew up to become a doctor, 'and our parents tore their hair out. Verity would say, "That's how you do it" – she could be quite combative – and I'd say, "No, it isn't."'[2]

Verity's upbringing was underscored with all the rituals and traditions of a well-heeled middle-class Jewish family. Her mother was quietly religious and Verity was taught Hebrew. All her life she treasured the beautifully illustrated copy of the Children's Haggadah given to her by her parents (inscribed, 'To Verity Ann, with best love').[3] Corrie Lambert was a practical person whose ambitions for her daughter were traditional and confined to the making of a suitable marriage. Carefully, she instructed her daughter in the arts and science of keeping house, and among these skills was the making of that Jewish culinary essential, chicken soup. But there was little emphasis on worship in the Lambert household and no strict observance. Even so, it pained Stanley when his older brother Baron transferred his religious allegiance to the Catholic church. Many years

---

[2] Verity was in touch with another cousin, Sylvia, right up to her death but alas I have been unable to trace her

[3] This is now in the possession of Verity's close friend, Kate Kagan

later, when Baron died, Stanley only agreed to attend the funeral out of a sense of familial duty. While he was making his way there, he chanced to come across a synagogue. Acting on a sudden conviction, he swiftly put on his kippa, the traditional Jewish head covering, and went inside, where he intoned the mourner's Kaddish, the Hebrew prayer for the dead. Only then did he make his way on to the official service, held in a Mayfair church. Stanley may not have been spiritual but this does not mean that he abnegated what he regarded as his responsibilities to the local Jewish community. For a time, he put his considerable gift for figures at the disposal of the Finchley United Synagogue, acting as their treasurer. For him, being Jewish was more a question of his cultural identity and strong sense of family than a matter of pure faith. It was tribal rather than spiritual. In this, as in other respects, Verity followed in his footsteps. To friends, years later, she would sometimes laugh and dismiss herself as a 'crap Jew'. When she was on location, those who shared her faith sometimes had to conceal their surprise at her undisguised enthusiasm for that perennial crew pick-me-up, a bacon sandwich. Yet undoubtedly, like her father, although she wasn't religious, being Jewish was never an irrelevance to Verity. Given the state of the world during her formative years, it scarcely could have been. Later, as she made her way within the entertainment industry, replete with a wealth of Jewish talent, she was to discover it had professional significance. Many of her show business friends and colleagues shared the same faith and it provided a reassuring shorthand, a point of contact and association.

When war was declared in 1939, Stanley Lambert volunteered to serve on submarines but he was quickly ruled ineligible for any of the armed services. The reason was that, as a young man, he had contracted tuberculosis. At this time, the disease was still virulent, widespread and without cure. Indeed, he was lucky to recover. His first cousin, Roland, who also caught TB, died from the infection while still only a teenager. Seeking an alternative means of contributing to Britain's war effort, Stanley was eventually put in charge of looking after various factories, which meant that he had to remain in London for the duration.

A favourite family story from this time has survived and was told to me by Verity's cousin, Dr Anthony Joseph. At the start of the war, before rationing had really begun to bite, the government asked car owners to economise by sharing their journeys. Stanley dutifully placed an advertisement in the local newspaper offering a lift into town for anyone sharing his route. Soon afterwards, a local man called him to accept the offer. He asked how much Stanley would want to be paid. 'Just the cost of the petrol...' came the reply. 'No, no,' argued the man, 'There's the overheads and the insurance and so on.' When Stanley hung up, he turned to his wife and exclaimed, 'Goyim! I offer him a price and he offers me twice the price!' 'Goyim' is the Hebrew word for nation and in slang terms is used to indicate someone not of the faith. When the other man put down his phone, he too turned to his wife and said, 'Goyim! He only asked half what he should have!' Only when they met did they realise that they were both Jewish.

Although four-year-old Verity was briefly sent to boarding school while her parents adjusted to the sudden upheaval in their lives and found somewhere relatively safe to live, she was unusually lucky by the standards of most wartime children. The Lamberts settled in Woking for the duration and were able to stay together throughout the uncertain and frightening years of war. Their bond, already strong, intensified. Verity attended the fee-paying Flexlands school in Cobham, Surrey, and was happy and did well there. Her memories of this time unsurprisingly echoed those of many of her contemporaries and they consisted of sirens and air-raid shelters, making toys from lumps of shrapnel and watching, fascinated, while her mother boiled up the crimson stubs of nearly spent lipsticks to make sure absolutely no precious carmine was wasted. As for millions of wartime British families, the cinema was a fixture of their lives, and they often went three times a week. There were other treats, too, theatre outings, birthday parties and a menagerie of assorted family pets including a dyspeptic terrier named Gerry, whom Verity cordially disliked. There were even holidays on a farm in Cornwall. 'I remember learning to milk cows,' Verity told *The Sunday Times*, 'skimming the cream and bicycling down the hills. It was just wonderful.'[4]

Despite the privations of the time, the Lamberts enjoyed a relatively comfortable and secure lifestyle. Verity was carefully protected from whatever terrors her parents must surely have felt at the prospect of defeat, a threat which loomed over every Jewish family in Britain. Although the full horror of the Nazi holocaust would only be uncovered after the war, most Jews had some sense of the fate that would befall them if the Allies were defeated.

Verity was nine when the glorious excitement of VE Day signalled an end to the carnage. It is perhaps surprising that, having stuck together throughout the uncertainty of the war, a year later, the Lamberts decided to send their daughter away to school. But with the pernicious evil of Nazism swept away, it was again possible to take a long-term view and both parents were anxious that their only child should learn to share. Wanting only the best for her, they chose what is still one of Britain's most elite boarding establishments for girls – Roedean. At first, Verity was excited at the prospect of boarding school. Like thousands of other little girls, she had eagerly devoured the stirring school stories of Angela Brazil, whose heroines were capable and independent young girls, making the most of the fun and adventure of school life. The reality was rather different.

Verity joined Roedean as a junior in the Michaelmas term of 1946. Approached by a long gravel driveway, the sprawling school buildings had the austere look of an old asylum. In her navy wool suit and matching felt hat with the school logo embroidered in red on the front, and her red-and-blue striped tie, the ten-year-old Verity found herself cloistered in a strange new world of housemistresses and prefects, trunks and tuck boxes, dormitories with rows of iron bedsteads and common rooms crammed with desks and hard chairs. For Verity, deposited here for weeks on end, surrounded by strangers, expected to find her way around and learn all kinds of new rules and rituals, it must have been an appalling shock. She could not remember her brief infant experience of boarding

---

[4] Quoted in *The Sunday Times* (07.01.96)

and so could draw no comfort from it. Any child who has been away to school can easily conjure up the dull, heavy sensation of homesickness that is the unwelcome accompaniment to the start of a challenging new life.

The school's position, set high on a cliff overlooking the main road from Brighton to Rottingdean, provided little defence from the sometimes harsh sea winds. The winters following the war were especially bitter and, with central heating the stuff of science fiction, chilblains were endemic. Stringent rationing robbed school meals of any variety – dried eggs and dripping on toast were standard fare. It was a Spartan existence for the girls whose parents could afford to pay for the privilege of sending them there. Mistresses were addressed to their face as 'Madam' but all had their own nicknames. The formidable headmistress, Miss Horobin, who on her appointment described herself to the local press as 'frightfully gamesy', was known to her charges as 'the Horror'. Most of the girls acquired their own nicknames too. Verity's was Tig. Although the precise reasons are lost in time, it is perhaps an abbreviation of Tigger, the bouncing tiger from A.A. Milne's *The House at Pooh Corner*, and a logical reflection of her natural effervescence. In 1948, Verity emerged into the senior school, where she was a member of House One. There were four houses in all, each diminutive communities in their own right. There was little privacy. Like many who undergo the boarding experience, Verity swiftly learnt to conceal her emotions when it suited her, as a natural form of self-protection. In years to come, her reticence to share or express her more private feelings would be noticed by many of her friends.

Everyone's schooldays leave traces and sometimes scars but boarding undoubtedly intensifies these. Whenever she was interviewed about her youth, Verity acknowledged that her experiences at Roedean taught her to be independent and self-reliant, and to work effectively in a group situation, something that was to stand her in good stead in the take-no-prisoners world of television. Also useful were some first-rate English lessons, which she enjoyed, and in which the teacher taught her to question a text thoroughly and examine the motivations of the characters involved. 'My English teacher never *told* you anything,' Verity recalled. 'She made *you* tell her what something was about. Even if you were wrong, she would say, "Why do you think that?" If you produced some idiotic reason, she would say, "That clearly is not right, is it?" And you would go back and try to find out what was right.'[5]

While recognising that all this was, albeit unintentionally, useful training for her future life, neither did Verity fail to point out that Roedean also left her with a powerful sense of otherness, of not fitting in or belonging. This had several aspects. Like most boarding schools of the period, there was terrific emphasis on games. Lacrosse loomed large. 'I always found the game very scary,' Verity told *The Times* in later life. 'I used to drop the ball and run in the other direction.'

---

[5] Quoted in *Women with Attitude* (see bibliography)

This was a modest assessment of her actual ability. Verity was, in truth, a creditable lacrosse player, ending her time at Roedean as Vice-Captain of her house team. She played in the First XI cricket team, too, for which she was also House Captain. But, in general sport bored her rigid and she detested having to brave the elements when, as was all too frequently the case, the weather was foul. After Verity's death, one of her contemporaries, Phebe Tyson, recalled, 'One afternoon, when the weather was so bad that games were actually cancelled, several of us were sitting in the boot hole discussing our futures. Verity announced firmly that she was going to be a beautician; silence – and then the rest of us fell about laughing. She was always a live wire.'[6]

Although clearly a girl of above average intelligence, Verity did not apply herself academically. 'I couldn't knuckle under,' she explained years later. 'My housemistress thought I was wilful, and so did my teachers. If you are an individual who doesn't fit the mould, you become a difficult person – which is not the same thing as being naughty. English boarding schools like to mould you into a pattern and for some reason I could not conform to that pattern.'[7]

Almost certainly, her faith contributed to this feeling. In any highly traditional boarding school, especially in this era, conformity was essential. Being Jewish set Verity apart, together with the handful of other girls who shared her faith. Whenever bacon or pork was served, they were given 'specials' instead. 'Although I never had a sense of anti-Semitism,' says Jean Naggar, who was one of this group, 'we knew that there were many more Jewish girls in the school who did not confess to being Jewish. They just fitted in.'

On Sunday mornings, instead of trooping into chapel with the rest of their friends, the Jewish contingent – 'about ten to twelve of us of different ages and from different houses' – were placed in the charge of the scholarly Dr Blumenthal, who travelled from London every week to instruct them in aspects of their faith and heritage. Each session would start with the girls forming a semi-circle and reciting a Jewish prayer, the Shema, together. 'Then she would talk about a forthcoming Jewish holiday,' recalls Jean Naggar, 'or sometimes she would talk about a Bible story and encourage discussion. It was quite lively.'

Unfortunately, Dr Blumenthal had a pronounced stammer and, inevitably in a group of teenage girls, this sometimes led to giggling and unkind behaviour but, as Naggar acknowledges, 'the intention was to create a sense of identity so that the Jewish girls wouldn't feel that they were just pushed aside.'

In 1950, while Verity was still incarcerated at Roedean, the Lamberts settled in a new home, number 19, Crooked Usage, Finchley. The quaint name Crooked Usage is a reminder of its former notoriety as a route for highwaymen. The house was detached

---

[6] In the Roedean school magazine

[7] Quoted in *The Executive Tart* and *Women with Attitude* (see bibliography)

and set in a large garden. The interior was substantial, decorated and furnished in the traditional English style of the time with a lot of dark oak furniture and muted colours. The Medways, the Lamberts' new neighbours, were, like them, middle-class, professional, Jewish people. Murray Medway ran the family footwear business, Elliotts, and was involved in local politics (he later became the last Mayor of Finchley and a close friend of Margaret Thatcher). As well as an abiding love of golf, Murray Medway and Stanley Lambert had similar values and soon became fast friends. Like Corrie, Anne Medway was a dedicated housewife. The Medways had two children, Jill and David. Jill was just a year younger than Verity and the two girls formed an immediate bond. It was around this time, during the school holidays, that Verity started smoking, a habit that stayed with her for decades to come. Together with Jill, she would sneak into the garden for an illicit cigarette. Both girls kept their contraband carefully hidden.

David Medway, who was only 11 when the Lamberts moved in, might easily have been left out of their childhood alliance. The fact that he wasn't, he believes, owes much to Verity's good nature. 'She was very, very kind to me and never pushed me aside. She was always willing to talk. She was joyful, full of fun. I liked her very much.'

Once, when Verity was about 16, in his eagerness to get downstairs, Medway pushed past her. She fell down the stairs, breaking her ankle, something about which he still feels guilty to this day.

Both families shared several holidays together, driving down to the south of France and staying in a hotel, playing games on the beach, going on trips, shopping and seeking amusement and diversion. Only Corrie, who disliked the sun, would remain shuttered inside. 'I always felt quite sorry for her,' says Medway. 'She was pretty sad most of the time. She never had much of a personality. She was always sitting in the background and hardly ever talked at all, whereas Stanley was very open and full of fun.'

Medway believes that, by now at least, the Lambert marriage was no longer a happy one. He vividly remembers spending a weekend with the Lamberts when his own parents were away. 'It was pretty miserable. They didn't talk at all. Corrie was definitely depressive. The marriage hadn't gone well but in those days, people didn't want to divorce.'

Verity's favourite record of 1951, the year she turned 16, was Nat King Cole's mournful ballad *Too Young* ('They tried to tell us we were too young...'). '"The theme song of the teenager," she called it. 'I remember being driven down to the south of France by my parents with my best friend and we sat in the back of the car and sang this song interminably all the way from London. I think my parents must have been driven totally mad by it.'[8]

---

[8] Verity chose the song as part of her selection of favourite tracks during her appearance on Eve Pollard's Radio 2 show (22.05.93)

When Verity left Roedean the following summer, she took with her a disappointingly meagre haul of six O Levels. However she occasionally sought to dismiss this in later years, it was a conspicuous lack of attainment that always embarrassed and annoyed her. She was later to find herself working in an industry with some of the finest creative minds of her generation so it is understandable that she felt undermined and self-conscious about it. She sometimes claimed that, as well as the half a dozen O Levels, she had an A level too, but I can find no record of this.

To friends, Verity later confided her belief that Roedean was little more than a factory to turn out meek, eligibly marriageable daughters of well-to-do families. To some extent, this is a fair criticism but it cannot be denied that there was a reasonably high academic standard at the school. She was perhaps blaming others for her own failure to realise her undoubted potential. As she explained to one interviewer: 'My headmistress told my father that I could not possibly go to university, which was ridiculous.' But university entry in those days was much tougher and more selective than it has since become. It is difficult to imagine how she would have been able to proceed without additional study and further qualifications. Faced with such complications, her teenage reaction was to give up. 'I was 16 at the time and not very sensible,' continued Lambert in the same interview. 'I didn't want to spend any more time at school with people trying to make me into something I wasn't. I transferred my feelings about authority to further education in general and took the opportunity of leaving school altogether.'[9]

Over the following decades, Verity kept in touch with Roedean, carefully sending them updates of her many achievements (which were duly printed in the school magazine). Maybe she felt she still had something to prove to them and that news of her latest award or achievement was one in the eye for an establishment which she always felt had failed to recognise or channel her considerable abilities. When, in 1985, she didn't receive an invitation to the school's centenary celebrations, she admitted that she was hurt and annoyed. Even if it was an oversight rather than a deliberate snub, it acted as a blow on a bruise that never quite healed. Tellingly, for a woman who developed a profound gift for discovering, nurturing and sustaining friendship of all kinds, she did not keep in touch with anyone from her school years.

Leaving Roedean was the first major independent decision of Verity Lambert's life and her father was both horrified and bemused by it. He very much wanted her to stay on, study for A-levels, go on to university, and then perhaps seek a future as a lawyer or doctor. He received no encouragement from the school, while Verity herself adamantly refused to countenance his wishes. She was sick to death of studying and, like many who have taken against school, had formed the impression that university would only be more of the same. Roedean had drilled a sense of independence into her and now she was acting on it, no longer biddable and content merely to do as her parents wished. She later admitted to a 'certain emotional resentment against my parents for sending me

---

[9] Quoted in *Women with Attitude* (see bibliography)

away, which is rather ungracious because they were trying to do their best for me.'[10] Family harmony, previously unthreatened, was destabilised and for a time there was an atmosphere of tension at home. 'I obviously had a brain and I wasn't using it,' said Verity, years later. 'But it seemed to me that I just wanted to be independent.'[11]

Stanley was upset and worried by his daughter's insouciant attitude to her education, but Corrie Lambert did not entirely share her husband's dismay. She held firm to the traditional view that the best hope for a girl's future happiness and fulfilment was to make a good marriage and have children of her own. She had every confidence that her daughter would make a suitable match and in this she was not merely blinded by love or mere expectation. Verity may have underachieved in actual qualifications but her quick wits and vivacity were immediately apparent to all who met her. She is variously described as strikingly attractive, without being a classic beauty, possessed of a good complexion, plenty of thick, dark hair, natural curves and excellent legs. But her best feature was her obsidian eyes. The very deepest black, they commanded attention and were a clue to her state of mind; whether sparkling with fun or desire, set hard and unflinching or filled with tears of rage and frustration. All her life, people noticed and commented on them. Even the best photographs fail to do them justice.

The dating game played out in Jewish youth clubs and groups like the Maccabi associated with local synagogues where young people from respectable backgrounds could socialise, play sport, organise entertainments, theatricals, outings and parties. Their parents were moneyed middle-class, professional and shared Corrie Lambert's hopes of a good match for their offspring within their own faith. 'Nice Jewish girls went to meet nice Jewish boys,' chuckles Freddie Hancock, later a top agent, who was involved in these clubs at the same time as Verity. 'You got involved with different things – a group of very attractive young men played badminton and girls would go to watch them. It was the thing to do to prove to our parents that we were meeting nice Jewish people. But, funnily enough, few of us actually married Jewish people.'

It was in this sociable environment that Verity first met another girl who would become a lifelong friend and surrogate sister – Marilyn Heller. 'She had just done her exams and left Roedean,' Heller (now Gross) recalls. 'There was lots of going to dances in pretty dresses. This one was for charity. She was wearing a pink satin dress and she looked absolutely gorgeous. She was all agog with excitement.'

The two girls, both without siblings, quickly formed a bond.

'It struck me when I first met her how independent she was for her age,' says Gross. 'I was a couple of years older but she was already more independent than I was. I think what we had in common was that neither of us wanted to go with the flow, so to speak.

---

[10] Quoted in *The Sunday Times* (16.01.83)

[11] Quoted in *Winning Women* (see bibliography)

We were expected just to be pretty and find a husband – which was very much the era. But we were both independent-minded. There was something else out there that we wanted to do, though we didn't yet know what.'

In the meantime, there was plenty of fun. 'In those days we had little dressmakers and she always knew what she wanted. Once, we were bridesmaids for a distant cousin of hers and had lots of giggles choosing our own dress fabric. It was turquoise. Of course, instantly afterwards we thought we'd made a mistake and would never wear the dresses again.'

As well as dresses, they shared boyfriends. 'They used to go backwards and forwards between us,' smiles Gross, 'which we used to have a good laugh about in later years.' These boys tended inevitably to be young professionals – doctors, lawyers and businessmen. 'We probably bored and scared a lot of them by saying, "Why don't you do this?" She had a strong sense of her self – something under the vivaciousness. It wasn't just the coquettishness of the young girl.'

One handsome young man, Dennis Meyer, caught the eye of not just Verity, but Marilyn Heller and Freddie Hancock too. 'We all dated him,' says Hancock. 'And he turned out to be the most boring date you could possibly have. It was all a fantasy that we had created. We never admitted it to each other, though!'

Amidst all these dances and parties and while the ceaseless flirtation was afoot, Stanley Lambert had yet to accept total defeat as far as his precious daughter's education was concerned. Eventually, a kind of compromise was reached. Inspired by his own youthful experience, Stanley suggested that Verity spend a few months in Paris, so that she could learn to speak French as fluently as he had done and immerse herself in the culture and cuisine of one of the world's great civilisations, to which she was, after all, linked by blood. 'It was about rounding her off a bit,' explains Marilyn Gross. 'A traditional thing to do, if you could afford it.'

Verity was enrolled on a six-month course, run by the University of Paris, called the *Cours de la Civilisation Française*, studying eighteenth to twentieth century French literature, history, politics and, in the evenings, history of art. She also took French grammar lessons and, interested in food even then, learnt to cook in the French fashion. She lived with a family who refused to speak English, which was brutal but effective. 'I am quite garrulous,' she recalled. 'But I didn't open my mouth for about three months. I was so afraid that they would laugh at me. By the time I started speaking, I could understand everything. Once I realised that people wouldn't laugh at me, I started to speak.'[12]

Her natural confidence returned and she settled and learnt to love the great city. An abiding memory was her very first trip to the opera, for a production of George

---

[12] Quoted in *Women with Attitude* (see bibliography)

Gershwin's *Porgy and Bess*. She was only 17 years old and was beginning to experience the many pleasures and possibilities of an affluent and cultured life.

One of the oft-quoted 'facts' about Verity Lambert is that she was a graduate of the Sorbonne. This is not the case. Although perfectly respectable, the *Cours de la Civilisation* was a diploma, not a degree, and yet for the rest of her life, in interviews and biographies, Verity allowed it to be known that she had achieved something rather grander. Periodically, some of her close circle attempted to question her about it. 'What's all this nonsense about the Sorbonne?' asked Kate Kagan, who was one of her closest friends. 'You never went to the Sorbonne!' She laughs as she imitates the expression of great hauteur that came over Verity's face as she asked the question. '"Oh didn't I?" was all she would say.'

It is fascinating that both the elusive A Level and her time in Paris are among the few untruths perpetrated in public by Verity throughout her adult life. Early in her career, perhaps these academic white lies were a useful way of massaging the facts so that she appeared a better prospect on paper. Later, when she no longer had any need of them, she had to stick to her story. She is scarcely unusual in employing a little creativity to add lustre to her credentials. But what is illuminating is how much she clearly resented the lack of a formal education at which, in different circumstances, she surely would have excelled.

When Verity returned from her sojourn in Paris, her father again attempted to persuade her of the wisdom of studying for some kind of degree. Again, she refused. Instead, at her mother's insistence, Verity was persuaded to undertake the best secretarial course that money could buy, courtesy of the renowned St James' College. This should have taken three months, but, as she hated every moment, in the end it was 18 dreary months before she could consider herself qualified. She had acquired the essential core skills of shorthand, achieving an impressive speed of 140 words a minute, and of touch-typing but she also found herself proficient in more obscure accomplishments, like double-entry bookkeeping. Her social life was far more interesting. There were parties and dances, trips and holidays abroad, still a great luxury at this time. It was useful having a really close girlfriend, Jill Medway, living just next door. They went to the cinema together and spent hours chatting and chain-smoking in their bedrooms, sharing secrets, discussing clothes and boyfriends. 'Her mother was always wanting to know which boy she was going out with,' remarks Medway. 'The two of them used to scamper off and they were obviously going out with Christian boys without the parents knowing. It was always very secretive. But then parents of that generation were living in the Ark.'

When she was 19, the Medways introduced Verity to a young man called Laurence Blonstein. Blonstein was a cousin of theirs and had graduated from Cambridge. His ambition was to train as a doctor. 'My father was trying to get a wife for Laurence,' explains Medway, bluntly. 'Verity was available and he decided to introduce them. Stanley welcomed it and she went along with it.'

'They wanted me to marry her because I was going to be a nice Jewish doctor,' says Blonstein himself. 'Stanley was very keen on me. I think that he thought that I came from a good family – my father was a doctor too. Verity had a nice long neck. I rather liked that. Whereas she used to say I looked a bit like Louis Jourdan.'[13]

A courtship followed and before long, Blonstein proposed and was accepted. He gave Verity a diamond engagement ring, which had belonged to his grandmother. An exuberant Stanley paid for a celebratory holiday for himself, his wife and the young couple at the Lido in Venice. But on their return, the stark reality of their situation soon became apparent. 'Because of my studying, it was very difficult to keep up any relationship,' says Blonstein. 'I was working at the Middlesex Hospital. In those days, doctors really worked very long hours, even more than they do now. Also, I had deferred my National Service but was going to have to do that once I'd finished my training. I pinned my hopes on her carrying on with her interests until I was out of the Air Force and ready to settle down.'

With this in mind, Verity continued to work. After some desultory temping, she obtained her first proper job as a secretary in the Kensington de Vere hotel. Because of her knowledge of French, she was assigned the task of typing the lunch and dinner menus, which were presented in the most formal version of the language. 'Deadening and awful', she branded the experience.[14] Next came a spell in a lawyer's office. It was no better than the hotel job had been. She couldn't get used to the eccentric legal requirement to type contracts without any punctuation. 'You weren't allowed to punctuate as punctuation changes the meaning,' she explained to Jody Brettkelly of the *Mail on Sunday*. 'One of the few things I was good at at school was English language and I had this completely Pavlovian desire to punctuate.'[15]

Bored to tears, she began to look for an alternative.

Despite their affluence, the Lamberts hadn't acquired a television set of their own until Verity's late teens, so it was only slowly that she began to take notice of this new phenomenon. 'I had a boyfriend and his family had one,' she told Susan Vinnicombe. 'On Sunday nights, there was always a play on the BBC. They used to line the chairs up as if you were watching in a cinema. So when people say to me, "Did you want to work in television?", I really had not the faintest idea what it was. It just wasn't part of my culture at all when I was growing up.'[16]

---

[13] Louis Jourdan (1921–2015) Darkly handsome French film actor who found success in Hollywood movies, among them *The Paradine Case* (1947) and *Gigi* (1958)

[14] Quoted in *Tactics: The Art and Science of Success* (see bibliography)

[15] *Mail on Sunday* (02.10.94)

[16] Quoted in *Women with Attitude* (see bibliography)

Her eventual entry into the world of television in 1955 was quite without fanfare or expectation. It was just another secretarial position, this time working for the press officer of the fledgling Granada Television. This company was dominated by its founding fathers, the impresario brothers Sidney and Cecil Bernstein, always known to their staff as 'Mr Sidney' and 'Mr Cecil'. Stanley Lambert happened to know Sidney Bernstein well enough to ask him a favour and find his daughter a job. Bernstein obliged by giving Verity a chance to become secretary to Granada's press officer, in their London offices. 'I thought it would be more interesting,' she said, 'and I would get to meet actors and actresses. Of course I didn't get to meet any.'

She was terrified of both Bernsteins and, years later, she admitted: 'Whenever the internal phones lit up for Mr Sidney, I would resolutely ignore them, thinking that I would cut them off if I picked them up. They thought I was out all the time. The press officer knew as much about running a press office as I knew about being a secretary, so it was a rather disastrous coupling.'[17]

Verity spent most of her time typing envelopes and practising yoga on the office floor. Six months into the job, she was fired, ostensibly on the grounds that she was the youngest member of staff and it was a case of 'last in, first out'. 'A week later they changed their minds and asked me to stay,' she told the *Mail on Sunday*. 'But I said I would only do that if they would guarantee they wouldn't fire me again.' They wouldn't, so she refused the offer. 'I was just stupid, really, and bloody-minded. And I also felt slightly uncomfortable that I had got the job as a favour to my father. I thought I wanted to do this on my own, so nobody could ever say, "She got her job because of her father", or "She slept with someone."'[18]

Despite her professional deficiencies, Verity had become at first curious and interested and then excited and enthusiastic about the burgeoning industry of television. 'It seemed like it was fun and there seemed to be other jobs that weren't secretarial that could be attained at some point or another. I was just star-struck and it seemed glamorous and better than being a suburban housewife.'

She broke the engagement to Laurence Blonstein. 'We never had a row,' he says, somewhat wistfully. 'I think I understood why she wanted to end it. She saw that there was a chance of a better quality of life. She was very decent about it and gave me the ring back.'

The break-up was another disappointment for Stanley Lambert. 'It left a sour taste in his mouth,' says Medway. 'But it was doomed from the start because that relationship would never have worked. They were completely different people. She wanted a career and he just wanted a wife and kids.'

---

[17] Quoted in *The Executive Tart* and *Women with Attitude* (see bibliography)

[18] *Mail on Sunday* (02.10.94)

This may be true but Blonstein's feelings remained deep enough for him to hold out the hope of an eventual reconciliation. In 1959, he was invited to his cousin Jill's wedding in Paris. Knowing that Verity would be among the guests, he decided to see if there was any way he might persuade her to try again. She agreed to have a meal with him but, to his disappointment, was non-committal. 'When it came down to it, she realised that life was going to be much more exciting in television than being my wife. Had she married me she would never have reached the heights she achieved. I just watched her success from afar and I was very thrilled, in a way, to have been close to someone of that ability.'

According to Verity's second cousin, Anthony Joseph, this engagement was the first of three others that followed 'in moderately quick succession'. Unfortunately, I've been unable to trace any further details but at this somewhat gauche stage in her life, it seems entirely credible that Verity was casting out the net, experimenting with the idea of love and marriage and attempting to live up both to her parents' expectations and those of the society in which she had grown up. 'On the occasion of the fourth engagement,' says Joseph, 'I do most clearly recall my late mother complaining to my dear father that "if that girl gets engaged any more, I am not buying her another present. We have never had back any of the presents we bought before!"'

When the engagement to Laurence Blonstein came to an end, Verity switched her considerable energy to taking the next step in what she was finally beginning to see as a career rather than merely a stopgap. She was undeterred by her recent dismissal from Granada. 'Being fired was very good for me,' she said later. 'I hate to fail so I became quite determined to prove I could do the job and that they were foolish to fire me, which got me over two years of hateful secretarial work, which otherwise I would have moaned and groaned about.'[19]

She applied for and was appointed as a junior secretary in another fledgling ITV company, ABC Television, reporting for duty at their Pathé House headquarters on the corner of Wardour Street and Oxford Street. Placed within the office of the managing director, Howard Thomas, she was to work to the hawkish and highly experienced principal secretary, Eve Hockman. Verity later paid tribute to Hockman for teaching her to be 'a proper secretary'. Technically, the job was a step down from Granada but, strategically, it was a very good place in which to make her mark, as ABC executive Brian Tesler recalls: 'You noticed Verity because when you wanted to see Howard, you had to go through Eve, and Verity was always there. If Eve wanted something done for Howard, she would often send Verity to do it. She was very visible and very capable. I think her qualities were obvious to everyone.'

She was all the more noticeable because ABC wasn't a big company, as Jackie Davis, then a production assistant, recalls. 'It was only one corridor and it had everyone on that corridor from drama to light entertainment. It was an exciting time, very, very vibrant.'

---

[19] Quoted in *Winning Women* (see bibliography)

With her natural sociability, Verity quickly got to know her new colleagues, making friends with those she liked the look of. 'All our lives were tied up with work and colleagues,' remembers Jill Horwood (now Sampson), who had joined as secretary to programme controller Roland Rowson. 'I remember Verity coming into my office and saying who she was. She was always very sociable. Forthright and down to earth. She was direct but always charmingly so.'

The head of drama at ABC was Dennis Vance, an ex-actor and, during the war, a Fleet Air Arm pilot in the RAF.[20] He was heavy-drinking, eccentric, occasionally erratic and the creator of ABC's flagship drama slot, *Armchair Theatre*, which went out live every Sunday from studios in Didsbury, Manchester. 'He was great to work for,' recalls director Ted Kotcheff. 'I did a production of Eugene O'Neill's *Emperor Jones* and we literally built a whole jungle in the studio. I went into his office and said, "Jesus, Dennis, I'm building a whole jungle, it's going to cost a fortune," and he said, "Just do it, get on with it, don't waste my time – do what you please!"'

'Everybody loved him,' smiles Jill Horwood, 'though he was always blotting his copybook. He was working for nothing because he owed the company so much. I was his production assistant [PA] for some time and he was an absolute nightmare because he didn't do his homework. It would get to about 24 hours before transmission and he still hadn't produced a camera script. He'd say, "Come over at two o'clock and I'll run it through for you," and he used to do it at speed. Then, when you got into the studio everything changed. He was a livewire.'

When a vacancy arose as secretary to Vance, Verity immediately applied.[21] The story goes that whoever was looking through the applications misread Roedean and thought instead that she had been to RADA, the leading drama school.[22] Whatever the truth of this, she got the job and joined a department that was on the cusp of one of the most exciting and creative periods in British television history. More importantly for Verity herself, it was an opportunity that ignited and informed her professional future, and introduced her to the man who became the first great love of her life.

---

[20] Dennis Vance (1924–1983) Eventually returned to directing and his credits include a couple of episodes of the daytime soap, *Rooms*, produced while Verity was director of drama at Thames Television

[21] The first mention of Verity in the trade journal *Television Today* is on June 21 1956, where she is named as Dennis Vance's secretary

[22] She tells this entertaining story in *Myth Makers* (Reeltime Pictures 1996)

CHAPTER TWO
PISS AND VINEGAR
1955–1963

'You've got to let people know that you want to get on, otherwise they'll leave you where you are, particularly if you're good at what you're doing. You have to keep reminding people that you want to do something different.'

Verity to Sophia Watson, *Winning Women*, 1989

Almost by accident, Verity found herself working in an industry rapidly expanding and teeming with opportunity and, better yet – within the sub-culture most suited to her personality and interests – drama. The arrival of independent television signalled an end to the cautious innovation characterised by the BBC over the previous decade. In the latter half of the 1950s, there was a creative free-for-all, as the infant ITV companies jostled for position and sought to establish their own identities. Drama, whether popular or usefully prestigious, was always one of the defining cultural and commercial battlefields. There wasn't enough talent to meet the ambitious demands of this new age of competition, so in order to find the influx of directors and producers they needed, managements looked abroad. Canada became the great hunting ground. Not only was its television service well established and full of ambitious young professionals with the necessary experience, Canada was part of the Commonwealth. Canadians could work in Britain without the prohibitive restrictions of visas and permits.

As a result, some of the great names of British television drama arrived on these shores, among them Alvin Rakoff, Silvio Narizzano, William 'Ted' Kotcheff and Sydney Newman, all of them eager to create their own style and to explore the huge visual potential of the medium, not just adhere to the frequently turgid theatrical standards that often prevailed in television at the time. Under the occasionally haphazard leadership of Dennis Vance, the ABC drama department set out their stall under the banner of their weekly *Armchair Theatre* and, as Vance's secretary, Verity was at the heart of this creative machine, albeit in a subservient role. She continued to make an impression.

'Verity had a terrific aura about her,' says Jackie Davis. 'I think it came from her background. I don't think she was ever scared of anybody. And she was very striking to look at – very attractive.'

The eminent director Herbert Wise echoes these sentiments. 'There was a self-confidence, almost arrogance, not necessarily an unpleasant arrogance. She used quite a lot of feminine charm. In those days, women were so disenfranchised – they had so much more difficulty getting a job. I think she *used* her sex. I'm not critical of it because I think women had to do it. Verity was too intelligent to let it show; she was more than anything *clever*, using her femininity, her education, her sex. She kept her true self very close to her chest.'

Perhaps her closest confidante during this time was another of the Canadian emigrés, Nora Fielding. Fielding was older than Verity and had travelled to England with her husband Wilf. He became established at Granada while she worked for ABC as a PA in features, where she quickly acquired a reputation as supremely professional and was, according to Jackie Davis, 'incredibly confident'.

'She was even tougher than Verity,' adds director Alvin Rakoff. 'There was a mutual respect.'

'She was like a sort of Hello Dolly, organising boyfriends for people,' recalls the actress Judy Cornwell, who worked with Fielding on an ABC quiz show at the time. 'Nora came up to me one day and said, "Oh Judy, you're so pretty, do you have many friends?" and I said, "Well, I'm working most of the time." She said, "I've got a very nice girl, just like you and she needs a friend. I think you'd both get on so well together. I have found this wonderful shop in Soho where they do the best cakes in the world and beautiful coffee so why don't we meet up there and I'll bring my friend along and you can meet her?" That's how I met Verity. We stuffed our faces with Nora picking up the bill and then Nora said, "Have you both got boyfriends?" and I said, "No," and Verity said, "No, I haven't either." So she and Wilf threw a dinner party at their cottage in Haywards Heath with two young Canadian directors for us to meet. The cottage had very low beams. The fellow who had obviously been lined up for Verity was very tall and he knocked himself out on one of the beams. Verity looked at me and we got the giggles. We whispered to each other; "I think we're better off getting our own boyfriends, don't you?"'

Verity's income was minimal but few economies were necessary. Although her father scolded her, 'The trouble with you, Verity is that you have a Rolls-Royce outlook and a Chevrolet income', his generosity meant that, unlike many of her peers, Verity was able to run a car, spend money on her clothes and personal appearance, dine out in restaurants and book occasional holidays abroad.

Cushioned from many of the harsh realities of earning a living, Verity later admitted that she 'didn't feel the need to apply myself in any way. I led quite a trivial life.'[1]

The sum of her career strategy, such as it was, was to win eventual promotion from secretary to production assistant. There was a minimum age requirement of 21. As soon as she had attained the magic number, Verity put herself forward and it wasn't long before she was given the go-ahead to begin her PA training. 'I wanted to stay with drama,' Verity recalled, 'but they put me through a learning process where you do lots of things including quiz programmes.'[2]

Her first appointment – and a personal low point – was on a consumer programme called *State Your Case*. She branded it 'One of the most horrible programmes I could ever imagine,' explaining that 'it consisted of two lawyers, a prosecuting lawyer and a defence lawyer. Poor unfortunate members of the audience, who had written in with really terrible tales to tell about what bad luck had befallen them, were chosen to come up and they were then in the witness box and were asked nice questions by the defence lawyer and very unpleasant questions by the prosecuting lawyer. We had a jury who then voted on who was the most worthy of these poor unfortunates and [the winner] got one hundred pounds. It was absolutely frightful.'[3]

After a few months of this relative purgatory, Verity was back where she started, in drama, assigned to *Armchair Theatre*. In this era of live drama, the importance of the PA cannot be underestimated. They worked closely, often obsessively, with their director and their duties ranged from typing up scripts and camera cards (which numbered and described every shot the director required from each of his studio cameras) to the essential exact timings of every act. During camera rehearsals and live transmission, the PA sat in the control room or gallery, next to the director and surrounded by stopwatches. Their job was to shot-call, calmly and clearly, as the action played out on the bank of monitors showing the output of every camera on the studio floor. In doing so, their function was an absolutely vital one as not only the vision mixer (who sat on the other side of the director and physically cut the shots using a bank of switches) but the camera crew, listening in via their headsets, relied on being able to hear which shot was 'live' and which was coming next. The PA was also the first point of telephone contact between the live gallery and transmission control, liaising the moment anything went wrong. Theirs was the voice everyone heard at the stomach-turning moment when the countdown to live transmission began and again at the end of the process, counting a production off air.

'She was a bloody marvellous PA,' says Pamela Lonsdale, who was doing the same job

---

[1] Quoted in *The Executive Tart* (see bibliography)

[2] Quoted in *Women with Attitude* (see bibliography)

[3] Kaleidoscope convention interview (09.12.06)

at the time. 'She worked very, very hard – a brilliant person, but slightly aloof.'

Rising director Philip Saville first spotted Verity hurrying here and there in the corridors of ABC. 'She had great legs,' he recalls, 'and dressed up quite a bit, high heels and swish. She was a glowing young woman with lovely, pretty eyes. In the control room she was very good. She'd always have a sweet or chocolate, and she was very good at jokes – an excellent PA, very ambitious.'

In the autumn of 1958, Saville was scheduled to undertake an ambitious *Armchair Theatre* production of William Saroyan's play *The Time of Your Life*.[4] The first challenge was to negotiate the rights to the piece, which was then being performed by an American stage company in Brussels. Another problem was that it was going to need substantial pruning for the available slot. 'Why don't you go there and see what can be done?' suggested Dennis Vance. Saville was concerned about his rusty French but then he remembered that Verity could speak the language fluently.

'So we went to Brussels together,' he says, 'and that's how I first worked with her. She had the ability to be very precise about things, which is always a sign of people who want to be ahead of the game. You couldn't just get away with a casual remark, you had to substantiate it. She'd say, "What do you mean exactly? Explain yourself." Anyway, I said to her, "I've got to reduce this production by at least half an hour, if not more." She said, "I'm sure you can do it and if I can help in any way, just ask." We had to deal with these Hollywood stars of that period, Franchot Tone and Ann Sheridan. They were mostly drunk all of the time. Verity wasn't afraid of them because she was eloquent. It was confrontation in a good sense. She was so much into theatre and television and the workings of it all.'

But the director with whom Verity worked most closely and the man who would have the most profound impact on her life was 26-year-old Ted Kotcheff.

'Anybody that could work with Ted Kotcheff could work with anyone,' observes George Taylor, who was an ABC producer at the time.

'Verity absolutely adored Ted,' says Jill Sampson. 'He was very good-looking and had a very strong character himself – terrific vitality, all go. Verity was a very good match for him. I think they were the love of each other's lives.'

'We certainly were in love with each other,' sighs Kotcheff himself. 'I remember being in the pub right round the corner from Pathé House and I said, "I think I'm in love with you" and she said, "I *know* that I'm in love with you, Ted." It was very easy for us – it's a seven-day-a-week business and we were thrown at each other all day long and night. When you work so closely with somebody, with such intensity and you share that intense experience, you're halfway there to being in love. So when you do, it makes the whole

---

[4] Transmitted 19.10.58 – no recording survives

experience even more intense. To me she was a total woman – intelligent, sexy, affectionate, capable of love and emotion and she was contributive to our work together.'

Born in Toronto in 1931, to parents who had emigrated from Bulgaria in Eastern Europe, Kotcheff graduated from the University of Toronto with a degree in English literature and started his television career at CBC in Canada. He worked under Sydney Newman, who was then head of documentaries.

'I would write the scripts for these documentaries,' recalls Kotcheff, 'and of course he would rewrite every word. He said, "Ted, you've got the words saying the same thing as the pictures – you've got a chance to do two things at the same time, words and pictures! Words should not be underlining what you're seeing on the screen, they should be counterpointing it." He taught me great things.'

When Newman became CBC's head of drama, he invited Kotcheff to help run the script department. 'I used to rewrite the scripts sometimes because this was live television and the scripts would come in too short, so all night long I'd type 'em out, comedies, dramas, history plays, whatever they were, I'd write a scene or two. And then one day, Sydney comes into my office and says, "Ted, you're a pretty good writer, not a great writer, but a pretty good writer. You know what you'd be great at? You'd be a great director." To this day, I kick my ass that I never asked him why I would. He said, "Do you wanna have a go?" I said yes and he said, "I tell you what, I'll let you direct one play. If I like it, you'll get a year's contract. If I don't like it, you're on the streets and you can't come back to this job. So if you don't want to risk it, you're doing a good job here in the script department and you can stay." I said, "I wanna risk it..."'

For two years, Kotcheff absorbed himself in the craft of directing television drama under Newman's demanding scrutiny. There is an oft-told anecdote that illustrates their frequently combative relationship. The story goes that during an especially fraught studio day, Newman was holding his head in his hands and berating Kotcheff, shouting, 'What are you doing to me? After all I've done for you – I brought you up from the gutter!', to which Kotcheff snapped right back, 'From the gutter to you is up?'

Kotcheff's interests were not confined to the small screen and he quickly became frustrated that Canada offered little prospect for him to work in either theatre or film, as well as in television. Taking advantage of the British television explosion, Kotcheff arrived in England at the end of November 1957 with a contract to work for ABC as a director. He was given Verity as his PA. Ted Childs, later a highly successful producer himself, remembers an encounter with Kotcheff which gives a revealing insight into the director's mind-set: 'He was having a stand-up row about a play,' recalls Childs. 'Kotcheff stormed up, turned to me and said, "I'll give you a tip, kid – never have ugly broads working for you. Nobody fucks up in front of a good-looking chick but a dog – who gives a shit?"'

Verity, attractive, intelligent, opinionated, inspired Kotcheff from the outset. 'She functioned like my associate producer,' he explains. 'She did everything. It was like going to TV school, doing these amazing plays every month. Two weeks working on the script and doing the casting, then rehearsing for almost two weeks, then up to Didsbury in Manchester to put the play on. She knew the shows inside out. We had two days in the studio. Around two o'clock of the second day we would do a run-through and then four o'clock a dress rehearsal – I would give the notes to the actors and then the cameras, with Verity, of course, and then we went on the air at nine o'clock. Verity was a very intelligent woman and made excellent suggestions to me and also she knew the whole acting scene. My casting director might suggest somebody and I wouldn't be sure and she'd say, "He's very good." "OK, go ahead, let's have him!" Verity always knew her mind and had insightful opinions.'

Within a few weeks of their first working with each other, everyone at ABC knew that Ted and Verity were an item. As a couple, they became fixtures on the thriving social scene that came with the job. There were dinners with Kotcheff's best friend, the writer Mordecai Richler, and his wife.[5] 'Ah, Ted, you're a very lucky guy,' enthused another friend, the writer Terry Southern, later to provide the screenplay for the seminal 1960s movie *Dr Strangelove or: How I Learned to Stop Worrying and Love the Bomb*.[6] Verity became an enthusiastic participant in a poker school, mainly comprising the Canadian contingent and their cronies, among them Alvin Rakoff and his actress wife, Jackie, with whom Verity struck up an immediate friendship. 'We used to take it in turns at each other's houses,' says Rakoff. 'You used to supply the beer, the wine and the sandwiches and the cards, tables and chips. We all had chips. The regulars were Ted, Verity, myself, Jackie, the actor Gaylord Cavalerro, George Baxt, who was an American writer, and whoever his boyfriend was at the time, and Henry Kaplan, another Canadian director, who was also gay. Sean Connery came a few times. Faced with all this male competition, the girls were quite ruthless!'

Like so much early television, there are yawning gaps in the *Armchair Theatre* archive. Television was regarded as a transitory medium, an attitude only encouraged by the crude and expensive methods then available to preserve it. But some of the plays that Kotcheff directed with Verity by his side do survive and, despite the ravages of time, give some sense of the energy and creativity that established the strand as both a critical and commercial success, among them *The Emperor Jones* by Eugene O'Neill, *The Greatest Man in the World* by James Thurber and *Hot Summer Night* by Ted Willis.

One *Armchair Theatre* on which they collaborated has become a notorious footnote in the history of live television. *Underground*, adapted by James Forsyth from a 1955 novel, *Few Were Left*, by Harold Rein, is one of the many that no longer exist but the traumatic experience of making this play seared itself into the memories of those involved.

---

[5] Mordecai Richler (1931–2001) Eminent Canadian novelist and writer. Kotcheff later directed *The Apprenticeship of Duddy Kravitz* (1974) a film for which Richler wrote an Oscar nominated screenplay

[6] Released 1964

'It was a very good play,' asserts Kotcheff, 'very well written. The H-bomb had hit London and destroyed it and we follow a handful of people who survive because they are 300 feet down in a subway station. They go wandering through the tunnels to find if there are any other people around.'

It was a typically ambitious Kotcheff production with the entire studio converted into a ruined underground station. Designer George Haslam carefully positioned heaps of debris to act as hides for the bulky cameras. The director assembled a talented cast, among them the well-known character players Donald Houston and Andrew Cruickshank, a yet-to-be famous Warren Mitchell and two up-and-coming actors, Gareth Jones and Peter Bowles.

'The funny thing is that Ted Kotcheff looked very like I did in those days,' remembers Bowles. 'My very first moment of fame was when I was in The Salisbury pub in St Martin's Lane, having one or two actors offering to buy me drinks because they thought I was him! I liked him very much – he swore a lot, I recall. Verity was very attractive and wore short skirts and had very good legs. There was a tremendous camaraderie – we felt that even though the script might not be very good we were doing something important. We knew it was going to be watched by millions of people.'

Gareth Jones was a stocky Welsh actor in his early thirties. 'A very exciting actor', according to Philip Saville, who had directed him in another *Armchair Theatre* earlier that year. 'Rather like a young Charles Laughton or Simon Russell Beale. He could have had an amazing career.'

The play was thoroughly rehearsed and then, as was the well-established *Armchair Theatre* tradition, all the cast and crew took the Friday night train from Euston in London to Manchester, ready for the busy weekend in the studio and the culmination of their efforts. On Sunday night, Verity counted the production down into transmission, and it had reached Act Two when something went badly wrong.

'Because we had to climb over all this rubble,' explains Bowles, 'they'd asked for a nurse to be present during the shooting in case anybody turned an ankle. I was in this little group and the character played by Gareth Jones [Carl Norman] was supposed to join us and share dialogue. We saw him coming down the tunnel towards us and then we saw him fall. We presumed he'd tripped up and we could see people apparently tending to him. So we had to carry on and extemporise to cover it.'

Kotcheff recalls the make-up girl running into the gallery. 'She says, "Ted, Ted, Gareth has fainted, he's passed out." The problem with losing him was that he was the villain – the Judas figure – he had betrayed the other five so without him, there was no story. Somehow we staggered to the end of Act Two.'

As soon as the commercial break was called, Kotcheff intended to race to the studio floor and improvise a way of out of the situation. Before he could do so, he was informed that Jones had not fainted but died. The adrenaline of the crisis, already intense, now induced an extraordinary team effort to keep the show on air. 'I turned to Verity,' he says, 'and told her, "I'm going to talk to the actors, you phone master control, and get them to have a Charlie Chaplin film on standby because we could grind to a halt."'

'Master Control were unable to give me any kind of definitive answer,' said Verity when interviewed about it years later. 'It was one of these things where nobody knew what to do. Nobody could prepare for it. You had to think on your feet. I don't know, rightly or wrongly, we just ploughed on with it.'[7]

'The cast were told that he had fainted,' says Bowles. 'Certainly we weren't told that he was dead and if we had been, I know that Donald Houston would not have been able to carry on because he was a close friend of Gareth's.'

Kotcheff got the actors together and delivered some quick-fire explanations. 'Listen, Gareth is not feeling well, he's passed out so we have to go on without him. Here's what we're going to do. You're going to be the Judas figure...' As he frantically went through his makeshift plan, time was running out and up in the gallery, Verity, her eyes glued to her stopwatch, was announcing, 'One minute to go...' then '30 seconds'. Just as she began to count down the end of the commercial break from ten, Kotcheff told her that she would have to take over the directing of the cameras so that he could concentrate on troubleshooting the rest of Act Three, to try to avoid any additional catastrophes.

'So she started directing,' he says. '"Camera 3, get behind that pile of rubble – take 4..." The choreography was so complicated and because the actors were improvising, I would suddenly yell out, "Camera 2, quick, go to the end of the subway tunnel," because that's where they were heading. On it went like this. Verity was great at directing the on-air cameras whilst I was looking a few pages ahead so that we didn't grind to a halt, or have cameras looking at each other. Don't me ask how but with Verity calling the shots and me anticipating what the problems were going to be, we got to the end.'

Christopher Morahan, a rising director himself, was watching at home. 'It was an imperative, you had to watch *Armchair Theatre*, it was bound to be interesting. I remember this one clearly. Every time someone went to a door, there was a camera there. So I said, "I think we're watching a live disaster!" It was fascinating to read [about] the next day.'

Only when the red transmission lights went off were the cast allowed to know the sad truth about Jones' collapse.

'We were extremely upset,' says Bowles. 'It was so tragic. Gareth was a very nice man.' There was no anger at the ruse that had enabled them to keep going, rather a deeply shared, unstated acceptance of the oldest cliché in the theatrical book – that the show

---

[7] Kaleidoscope convention interview, 2006

must go on. 'After we faded to black,' says Kotcheff, 'there was dead silence in the studio. Nobody moved when I went out. I spoke to Donald first and he was sobbing. I said, "I don't believe this. I'm so sorry, Don, I know he's your friend." He said, "He was going to get married in ten days. I can't do it, I can't tell her. Can you do it?" So after talking to the whole crew, I asked Verity to get his fiancée on the line and I had the doleful job of telling her too. It was just an extraordinary experience and became mythological.'

Everyone was booked onto the late-night return train to London. Bowles vividly remembers how the cast had been out and bought a crate of beer to liven up the trip home. Now that their journey home had become a wake, they all refused to touch Gareth Jones' share of the alcohol. 'The next day,' recalled Verity, 'the front page of the paper was saying how awful that an actor had died during it, but the back page was saying what an awful play it was.'[8]

The *Daily Mirror* carried a quote from an ABC official claiming: 'The viewers never guessed what had happened. We haven't had a single enquiry from them.'

'It proved,' believes director Alvin Rakoff, 'how exciting, strange and panicky live television could be. It was the ultimate.'

The producer of *Underground* and head of drama at ABC since earlier that summer was a man himself to attain almost mythical status in television history. Sydney Newman, Kotcheff's former mentor, had been drafted in from CBC to take over from Dennis Vance, whose sometimes exasperating behaviour had pushed ABC chairman Howard Thomas to the limits of his patience. Knowing of their earlier association, Thomas approached Kotcheff and asked for a character reference for Newman. '"He's a brilliant drama producer,"' replied Kotcheff, '"great with people. His choices of people and material are impeccable, I couldn't recommend him more highly." I helped to get him the job.'

As soon as Newman arrived at ABC, he began to impose order on chaos. He established a script department to sift the wheat from the chaff and ensure that good material didn't get lost through the lack of a system. He paid well, offering more to writers and directors than any other company and keeping their loyalty through ongoing contracts. Most significantly, he imparted his belief in the cultural relevance and dramatic potential of popular television. As he stressed to his directors back in Toronto, 'Listen, television is a contemporary instrument and I want it to reflect what's happening in a contemporary society.'[9] Now he was in Britain, he would say the same to the writers he met. 'Write what's going on in Liverpool – I want all television to be like that – life as it's being lived at this very moment, that's what television was made for. Make it new.'

'Verity was heavily influenced by this belief,' says Kotcheff, 'and she felt the same way.'

---

[8] Kaleidoscope convention interview, 2006

[9] Quoted in *Armchair Theatre: How to write, design, direct, act and enjoy television plays* (see bibliography)

'He had an infallible way with public taste,' believes Philip Saville. 'He lived in Crediton Hill in West Hampstead and when he said, "I'm having a cocktail party," you never said no because after two or three martinis he eased up a bit and would tell you his plans.'

'Sydney's great talent was to spot talent,' says Kotcheff. 'He made me believe in myself and that's half the battle. You go out there and expose yourself to do this work and you better believe in yourself if you want everyone else to believe in you. He fired this director one day and I said, "Why did you fire him?" and he replied, "He always agreed with me. I want somebody to argue with me and have some point of view." Sometimes when Verity was my assistant, she gave Sydney a hard time and would stand up for me. "Leave Ted alone, that's a great approach to that scene – your approach is crap!" Although he'd be mock-angry, he'd have respect about the fact that she had a point of view and wasn't self-conscious about expressing it. If you want to be a producer, you've got to know what you want and you've got to pursue it with all your power.'

'She's got a lot of guts,' Newman told Radio 4's *Profile* in 1987.[10] 'She would chip in and I would say, "Verity, know your place." She would keep quiet for two minutes and then break in [again].'

At this stage, Verity's ambition was not to produce but to direct. 'That was all I wanted to do, actually,' she admitted. 'It seemed to me to be the most glamorous job behind the scenes. I was like the original Yosser saying, "I could do that," always telling Sydney that I wanted to direct.'[11]

Newman himself remembered her as 'a very sassy lady. She was never foolish. She was very electric and a bloody good person to have around.'[12]

Despite this, Verity felt increasingly undervalued and overlooked. For all its responsibilities and compensations, she still felt that being a PA was, in many respects, just a glorified form of secretarial work. She was vocal about her frustration and kicked against the system whenever she could. Anne Summerton (now Mills), then a junior PA, remembers Verity absolutely refusing to conform to a starchy ABC rule dictating that women employees should not wear trousers. 'The rest of us were grumbling and moaning about this,' recalls Mills. 'Only Verity did something about it.' To the envy and amazement of her female colleagues, Verity sauntered into work wearing an expensive pair of leather trousers. 'She looked terrific,' Mills continues, 'She could ignore the rules and get away with it. That's the kind of woman she was.'

But despite her *chutzpah* and aptitude, Verity's pleas to be given a chance as a director

---

[10] *Profile*, Radio Four (12.03.87)

[11] Kaleidoscope convention interview, 2006

[12] Quoted in *The Executive Tart* (see bibliography)

were not taken seriously. Feeling that her professional life was at a standstill, she began to consider ways in which she might overturn the frustrating status quo. Still very much in love with Kotcheff, she later claimed that it was only when she started to take her own career seriously that her relationship with him began to unravel.

The truth is that there were other serious tensions at play from the start. Stanley and Corrie Lambert were frankly disapproving of the relationship throughout and this understandably put Verity under immense strain. 'They were very cool towards me when I met them at their home,' remembers Kotcheff. 'Her father never liked me and tried to discourage our relationship. They were like a lot of the middle-class bourgeoisie in England. They always want their daughters to be marrying a prince or a count or something. They had an only child who they wanted to marry up and here was this upstart director from Canada.'

Their principal objection was that Kotcheff wasn't Jewish. There was a series of bitter rows and painful confrontations between Verity and her parents. In September 1958, the Lamberts wrote to Kotcheff, urging him to give up their daughter, reasoning that her long-term happiness was at stake, and that she would be far better off marrying someone of her own faith. In a highly emotional state, Verity fled to Torremolinos in Spain, in those days a little fishing village, a holiday spoilt by the angst and upset she'd left behind her. While she was there, Kotcheff wrote to her with characteristic vehemence, rubbishing every line of her parents' entreaties and encouraging her to dismiss their concerns; 'You are less Jewish than I am. I have been in a synagogue more often than you have.' It is perhaps significant that she kept this letter for the rest of her life. Realising that their daughter had no intention of giving Kotcheff up, in the short term, the Lamberts could do little, but the knowledge of their unwavering opposition and the unhappiness and doubt this caused Verity had a slow and corrosive effect on the relationship.

'It was a big deal,' says Alvin Rakoff. 'I think they both wanted it to continue. She was a non-practising Jew – when you join showbiz, you join a different religion. But they felt the pressures of that time enormously, with both parents objecting. I think it was heartbreaking for both of them. They should have got married. It affected both their lives. It's tragic. She would have been totally different. Softer. Happier.'

In 1961, the couple travelled to Los Angeles together. Verity brought various letters of introduction with her, in the hope that they would open the door to television work in Hollywood. 'I thought it would be easy...but it wasn't,' she explained to reporter Elsie M. Smith in 1965. 'All the letters of introduction were useless. I spent two or three terrifying months out of work but finally got a job.'

This was an offer to work for David Susskind's company in New York. Kotcheff told her: 'David Susskind is one of the biggest figures in American television – you're going to learn things you could never learn anywhere else. You've got to take this offer.'

Revealingly, Kotcheff says that this was one of the few occasions when they had a row.

Perhaps his encouragement that she should take up the offer was the last thing that she wanted to hear. But this is what she did, and the relationship came to an end. Over 50 years later, Kotcheff claims still to be puzzled by what precisely caused the final split. 'We were friends to the end,' he sighs. 'I don't know why we drifted apart.' He stops to think for a moment and then continues. 'What happened, I think, was that neither one of us was ready for marriage. She didn't want marriage or children because she had other aspirations. I'm very temperamental but I don't recollect having a lot of emotional fights with her. We didn't have anybody else. Worked seemed to get in the way. I wanted to go off and make films – she wanted to get further in television. We split not out of any rejection or emotional complexities [but] this desire to find ourselves in our work, which was taking us in opposite directions. It happened quite suddenly and quite subtly. I missed her a lot.'

In later years, Verity told friends that she 'fled' to New York, attempting to bury her broken heart in the shock of the new. She had a least one good friend there, in the form of Marilyn Gross, who had married an American and was now based in the city.

On the surface of it, the job waiting for her there might have been regarded as a step, if not backwards, then certainly sideways. Verity was to join the secretarial team in the hub of Talent Associates, then the leading independent producer in the city. David Susskind, whose company it was, remains a significant figure in the pioneering age of American television, both for his enterprise and personality and because he combined his production interests, which ranged from one-off dramas and series to fronting a popular weekly talk-show that ran for over 25 years. He was a man of immense energy and purpose, charming, persuasive and inevitably influential. He was also demanding, quixotic, sometimes unreasonable and occasionally an out-and-out bully. His office was necessarily staffed by women with the strength of character to withstand his rages and interpret his dictates. With her own considerable force of personality, and just out of an intense relationship with one of the most volatile men in the industry, Verity was not daunted in the slightest. It is worth noting that Susskind was extremely unusual at the time for the sheer number of women that he employed – 32 out of a total staff of 45. A 1959 *TV Guide* spread about the company proclaimed 'Where Women Are Welcome'. The less savoury side to the spin was that Susskind was also notorious for propositioning his female colleagues, although he was not known to hold a grudge if they refused him. One of Verity's friends and long-term collaborators, the director Herbert Wise, believes that she was no exception and, indeed, 'that was how she got on there. Women had to do this then. She certainly had been in love with Kotcheff, [but] I think that was her only real love affair. Verity was out for herself, which, in this business, is a wonderful quality. She was a very ambitious woman.'

As well as satisfying his own predilections, Susskind also knew only too well that women could be paid less than men and were invariably prepared to work longer and less reasonable hours. Facing this accusation during a television interview, Susskind admitted that 'they will work New Year's Day, Christmas and Easter.' At first, he insisted that Verity was put on reception as it amused him to have callers greeted by her cut-glass English accent. This unrewarding position came to an abrupt end when Susskind was calling his office from Los Angeles and Verity managed to cut him off 12 times.

'He was a slightly crazy man – bizarre, I think,' says Marilyn Gross. 'He was mercurial. She kept saying, "It's crazy," but she was used to the hard work and the odd hours and she didn't have anything that she had to be home for, so she worked all the strange hours and she knew that in the end it would be good experience. It was fun for me – she would come over and have a drink or one or two or three!'

Verity later told Susskind's biographer that she 'felt I was working in a place I wanted to work that was making programmes that were respectable and I could admire. And I was learning.'

But, although this may have been true, she was still at a significant remove from the creative process, despite occasional stints stage-managing on the studio floor. Whatever her feelings about the work, she loved the city and the wit and cynicism of the native New Yorkers. She had learnt to cook in the French fashion during her time in Paris and now she found the time to further study the skills of *cordon bleu*. She enjoyed the constant hum of life here, too, the culture on tap in the theatre, cinemas and museums and the myriad choice in the shops. She wasn't totally in thrall to the Big Apple, however. One day, walking down Fifth Avenue, she was just thinking how terrible were all the women's hairstyles when she spotted a startling exception on the other side of the street. Seconds later, she realised that the woman in possession of this perfect cut was her old friend from London, the actress Jackie Hill.

Verity rushed over and discovered that Hill was here with her husband, Alvin Rakoff, who had just been contracted to direct a show for none other than David Susskind. 'Of course, they teamed up immediately,' smiles Rakoff. 'Two English girls in New York. Verity discovered that Jackie was going to a young Vidal Sassoon, which is why she had such good hair. They became very close during our stay. They were both straightforward and shared a basic honesty about life, men and each other. They would have a great old time. They would go into [the department store] Bergdoff Goodman and because they had these English accents, people would sort of faint and dance attendance on them. In the fur department, they'd bring out all the big expensive furs they couldn't afford for them to see. They'd be given a drink and a cigarette while all these minks were paraded and then they'd walk away saying, "Yes, thank you, we'll let you know."'

When Verity returned to Britain, she bypassed her fear of flying and booked herself an ocean passage instead. She was travelling in style, and with a new sense of purpose, determined to achieve her goal of becoming a director. In the meantime, she accepted an offer to return to her old job as a drama PA at ABC, where, among other shows, she worked on the early *Avengers*. But the hurdles ahead were not just professional ones. Having reached some kind of equilibrium about the end of her affair with Ted Kotcheff, she was now confronted with another devastating loss. On 1 December 1961, Corrie Lambert, had a heart attack and died in Westminster Hospital. She was only 56 years old and had been battling cancer for some time. The shock of the bereavement was intensified because Verity's father, Stanley, had fallen in love with his secretary, Betty, whom he now proposed to marry without delay. Verity never stopped adoring her father but their relationship had already taken a battering over Kotcheff and this development, which she resented for her mother as much for herself, only triggered more rows and added to the wretchedness she felt at the premature loss of a parent. She disliked and mistrusted Betty, who had been married before and had a son, Kenneth, of her own. It was to be years before the two women were reconciled and, in the meantime, the atmosphere between them was polite but strained.

Shortly after her mother's death, Verity did agree to go away with her father on a recuperative skiing holiday. 'I was completely fearless,' she said later. 'I had this idea that the snow would be soft. When I finished I had bruises that literally went right down each side. I told my instructor that I thought I was lucky not to break my leg. He said, "No, you were lucky not to break your neck." So I thought, "This isn't a very good idea." And I haven't been since.'[13]

Back home, Stanley Lambert bought a tiny house in Belgravia, ostensibly as a family investment, but principally as a base for his daughter, who needed somewhere of her own to live. Situated at the back of Belgrave Square, 59 Eaton Mews West was once the humble province of the servants who worked in the stables and garages belonging to the big town houses round the corner. Now it became Verity's first real home and her father hired an interior designer to decorate and furnish it exactly according to her tastes – neutral, modern and understated. The front door opened straight into the open-plan sitting room, with sofas made to fit the space and underfloor heating concealed beneath a parquet floor covered with rugs. There was a small kitchen at the back of the house and this had to have frosted windows as a condition of the lease, to protect the privacy of the posh neighbours of Eaton Square. Stairs ran up directly from the sitting room to a first floor into which were crammed two bedrooms and two bathrooms. Verity had the bigger of the two bedrooms, which came with its own dressing area. A cleaner was engaged to come in once a week and keep the place spotless. The house also had a garage in which she kept her car, a Sunbeam Alpine.

This de luxe *pied à terre* made a lasting impression on the television presenter Joan Bakewell, who was herself at the beginning of a career of durability and distinction. 'For some reason I had to go round to her place,' she explains. 'I remember thinking, "Oh my God! This is a wealthy young woman." I'm from modest means up North and she had something I'd never seen before – heavily interlined curtains which kept the cold out. I remember thinking that this was the height of luxury and how did one get them? And how did she know? Gradually, it bore in on me that she was what we called then a Jewish princess.'

---

[13] 'My Hols' *The Sunday Times* (07.01.96)

Initially, Verity shared the house with her old friend and fellow PA, Jill Horwood, who paid a peppercorn rent. Later, they were joined by another close colleague, Nora Fielding, who shared Verity's room, moving in when her marriage collapsed and an unpleasant divorce ensued. 'Verity was very good to other women,' says Jill Horwood. 'Very, very loyal to her women friends. Somebody said to me once, "Well, of course, it was easy for Verity because she was so rich." I don't actually think that that rang true. I mean, her father was rich but she never threw money about. I never saw her wasting money or being ostentatious at all.'

The house share was a great success. On Saturday afternoons, the three friends would often treat themselves to a long lunch at a restaurant they could ill afford. Each of them had a cat. Verity's was a Burmese named Castro, or Cassie for short, while Jill and Nora had the Siamese double-act, Albert and Henry. 'We couldn't let them out because we had no outdoor space,' says Horwood. 'But very often they would escape. There was an enormous garage opposite us and the cats would make a beeline for this. Then there would be a mad dash with all the mechanics looking for the cats.'

Verity and Nora were both passionate about cooking and evenings would be spent preparing elaborate dinners, which weren't served till late. 'There was one particular occasion,' recalls Horwood, 'when I had friends over from Spain. Nora and Verity were doing the cooking and I was supposed to go and meet these friends who were staying at the Athenaeum. I got them back to the mews and Verity and Nora were on the floor in the kitchen absolutely convulsed with laughter because something had gone wrong. It was just one of those hysterical evenings. We had to pretend that we always ate at eleven o'clock at night!'

There was a lot of entertaining and guests for dinner included actors, writers, directors and executives, everyone from the celebrated critic Kenneth Tynan to their erstwhile boss Dennis Vance. The writer Hugh Whitemore vividly remembers Verity telling him 'about a night they had some boyfriends coming to dinner. They decided to make tagliatelle verde. They put out the starters and then discovered that Verity's cat had eaten the tagliatelle so they had to make some more. Dinner was underway and everyone was enjoying themselves when Verity's cat, who had been sitting and watching them all from the top of the television, started to be slowly and copiously sick, vomiting out great long strips of green pasta.'

It was, admits Horwood, often a struggle to get going in the morning. 'We all smoked from the moment we woke up,' she says. 'That was breakfast. We were always late in to work but one did work very long hours. All our lives were tied up with work and work colleagues. We were deeply into it and it came first. Once you were in production on something, your life wasn't your own.'

Not surprisingly, going back to a job Verity had already mastered so convincingly was less than satisfying, especially when she was called upon to camouflage the inadequacies of an incompetent director called Jack Dixon. 'He came from Holland to direct an

Armchair Theatre,' she recalled. 'In those days we had to do a camera script and work out where your cameras were going to be. It transpired he wasn't particularly interested in [this] so it fell to me. Because I had worked for Ted Kotcheff, I knew what would look good, so he got quite a classy thing from me, I have to say. He got another job out of it actually, didn't have me and didn't do quite as well. Sydney [Newman] said, "I don't understand it, Verity. He did the last show and it looked great," and I said, "That's because I did that one."'[14]

Newman was by now in overall charge of drama at ABC but even he seemed unable or unwilling to promote Verity further or faster. She had been promised that when the company was next looking for directors, she would be put before the interview board. When it came to it, no women were even short-listed. 'I'm absolutely sure it was because they did not want a woman director,' she said later. 'They did not even bother to make an excuse for not keeping their promise. They didn't have to in those days. I made a lot of complaints because I'm quite vociferous but there were no means of really complaining in 1962. There wasn't a sexual discrimination board. I don't think anybody had even taken their bra off in those days. I decided that if I couldn't move up somewhere within a year, I would forget about television and do something completely different.'[15]

In December 1962, Newman joined the BBC as head of drama. He'd actually been headhunted by director of television Kenneth Adam some months before but ABC had initially resisted his requests to be released from his contract. The new job was prodigious in scope and potential.

'He really revolutionised drama,' believes former BBC executive Paul Fox. 'He was the man who made BBC drama work. Until then it had been boring and dull. He was the great Canadian showman and would say 'fuck' round meeting tables when women were present and when nobody said 'fuck'. He had this transatlantic bravado and drive and gung-ho spirit which was needed at the BBC at that particular time – to give it a kick up the arse hard and try something different.'

'Sydney was a wonderful rough diamond of a man,' says Joan Bakewell[16]. 'He was a bit of a bruiser, absolutely terrific but gave no quarter and wouldn't stand fools.'

Newman's arrival caused consternation among those who regarded him as a vulgarian, noisy, brash and brutalist. 'He was a catalyst for change,' says director Christopher Barry, 'and had such a explosive effect on the department it went on to different kinds of success. He interviewed me and I remember I was very surprised to find him putting his feet up on his desk in front of me. I was facing the soles of his feet before I saw his face!

---

[14] Kaleidoscope convention interview, 2006

[15] Quoted in *Winning Women* (see bibliography)

[16] Newman appointed Bakewell's then-husband, Michael, as head of the plays department

He may have done it just to see if I was shockable.'

'I couldn't cope with all that swearing and shouting,' admits Betty Willingale, then the script editor of the Sunday classic serial.[17] 'He absolutely didn't like them at all – he was always nit-picking and driving us mad.'

Whether fair or not, to Newman, these serials were a symptom of precisely what was wrong with BBC drama. He regarded them as staid and predictable, based on a literary and historical tradition rather than rooted in the fresh and contemporary. Perhaps even more of a cardinal sin from his point of view, many of them failed to attract or sustain a substantial audience.

'Above all,' stresses Fox, 'Sydney wanted audiences. He wouldn't only say, "It's a wonderful play," but also "What are the audience figures?"'

Newman relished the opportunity he had been given. Rapidly, he revolutionised the department, dividing it into three distinct component parts – plays, series and serials, each with its own head who would report to him. He also took charge of the BBC's commitment to screening lavish television operas. Looking back in a 1986 interview, he said that his 'main task was to strike a balance between high cultural tastes and vast average popular tastes. It was a matter of finding a balance and at the same time pushing forward to be the most creative and discerning about the changing moral and political climate. I wanted to be the best and I wanted big audiences.'[18]

One of the problems inherited by Newman and that he was required to address was the critical performance of the BBC's Saturday night line-up. Between the big-hitting ratings of the afternoon's sports coverage and the start of the popular youth show *Juke Box Jury*, there was a sudden and significant drop in audience figures. He recalled: 'I was asked, "Could we do another kind of children's drama which would sustain the ratings and start building towards Saturday evening?" I always had a love for sci-fi and I thought of a time/space machine and the cute thing about it was that it was to be a very commonplace object. It could have been an old car or anything. I've never claimed that the police telephone box was my idea, only that it be a kind of space machine that would be small on the outside and enormous on the inside.'

Newman's other conviction was that whatever this new serial became, it should first and foremost be appealing to children, with a certain educational element. 'That's why I wanted it to be a time machine, to go back in history.'[19]

---

[17] 'When he left,' says Willingale, 'he came and shook my hand and said, "It's the greatest regret of my life that I couldn't kill the fucking classic serial."'

[18] Interviewed for *DWB (Doctor Who Bulletin)*, August 1986

[19] Quoted in *DWB*, as before

A script department working party was put in place to brainstorm concepts and characters. The serial was given the name *Doctor Who*, a reference to the leading character who would, as Newman put it, 'be an old man of 760 years of age who had fled from outer space. A crotchety old guy who really is acutely intelligent and intrinsically kind.'

When Newman began to think about who might produce this new series, he knew it had to be someone new to the job, fresh, dynamic, and ambitious. He was troubled by what he felt was a lack of suitable candidates. The launch of the new channel, BBC2, just months away, was creating a plethora of opportunities and soaking up much of the available talent. He offered the job to a bright young director called Don Taylor, who turned it down. Shaun Sutton, who had directed a string of children's serials with some flair, was also uninterested. Also briefly in contention was Richard Bates, who had impressed Newman as story editor on ABC's *The Avengers*. Bates politely refused and claimed that almost as soon as he'd put down the receiver, he heard the phone ring in the office next door where Verity was working. Newman had 'remembered Verity as being bright and to use the phrase, full of piss and vinegar. She was gutsy. The best thing I ever did on *Doctor Who* was to find Verity Lambert.'[20]

Verity herself always said that the call from Newman started with the question, 'What do you know about children?' – the answer to which was next to nothing 'except for my own childishness.'[21]

According to Linda Agran, her friend and future colleague at Euston Films, 'when Sydney Newman told her that she'd be doing a children's programme, she went completely ape-shit. She said, "I don't know any children, I don't want children, I don't fucking like children!"'

But she accepted his invitation to BBC Television Centre to meet head of serials Donald Wilson with alacrity. 'I don't think he quite liked her at first,' said Newman. 'She was too good-looking, too smart Alec-y, and too commercial television minded, and he was a rather snooty, typical BBC pipe-smoking type.'[22]

Newman stressed that he was considering other candidates. 'I'm not sure that was true,' said Verity, looking back, 'but I think he said that so I wouldn't get overconfident.'

She needn't have worried. The job was hers, and it can only be imagined with what satisfaction she tendered her resignation from ABC. She had been toying with the idea of trying the antiques trade, abandoning a television career that had seemed moribund

---

[20] Quoted in *DWB*, as before

[21] Quoted in 'A Woman's Tale', *The Sunday Age*, 1990

[22] Quoted in *DWB*, as before

– until now. 'It didn't matter if she had been offered the news,' chuckles veteran director Herbert Wise. 'She was sharp enough to know it doesn't matter what rubbish it was. It was a toe into the BBC. Once in, particularly with Sydney there, she'd do all right.'

Asked about this critical turning-point in her life, Verity herself was characteristically blunt: 'I would have taken a job producing anything,' she said, 'because I wanted that opportunity. I had the glorious ignorance of not really knowing what was in store for me.'[23]

Whatever doubts she may have privately felt about the prospect of producing a series for children, it was nonetheless an extraordinary vote of confidence and the chance for which she had been longing, to galvanise her abilities and prove her worth. 'I thought, maybe if I take this job I might be able to direct...' she later admitted[24], unable to imagine the extent to which this thrilling appointment was going to transform her life and define her legacy.

---

[23] *Doctor Who Magazine* Issue 234 (17.01.96)

[24] Kaleidoscope convention interview, 2006

CHAPTER THREE
ADVENTURES IN TIME AND SPACE
1963–1965

'I have strong views on the levels of intelligence we should be aiming at. Doctor Who goes out at a time when there is a large child audience but it is intended more as a story for the whole family. And anyway, children today are very sophisticated and I don't allow scripts which seem to talk down to them.'

Verity to John Sandilands, *Daily Mail*, 28 November 1964

Verity joined the BBC as a producer on a six-month contract on 17 June 1963. The excitement of being offered the job had been tempered by the subsequent salary negotiation. 'I don't know why we're employing you when we have people with much better qualifications,' she was told.[1] Verity had to fight for a fee only nominally greater than the one that she had been receiving as a PA. She was at least allowed the privilege of parking at the front of Television Centre but there was a lull of several weeks before she could get started. In those Cold War days, it was standard BBC practice to security-vet prospective staff.

Other than this official scrutiny, Verity knew that she was likely to be the focus of a different kind of attention in her new role and, as a consequence, she was careful with her image, choosing well-cut expensive clothes to offset her well-cut, expensive hair, discreet jewellery and killer heels. She was adopting her version of what would later be termed 'power dressing', acquiring a style to belie her youth and counterpoint her natural authority. She was, she later said, 'a bit of a freak' and arrived when both her new bosses, Sydney Newman and Donald Wilson, were on leave so must have felt all the more

---

[1] From *The Executive Tart* (see bibliography)

exposed. But it is not true that she knew no one else at the BBC; Newman had already brought over some of the old crowd from ABC and her friend Irene Shubik would soon follow her.

There were several women in relatively powerful positions at the BBC but Verity had the distinction of being the very first female producer in the newly formed drama group, as well as by far its youngest. Some of those working at this time still dispute Verity's right to claim this achievement but their objection is based on an understandable confusion. Until Sydney Newman's reorganisation of the department, there had indeed been other women credited as producers. However, these women, among them Naomi Capon and Chloe Gibson, were, in truth, directors (the title they now assumed). Newman wanted producers to be quite distinct from directors and the credits to reflect this.

There were three departments in his newly forged drama group – plays, series and serials. *Doctor Who* came under serials and its head, Donald Wilson. A few weeks earlier, Wilson had offered the position of *Doctor Who* story editor to Betty Willingale, who was then doing the same job on the Sunday classic serial. Willingale had been horrified. 'I wasn't at all happy,' she says. 'I didn't want to do it. I'm not interested in any kind of science fiction. Then Verity was appointed. And Donald said, "We've decided that it wouldn't be a good idea to have two women working together," which made me laugh. But, because I didn't want to do it, it was also a great relief.'

Instead, Wilson chose David Whitaker, a thoughtful and quietly creative man, who was to be a great support to Verity over the coming year.

When she first walked into the *Doctor Who* production office, Verity found, as well as Whitaker, a small team already in place, including the experienced director Rex Tucker and what had been termed an associate producer, Mervyn Pinfield, seconded to the new programme because of his technical expertise and, according to the actor Russell Enoch,[2] 'like a wonderful sort of head prefect. She was always trying to tease him.'

There were also a couple of capable secretaries, Margaret Turner, who worked for Whitaker, and Val Speyer, who was assigned to Verity.

This compact group, based first on the fifth floor of Television Centre and then in a cramped set of offices in Threshold House on Shepherd's Bush Green, had just a few weeks to turn a collective idea into a thriving and functional series, with a projected run of a year, to be delivered on a tough weekly turnaround. But for Verity, the immense practical and creative challenges ahead had to be accompanied to a background noise of suspicion and spite. 'Verity arrived with a great deal of sniggering,' admits director Richard Martin. 'She knew she was being scrutinised. She looked out of place and felt

---

[2] At this stage, and for many years, Enoch acted under the name William Russell, which is how he was credited throughout *Doctor Who*

out of place and was out of place but she had so much bloody nose on her, that woman, and Syd knew that and just believed in her. People would come out of their offices and say, "What's she wearing today, Richard?" She was tough enough to take it.'

Someone with a good understanding of Verity's situation at this time is the presenter Joan Bakewell, who had for years to contend with the condescending by-line 'the thinking man's crumpet'. 'We put up with a good deal of sexism,' she says. 'I was patronised and generally treated as a woman and I'm sure she was too. I think what we both did was keep our heads down and get on with our work. We didn't mix with the kind of people who would be snide about us. Verity was a very determined person and so was I. If there were issues that arose, you toughed it out.'

During the many meetings involved in setting up the series, some of Verity's male colleagues would occasionally make goading and impertinent comments such as, 'Oh, you're not going to cry, are you?' and 'Don't you worry, dear.'[3]

'Meeting me was a shock to a lot of people,' said Verity herself. 'I would be introduced to someone and I could see horror flit across his face before he rearranged it into a sort of smile. I was aware that I was an oddity. I had never produced anything, I hadn't got a university degree, I was not a BBC-type person. People looked at me and said, "Well, what's *she* done? Why is *she* here? Why isn't one of *our* people doing this?" I am sure they thought I was sleeping with the head of the department. People did ask me.'[4]

In 1990 she told the Australian newspaper, *The Sunday Age*: 'The fact is, it wasn't true and I couldn't give a shit.'

But her promotion and arrival were so conspicuous that the assumption that she must be sleeping with Newman was inevitable. 'We all thought, "Well, we know how she got in,"' says Val McCrimmon, who was to be an assistant floor manager on the new series.

Waris Hussein, who was yet to be appointed to the programme, remembers having a drink in the club at Television Centre one evening and overhearing two women, 'like characters out of *The Killing of Sister George*,[5] bitching, "She didn't *walk* into this job, did she?" I was fully aware of the prejudice and so was she and she was determined not to let it fail.'

'Everybody thought you slept your way to the next job,' observes agent Freddie Hancock. 'She had a very close-knit circle around her that she trusted and part of that was because there was so much bitchery that went on about women. No one really relished

---

[3] Quoted in 'A Woman's Tale' – *The Sunday Age* – 1990

[4] Quoted in *Women with Attitude* (see bibliography)

[5] 1964 play about the dysfunctional lesbian relationship between an older and younger actress. Written by Frank Marcus, it became a celebrated film in 1968 and starred Beryl Reid as the butch June Buckridge

your success, they relished you falling apart.'

'It's a sign of those times,' shrugs vision mixer Clive Doig, 'because there was a lot of sexism. Men were resentful of women taking their jobs so it was thought that she was just Sydney's little plaything.'

'Having affairs with people like Ted and Sydney was part of the ladder – it happens,' says director Piers Haggard. 'She was wonderfully driven and wasn't the sort of person to cross her legs and hold it back. I think she was more liberated – if she wanted to do it, she'd do it. Years later, Verity and I were involved in a discussion on stage at the National Film Theatre. Sydney was in the audience and I remember him calling out something like, "And how's my little sugar pot?" – a shameless, unmistakable sexual endearment. No decorum at all. Talking in almost lascivious terms about Verity. It was so clear. You got the vibration that he remembered those long, hot afternoons.'

'She didn't have a love affair with him,' asserts another eminent director, Herbert Wise, 'but she certainly went to bed with him. The French are much more grown up about this. She was quite busy jumping in and out of bed. Women had to do this then. I was present when she once gave some advice to Irene Shubik. Irene was complaining about not getting the opportunities. Verity said, "Come on, girl – stop moaning. Open your legs and get on with it."'

Given Verity's sense of humour, it is entirely likely that this remark was made in jest, simply to tease Shubik, who had a neurotic tendency to take herself too seriously. But Wise remains adamant that Verity used her undoubted allure to her professional advantage.

'She was a gorgeous kid,' said Newman of Verity, years later. 'And the fact that she was pretty certainly helped. In the first two or three months, people imagined she must be my mistress – which she wasn't.'[6]

'*Of course* he lusted after Verity,' says BBC executive Paul Fox. 'In a big way. There's no question about that. She was unbelievably sexy, stunning, lively and fun.' Despite this, Fox is among the sceptics. 'She wasn't going to have it off with the head of department,' he says.

'We all adored Sydney,' points out Verity's then housemate, Jill Horwood. 'But I don't think she had an affair with him. I really don't think she did. She was very clever and she knew how to play him. He wasn't into offering jobs just because you were pretty – he wasn't that sort of person at all.'

'He was something else,' believes designer Eileen Diss. 'A man of tremendous liveliness. Verity was very much the sort of person he would have backed because they both had this spark and energy.'

---

[6] Quoted in *The Executive Tart* (see bibliography)

'Syd wanted to shake the fuck out of the BBC,' says director Richard Martin, 'and he had a belief in her. It was a sort of Jewish dad with Jewish kid. He saw, quite rightly, that she was going to make a success somewhere along the line, somehow.'

Did it help that she was Jewish too? Some have theorised that Newman's patronage was in part due to their shared cultural heritage. 'There was a loose, unreligious, very joyful sense of Jewish friendship in the business then,' says actor and writer Douglas Livingstone. 'Because they are so good. They know what they're bloody well doing, they really do. Television is just something that as a group of people they are very good at.'

In the run-up to its launch, *Doctor Who* was very much Newman's pet project and as the producer who had to realise it, Verity necessarily had to spend a lot of time with him, discussing and debating decisions. This only intensified the whispering within the corridors of the BBC. Verity faced it out. She was never one to hide herself away and, indeed, she rapidly became a stalwart of the various BBC club bars, holding court, usually laughing, always vivacious. When not lunching off the premises, she would get one of the secretaries to book her a table at the waitress-service section of the staff canteen and there, over the subsidised BBC three courses and plonk, she would foster friendships with colleagues attracted by her obvious intelligence and unselfconscious *joie de vivre*. If anyone had the guts, or lack of tact, to quiz her about the relationship with Newman, she would answer without rancour but deny anything improper.

'I didn't think about it at the time,' she told *The Daily Express* in 1982, 'because when I was in my twenties, I didn't think I was attractive. I wanted to look like the stereotype of the day, gamine like Audrey Hepburn, and I didn't. When people told me I was attractive, I didn't believe them. But looking back, I'm sure the fact that Sydney Newman found me attractive helped enormously.'[7]

Over 50 years later, no one can be sure of the truth. During their lifetimes, both parties consistently denied there was anything physical about it. Throughout her career, Verity was willing and able to use her sexuality when she needed to, and to enjoy doing so. But there is a wealth of difference between flirtation and surrender. She would surely have been aware of the risk of giving any man in thrall to her what he wanted, only to watch him rapidly lose interest afterwards, which is so often the nature of the beast. Whatever physical attraction existed between her and Newman, and however it was acted out, there was clearly more to their relationship. She respected and admired him, feelings which he reciprocated. Crucially, she also had the talent to deliver what Newman was looking for. So, whether she slept with him or not, it was still a far-sighted and intelligent decision to give her the chance to demonstrate her abilities.

---

[7] *Daily Express* (12.10.82)

'I modelled myself on Sydney,' Verity told an audience at a university conference in 2004.[8] '[He] was quite an interventionist producer and very much wanted to be part of the creative process and so that was my role model. I felt that the producer had a very creative role.'

Perhaps it was this belief, allied with the distraction of both her sex and her youth, which set the incumbent director Rex Tucker against her from the start. Verity said later: 'I could hear him thinking, "Here's a young girl I can walk all over."' Tucker was pushing to cast an actor called Hugh David in the title role, made up to look older. As well as disliking the idea, Verity felt it was impractical given the time pressures they would be working under in the studio. There was a brief battle of wills until Tucker withdrew from the process, an early signal that, although supremely collaborative, Verity was absolutely determined that her authority would prevail.

Always a hard worker, and with a lack of domestic distraction, Verity imposed an energy and purpose on her team. Her secretary, Val Speyer, became the first in a long line of personal assistants to fall completely under Verity's spell. The BBC's Written Archives are full of the little notes Speyer carefully typed when Verity was out of the office, full of queries, requests and information for her boss ('Madelaine in Costing Unit rang…as you know, there is considerable overspending on some things…') Speyer, plain, kindly and thorough, was dazzled and motivated by the energy, glamour and sheer fun of her producer.

Every day, Verity would arrive at Threshold House ready to attack the day. 'She'd sort of rush into the office and there was quite a fraught atmosphere, hectic,' recalls David Whitaker's secretary, Margaret Turner. 'She was very much in charge. Once she was in, everybody knew that she was there and it was all go, go, go. She always knew exactly what she wanted. There was a lot of shouting but she was very nice.'

Maggie Allen was a trainee producer's secretary, working with Peggy Lupton, who had been assigned to assist the first director. Allen, later to become a prolific writer and script editor, vividly remembers her time with Verity. 'We got on like a house on fire,' she recalls. 'She used to take me around with her to take notes. I wonder if, having been a production secretary herself, Verity thought it would be extremely useful experience for me, learning how a drama series was set up. She was only two years older than me but she had this great confidence and presence. She was really classy. I remember how I nearly choked when I was nominated to walk forward towards the camera through different clouds of 'fog' in a studio in Lime Grove, while she decided which effect to use for the opening when you first see the TARDIS. I was coughing my lungs up and I thought, "This is the glittering world of show business!" I also remember going to the Radiophonic Workshop, where Delia Derbyshire played her the title music for the first time.'

---

[8] At the Producing Popular Television Drama conference at the University of Reading, 16 October 2004

'I want a new sound – way out and catchy,' Verity had briefed Desmond Briscoe, the head of the Radiophonic Workshop. He replied, 'Then we want Ron Grainer to write it for us.'[9]

Grainer was an Australian composer who had already made a name for himself devising the themes for series such as *Maigret*, *Steptoe and Son* and *That Was The Week That Was*. Delia Derbyshire and Brian Hodgson arranged his score for *Doctor Who* using an oscillator, a 'white noise' generator and another machine similar to an electronic guitar. This collaboration created one of the most distinctive television themes ever. 'I'm delighted with it,' Verity told the *Daily Mirror*'s Clifford Davis. 'It's just what I had in mind.'

With the recalcitrant Tucker out of the way, a new director was given the job of launching the serial. At 23, Indian-born Cambridge graduate Waris Hussein was even younger than Verity. Having survived the rigours of the BBC's directors' training scheme, he had cut his teeth on the twice-weekly soap opera about a women's magazine, *Compact*. This followed a pattern of one live show, followed almost immediately by one recorded as live. Hussein had proved himself on his very first live edition when, seconds into transmission, one of the four cameras failed. 'I had to direct the rest of the three to cover the gaps,' he grimaces. 'It was like one of those awful Hollywood movies where Doris Day lands the plane. I managed to land the plane. Because I managed to avoid the catastrophe that it could have been, I got an annual ongoing contract.'

Hussein is under no illusions as to why he was given the new serial. 'Nobody wanted to touch *Doctor Who*,' he says. 'Nobody thought it was going to get made. They thought it was crap. The attitude was, "If it's going to fail, it might as well fail with this young Indian."'

Hussein made his way to room 5014 at Television Centre. 'There was this woman with this fabulous Vidal Sassoon hairdo, dressed simply but incredibly elegantly. I said, "Hello, I'm Waris," and she said, "Hello, I'm Verity," and I went on, "What are we going to do with this?" She smiled and shrugged. "Well, we're going to have to make it work."'

Hussein, beautiful, clever, talented and waspish, was a stroke of luck for Verity. Like her, he had something to prove, was passionate about his work and fun to be with. 'He made that first serial work by going into it with the right attitude,' she later recalled. '"This is going to be a good story and I'm going to enjoy it." I felt the same way. We used to fall about with laughter at the fact that he had actors coming into audition and he had them showing their legs because they had to wear bear skins on set. We had a very good time and it was absolutely the right atmosphere to start making the series.'[10]

Their friendship would last for the rest of her life. 'Sometimes,' he says, 'you're

---

[9] Quoted in 'Verity's Tune Is Way Out of This World', *The Daily Mirror* (07.12.63)

[10] *Doctor Who Magazine*, Issue 234 (17.01.96)

conscious of evolving or creating a friendship. In this case, I don't think I was ever conscious of it – I think it just evolved by itself because we were so much put together by this task of proving that we could succeed in the face of adversity. I was very conscious of my ethnic background – of walking on the studio floor and having these redneck crews looking at me askance and wondering when I was going to stumble and fall. I knew I would have to be absolutely prepared, my camera scripts immaculate. For Verity, the whole attitude to women was they don't do this job, they were secretaries or PAs – it was a testosterone-driven thing.'

Douglas Allen, a senior producer in the department, was not alone when he complained that she was 'apt to turn on the water works'[11] if she didn't get her way. This wasn't entirely without foundation – but if there were tears, they were real and induced from outright frustration at the frequent obduracy of BBC bureaucracy. This was nowhere worse than in the design department, who were sceptical about the practicality of supplying a weekly science fiction series on the available budgets. Verity's first designer, Peter Brachacki, behaved with outrageous lack of professionalism, repeatedly stonewalling her attempts to get him to engage with the task ahead. 'Incredibly patronising' was how Verity herself remembered him.[12] But such opposition only made her more combative and determined.

Newman wanted to be consulted on the major issues, yet he allowed her the room to make her own decisions too. Casting was, as in all drama, critical. There were four principals to find. Various names were discussed for the most important of these, the man who was to play the Doctor, among them Leslie French and Cyril Cusack. It was Verity's idea to approach the 55-year-old character actor William Hartnell. Along with millions of others, she had seen him play the fierce sergeant in Granada's long-running comedy series, *The Army Game*, and she remembered him, too, from earlier film roles in *Odd Man Out* and *Brighton Rock*. But it was his recent, small supporting role in the Lindsay Anderson film *This Sporting Life* that did just as much to convince her. 'It seemed to me,' she explained later, 'that he was an actor with the range to show us all sides of the Doctor.'[13]

On 12 July 1963, Hartnell travelled up to London from his home in the Sussex countryside to meet Verity and Waris Hussein for lunch to discuss the idea. Much has been made of Hartnell's bigotry and the resulting irony that the producer who cast him in the role for which he will forever be remembered was an inexperienced young woman – not to mention the fact that his first director was a gay (albeit necessarily closeted) Indian. But inevitably, the reality was subtler than this. Hartnell, while undoubtedly a product of his upbringing and generation, with the attitudes to match, was also a man

---

[11] According to Christopher Barry

[12] *Doctor Who Magazine*, Issue 234 (17.01.96)

[13] *Doctor Who Magazine*, Issue 234 (17.01.96)

of the theatre. He listened, was charmed and persuaded. He could see the potential of the part and the appeal of a long contract in what had so far been a lean year. Within a couple of weeks, he accepted the contract to become Doctor Who. 'Obviously, he was my casting,' said Verity, 'but for me he was the best. He was the one who embodied the most complexity – sometimes dangerous or unpleasant, sometimes kind, sometimes foolish. But, most importantly, he was never a member of the establishment. He was always an outsider.'[14]

Newman called her decision a 'brainwave'[15] and future showrunner Russell T Davies hails it as 'brilliant' but not everyone at the time agreed. 'Bill Hartnell was fucking awful,' snorts the director Herbert Wise, 'the most terrible casting. I don't know what motivated her to cast him.'

Within the business, Wise wasn't alone in questioning the choice or rubbishing the outcome. But the audience disagreed and the series made Hartnell a star. He adored Verity and trusted her absolutely and she treated her leading man with respect and thoughtfulness. She could recall only one occasion on which she had any serious confrontation with him and that was when he allowed his irritation at some perceived failing of the *Radio Times* to affect his performance. After the recording, in the bar, she rebuked him. 'I said, "You're much older than I am and a great professional, but it was very unprofessional of you to do that. You let everybody down." We argued. He was very contrite.'[16] On the following Monday, a huge bunch of flowers and a note of apology arrived on Verity's desk.

The pursuit of talent is a key function of any producer but Verity soon learnt that her boundless enthusiasm and persuasive skill were not enough to entice writers and directors of the calibre she had been used to at ABC. 'She was very anxious for me to direct *Doctor Who*,' remembers James Cellan Jones, 'and I was a frightful snob and said, "No, I don't direct that class of material."'

She collected further refusals from directors Philip Saville and Alvin Rakoff. 'It was very much small beer,' says Rakoff. 'She was very upset that I would never do it but it was way beneath me; it was a kids' series.'

Rakoff's wife Jackie was a different story. The couple were on holiday in Italy when Verity rang to offer her old friend the part of teacher Barbara Wright. 'There wasn't that much work around for her at that time,' says Rakoff. 'A lot of directors wouldn't hire her because she was my wife. It was a real stumbling block. She enjoyed working, having the money and she had great respect for Verity, as Verity had for her, so she said "yes".'

---

[14] *Doctor Who Magazine*, Issue 234 (17.01.96)

[15] *DWB*, August 1986

[16] *Doctor Who Magazine*, Issue 234 (17.01.96)

The third member of the company was Russell Enoch, known professionally as William Russell, and familiar from a range of series and serials, including *The Adventures of Sir Lancelot, St Ives* and *Nicholas Nickleby*. He was handsome, confident and established, and Verity thought he would be perfect as the second lead, a rather more conventional hero than the Doctor and able to shoulder the burden of any action or fisticuffs. She invited the actor to lunch and 'she came in looking very smart,' as he remembers. 'I was very impressed. She was a very attractive young woman. She was wooing me to do the part and she won. I gave in very quickly. We didn't talk much about it, we were talking about what we had seen on telly the night before and having quite a nice lunch.'

The final member of the quartet, 23-year-old Carole Ann Ford, was spotted by Hussein in another production, who noted her powerful scream. Ford was invited to an interview to meet Verity, who was taken with her slightly 'strange' look. 'She was very friendly but she had this very strong presence,' says Ford. 'A very strong personality. I was slightly in awe of her. Even though she was so young, she came across as being older. She was very much in command of herself, full of authority, and she had a slightly icy quality to her. I think she was always sizing up situations. There was something about her which made you think you've got to watch her. She immediately engendered your respect.'

'What Verity did was launch a brand-new series with two men and two women,' observes Russell T Davies. 'A phenomenon for the time. She was way ahead of the curve. I'm struggling to think of other series at that time which could equal that. Even *The Avengers*, as much as we love that, has one man and one woman but the woman is a dolly bird, there to look beautiful and it's quite remarkable when you look at *Doctor Who* that Susan is not there to slip into a bikini and Barbara is not doing high kicks – and they are not just dressing either. Barbara is so classy and strong. Susan is clever. Yes, she ends up screaming – frankly, if you put me on board a spaceship with a Voord, I'd scream! All those four are great casting. Two women leads – *now*, you don't get that often.'

The first idea for a launch story – in which the TARDIS and its crew are miniaturised – had already been postponed because of the inevitable technical difficulties it presented. In its place, and before Verity's arrival, an Australian writer, Tony Coburn, had been commissioned to deliver four episodes. Having established the premise and the principal characters, these took them back into Stone Age times for an adventure with cavemen. 'I don't think I would have chosen to start with that,' admitted Verity, later. 'There wasn't a huge amount of dialogue – there was a lot of grunting – and they weren't exactly the most accessible [characters]. I was very worried.'[17]

She tried to sideline the scripts and offered the chance to write the opening serial to Hugh Whitemore, a writer she'd liked and admired at ABC, and who was at the start of his own prestigious career. Whitemore was interested and thought the series was 'a terrific

---

[17] Quotes from DWAS (*Doctor Who Appreciation Society*) convention interview (01.08.81) and *Myth Makers* interview, 1996

A sense of determination – even in the high chair

Stanley and Corrie Lambert, either side of Verity's redoubtable Great Aunt Sheba

Verity with Gerry, the family dog she disliked

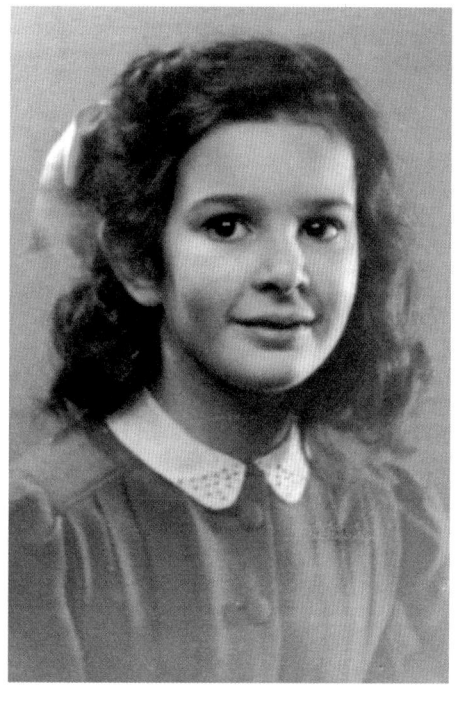

'An individual who doesn't fit the mould'

Celebrating her engagement and soaking
up the sun in Venice, 1955

'I never had any thought of what I
was going to do'

Verity at home
in Crooked Usage

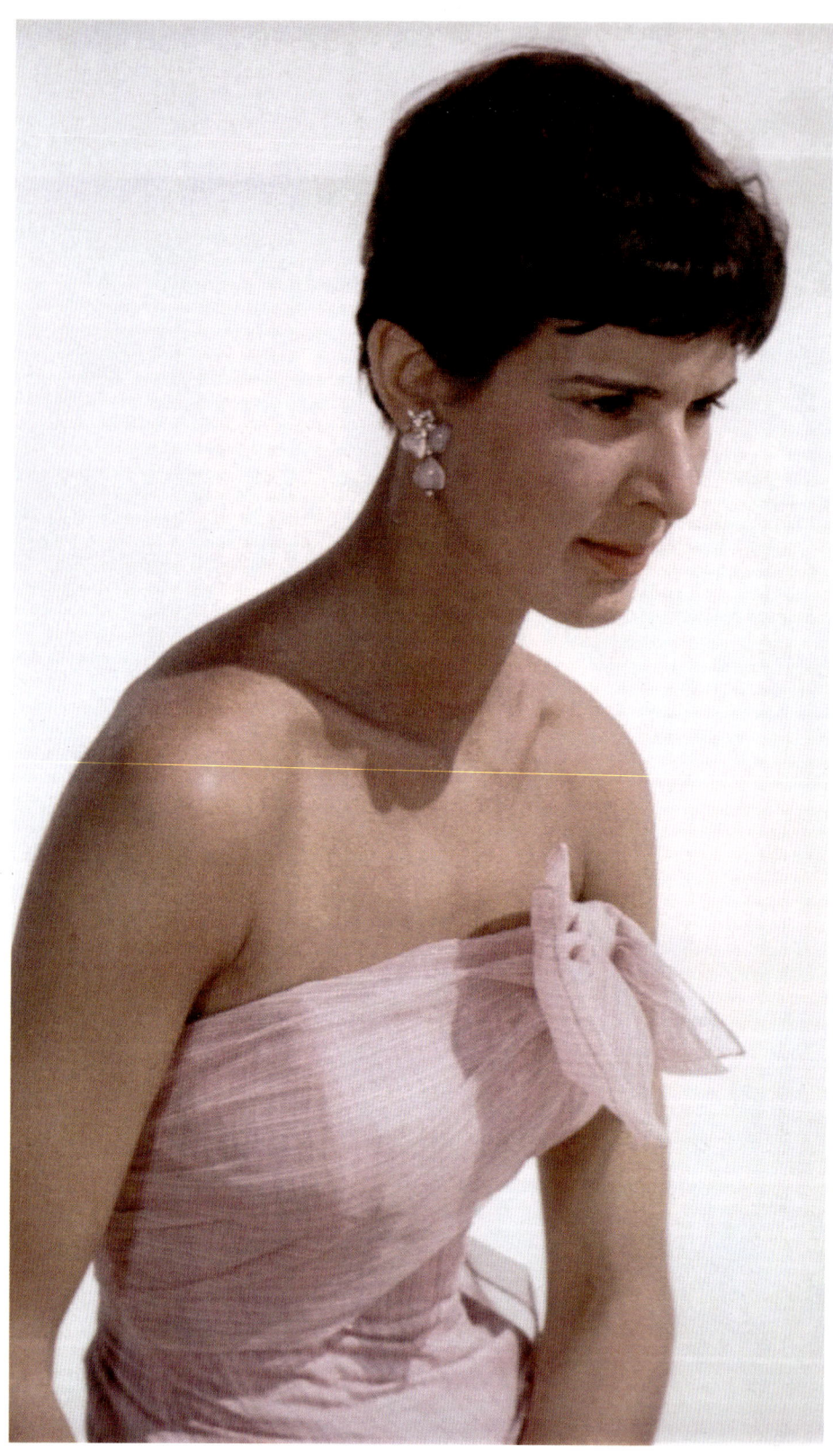

'I wanted to look gamine – like Audrey Hepburn'

In the gallery for *Armchair Theatre*. L to R June Howson, Ted Kotcheff and Verity – 1959

With Kotcheff at an industry dinner. Fourth on Verity's left is Irene Shubik, a friend who later became an implacable enemy

Verity, with friends Cissie and Angela,
in New York, 1960

Taking tea on the set of *Doctor Who*, 1963
L to R Verity Lambert, Maggie Allen, William Hartnell and Russell Enoch.
In his 1965 *Desert Island Discs*, Hartnell described Verity as 'a very charming
and loveable person.'

A rare shot of Verity in characteristic pose in her office.
To the left is Anthea Browne-Wilkinson

Friends were baffled by the unlikely engagement of Verity and flamboyant
director David Sullivan 'Prouders' Proudfoot

'I definitely wanted to succeed, for both myself and my father...'
Showing off the leather trousers with which
she defied the rules at ABC

idea' but was busy elsewhere and had to decline. Other writers failed to deliver too[18], so Coburn's effort remained. It was his idea to make Susan the Doctor's granddaughter, to which Verity agreed. She thought it gave a logic to the characters and a reason for them to be travelling together. This development did not go down well with Newman, though, who thought it implied that the mysterious Doctor must have had some kind of sex life. 'They pulled that thing on me and I was livid with anger,' he said in retrospect. 'Verity cocked it up – it was so stupid to have a character like Doctor Who randy as well, in a children's series to boot.'[19]

Used to his grumblings, Verity was undeterred. The 'ugs' and 'gugs' of Coburn's dialogue remained too, with pages of turgid exposition.

'I mean, what do you do with cavemen?' snorts Hussein. The answer, it transpires, was considerable. Between Whitaker and Hussein's exhaustive rewrites and the clever and imaginative way in which it was directed, the first *Doctor Who* was, and remains, a remarkable piece of work. Achieving it was a fraught process. Ironically for a supposedly futuristic serial, recording was not to take place at the BBC's ultra-modern Television Centre but down the road at the ramshackle Lime Grove, where for months it would struggle to cope with the inadequate dimensions and antiquated kit of Studio D.

'We are working under many difficulties,' Verity wrote in a memo dated 5 December 1963. 'Each episode of this serial (with very few exceptions) is technically complicated. The nature of our work requires numerous sets and the studio is, in most cases, filled to capacity with scenery. We are using cameras which cannot take either wide angle or zoom lenses.' She ended with a plea for additional cameras. All too often, such pleas fell on resolutely deaf ears. Later, when she could afford to joke about it, she referred to it as working 'state of the Ark'.[20]

The design department continued to behave badly. Brachacki's original TARDIS was too heavy to set and strike on a weekly basis, so it was decreed that it would have to be redesigned. The cost implications were obviously going to be significant and yet James Mudie, the head of scenic servicing, simply attempted to bypass Verity and authorise the work himself. She fired off an understandably furious memo to all concerned: 'The original designer should have considered this aspect and, under the circumstances, the man hours and money required for this should not be taken from my budget. I [am] most emphatic about this. I only found out about the redesign of the spaceship having been put into operation because the designer called me to check.'

---

[18] In a 1993 interview with *The Times*, Dennis Potter claimed that Verity had rejected an idea he'd had for *Doctor Who*. The story he pitched apparently concerned a 'schizophrenic who thinks he is a time traveller' – an idea explored in the 2008 episode *The Next Doctor*.

[19] *DWB*, August 1986

[20] Quoted from *The Time Meddler* commentary for episode one

Newman had decreed that there should be a pilot recording of the first programme, and this was scheduled for Friday 27 September 1963. Verity's first experience of being in a studio gallery as a producer was always going to be tense but the whole day was exceptionally difficult all round. As Hussein and his crew tried to work around the serious limitations of the space and equipment, Newman declared himself unhappy with the extraordinary 'howl-around' title sequence and the spooky BBC Radiophonic arrangement of Ron Grainer's signature tune. On both, Verity stood her ground. During the actual recording, there was a series of technical errors and Newman was unhappy with some aspects of the characterisations. He condemned the effort as unacceptable. Although it had been hoped it might be possible to transmit the pilot, the schedule and budget had always been allocated so that a re-recording was an option. This was now booked in for Friday 18 October. In the meantime, Newman took Verity and Hussein for a debrief over dinner in a Chinese restaurant. Contrary to popular myth, 'Sydney didn't really nearly fire us after the pilot,' smiles Hussein. 'He was just cracking the whip. We were totally aware of the limitations of what we'd just done. We were like the Three Musketeers – we were the aliens fighting the establishment. Sydney was Canadian Jewish, Verity was an upper-middle-class Jewish princess and I was an Indian. How much more can you be outsiders? You've got to understand the atmosphere under which we made that show.'

The remount went well. 'The first episode is a piece of glory,' exclaims Russell T Davies, the man who revived the series in 2005. 'It's very hard to capture how absolutely extraordinary it must have been for a woman to be producing something with a gay Asian director, both in their twenties. That would be fairly remarkable now but in 1963!'

In theory, cast and crew were now locked onto a treadmill of weekly production that would occupy them for the next year. Story editor David Whitaker had been stockpiling scripts for this eventuality and new directors had joined: Richard Martin, another *ingénu* like Hussein and Christopher Barry, older and more experienced and, as he put it, 'seen as a safe pair of hands.'

But even as episode one was being put onto tape, controller of BBC1, Donald Baverstock, was being advised that *Doctor Who* was simply too expensive. He requested that production cease after the first four episodes, dropping his bombshell in memo form and promptly departing for a three-week holiday. An intense period of meetings and tense negotiations followed. Verity had to answer for her decisions and make her case for her show to continue. Particular concerns had been raised about the exorbitant expense of the TARDIS interior. The construction of the brilliantly eye-catching hexagonal spaceship had been farmed out to an external company in the face of the inertia of the in-house design department. Verity argued forcefully that she always planned to amortise the cost of this across the year-long run and that it was not an example of profligacy, rather the reverse. While all this internal drama was going on, she protected her cast and crew from any uncertainty and continued to be fully involved in planning episodes she now realised there was every possibility might never get made.

Her working week was rigidly structured. On Monday there was a read-through for the next episode. On Thursday, her producer's run took place, which was her opportunity to see each show in full and give the director her notes before the studio day on Friday, with the critical recording following the supper break in the evening. She was under relentless pressure. Many others might have buckled in the teeth of such a gale and looking back years later she did acknowledge that it was 'a horrendous way of working'. But inherent in Verity's personality was an essential positivity. She had an in-built faith that good things would come to her. If they didn't, she was able to let them go and move on. Time and again, close friends and colleagues have told me how she could immerse herself in the most trying situations at work, fully engage with them but then walk away at the end of the day, switch off and relax. A great asset in any walk of life, this gave her a robustness in the sometimes hysterical amphitheatre of television drama and its need for ceaseless crisis management.

Eventually, the powers that be accepted Verity's assurances that she could deliver the series on its meagre budget and gave a grudging commitment to an initial run of 13. Further extensions followed throughout the next few months but the uncertainty of this real-life 'will they, won't they?' cliffhanger was far from ideal.

Transmission, which ultimately would determine all, was scheduled to begin on Saturday, 23 November and by then, the production had built up a small backlog of episodes, though frustratingly, one of these later had to be re-recorded as the microphones picked up sound bleeding from the production talkback[21]. On Friday 22nd, episode six was just about to be recorded when, at 6.42 p.m., news reached Britain from America of the shocking assassination of President John F. Kennedy. There was no question of stopping but when people asked the question 'Where were you when Kennedy was shot?', Verity was able to provide a more unusual answer than most.[22]

As was standard BBC practice at the time, an Audience Research Report was compiled to synthesise public reactions to what they were being presented with. When Verity scanned the closely typed memo, she must have been relieved to read that 'a good many viewers in the sample...regarded this as an enjoyable piece of escapism, not to be taken too seriously, of course, but none the less entertaining and, at times, quite thrilling...children, they were sure, would love it.' A reaction index of 63 was noted, roughly typical for other dramas at the time, and the ratings of 4.4 million were respectable, despite being diminished by a power cut, which excluded a sizeable slice of the potential audience. For this reason, it was decided to repeat the first episode

---

[21] This was *The Dead Planet*, the first episode of the serial that introduced the Daleks

[22] In 1993, Verity was filmed talking about her memories of this night for the programme *Where Were You?* (22.11.93 Bamboo Films for ITV) Alas, her contribution was not included in the final cut. 'It was an incredibly difficult choice,' director Paul O'Dell wrote to Verity. 'I'm sure you're familiar with the problems. We ended up with literally hours and hours of splendid material...obviously it's only possible to carry so much in a one-hour documentary.'

immediately before the second went out. Verity always felt that this imaginative scheduling contributed much to successfully launching the programme. The other major factor was a monster, which was to become one of the most famous of all – the Daleks.

An inherent part of *Doctor Who*'s premise was that the TARDIS crew would adventure in time as well as space. Stories would alternate between futuristic fantasy-based science fiction and more educational historical yarns. Underwhelmed by Anthony Coburn's Stone Age opus, Verity was equally lukewarm about his proposed second contribution, *The Robots* and, indeed, about the man himself. Trained on *Armchair Theatre*, where the script took centre stage and the text was everything, she could already sense that some writers might easily deviate from what she felt she had been charged to achieve. She liked and trusted her story editor, David Whitaker, and together, they decided to shunt *The Robots* sideways and move forward another commission into its place.

Terry Nation's seven-episode Dalek epic would take the show from modest success to a must-see weekly television event. Ironically, Nation was another writer who felt half-hearted about contributing. 'I remember feeling vaguely insulted at being asked to write for "children's hour",' he admitted years later.[23] Whitaker had seen Nation's episode of ABC's science fiction anthology series, *Out of this World*, the previous year. Nation accepted the job on a purely pragmatic basis because he had just parted company from the comedian Tony Hancock. 'Terry himself was finding his feet as a writer and exploring new things,' comments Beryl Vertue, who was his agent at the time and had the sense to negotiate a share in any royalties resulting from his creations. 'He had the good fortune to think of this thing called the Daleks without knowing quite where that would lead.'

He wasn't alone. The regular cast, who had laughed their way through rehearsals for much of the cavemen serial, now picked up these new scripts with equal scepticism. 'We were very critical of the Daleks,' laughs Russell Enoch. 'I mean – a man with a lavatory brush!'

'We all thought that the Daleks were a huge laugh,' agrees Carole Ann Ford. 'But Verity didn't mind the fact we had such giggles in rehearsals. She was astute enough to know that if you get over the giggles then they don't come later.'

Richard Martin was one of the directors whose job was to realise Nation's scripts. 'He was a fucking awful writer,' he says, with feeling. 'Lazy and arrogant. He would have been excellent at writing cartoon strips in the *Daily Express*. It was that standard. The story was a direct pinch from *War of the Worlds*. Having invented the Daleks, he hadn't ever bothered to think how they reproduced, how they eat – none of the detail. We filled in all of that, me, Chris [Barry – the other director] and Ray Cusick [the designer]. David Whitaker was a nice guy but, unfortunately, also couldn't write dialogue. He had to patch up Nation's appalling scripts. It was bad, derivative writing – awful.'

---

[23] Quoted in *Doctor Who: A Celebration* (see bibliography)

But Verity thought the story 'terrific...full of incident...a jolly good adventure. It was like a proper thriller serial with our people involved. Every episode made you want to read the next one.'[24]

That was her opinion. But when the scripts reached the desk of her head of department, Donald Wilson, he, too, detested them and summoned Verity and Whitaker for a meeting. They went expecting praise and instead were dismayed to hear him pronounce, 'I think this is one of the worst things I've ever read. It's utterly appalling. It can't go out.'[25]

When Verity explained that it would have to, as there wasn't anything else to replace it, Wilson had to concede but expressed his view that the serial was so deficient that it would probably kill the entire project. 'You think about how fast they were working,' exclaims Russell T Davies, 'and her standing in that office and saying, "It's too late – the scripts are done, we're in production now." She was brilliant enough to force that through. But it was nonsense. One day's rewrite on that and you could have taken the Daleks out and had old, wizened men in chairs who were scarred by the war. She could have changed it and there was something fantastically pig-headed about her saying, "No, this works and it's going to be brilliant."' Davies pauses before adding, 'There might have been part of her saying, "We've spent the money as well..."'

However demoralised she may have been, when Raymond Cusick's brilliant Dalek designs were ready for inspection, Verity, like everyone else, couldn't wait to clamber inside one and have a go. The serial was recorded and, perhaps serendipitously, the first episode went out just before Christmas.

Newman had, by now, taken a back seat and left Wilson in charge. Given Wilson's own views about the Dalek scripts, it is interesting that he didn't feel moved to warn his boss about what was coming. Whatever the reasons, it was only on transmission that Newman first set eyes on the Daleks. He was incensed, principally on the basis that one of the ground rules he had set for the series was that there should be no BEMs – or bug-eyed monsters – which he classified as 'cheap science fiction'. 'I was so angry with her,' Newman recalled. 'I phoned her up and said, "I want to see you in my office on Monday morning." I really ripped into her. "You've betrayed the whole concept." She was protesting at the top of her voice but feeling guilty and she blurted out that these were actually human beings who were so far advanced their bodies had atrophied.'[26]

Newman saw the sense in her argument, calmed down and listened. But it was the serial's phenomenal success with the audience that finally vindicated Verity and silenced her critics. The viewing figures soared. Vision mixer Clive Doig still remembers visiting

---

[24] *Doctor Who Magazine*, Issue 235 (14.02.96)

[25] *Doctor Who Magazine*, Issue 235 (14.02.96)

[26] *DWB*, August 1986

the production office and witnessing Verity's excitement at the latest ratings. She embellished her office by appropriating the Magneton, a metal creature specially made for the serial, telling a reporter: 'He's my favourite. I couldn't bear to part with him.'

Her unabashed delight in the Dalek phenomenon was shared by millions of children, and all over Britain, playgrounds buzzed with the sound of small-fry imitating Daleks and intoning 'Exterminate!' at each other. Wilson had the charm and good manners to apologise for doubting Verity, saying, 'I clearly know a great deal less about this than you. I'm going to leave you alone.'[27]

On 6 January 1964, Newman sent her a written pat on the back: 'Congratulations are due to you and those working with you on the splendid progress being made on *Doctor Who*. Many, many people have told me how much they enjoy it. Despite the blonde faeries this last episode, *The Escape* contained one very marvellous thing which you should attempt to duplicate as often as possible. I am referring to the demonstration of intelligence by our four heroes – you know the way they figured out how the Daleks operated their machines and how to disable them.'

Newman was evidently as hooked as the rest. For Verity, all this meant much more than merely proving a point. Against considerable odds, she had delivered an emphatic hit for the BBC and had proved herself more than capable in the process. One of the initial sceptics, director Chris Barry, admits that 'I was really quite pleasantly surprised at her professionalism. Mervyn Pinfield and I would occasionally discuss how she was doing and we were happy with how things were going along. She was a woman on the go, determined to have success.'

When it came to managing her teams, inevitably most of whom were men, Verity used her intelligence and experience. While she made it perfectly clear that she expected to be heard, she was willing to listen and learn as well. It helped that many of her colleagues were in their twenties too, just as keen to make their mark and be noticed as she was. She was able to encourage and harness their energy and excitement, but she was also skilled at using patience and tact to get the best from older and more reserved colleagues, like Barry and Pinfield, with the result that both she and the series benefited from their wisdom and knowledge. 'Unlike some producers, she didn't burden you with too many notes,' says Barry. 'And she was sympathetic to my ripostes if I had to make them. It is fatal in a producer if they can't see the director's point of view. Not having directed may have helped her in that way.'

Barry was grateful, too, for the solidarity she offered him when one recording went badly wrong. 'I was feeling as low as it is possible to feel,' he comments. 'And I left the studio and went out to my car. I had 35 miles to drive home, feeling really terrible. She came out to me so I wound down the window and she bent down and told me not to

---

[27] *Doctor Who Magazine*, Issue 235 (14.02.96)

worry, that it would all work out and it would be quite all right. I found that so helpful and reassuring that I didn't go home quite so depressed.'

Another early director of *Doctor Who* was 31-year-old John Gorrie, who was working in serials on loan from the plays department. 'I was sitting in my office in Threshold House one day,' he recalls, 'when Verity, who had an office down the passage, came in and said, "Now John, I want you to come and do a *Doctor Who* for me." I'd seen her about but I didn't know her. "That's not at all a good idea, Verity," I said. She immediately asked, "Why not?" "Well, because science fiction bores me into a coma," I explained, "It's just not my bag..." She looked at me and smiled and said, "*Nevertheless*, I want you to do it," and I realised then that this was a woman with an iron will and I had to do it. The trouble was we recorded in a studio the size of a hen coop and my story had six different sets in each story. I think it's quite simply the worst directed production I've ever done in my life. It's so static – the camera never moves.[28] But she was hugely supportive and I enjoyed it in a punishing sort of way. And I loved her. I always loved her. From the moment she said, "*Nevertheless...*"'

Gorrie is at the centre of a minor *Doctor Who* mystery. On the official paperwork for this most documented of shows, his name is listed as the director of the third episode of the French Revolution story, *The Reign of Terror*. Gorrie was apparently a last-minute substitution when Henric Hirsch, the scheduled director, was taken ill and dropped out of the recording. But, despite the records, Gorrie disputes his involvement and he has a compelling theory about what actually happened. 'It's a total myth,' he says. 'It really wasn't me. They sent me the episode when they brought it out on DVD and I hadn't ever seen it before in my life. I would have remembered if I had directed it. When Henry Hirsch keeled over, I think probably what happened was that Verity sat in the director's chair and called the shots. I imagine that some officious union person then said, "Was there a director in the gallery?" because that was the rule then – there had to be – and she said, "Oh yeah – John Gorrie was there," thinking, "I'll tell John later that's what I've said." That's just my theory.'

Doctor Who historians have theorised that in the emergency perhaps Verity turned to her reliable and experienced associate producer, Mervyn Pinfield and asked him to take over. But I believe that Gorrie's theory is more credible. In such fraught circumstances, producers were expected to be able to take over and Verity would have been familiar with this etiquette. We know, too, from her experience on the *Underground* play that she was more than capable of holding her own in a studio crisis.[29]

---

[28] The serial was *The Keys of Marinus*.

[29] Verity herself stuck to the story that Gorrie had directed but in *Doctor Who Magazine* (14.02.96), she admitted that had a substitute director not been found: 'I probably would have done it myself. I'd been a PA and worked with directors long enough. It would have been camera-scripted, so although it might not have been brilliant, I could have made it work.'

Whatever the truth, schooled by the hyperbole and temper tantrums of Ted Kotcheff and Sydney Newman, Verity was unselfconscious whenever she felt the need to assert her authority. 'We had a lot of arguments,' recalls director Richard Martin. 'She had enormous boobs and once, by mistake, I called her "Very-titty" to her face; I said, "You can't do that, Very-titty." We both froze and never mentioned it again. I used to upset her and she used to upset me. I don't work well with people looking over my shoulder and Verity was so determined to make her mark in the very early days when we were in Lime Grove, she sat behind me in the studio. On one occasion, we'd got about quarter of an hour of the programme left to do and ten minutes left to do it in. I was, as usual, screaming my head off and trying to talk it all through. Verity suddenly said, "Richard, Richard, stop recording." I said, "What?" "Richard, stop recording!" "All right, hold recording. Yes, Verity?" "I can't allow that hat." She didn't like a hat someone was wearing. And I smashed my hand so hard against the table with all the expletives I could muster that my finger has never been straight since. I just tore into her. She said, "I still can't allow that hat." "All right, take the hat off and let's get on with the show."'

After the recording, at the usual drinks and still fuming about the incident, Martin decided it would be best to keep a wide berth from his producer. She had other ideas. 'From right across the room she yells, "Richard, come here." "Oh fuck, here it comes – dismissal" I went over and she said, "You were quite right to shout at me." The temperature went down like that. "But I was quite right to stop the recording. I'm not going to sit behind you any more – I'm going to sit in a room downstairs but I'm still going to phone you if I don't like it." She was asserting her right. That was our relationship. I was always getting my hands slapped but when the stuff was good, Verity would support you.'

It is telling that, despite their clashes and the obvious animosity Martin sometimes displayed towards her, Verity didn't just continue to employ him, she attempted to include him in her life, too. She offered him the services of her father as an accountant and even asked Martin and his wife Sue to spend Christmas with her. '"Come around and celebrate it at my place," she said. "We're going to spend it under sun lamps drinking hi-balls."' Martin laughs at the memory. '"That's not me," I said. "In our house, Verity, we still have Christmas trees."'

Many of Verity's colleagues tell stories of similarly impulsive suggestions. This attitude was, in fact, typical of her and remained habitual to anyone in her orbit. If she liked you enough and you were part of her circle, there would be invitations, introductions, and presents, and, once offered and accepted, underneath it all an unshakeable loyalty. It is one of the most attractive facets of her personality and it remained with her to the end of her life. It isn't too Freudian a leap to suspect that perhaps it stemmed from being an only child and, as time went on, from never having a family of her own. Verity's friends were her family and she made real and lasting connections with scores of disparate people all attracted by her impulsive generosity, spirit of fun and willingness to enjoy her life. She joined Russell Enoch and his family on holiday one summer and he treasures the memory of her performing handstands and trying to teach his young daughter, Vanessa, to follow her example.

As well as her friendship with Enoch and Jackie Hill, Verity often asked Carole Ann Ford out to lunch, though here her friendly overtures were less successful. 'I had the odd lunch with her,' says Ford. 'But I was so much in awe of her. Now I can see that she was quite obviously reaching out to me.'

As a result of the actress' reticence, it would be many years before any meaningful friendship developed between them.

Maintaining success can be just as tough as achieving it in the first place and this was true for Verity throughout the rest of her time with the programme. 'Verity loved the series and was a real pro,' said Sydney Newman, when he reflected on her achievements. 'Whether she liked the script or not, she knew she had to make the script work, which is what any good producer does.' [30]

Newman nagged her to read *New Scientist* magazine every week, in the vain hope that some real scientific principles might translate into the programme's storytelling. Verity did as she was told but admitted, 'I was hopeless. I couldn't understand a word. I had to rely on imagination.'[31]

Scripts continued to be a problem on *Doctor Who*. Even the director of television, Kenneth Adam, took the time to send a concerned memo: 'If it is to survive, it needs a touch of discipline – especially in the writing. They couldn't really be so stupid by now as always to split up the way they do when danger threatens. Even my three-and-a-half-year-old granddaughter remarked on it on Saturday.'

Sydney Newman scribbled a hand-written response, noting that both he and Donald Wilson had 'rather forcefully brought these to Verity's attention. The scripts are what is difficult!'

'They were really, really bad,' says director Richard Martin. 'Appalling. She knew that it could be something better but she didn't know at that time how to achieve it. She was making it up as she went along'

Some of the cast, and notably the star, occasionally attempted to do the same, prompting a sharp response from Verity who wrote to Richard Martin, admonishing him. 'I am very concerned about the amount of line changing that is going on during rehearsal of *Doctor Who* scripts. I am not against rewrites, particularly if they improve the finished product. If, however, artists are continually changing lines purely because they can't remember what they are supposed to be saying this does not end up as an improvement. I feel that it is your responsibility as a director to exercise control over this.'

---

[30] *DWB*, August 1986

[31] Interviewed on Reeltime Pictures' *Myth Makers*, 1996

The battle over the calibre of the writing continued. 'We used to have terrific arguments every Monday when the script arrived,' says Russell Enoch. 'They were very variable and you'd protest, "I can't say this rubbish." We'd all have a go during the read-through. Carole always wanted something to do and we all wanted it more grown up.'

On 23 February 1964, Enoch wrote to his agent, Terry Plunket Greene, formally complaining about the situation. 'We are going through a very trying time with that script and a great deal of last-minute work is having to be done. Last Thursday lunch time we added a six-minute scene and we are in the studio on Friday![32] It was not good enough in a four-day rehearsal schedule with a new and probably inexperienced director. We have had four new men in the past four weeks. The main trouble stems from the fact that they have written a story in which the four of us are virtually superfluous.'

The agent passed these comments on to Donald Wilson, who sent a note, 'Verity – please speak urgently.' She then held a series of discussions with her principal cast, to reassure them that now the series had been confirmed to run for the 52-week period originally suggested, scripts could be worked on 'much further ahead', a promise reiterated in the comprehensive reply composed to mollify Plunket Greene.

The regular cast were thrilled to be presented with a two-part story set entirely inside the TARDIS, focused on the psychological tensions between them. It didn't matter to them that it was actually an exercise in balancing the books, always the most precarious of Verity's responsibilities. Unfortunately for her, a sequence in which the Doctor's granddaughter, Susan, menaces Ian with a sharp pair of scissors triggered the considerable wrath of the children's department. They were already in an almighty sulk because although *Doctor Who* was intended principally for children, they were not trusted to make it or indeed any drama, since the BBC's organisational overhauls of the previous year. The scissor sequence gave them an excuse to pounce as they knew that it was a long-established BBC protocol that household objects should not be used as weapons in output aimed at juveniles. Here was *Doctor Who*, now apparently watched by most children in the land, flagrantly breaking the rules. 'Memos were flying all over,' said Verity, who never forgot the huge fuss that ensued. 'We made a mistake, we admitted it and apologised.'[33] Russell Enoch remembers that 'Verity came in on that Monday and said, "Oh my God, the heavens have opened! This is a children's programme, you see." But, really, she was aiming much higher than that.'

Complaints that the programme was too frightening for children continued. On 28 July, 1965[34], Verity was invited onto BBC2's topical review *Late Night Line-Up* to discuss the

---

[32] This was for the story *Marco Polo*

[33] *Doctor Who Magazine*, Issue 235 (14.02.96)

[34] Alas, no recording of this edition survives but this book's cover does feature a 'telesnap' of Verity, believed to be taken from the screen at the time of transmission

charge. Here she was ambushed, not by a hostile presenter, but by the writer and creator of *Quatermass*, Nigel 'Tom' Kneale. Kneale felt that *Doctor Who* was irresponsible in the extent to which it engendered fear in its juvenile audience. 'He felt they were disturbed by it, so he had no interest in writing for it,' said Verity. She later remarked that he was 'very offensive about it. I said to him that children are brought up on fright. Look at Hans Christian Andersen – that isn't frightening? Children like to be scared. They enjoy hiding behind the sofa but their parents should be there supporting them.'[35] But Verity faced his onslaught with equanimity. She enjoyed an argument, especially with someone whose talent she admired and when she felt on sure ground herself.

One of the compensations of the Blitz spirit needed to shoulder the burden of a weekly turnaround was the bond that was quickly forged, not just between the four regulars but their producer, too. 'We really did like each other, all of us, that was a really nice thing,' smiles Russell Enoch. 'We'd have a drink after a show and then she'd say, "Come back to my place," and we used to all go back to Verity's and then the conversation would go on, sharing all our opinions about this, that and the other.'

'She was very much a social animal,' agrees Carole Ann Ford. 'There was one wonderful Greek restaurant that we all used to go to and she introduced me to a wine called Aphrodite, which I thought was terribly naughty at the time. We used to have these lovely wine-y, houmous-y Greek lunches.'

On studio days, when there wasn't the time to eat out, Verity and her cast avoided the dire BBC canteen cuisine and held civilised picnics instead, usually in Bill Hartnell's dressing room. Everyone would contribute, whether a starter or main course, perhaps some wine or a selection of cheeses. Although it was unusual behaviour for a BBC producer, it suited Verity's personality and her abiding interest in good food and drink.

The apparently unstoppable success of the Daleks unleashed a juggernaut of merchandising, all of which Verity had to approve. One Saturday she was having lunch as usual with her housemates in the George and Dragon, a modish and expensive restaurant of the time. As they lingered over their drinks, it grew later and later until the place was empty except for them and another table of four. 'We started talking,' remembered Verity, 'and this man introduced himself. His name was Walter Tuckwell. When I told him my name, he said, "You made me a millionaire." I asked him what he meant and he said that he'd bought half the franchise for the toys for *Doctor Who* from the BBC. He had made millions. I never received a penny, apart from my salary.'[36]

The pinnacle of 'Dalekmania', as it was termed, was a pair of feature films loosely based on their first two television outings. Verity was not impressed. 'I would have liked some paid input,' she commented years later. 'Instead, the producers took me out to lunch

---

[35] *Doctor Who Magazine*, Issue 235 (14.02.96)

[36] Quoted in *Women with Attitude* (see bibliography)

and picked my brains. I thought it was awful, just so shoddy. They just made a terrible cheapo version. I think a bit more money, a better script and the television cast would have made it work better.'[37]

In the early part of 1964, Verity had a shock. Donald Wilson summoned her to his office and said that he wanted her to leave *Doctor Who* in order to take on the production of a new serial called *Swizzlewick*.[38] She immediately protested that she wasn't ready to leave *Doctor Who*. Wilson explained that because the new show was going to be made in the BBC's Birmingham studios, it was unreasonable to expect a producer with a family to take it on. She had been chosen because she was a single woman without such commitments. Verity was infuriated. It is unclear how she got out of it. Veteran children's producer Joy Whitby recalls Verity contacting her around this time: '*Play School* had just begun and she rang out of the blue to ask if I could take her on. I remember being absolutely amazed that she should bother to call me. We hadn't met and I didn't know her at all, except by reputation – which was good. It seemed to me incredible that she should want to come to the children's department and work on a small children's programme and, to my shame, I didn't accommodate her. The truth was I had a full complement of staff. I'd already taken on some very overqualified people like Dorothea Brooking, who had been a very successful drama director[39]. I must have been a bit weary of having an overload of high-powered staff. So I just said I was terribly sorry but I couldn't help her. But I always regretted not getting to know her.'

Did Verity ever seriously consider a move to children's TV? It seems unlikely. So was the call to Whitby merely a ploy to explore Verity's options within the BBC and call Wilson's bluff? It seems possible. It is equally likely that she threw herself on the mercy of Sydney Newman, or simply persisted in arguing the case for her to remain in situ. *Swizzlewick* went ahead without her and was, briefly, a topic of debate because it upset a housewife beginning to make a name for herself with her attacks on the supposedly lax morality of the BBC – Mary Whitehouse.

Verity's remarkable gusto propelled her through an intense, unrelenting first year as a producer. Even when plans were drawn up to rest *Doctor Who* for six weeks over the summer, she was proposing to produce an alternative serial to run in its place. 'David Whitaker and myself are, at present, discussing ideas for this,' she wrote nonchalantly to Donald Wilson in April 1964, 'and we hope to let you have something definite by the end of next week.'

In the event, this additional effort was not required. By the time the first series of *Doctor*

---

[37] *Doctor Who Magazine*, Issue 235 (14.02.96)

[38] Twice-weekly serial, transmitted in 1964, about a local council in a fictional Midlands town

[39] Dorothea Brooking (1916–1999) Eventually made her way back to children's drama, where her credits included *The Secret Garden* (BBC 1975) and *The Haunting of Cassie Palmer* (TVS 1982)

Who came to an end, it wasn't Verity who was flagging. At this point, David Whitaker departed and a new story editor, jovial, sweet-natured Dennis Spooner took his place. Front of house, Verity gave in to Carole Ann Ford's frequent moans about the inadequacy of her part and didn't offer to renew her contract. In her place came an almost identikit 'teenage' character, Vicki, played by Maureen O'Brien.

'For me, Verity was like one of the gods,' says O'Brien, now a highly respected author as well as an actress. 'Strong and vibrant. In my mind's eye, I always see her in red. She chose me – I was 21 and she seemed at least 35 and one of the grown-ups. She was from a different world. She was so completely assured and in charge. She was the boss. In those days, as a woman, you had to be furiously ambitious to achieve what she had. But she was not a bitch, primarily and absolutely, not ever. She was kind and she was good and you felt that she had very high standards. The passion for getting it right, the best it can possibly be, is what she shared with the actors. You felt she was absolutely on your side and would fight for you. I was in awe of her.'

The regular cast quickly accepted O'Brien, and Hartnell, who hated change and had remonstrated with Ford not to leave, was eventually reassured. She was integrated into the studio 'lunch club' and was talented and diligent enough to do her best with a thin part. But she loathed the public attention that came with appearing in such a successful show and was aghast at the poverty of the writing. Soon, tentatively at first and then more insistently, her voice was added to the chorus of disapproval at the weekly run-through. 'I was taking it seriously. I felt that often they underestimated the intelligence and the sensibility of the kids in the audience,' she says. 'They'd think, "Oh, here she goes again." They all thought I was mad and patted me on the head. I was frustrated because I thought the scripts should be better. I really didn't like being in *Doctor Who*. I had a sort of breakdown – I was just clinging on by the skin of my teeth all the way through. Now when I look back I think why did you despise it so much? I was such a culture snob and absolutely passionate about theatre and to me, it was just like nothing.'

The struggle for standards, in storytelling and in execution, remained a headache. With hindsight and years of experience, Verity was able to be philosophical about it. 'It is a terrible strain making television,' she said. 'Everything about *Doctor Who* was difficult because we were as ambitious as we possibly could be. We wanted it to be as marvellous and wonderful to look at as we could make it. You have to make so many compromises along the way that if you enter into a project in a spirit of compromise, you don't do good work. You have to start off demanding as much as you can possibly get on the basis that you won't get it all but you may get a bit more than if you didn't try.'[40]

She fought to resist the temptation to bring back her reliable metal monsters, the Daleks, too frequently. One *Daily Mail* reporter, who referred to her as 'talk, dark and shapely', quoted her sniffy response to his comment that the Daleks might one day take

---

[40] *Doctor Who Magazine*, Issue 235 (14.02.96)

over *Doctor Who*: 'I feel in no way obligated to bring them back even if this present story is a tremendous success.'[41]

The reality was that they were now as popular with some senior BBC management as they were with viewers. Erudite sixth-floor executives like Huw Wheldon displayed childlike enthusiasm and nagged Verity for their return. With no more talk about the dangers of 'BEMs' and 'cheap science fiction', she pushed her team to find new enemies that would capture the imagination of the audience in the same way as the mutants of Skaro. But neither the rubber-suited Voord, the flat-footed Sensorites or the insect Zarbi held the same magic.

The Zarbi featured in an almost recklessly overambitious story called *The Web Planet*, which stretched the budget and tried the patience of its fiery director, Richard Martin. 'A sweet little Australian guy [Bill Strutton] wrote it,' chuckles Martin, 'He was tiny! And so pleased with what we'd done with it. "I've never been asked to do anything like this before. It's really wonderful, Richard." Sadly, he couldn't write dialogue at all. But I was excited by the visual possibilities of such a story. I was so conceited and sure of what I could do with it.'

Martin set to work with a will. The studio recordings, now at Riverside, were even tenser than usual. Verity agreed additional camera rehearsal for one episode, only for scenic servicing to let her down again. Two of the sets failed to arrive as scheduled, the extra time evaporated and the advantage was lost. Viewed dispassionately on DVD today, *The Web Planet* is, in many respects, jaw-droppingly awkward, clunky and embarrassing. Yet there is something magnificent about the sheer ambition and imagination in evidence. Everyone is trying to be extraordinary. The Audience Research Report for episode six, *The Centre,* carried the unwelcome news that the reaction index was well below the average for *Doctor Who* together with the comment that 'the whole series based on the Zarbies [*sic*] was "like a third-rate kiddies pantomime." Another [housewife] declared that "even the children were critical of the centipedes' costumes. They looked like something left over from a children's fancy dress party."'

'I don't think it really came off,' Verity admitted, '[but] I thought we took a really good stab at [it]. It was very difficult because we had these bloody things flying about. People were pushed to the limit, which always makes them obstreperous.'[42]

In marked contrast to the schlock horror of the futuristic serials, the historical adventures that interspersed them were often of a very high standard indeed. Even here, Verity was content to allow experiments, agreeing to Dennis Spooner's suggestion that they should try a comedy, which he delivered in four episodes about *The Romans*.

---

[41] *Daily Mail* (28.11.64)

[42] *Doctor Who Magazine,* Issue 235 (14.02.96)

Unfortunately, the dreaded Audience Research Report delivered a damning verdict on this deft cocktail of farce and slapstick, with a below average reaction index and comments like '"So ridiculous it's a bore!!!" declared one of a number of viewers who apparently agreed that *Doctor Who* was only for morons.'

Happily, the report did include some rather more encouraging sentiments too. 'As with all the *Doctor Who* stories, it seemed, it had maintained its hold over viewers of all ages. "It's about the only programme we all rush home to see."'

Verity was always open to trying a different approach and she was realistic about the various cast changes that came her way. Bill Hartnell didn't share her philosophical attitude. When Russell Enoch broke it to Hartnell that he was not going to continue with the series, Hartnell admonished the younger man. 'You've got your arse in butter but you want to leave?' He had hated losing Carole Ann Ford and now he was thoroughly destabilised as Enoch departed with his co-star, and Verity's friend, Jacqueline Hill. 'He was in a terrible state about it,' recalls Maureen O'Brien. 'Upset and worried. It was very difficult to reconcile him to having another person at all. Peter Purves had appeared on this earlier show – and Bill had liked him very much. I remember discussing it with Jackie and Russ and saying, "If we suggest Peter as your replacement maybe it would comfort him a bit?" So I suggested it to Bill and he went, "Hah! Why not?" and he then suggested it to Verity.'

Peter Purves became one of the most rapidly cast companions in the history of *Doctor Who*: 'I'd only seen the bosses – Verity and her story editor, Dennis Spooner – twice – at the producer's run through on the Thursday, and then when we recorded on the Friday. Immediately after that, they came up and invited me for a drink where they offered me the part. Three weeks later I'm in the show – it was absolutely amazing.'

The exodus continued when Verity realised that, despite her best efforts, Maureen O'Brien remained unreconciled to the job and wanted out. 'I remember,' says O'Brien, 'that before one of the recordings, Verity brought Sydney Newman down. She said, "Syd would like a word" – and I can remember her looking at me in a rather hopeful kind of way and Sydney said to me, "We want you to cut your hair short and dye it dark." I said, "Sydney, if you want somebody with short dark hair, why don't you get Carole Ann Ford back?" So he sort of shrugged. I now think that Verity had brought him down to talk with me because she didn't want me to leave – she was giving me a chance to redeem myself and of course I stepped right into it.'

By the spring of 1965, as production drew near to an end on the second season of *Doctor Who*, Verity herself was ready to leave. She realised that there was nothing left to prove and she was hungry to reach for the next rung on the ladder. 'The time had come,' she said. 'I felt (it) needed someone to come in with a different view. It was a fantastically interesting and enjoyable experience and a lot of fun. The beauty of *Doctor Who* was that it was a format show that didn't really have a format. You could try anything. There were no rules laid down and consequently, I could do almost anything I wanted.'⁴³

Throughout her time on the series, attending photo calls for the press, she had become used to the lens being focused on her. She was always stylish and photogenic and being a female producer was still such a novelty; it was often the shot featuring her that made the final edition, usually with some patronising prose to accompany it. The *Oxford Mail* piece of 5 February 1965 verbally ogled her: 'The dark-haired girl with the big brown eyes and slender figure looked much too glamorous to be merely a name on the television screen – even though it is the one that comes up on Saturday afternoons at the end of each *Doctor Who* episode.' This sexist rhetoric was typical. In another story, about the sale of 26 episodes to Canadian TV, their *Globe and Laurel* described 'Miss Lambert' as 'decorative enough to appear in any show she might produce'.

To coincide with her departure, Verity was photographed on set, surrounded by an array of aliens, looking soignée and pleased with herself, as well she might. Not yet 30, she had risen magnificently to the many challenges of the previous two years. 'Anybody can get an idea,' said Sydney Newman, 'but it's what you do with it and the biggest right thing [I did] was getting Verity.'⁴⁴

'She was very much Sydney's protégé,' points out Chris Barry, 'but she was eager to show her own abilities. Lady Luck played a part but she deserved it too.'

'Syd put her in charge of *Doctor Who*,' says Peter Purves, 'and he came up with it but it was a success *because* of Verity and the man she cast, Bill Hartnell, who created a character which suddenly caught the imagination.'

'I think there was some sort of chemistry she must have seen that worked between the four of us,' suggests Carole Ann Ford. 'She got everything right. It was her entré into the world of high-powered producership.'

'She was always in control,' admits Russell Enoch. 'There was never a question that she wasn't in charge. She was determined and so bright.'

'She was a very hard worker,' says producer's secretary Margaret Turner. 'She had such a presence. Nobody thought it was going to be a success. To think, it was looked down on at the start...'

'I do feel,' says Richard Martin, 'that it was a bed of nails that she came into and I do salute her for having turned it into a bed of roses.'

Her departure was carefully scheduled so that there could be a handover with her

---

⁴³ *Doctor Who Magazine,* Issue 235 (14.02.96)

⁴⁴ *DWB*, August 1986

successor, John Wiles[45]. Inevitably, her principal concern during these final weeks was – what next? She still had the ear of Sydney Newman and knew that he was planning a major new series partially inspired by the pulp fiction books about Sexton Blake. Never one to dissemble, she made her interest in the project clear but her immediate boss, Donald Wilson, had other ideas. He wanted to put her obvious stamina to further use on a new twice-weekly soap opera that had been floating about the serials department since 1963 and was only now going into production, as a replacement for the long-running *Compact*.

Titled *199 Park Lane*, the intention was to present a sophisticated saga about the wealthy occupants of the various apartments in a London mansion block. On 1 March 1965, the press reported the cancellation of *Compact* and the imminent prospect of *199 Park Lane*, along with the news of who was to produce the new series. As the *Daily Sketch* put it: 'Verity Lambert, the attractive young girl producer of BBC's top science fiction serial, *Doctor Who*, will be in charge of *Park Lane*.'

Except that Verity thought it a dreadful, dated idea, with no truth or purpose and naturally, being Verity, she said so. 'Donald said he could fire me if I didn't take it,' she recalled. 'He said, "You do realise you're on a contract and not a staff producer. If you don't do it we can just get rid of you[46]." I said, "I do realise that, but I can't do this show."'[47] Grudgingly, she agreed to read some of the scripts. These only hardened her resolve. 'I said I would only do it if we rewrite the scripts, so they were rewritten and the guy that had written them objected strongly.'[48]

She stood her ground and said that she would only produce the series if she could take her name off it. In the face of such resolve, Wilson relented and *199 Park Lane* was assigned elsewhere. Viewers, it soon transpired, shared her disdain, and the serial was rapidly cancelled[49]. It was a victory for Verity but it came with a condition. Newman now

---

[45] Wiles trailed Verity for around six months, sitting in on meetings and story conferences and getting to know the key personnel. He formed a high opinion of her abilities, telling *Doctor Who Magazine* (Winter Special 1983) that she was one of only two people throughout his career whom he felt truly mastered the job of producer. He called her 'an extraordinary woman, capable of that rare talent of working like a spider in a web and getting a creative kick out of bringing together personalities and sometimes making something out of a clash of personalities. Verity seemed to generate activity all around her.'

[46] It is possible that Verity's call to Joy Whitby was prompted by this latest spat with Wilson. The dates may even be indicative that this is more likely, given that Whitby reasons that *Play School* needed to have been running for long enough for Verity to have identified it as a success

[47] Interview for the *Adam Adamant Lives!* DVD, March 2006

[48] Interviewed at Kaleidoscope convention, 2006

[49] Michael Ferguson, who directed some of *199 Park Lane*, recalls: 'My abiding memory is of being summoned, together with Morris Barry, the producer, to Sydney Newman's office and subjected to an onslaught of criticism of every aspect of the production and the announcement of its imminent termination.'

told her that she could produce his *Sexton Blake* series only if she first launched yet another new soap opera. As with *Doctor Who*, time was not on her side. She had already booked a month's holiday in Spain where she planned to water-ski, read and recharge her batteries. When she came back, there would only be weeks to get the new show scripted, fully cast, thoroughly planned and transformed into a successful going concern. Verity was going to have to prove herself all over again.

CHAPTER FOUR

DO YOU DIG ME?

1965–1967

'As a woman I did have to work twice as hard. You really had to be good. Most of my role models were men. There just were not many women in positions of leadership.'

Verity to Susan Vinnicombe, *Women with Attitude*, 2003

Throughout the summer of 1965, Verity was busier than she'd ever been with just a couple of months to establish a brand-new serial and to spare some attention for the reward she'd been given for doing so, Sydney Newman's *Sexton Blake* project.

Even so, she found the time to respond in detail to Newman's additional request to devise some ambitious ideas for BBC2, a channel that was still finding its way and had just been given a new controller, David Attenborough. On 20 July, under the subject 'Special Programmes', Verity presented a creatively imaginative shopping list, at the top of which was 'a specially commissioned opera by Menotti, directed by Visconti/Zeffirelli/Peter Hall, with the Covent Garden Orchestra conducted by Solti.' Other suggestions included 'a specially commissioned musical written for Barbra Streisand', 'a television version of *Othello* with Sidney Poitier and Dirk Bogarde', 'a direct transmission of a major bullfight from Spain', 'a direct transmission of the Mardi Gras parade from either New Orleans or Rio de Janeiro' (to which she helpfully added in brackets 'This could be done via Telstar'), plays written for Jacques Tati and Frank Sinatra, and 'a television adaptation of *A Day in the Life of Ivan Denisovitch* by Solzhenitsyn'. The fact that none of these ideas reached fruition is not the point. The memo precisely illuminates Verity's ability to think in bold and potentially ground-breaking terms, in a way that might combine headlines, healthy audiences and a slew of good notices.

Her indefatigable reserves of energy were now absorbed in the more prosaic demands of setting up the new BBC1 serial. There were, in fact, two new serials planned for the main channel, both of them to run twice-weekly. *United!*, created by Brian Hayles, was the saga of a Second Division provincial football team, to be made in the Corporation's Birmingham studios. Verity was given responsibility for launching its stablemate, *The Coopers*, which, happily for her, was recording in London.

The Coopers had been devised to extract dramatic capital from the post-war new town boom, now at its height and part of the *zeitgeist*. The serial would follow what happened when the eponymous Cooper family moved into a fictional new town called Angelton. Verity recognised the merit and relevance of the idea. Unlike *199 Park Lane*, which she had dismissed as meretricious rubbish, there was some intrinsic purpose beyond the basic function of a serial to provide disposable popular entertainment.

Newman and his head of serials, Donald Wilson, had invited the highly regarded writer and producer Colin Morris to develop the new town concept. Morris worked on the format with Tony Coburn, the man who had written the very first *Doctor Who*. On 6 April 1965 Coburn had produced a document with their conclusions: 'We thrashed this out thoroughly between us, bearing in mind the original brief, which, stated in its widest terms, was; the content of the serial should arise from the influence of one dynamic man upon the workings of a traditional industry and the locality in which this industry operates. Or, stated in more general terms, the effect of the new, technological Britain on the old. We both like this idea but react against a setting of some smoky, dour, bleak Northern industrial town. We feel we might be typical of many viewers who have had a bellyful of the North and the Midlands and that if our serial is to have any freshness and originality, these things would stand a better chance of growing in some area which in television terms is virtually unexplored. We thought of East Anglia.'

Retitled *The Newcomers*, the series was launched with an introductory article, written by Morris for *Radio Times*, which neatly sums up the premise: 'Ellis Cooper, shop superintendent of a firm making components for computers, tells his wife Vivienne that his factory is moving to a sleepy country town in East Anglia and he has been offered promotion to works manager. Vivienne, city born and bred, a modern woman, marriage counsellor, content with her home and social circle, quails; her elder son, Phillip, faced with changing sixth form, hates the prospect... "Try and look on yourselves as pioneers, a sort of *Wagon Train*," they are told by the Town Clerk when they go to view their new home. For the 'strangers' on new housing estates there is loneliness, fear and boredom. But the children look healthier since they moved. Maybe it will be a generation before a balance can be struck for the newcomers? Meanwhile there are new boyfriends, new girlfriends, new babies, feuds with farmers, brittle industrial relations, and civic intrigue – copious material for a twice-weekly serial.'

Coburn was engaged as chief writer and would provide the opening scripts. Some have expressed surprise that Verity and Coburn were willing to work together again. There had been a bitter row over her decision to abandon Coburn's second *Doctor Who* serial, and he had walked away from the production vowing to have nothing further to do with it. But this time, Verity was essentially midwife rather than matriarch. She also had another highly competent script editor, Nicholas Palmer, to act as go-between. The *Doctor Who* reunion was completed when she insisted that Waris Hussein should be assigned as the director to set the show's style and treatment. Hussein himself was horrified. He was about to direct a Patricia Highsmith script when he received a call from Donald Wilson. '"Waris, we're taking you off," he said. "Why?" I cried. "Because Verity's doing a new series called *The Newcomers* and she's asked for you." I said, "But wait a minute, no; I've done my apprenticeship; I've got to do this drama." A pause. "Waris, you're going to have to adjust to the fact that you're not going to do that play." I went onto *The Newcomers* and I can't tell you how I resented it.'[1]

Hussein made his feelings plain – 'I was sulking,' he admits. One day, Verity had had enough and confronted him. '"Waris, for God's sake, come on," she said, and then I got on with it and actually ended up having a really good time.'

By the time he arrived, Verity had assembled her cast. 'All through her career she had a skill with casting,' says Hussein. 'She knew more or less the whole of *Spotlight*.'[2]

Verity made some interesting and intelligent choices. To bring to life the Coopers, the family at the heart of the saga, she first cast Alan Browning (later to find further celebrity as the husband of *Coronation Street* vamp Pat Phoenix) as the father figure, Ellis, with effervescent Australian entertainer Maggie Fitzgibbon as his wife, Vivienne. Their children, Philip and Maria, were to be played by two promising young actors, Jeremy Bulloch and Judy Geeson.

Bulloch, who was a talented amateur footballer, had simultaneously been offered one of the leads in *United!* but instead chose *The Newcomers*. 'Verity was very much involved in persuading me,' recalls Bulloch. 'She really pushed for me and that's when I decided, "Yes, I'm going with her." It's so nice to work with someone who smiles and gets on with it. She was terrific, absolutely adorable and so professional. She'd say, "Just keep doing what you're doing." Almost like "Don't act, be yourself." It gave you huge confidence.'

Verity ensured that all the principal actors were offered contracts with a series of options in the event of the programme's success. Just as with *Doctor Who*, it was decided to make a pilot recording before committing to the ongoing series. Eventually, the plan was for the first episode of the week to transmit live and the second to be recorded, the same production model that the BBC had used for their previous soap, *Compact*. The pilot would consist of two programmes taped back to back and then, if they were deemed

---

[1] According to Hussein, the Highsmith script was never made

[2] *Spotlight* is a large photographic directory alphabetically listing the majority of the actors available to work in British Equity

effective enough, these would serve as the first week's output.

Following an extended period of two weeks' rehearsal, to allow the cast to establish their characters as well as block and learn their moves, recording was scheduled between 8 and 8.45 p.m. at the BBC's Riverside studios in Hammersmith on Monday, 9 August and Tuesday 10 August, 1965. A minor overrun on the first day was caused by the breakdown of one of the cameras but the only other trouble that Verity encountered came as a result of the number of different brands of cigarettes ordered on the studio props list. A sharp memo ensued from Terence Cook, who managed the prop buyers: 'Verity, sorry, but I just don't believe that so many are really needed. It looks to me as though Bill Bloggs is saying, "I'd like to have a drag here and it has to be Disque Blue, thank you." 160 cigarettes of five different brands is going too far! Please to investigate...'

History does not record whether or how she did.

Recording complete, Verity took her leads out to celebrate. Afterwards, Maggie Fitzgibbon wrote to thank her for a 'very gay luncheon', adding 'Whatever way the pendulum swings, I hope the series is an enormous success.'

Scheduled between 7 and 7.30 p.m., *The Newcomers* launched on Tuesday 5 and Friday 7 October 1965. The internal Audience Research Report indicated a strong start, commenting: 'in a quiet, un-sensational way, this new serial proved distinctly appealing to a large minority of viewers – just under half of the reporting audience who sampled its opening chapters this week. They welcomed it firstly as presenting a very topical storyline...*The Newcomers* promised an entertaining focus on the human angle of such a situation, with members of one family, the Coopers, occupying the foreground of a picture of change and adaptation. Certainly, the tone of much comment...suggested that the writing and characterisation projected very well not only the central problem of domestic upheaval and readjustment confronting Ellis Cooper, his wife and their children, but also the industrial and economic considerations and nuances relative to the "difference between earning here or earning there."' Encouragingly, there was little downright criticism and even the viewers not as yet fully engaged indicated that they would 'nonetheless be keeping an open mind about the serial and its progress'.

True to her agreement with Sydney Newman and Donald Wilson, Verity only produced the first eight episodes, but the foundations she put in place helped *The Newcomers* to sustain a successful four-year run. Although she had dragged her expensive heels at the thought of launching another serial, she eventually looked back on the experience with a degree of both pleasure and pride. 'I enjoyed doing it,' she commented during a 2004 interview. 'It was completely different to *Doctor Who* because it was very much about reality and life.'[3]

---

[3] University of Reading, 'Cultures of British Television Drama 1960–82' (16.10.04)

For a few weeks, her duties on *The Newcomers* overlapped with the early stages of her next assignment, which would mark her graduation from serials to series, a significant step up within the drama group hierarchy. The shift to series meant reporting to a new boss, the 55-year-old ex-actor Andrew Osborn. Osborn had been elevated to management following the conspicuous success of two immensely popular shows that he had produced, *Maigret* and *Dr Finlay's Casebook*. Osborn was just as old-school as Donald Wilson in serials, and the tone of his memos that survive in the BBC Written Archive Centre are often chiding and cautionary. This caution was evident in his staffing decisions, too. Osborn once checked with producer Jordan Lawrence before pairing him with a female script editor in case Lawrence had an objection to working with a woman. His approach to Verity was headmasterly and dispassionate, but he was only too aware of her position of favour with Newman.

Such privilege came with a weight of expectation. Newman had been trying for months to breathe life into his *Sexton Blake* series but he hadn't got very far. Verity's job was to deliver the goods and do so fast.

Bizarrely enough, the initial inspiration was Mary Whitehouse, the Midlands housewife who, as the main spokesperson of the National Viewers' and Listeners' Association, had become the scourge of the BBC for what she and her members felt were the Corporation's increasingly lax moral standards. 'She was kicking the shit at me,' Newman commented later. 'To her, I was the greatest purveyor of plays of dirt, doubt and disbelief. I was trying to understand this woman and what she was on about. I thought she was mistaken in trying to force Victorian ideas on us today and from that I said, "Damn, I'm going to see if she's right and make fun out of Victorian ideas in the twentieth century."'[4]

Newman first attempted to acquire the rights to the popular stories about the Victorian detective Sexton Blake (a 'poor man's Sherlock Holmes' as he put it) and his faithful sidekick, Tinker. His idea was to take these familiar characters and update them into his own concept – a man out of time. After a few weeks' work, by April 1965, the concept had developed into a few pages of closely typed foolscap, outlining the proposed format for a series called *Sexton Blake Lives!*

The opening episode would begin with workmen, excavating a tunnel for the new Victoria line, stumbling upon a concrete bunker. When they break this open, they are appalled to discover a man tied to a chair, dressed in Victorian clothing and, though dazed, just as alive as they are. 'This is Sexton Blake,' wrote Newman, 'sentenced to a living death in 1895 but now, as the newspapers unhesitatingly declare, "Living To Fight Again!"'

The revived Blake teams up with a descendant of his old friend, Tinker, a lad of about

---

[4] *DWB*, August 1986

16. Except that 'he' turns out to be a teenage girl in disguise, working for her father, Edward Carter (son of the original Tinker), who is a private detective. 'Blake joins them and in the course of this, Carter is murdered. Blake joins forces with the girl, not only to avenge her father, but to recover his lost fortune and maintain and justify his international reputation as a fighter of crime.'

It was an early example of what is now commonly and rather nauseatingly called 're-imagining' and Newman went on to explain his reasons for choosing Sexton Blake as the focus of his format. 'From every indication we have,' he wrote, 'it seems as if we are going through a period of puritan revival. There is now too large a body of opinion expressing fear of amorality, if not downright immorality in our age. To meet this, series programme producers tend to make their heroes pure as the driven snow whether their names be Perry Mason or young Dr. Kildare. By purifying contemporary characters, they become completely unreal. What I want to do is to create a mid-twentieth-century hero who is genuinely puritanical. In short, by taking a man directly from the Victorian age and plumping him into the middle of 1965, we can get a genuine moral person who can act with bravery, positive moral convictions, his eyes glowing with the glorious tradition of a great Britain. Sexton Blake is alive – and he is the man!'

Verity was still producing *Doctor Who* when Newman first mentioned the idea to her and she was immediately intrigued by it. 'I'm attracted to interesting ideas, even if they don't work,' she said. 'He saw it as a way of looking at the world we live in an objective way, so there were some things that would be an improvement and some things that were distinctly not.'[5]

Unfortunately for Newman's original notion, the necessary rights to use Sexton Blake were not forthcoming so he had to think again. It didn't take long to realise that he could simply jettison Blake and create his own morally upright Victorian adventurer. He brainstormed a range of florid and evocative names and christened his hero Magnus Hawke. But there was still a long way to go. As Osborn somewhat wearily noted to Verity in his inaugural memo to her on the subject, dated 15 July 1965: 'This is all there is on Sexton Blake – Sydney's original format plus a pilot script which Terry Dudley was working on with Bill Barron. Philip Chambers was commissioned to write a pilot on the new character once we knew the name Sexton Blake was not available for us to use. Philip failed to deliver because of illness; it was to be called *The Queen's Surgeon* and was a good idea. I suggest you now start from square one. If this turns out really well, the idea is to slot it in on Saturday nights about the end of April '66, so please move fast and keep me completely in the picture.'

Never one to dither, Verity promptly commissioned a new pilot script from the established writer Richard Harris, whose work on *The Avengers* and *The Saint* reassured

---

[5] Interviewed for the *Adam Adamant Lives!* DVD release

her that he had the right experience to deliver the delicate mix of adventure, comedy and social observation to which she knew Newman aspired. The premise was unchanged; the leading character was a Victorian/Edwardian detective 'highly intelligent', 'extremely well educated' and 'superb physically' who is 'dedicated to fight evil in any form'. The supporting character was a 19-year-old cockney girl from the present day, 'not well educated but with a great degree of native shrewdness. She hero-worships the detective and would do anything for him.'

Anticipating that there were likely to be rethinks and rewrites, she suggested to copyright, the department in charge of negotiating the deal, that 'if there is a way of putting a clause in [Richard Harris'] contract that if rewrites be demanded above and beyond the normal he be paid an extra proportion of his fee, I should be most grateful, since it may involve more of his time than would normally be legitimate for a 50-minute commissioned episode.' To her intense irritation, copyright declined to do as she suggested.

Osborn suggested BBC staffer, Ken Levison, who had script-edited on the series *Thorndyke* and *R3* to perform the same function on *Magnus Hawke*. Verity had a long talk with Levison before agreeing but with *The Newcomers* to get up and running, it was late October by the time she was able to devote her full attention to the pilot script. On 12 November, she wrote to Newman, sending him a scene-by-scene breakdown and sharing some of her concerns. 'Some of the requirements are still only fulfilled shakily,' she noted, giving a couple of examples, including 'Magnus meeting a girl dressed as a boy. It is almost impossible to justify this without spotlighting the fact that it is a contrivance...would be most grateful if we could all have a meeting to thrash this out.'

Just as she had predicted, when the rewrites were needed, Harris, now out of contract, was unavailable and she had to draft in another writer, Donald Cotton, to perform them. She vented her frustration in a memo to Newman: 'I think it is a pity that the recommendations in my memo were not carried out and that because of this we had to approach a new writer.'

Alas, this was only the beginning of the endless script problems that were to beset the series. Production was delayed to buy more time to resolve the crucial pilot and to begin the commissioning of additional storylines. Newman dithered with another name change for his eponymous hero, flirting with Tom Devises as a slightly less fruity alternative to Magnus Hawke. Verity suggested the square-jawed leading actor Nigel Davenport to play him. Newman approved so an offer was put together with a sequence of options so that, should the series prove successful, the star would be committed to the role through to 1968. But, just before Christmas, Davenport declined.

Verity's fall back was Gerald Harper, a suave, handsome and mannered actor whom she had recently seen deliver a swashbuckling performance in *The Corsican Brothers*, an ATV

Play of the Week.[6] As she later explained: 'He was awfully good and elegant and moved beautifully. I wanted somebody who was stylish and who could look like he could handle himself and use a sword. Some actors [are] just of their time but Gerald had this ability, a kind of period feel about him, not too modern.'[7]

Conveniently, Harper was also working at Television Centre, recording *A Game of Murder*, the latest of Francis Durbridge's thrillers for BBC2.[8] During a break, there was a knock on his dressing-room door. 'Verity came in and we chatted,' he explains. 'She was a woman of immediate decisions. She said, "I'm doing this new show and I'm interested in you. Will you come and meet Sydney Newman?" So off we went and they told me the story and when it was going to start.'

Harper listened with interest but explained that he was booked to do a play on Broadway. 'Verity said, "Would you mind going and sitting outside with the secretaries?" So I sat outside for ten minutes and then I was called back and they said, "Now, listen. This is going to go out at nine o'clock on a Thursday night. It's taking over from *The Man from UNCLE*," which was a huge success at the time. "Within three months you will be famous. You've got to do it."'

Harper phoned his agent there and then and the Broadway producer agreed to release him. 'That's how we met and that's how we started,' he says. 'She had an extraordinary clear mind and was very forthright and could indeed be ruthless – you could smell that a mile off.'

On 13 January 1966, the series was finally christened *Adam Adamant Lives!* 'I looked up the word "Adamant" in the dictionary,' recalled Newman, 'and found out that adamantine is something very hard – almost as hard as diamond – so I called him Adam Adamant.'[9]

Verity cast 19-year-old Ann Holloway to play Georgina Jones, the fashionable young girl from 1966 who befriends Adam on his resurrection and teams up with him for subsequent adventures. A little-known character actor, John Dawson, was signed to play the third regular, William E. Simms, Adam's butler, who would join the cast with the second episode. Newman decided that Simms should be an 'ex-variety hoofer – song-and-dance man' with a propensity for reciting corny limericks, which he thought could

---

[6] Transmitted 08.11.65

[7] DVD interview, as before

[8] Transmitted 26.02.66 – 02.04.66

[9] Quoted in *Talkback – The Sixties* (see bibliography)

be used to inject a little humour here and there. Newman amused himself by coming up with a few examples.

'When the butler is worried about Georgina's innocent attitude to Adam – "Mary had a little sheep, And with the sheep she went to sleep, The sheep turned out to be a ram, Mary had a little lamb."'

Newman despatched this, and a few others, in one of the frequent memos he rained on Verity, concluding with the rhetorical question, 'Do you dig me?'

Verity did and, rather than relying on each writer to provide their own doggerel for Simms, she commissioned it all from Dick Vosburgh, a comedy specialist.

After more delays, the pilot was scheduled for recording in studio one at Television Centre on 8 April. The director, William Slater, shared her view of the potential dangers ahead, writing to her: 'I feel very strongly that any hint of camp acting or mannered delivery on Adam's part would be the kiss of death. At no time should we doubt the convictions of the character. I would kill an actor if he sent it up.'

But despite their best intentions and many hours of hard work, the pilot was not a success. Newman declared himself as unhappy as he had after the *Doctor Who* pilot nearly three years earlier. 'I think he felt that the writing wasn't witty enough,' said Verity, looking back.[10]

His other concern was casting. 'They threw the first girl [Ann Holloway] out immediately,' says Harper. 'Poor girl. She was quite nice, actually, and rather good, I thought.'

In her place, Verity cast 24-year-old Juliet Harmer, a former primary school teacher, who had been appearing in small roles on television for about 18 months. 'One of the reasons we cast Juliet,' said Verity, 'was because she epitomised that Sixties look, the long legs, long hair, boyish figure, very pretty, very good-looking and very relaxed. She was gorgeous and it was great fun to dress her in those clothes.'[11]

Harmer remembers Verity as 'a shadowy figure and a very, very cool customer. Somebody said, "You know she's only 28," and I said, "She's only four years older than me – she can't be!" I was so startled, I thought of her as being about 58 – she had that sort of charisma and confidence. Very grown-up. She was always very nice to me but I was a bit scared of her.'

---

[10] DVD interview, as before

[11] DVD interview, as before

Harmer was asked to knock four years off her age. 'They said, "We need to have a very young audience so you've got to pretend to be 20 instead of 24." To this day I think my Wikipedia entry says that I'm two years younger than I actually am.'

Despite the doubts about the pilot, the decision was taken to press ahead with a 16-episode series, to be recorded weekly between the end of May and early September. With so little time left before a set of satisfactory scripts was needed, it was the worst possible news when script editor Ken Levison tendered his resignation, having been offered a more lucrative job at ABC. Newman got on the phone to Tony Williamson, the one writer who seemed to be delivering material that captured the essence of what he wanted. Williamson arrived with a Herculean task ahead of him but, happily, he immediately bonded with Verity, of whom he later commented that she was 'one of the hardest working producers I have ever known.'[12]

'She was a genuine working woman,' agrees Robert Banks Stewart, one of the writers on the show. 'She didn't trade on her background. You never thought of her as being an ex-Roedean girl. If anything, she was always one of the crowd. Very go-ey, intelligent, funny and sexy.'

'I didn't find her sexy myself,' counters Harper. 'I found her quite masculine really. But she looked good. She was crisp and stylish. She didn't mess about. She had a clarity of mind which was always impressive. In those days, being a woman producer was like the colour bar. It was just something that didn't happen, but she took to it as if there was no problem at all. None at all. She'd got that authority.'

Scripts, unfortunately, were even more of a problem than they had been on *Doctor Who*. A wide range of writers were courted, among them her former script editor Dennis Spooner, thriller writer Patricia Highsmith, friends like *Armchair Theatre* contributor Clive Exton, and Hugh Whitemore, who disliked the idea and refused to get involved. 'I could see the writers I wanted but I couldn't persuade them to write for me,' Verity commented later. 'I think it taught me that everything wouldn't get handed to me on a plate.'[13]

In 1992, she told the journalist Lynda Lee-Potter: 'I had a crisis of confidence. I'd go to bed, take two really strong sleeping pills, sleep for four hours but I was so anxious I'd wake up again and I couldn't get back to sleep again. It was very frightening.'[14]

Many skilled and professional writers contributed storylines and even first drafts of

---

[12] Quoted in *Time Screen*, Issue 20, Spring 1999

[13] Quoted in *The Executive Tart* (see bibliography)

[14] *Daily Mail* (04.09.92)

scripts but, again and again, rejection ensued. None of them seemed able to establish a tone that worked. They were either too melodramatic, camp and fantastical or dull, mundane and ordinary. It was a constant headache. As Verity noted when sending the latest draft of one script to Newman and Osborn: 'This script will have quite extensive rewrites in terms of action and dialogue. It has already been worked over endlessly and shows it.'

Looking back many years later, she reasoned that 'the part which I don't think we ever really got right, and [it] was a very important part, was a way of seeing modern life in a witty way through the eyes of someone unaccustomed to [it]. The nearest equivalent is Mark Twain's *Connecticut Yankee at the Court of King Arthur*, which was very witty and [had] a sense of the ridiculous as well as the astonishment.'[15]

'I don't think she was very happy with the series,' remarks Gerald Harper. 'I don't blame her, neither was I. It was a brilliant idea, a comedy of manners. A man with Edwardian morals and values looking at the modern world. But the scripts were all done in such an incredible rush. It was a totally missed opportunity.'

It wasn't only the writing that presented difficulties. The practical problems were not inconsiderable, either. The series inevitably invited comparison not only with *The Man from UNCLE*, whose slot it would inherit and whose popularity the BBC hoped it might emulate, but also *The Avengers*. This was by now being shot on film, with all the considerable advantages this lent to a fantastical action-adventure. In sharp and unflattering contrast, *Adam Adamant Lives!* was locked into a gruelling weekly treadmill of four days' rehearsal culminating with recording crammed into the evening of the second of two long days in the studio. 'It was weekly rep with a better dressing room,' says Harper, with asperity. 'It was all done under ludicrous pressure of time. You just learnt the fucking lines and got on with it.'

Even the minimal location filming had to take place within the week of production and compromised the already limited rehearsal available for the leads. The inflexibility of this brutal schedule was no better demonstrated than during rehearsals for episode three. On 25 May, Verity was informed that there had been an accident involving one of the leads, John Dawson. The action called for him to pick up the body of a girl supposedly dying on the doorstep. As he did so, Dawson's back gave way and he collapsed. An ambulance was called.

'Before he'd got to hospital, he was recast,' says Gerald Harper, 'and Jack May was on his way to rehearsal to replace him. Jack was marvellous but Dawson had been utterly wonderful, just sensational. He'd worked for ten or fifteen years and never had a break.

---

[15] DVD interview, as before

I complained bitterly to Verity. "Jesus Christ, you can't do this to the man – it's the biggest break he's had in his life." She said, "Oh don't worry, Gerald, we'll give him an episode," and they did give him an episode.[16] But this had been the only chance he ever had to make his name and he was out in an hour and a quarter. That's decision. Don't misunderstand me. I liked her enormously. I understand why she had to do all these things but there weren't all that many people who could do it.'

Verity always professed to be mildly hurt that Harper saw her as ruthless. From her point of view, there was no choice. The accident had been 'enough to put the actor out of action for several weeks. With our schedule we just had to recast. Gerald says I rushed to recast him before he was even in hospital. I'm sure that wasn't the situation.'[17]

Harper used to joke that the preponderance of deadly female villainesses throughout the series were all based on different aspects of Verity. 'I can't say I was conscious of that,' she commented during an interview about the series. 'It was probably more to do with the fact that you wanted Adam to have a foil and with feminism and women of the Sixties actually running things [it] would be more bizarre to him.'[18]

Verity, as ever, was pushing the boundaries of what was achievable with the considerable constraints of time and money. She was imaginative in her selection of directors, giving chances to former designer and future film director, Ridley Scott. 'He was so slow,' says Juliet Harmer. 'Verity was doing her head in because he was way, way over time. But he was actually someone like her – he wanted everything to be perfect and look absolutely just so.'[19]

She also employed three women in the formative stages of their directing careers, Tina Wakerell, Anthea Browne-Wilkinson and Moira Armstrong. This was an unusually high ratio of female directors for the time and both Browne-Wilkinson and Armstrong became good friends of Verity's. 'She wasn't theatrical, which is what I liked about her,' remarks Armstrong, who first met Verity in the BBC club. 'She didn't go overboard with praising you. I liked her sense of humour – you could send her up and it wasn't resented. I didn't see any vulnerabilities. There's a sort of confidence that money always gives people and Verity had a built-in self-confidence. But it was ambition with charm not ruthless ambition.'

---

[16] Dawson appeared in *The Last Sacrifice* (25.08.66)

[17] DVD interview, as before

[18] DVD interview, as before

[19] In an interview in *The Sunday Morning Herald* (05.12.14), Scott explains that Verity gave him a chance because 'She discovered I was a real nuisance as a designer and I was always criticising the directors.'

Knowing that Newman was a keen aficionado of James Bond, Verity commissioned a pastiche Bond theme tune, sung by Kathy Kirby in the Shirley Bassey manner, to accompany the modish fast-cut photographic titles. These were provided by the talented Bernard Lodge, who had devised the strikingly eerie opening to *Doctor Who* for her.

Verity arranged for the episodes to be recorded onto 35mm film to allow for greater sophistication of editing, aware that fight sequences, of which there were plenty, really only worked when shot single camera and pieced together afterwards for maximum pace and impact. Enormous pressure was brought to bear on designers and worried memos flew around about the amount of sets and frequency of overruns in the studio, which incurred punitive overtime payments. On 16 June 1966, Osborn was moved to write to her: 'You have, I know, had more than your fair share of troubles since *Adam Adamant* began to record. I would however like you to be acutely aware of what has been going on and to take steps immediately to see that there is a dramatic improvement in this question of overruns. This is...something which must not be allowed to continue.'

Keeping within budget was a matter of pride to most producers but, to Verity, so was the necessity of delivering the best possible programme. In a struggle between balancing the books and finishing a recording to her satisfaction, there was never any contest about which would win. A month later, on 13 July 1966, Osborn was again scolding her: 'I am alarmed at the increasing debt into which you seem to be running. It is understandable that the first few episodes of a new series should overspend, this being absorbed as the series proceeds. The reverse seems to be happening with *Adamant*. Consistent overspending at the end of six recordings is now three and a half thousand pounds and I must ask you to take some immediate steps to recover this amount. I would suggest that you take a very hard look at the numbers in your cast and your filming, and the number of sets.'

But this time Verity had reason to fight her corner, using her response to detail the pressure under which she was producing the programme: 'I feel I must make a very strong complaint about the events in TC3 last Sunday and Monday. I am attaching a memo listing the pieces of scenery which were missing on the first day. On the Monday morning, there were still essential pieces of scenery missing. Some did not arrive at all. An important flat [piece of scenery] looked terrible but there was no time for us to stop and do anything about it. To add to our problems the property buyer had not sent half the correct props which had been ordered. The AFM could not contact her and he had to resort to going to the prop store himself and to making his own props. A lot of props did arrive which had nothing to do with our show whatsoever. I can only say this was a totally disgraceful situation. We eventually managed to record the programme...everybody on the production team worked 20 times as hard as they would normally have to. The show itself is only about 50 per cent as good as it should have been. The performances suffered through lack of time in the studio and the fact that we were not able to get a proper run-through and nobody knew what was coming next. I do not feel that the programme should be charged for any of the scenery and props which were not used and there is also a large bill for artists' overtime...I feel that Scenic Servicing must pay for both these items as I have no intention of paying for them on my programme budget.'

The much-reworked opening episode, *A Vintage Year for Scoundrels*, launched the series on Thursday, 23 June 1966. On that day, Sydney Newman sent her a memo: 'In lieu of a telegram (economy!), I want to tell you that despite all the ups and downs, I know you have virtually killed yourself to make tonight's, and subsequent episodes of *Adam Adamant*, the best it can possibly be. Let's pray together.'

Verity held a party at her house in Eaton Mews West to mark the occasion. 'We all went round and opened some champagne,' remembers Harper. 'Then we sat and watched it and after 20 minutes – something I've never known before or since – it went off the air. And she was on the phone like a rattlesnake...'

The fault, caused by a breakdown of the telecine machine from which the film recording was being transmitted, was rapidly resolved but it spoilt the party and felt like a bad omen. When the Audience Research Report came in, it indicated a reaction index of 46, doomily clarifying that this was 'considerably below the current average [62] for television serials. "Now I shall be able to attend to the garden on Thursdays as well as Mondays," declared an engraver and his disgust was evidently shared by a good many viewers in the sample who found this first episode far-fetched and ridiculous in the extreme. There was an unusually large volume of adverse criticism to both acting and production.'

Neither ratings nor appreciation figures ever really rallied throughout the rest of the run. Newman wasn't ready to let go yet. On 1 July 1966 he sent Verity a lengthy memo, which he called his 'last (I hope!) will and testament on *Adam Adamant*', detailing his thoughts about the entire production so far. As usual, he was splendidly candid and some of his opinions give an illuminating insight into a mindset that he realised Verity shared. 'No show will succeed if a sequence goes on longer than its story interest and content warrant. Excuses like, "The filming cost a lot of money", "The show will be short" won't wash. There's absolutely no excuse for dullness. So far the series seems to suffer from this weakness.'

He was especially critical of Juliet Harmer as Georgina Jones: 'Tell her to take lessons in speech and voice projection at her own cost – I'm not kidding about this. Her mumbling has ruined many good lines, confused the audience by making them worry that they are not getting it.'

When it came to the subject of Harmer's appearance, it was Verity he blamed: 'For Heaven's sake, you're a woman and supposed to know something about style and clothes and women's appearance. Georgina looks like something the cat dragged in. Her hair is still a mess. Surely she can look relaxed and informal and yet have panache and style. Frankly, I think you can get better advice and help on this whole question.'

He concluded by reminding her exactly what qualities he felt were needed for the show to be enjoyed: 'If it is fast...if it is realistic (believable people in conflict with an incredible Victorian); all pointing with humour and irony and tension to the contradictions in an amoral world.'

A few days later, confirmation of a second series was forthcoming, to go into production within a few weeks of work concluding on the first. There was no change to the relentless cycle of rehearsal and recording, however. Neither was there a change in the litany of overruns and over spending. In January 1967, Andrew Osborn noted: 'HDG Tel [Sydney Newman] had himself asked the producer, Verity Lambert, to record two scenes to cover another show. In spite of the fact that the recording was already thirty-five minutes over time, the producer took the decision to go ahead with these extra scenes. The over-run was therefore fifty-five minutes.'

It is striking that Verity put her allegiance to Newman over her duty to minimise the slide into overtime. Director Moira Armstrong shudders at the memory of these persistent overruns. 'It really was a very difficult show to do in two days,' she mitigates. 'They would have meetings about it afterwards and Verity defended me because she knew how tough it was.'

The results remained variable. There were some improvements but Verity herself only felt that one episode – *Wish You Were Here* by the highly respected playwright and producer James MacTaggart – really delivered the lightness of touch and ironic humour required. Moira Armstrong, who directed it, believes that MacTaggart's involvement was the key: 'We got the wrong writers. The trouble was that Verity didn't really aim for a high enough standard. We tried to make it sophisticated but we didn't have the material. I remember she gave me a script called *Black Echo* and I read it and thought, "Oh God!" I was going on holiday and I left a note for her saying, "Thanks for the half script!" and she said, "Oh nonsense, Moira, it'll be fine." If she'd gone to somebody really good, like Jimmy, all the way through, it could have lasted.'

Sadly for posterity, MacTaggart's contribution is one of the episodes subsequently destroyed by the BBC.

The second series was moved from Thursdays to a variety of time slots on Saturday night, always the biggest battleground for audiences in the television week. To the uninitiated, it might have seemed a promotion but in fact it was anything but. It was now being transmitted too late to attract the sizeable audience of children who had warmed to Adam the first time around. It was soon in direct competition with ABC's *The Avengers*, too, which was a show then at the peak of its charm. The obvious contrast in production values was also unhelpful. Verity complained about the inconsistency of the scheduling, writing bluntly to her superiors: 'I do not see how we can build up any kind of audience if the show changes transmission times as radically as this.'

Time did not mellow her view. In 2006, she commented: 'I hate that attitude of putting the same against the same. It's ridiculous and very unfair to the audience. I'm sure they did it as direct competition and it was stupid. It forced the audience to decide.'[20]

Ratings declined although it would not be fair to say that they were ever truly disastrous. But Verity was unhappy with what she felt were less than half-hearted efforts to publicise the programme. 'The coverage has been more or less non-existent,' she sniped in a memo to the Director-General, copied to her bosses, the drama publicity officer and the editor of *Radio Times* (which then existed solely to present and promote the BBC's schedule). 'I have tried to keep the Publicity Department informed of any events, actors etc. which might have been of interest to them. I do know that other programmes have to be given publicity but nevertheless when a programme returns to the screen at a <u>different time</u> and on a <u>different night</u>, it is essential it is put in the *Radio Times* to draw the viewer's attention to this. Series are put on the air to attract a large viewing audience. If the *Radio Times* does not promote them – who else is going to?'

The press were still interested in Verity herself. She was the story when, on 20 December 1966 the *Daily Sketch* ran a piece they headlined 'The Eve Who Aims to Put New Bite into an Old Adam': 'Being a TV producer, with the responsibility for millions of viewers and thousands of pounds, is tough,' wrote journalist Shaun Usher. 'Being the producer of a much-criticised TV series making a new assault on the audience ratings is considerably tougher. Yet the producer with just such a hot-potato assignment, when the BBC's *Adam Adamant* returns this month is a woman…a slender, glossy, very dolly girl called Verity Lambert. Without doubt, Miss Lambert will be under greater pressure than most of her male colleagues. About her work, she says: "I try not to use my feminine approach when working on a programme. People seem to accept that my instructions are for the good of the show, not another gambit in the sex war. If I were a man, I'd feel resentful, automatically, about having a woman as my boss," adds the ex-Roedean girl. "But I've never had trouble. Nobody calling me a silly moo, or anything like that." She sees nothing odd in the fact that a woman should be behind science-fiction thrills. "I love fantasy," she says. "There's a streak of it in all of us…and for that it doesn't matter a scrap whether you happen to be a man or a woman."'

There was a brief period during which it seemed possible that there might actually be a third series of *Adam Adamant Lives!* but no one within the higher echelons of the BBC was genuinely enthusiastic about the prospect. The star was fretting about the possibility of typecasting and didn't want to lose out on other work. On 6 February 1967, head of series Andrew Osborn wrote to the controller of BBC1 informing him that, in practical terms, it was essentially a choice between continuing with Adam or another show on his books, the boardroom drama *The Troubleshooters*. The controller, Paul Fox, needed little persuasion to opt for the latter: 'I didn't like *Adam Adamant*,' he says simply. 'It didn't

---

[20] DVD interview, as before

work in the slot. It was too fancy, too futuristic.'

Newman later acknowledged that 'it called for some pretty fancy writing and I think we failed script-wise and for a few other reasons. Verity knocked herself out trying.'[21]

'It was a good idea spoilt by the ridiculousness of the lack of time,' believes Gerald Harper. 'But I do remember that she was never for a minute fazed by it. She was always cool. You'd never know what she thought about it. It was only afterwards when years had gone by that I realised that actually she was disappointed by it and that it was not something that she looked back on with a lot of pride. But then, she did a lot of better things.'

'It just sort of missed,' was Verity's own judgement. 'My sorrow was that it wasn't as good as it should have been. You have to be honest about things you think work well and those that don't. It's as much my fault as anyone else's. It needed more wit. I still think it was the most brilliant idea.'[22]

In recent years, although still a relative minnow among shows of the same genre, *Adam Adamant Lives!* has undoubtedly acquired cult status as a supreme slice of Sixties kitsch. Verity was surprised but gratified that a series that had quite literally given her nightmares had somehow attained a kind of cachet and relevance.

Throughout the ceaseless challenges which producing the series threw at her, Verity remained buoyant, and this was for personal as well as professional reasons. A relationship had developed between her and David Sullivan Proudfoot, the director for the reworked episode one.

'She was very much in love with him,' says Ruth Caleb, then an assistant floor manager and later an eminent producer in her own right. 'She would turn up on location when I was working with him. Someone taught me to read hands at drama school and I read Verity's hand. She wanted to know how that relationship was going to go.'

Alas, Caleb cannot now recall what she saw when she examined Verity's palm but someone else who remembers this time is Maggie Allen, who had been one of the secretaries on *Doctor Who* and who worked with Proudfoot on *The Spies*, a thriller series he was producing towards the end of 1965[23]. 'We went filming in North Wales,' she recalls, 'and, even though the weather was bloody awful – bitterly cold and either raining or sleeting – she came out on location to support him.'

---

[21] *DWB*, August 1986

[22] Kaleidoscope convention interview, 2006

[23] There were 15 episodes of *The Spies*, transmitted on BBC 1 from 01.01.66

What Verity witnessed must have been impressive. Proudfoot had been forced to take over directing the episode because a scene-hands' strike had meant it could not be recorded in the studio. In those days, most programmes were transmitted quite soon after completion, so the entire episode had to be shot on location. Because the designated director was not available on the new dates, Proudfoot, as the producer, stepped in. It was a huge job, organising everything and persuading the scriptwriter to do a complete rewrite, finding locations, checking availability of staff, cast, transport, accommodation – and all at short notice. That was before he even started planning his shooting schedule. When the unit travelled to the location, only part of the new script was ready; the rest of it arrived in penny numbers and had to be retyped and duplicated on a Gestetner machine by Maggie Allen in her hotel room every night. Yet, despite all the difficulties, the entire unit responded to his cheerful leadership and supported him throughout the crisis.

When the first episode of *The Spies* was scheduled, Proudfoot, or 'Prouders' as he was nicknamed, bought several bottles of champagne and invited Verity round to his flat to celebrate. It was just the two of them. As he later told friends, they settled down to wait for the transmission but one thing led to another and it was 2 a.m. before either of them realised that they hadn't even switched on the television set.

Proudfoot seemed an unlikely choice for Verity. He was only slightly taller than her, a bit overweight, with an expressive face and eyes which, according to Allen, 'made him look a bit Japanese'. But matinée-idol looks were never one of Verity's prerequisites. She was attracted by talent, ambition, wit and intelligence, the same qualities which many found in her, and he made her laugh. She may also have responded to his vulnerability, masked by his sense of humour, anaesthetised by his drinking but obvious to everyone close to him. 'He had a very bad beginning in life,' suggests Allen, by way of explanation.

He was born in Bedford in 1935, the same year as Verity, but tragically his mother Catherine died when he was just 5 years old, after which two aunts looked after him. By the time he was 14, they too had died. His father had remarried and was living with his new wife and young son, and took the extraordinary decision to leave his son to fend for himself, alone in the aunts' house, a Dickensian image difficult for modern sensibilities to comprehend. There was at least the money to buy him a decent education and at Bedford School, Proudfoot flourished, enjoying drama, in particular. He was also a keen swimmer and diver. At a school diving contest, his best friend's mother, Molly Dalzell, was shocked to see Proudfoot walk up to the board with a huge safety pin holding up his trunks. Her son quietly explained how David had to look after himself. Horrified, and full of compassion, Mrs Dalzell insisted that he come to stay with them instead. Included in the Dalzell household (Mr Dalzell was the school's art master), Proudfoot finally discovered what he had always yearned for, the joy of living as one of a happy family.

A clever boy, Proudfoot went on to Oxford University, but, instead of studying, he devoted most of his time to the OUDS, the university's dramatic society, and, at the end of his first year, he was sent down. Another of the bright young talents to take advantage of the sudden expansion of television, he joined the BBC as a trainee and rapidly progressed up the ladder, propelled by his ability and lively personality. He prided himself on camera scripts with as many as twice the normal number of shots in them – exactly the kind of ambition that would appeal to Verity. But he wasn't just technically gifted. Actors responded to his sensitivity and love of the ridiculous and he was able to coax bloody-minded technicians to deliver the goods for him. 'I've never met anyone like David,' says Maggie Allen. 'He was the wittiest man I have ever met. He was a funny, lovable chap.'

'He was charming,' agrees Caleb. 'Slightly Nöel Coward-ish. Very, very witty.'

Adele Winston (then Adele Paul), who worked as Proudfoot's PA on a number of shows, still remembers an outing to the first night of a show starring Sammy Davis Jr at the London Palladium. 'Six of us went,' she recalls. 'Me, my date at the time, who was a director called Frank Cox, a PA friend who was single so I brought my mate Gareth Gwenlan for her and David brought Verity. I don't think that up to that point I had realised how rich women dressed up for a night out, but Verity was a vision. You could faint. Think of Audrey Hepburn at the top of the stairs in *My Fair Lady*. She had the hair and the jewellery and the dress and the make-up – she looked absolutely unbelievable.'

'Verity was a very private person in some ways,' says Gareth Gwenlan, 'and it did seem that David was not the obvious choice as a boyfriend but they were clearly having a great deal of fun and that's all people cared about, really.'

Like Verity, Proudfoot was utterly committed to his career and, when working at his peak, was a dynamic and effective director. Like Verity, he was an ardent party animal, with the stamina to match her appetite for drinks, dinner parties and evenings all dressed up and out on the town. It is a measure of how serious the relationship became that, for a time, the couple were unofficially engaged. But those in their closest circle were all aware of a major problem and once again, Verity's private life was the subject of whispers and conjecture. 'He really loved Verity and was very proud of her,' says Winston, 'but how he happened to have a relationship with any woman was totally unbelievable to me.'

It seems unlikely that Verity's 'gaydar' was truly defective. All her life, she was a magnet for homosexuals, who were, perhaps, attracted by some of the qualities which intimidated heterosexual men – her fearlessness, frankness and dynamism. To offset these, she had her own distinctive style and a sense of humour, both bordering on camp. Different herself, she was non-judgmental about other people's preferences. Within BBC drama alone, there was a phalanx of amusing and intensely talented gay men who became both her friends and her competition, men like Mark Shivas, Graeme McDonald and, most significantly for Verity, Andrew Brown. Would she really have missed what everyone else had identified in Proudfoot, even if he was in denial himself? It does seem entirely feasible that, under the spell and in love, she was deliberately fooling herself that there was a future in the relationship.

Despite Proudfoot's struggles with his sexuality, complicated further by his Christian faith, clearly he did have strong feelings for Verity and obviously wanted it to work between them. No doubt he was partly influenced by social pressure too. The Sixties may have been swinging but for gay men, this was still an era of extreme repression, even within the occasionally more tolerant climate of the entertainment industry. 'One never ever wanted to acknowledge one's sexuality,' sighs director Waris Hussein. 'I think he was very confused. In those days, we didn't discuss these things as openly as we do today but *of course* I knew he was gay. He desperately wanted not to be. None of us wanted to be outed.'

Hussein admits that he simply didn't understand the apparent relationship. 'To me, it was the ultimate form of neediness,' he says. 'I liked him a lot. I wasn't so intimate as to interfere. It would never have occurred to me to say, "Verity, what the hell do you think you're doing?"'

Eventually, but only after many months together, the unlikely couple bowed to the inevitable and, although they remained friends, there was no more talk of engagement. 'I think finally it must have become clear to her that it was never going to work,' says Ruth Caleb. 'He was gay.'

'There had always been a problem with his unreliability, too,' admits Maggie Allen. 'He would often back out of any difficult situation in his private life rather than deal with it. Probably his heart wasn't in it physically, though he would have loved to have had a family.'

'He certainly made inept passes at various blokes he was working with,' observes Adele Winston. 'He was very, very witty but that's not enough on its own.'

'David was a very gentle man,' says Hussein. 'He was very articulate, intelligent, funny – he lived in a world of make-believe in many ways and she liked being a part of that fabric. I think there was a huge comfort factor there. It wasn't going to last because David himself was so mixed up and confused.'

Like so many of their generation, Proudfoot was a persistent and heavy drinker. Within a few years, he was battling alcoholism, although he eventually conquered it after a long spell of treatment in a hospital rehabilitation unit. But his health continued to plague him, eventually forcing him to take early retirement. He moved from London to Portland, Dorset, where he lived a quiet life with two beloved dogs, until his death from liver failure in 2002. The following year his old friend Maggie Allen organised a celebration of his life, which was attended by a large number of former BBC colleagues. Despite the dreadful waste of his talents and the obvious loneliness of much of his life, they wanted to remember David Sullivan Proudfoot and what he had meant, not just to them, but to many other close friends, including Verity, who remained the only woman he had ever loved.

CHAPTER FIVE
THE DOOR OF OPPORTUNITY
1967–1970

'I get my satisfaction from working with people who I respect and admire. The idea of communicating to a lot of people also attracts me, and I don't think that popular means bad. You can do very high quality drama which is popular.'

Verity to Stephen Lacey, Producing Popular Television Drama conference, University of Reading, 2004

The Spanish island of Ibiza has changed radically since the 1960s. Then it was a still unspoilt backwater, a chic destination for London's liberal intelligentsia, and the new generation of free thinkers, hippies and creative types. In this idyllic space, they might indulge their senses and carouse by day and night without fear of judgement or suppression. Such was its allure that some nicknamed it the San Francisco of Europe. During this decade, it called to Verity, too, and she returned time and again.

Her life in London was defined by her ambition and work ethic and her social life reflected this. She regularly lunched with agents and television critics. Nights at the theatre enabled her to see who was 'in', up and coming or both. Parties were invariably packed with industry names and Verity, cigarette in one hand, drink in the other, could usually be found at the centre of the most lively, interesting and professionally useful conversations. It was networking before the phrase was coined. Verity's abundant high spirits carried her through a self-imposed schedule that many would have found unsustainable.

By contrast, in Ibiza, there was no routine and here she was able to fully relax in the warmth of the Mediterranean sunshine, enjoying herself without having to worry about what impression she was making. She loved the Arabic-inspired architecture, swimming in the sea and exploring the wildness of the countryside.

Sometimes she travelled alone, the confidence of her upbringing insulating her from fear or loneliness. Within the Ibiza 'set' there were always people she knew and could hook up with – among them a circle of interesting, talented actors who came to Ibiza to spend time in the orbit of charismatic American writer and director Howard Sackler. Although she was on the periphery of this group, some of them – including Eileen Atkins, Robert Stephens and Denholm Elliott – she counted as friends and would later employ.

But she discovered more than casual acquaintances on Ibiza. In the summer of 1962, Miriam Worms was staying with her husband, Jean-Pierre, in a friend's house in the picturesque little backwater of Santa Eulalia del Rio, 15 kilometres from the centre of Ibiza. 'There was one main road,' she remembered. 'The taxi driver could only change to second gear and drive forward. Uneven, beaten paths led to the houses. One day the bell rang and there was Verity with a straw bag over her shoulder.'[1]

From this chance encounter, a friendship flourished and Miriam Worms eventually became one of Verity's closest confidantes. Beautiful, chic and opinionated, Worms was born in 1929 in the German city of Danzig. Her family were Jewish and as the Nazi persecution grew worse, her parents decided to place their son and daughter in the hands of the Kindertransport, the humanitarian scheme designed to offer shelter overseas to Jewish children. Miriam and her brother were bundled off to a foster family in England. Unable to obtain the necessary papers to follow them, their parents were murdered along with millions of others in the death camps during the war.

'She lost all her family,' explains her husband, Jean-Pierre. 'The family she had afterwards were her friends. They were the most important thing in her life and Verity was the best friend you could have. They were not from the same world but they had a very, very close love between them. The fact that they were both Jewish was a strong connection. Neither of them were at all religious but both of them were very faithful to their culture and origins. Jewishness meant something to them, something that was part of their identity and which they would not betray for any price. Each appreciated the absolute authenticity of the other – Verity was a *real* person and they were people who didn't try to pretend to be anything other than who they were.'

Verity admired and identified with her new friend's irrepressible and joyful attitude to life and her indomitable nature. The year before they met, Worms had lost an eye when terrorists bombed the offices of the Paris newspaper for which she was working. She wore an eyepatch for the rest of her life and this became a hallmark of her style and defiance.

As well as her writing, Worms supported her husband with his political career – he

---

[1] Quotes taken from a piece Miriam Worms wrote to be read at Verity's funeral

became the MP for Màcon – and so, in its own way, her life was just as busy and involved as Verity's. But the friendship between them never faltered and they nourished it with long telephone conversations, discussing politics and the arts, or just chatting about *The Archers*, to which they were both addicted. They met when they were able, in Paris or London, and sometimes they went away together, the bond between them renewed and deepened. 'Her gift to enjoy life was boundless,' said Worms of Verity. 'She bore no grudges. Her warmth was enveloping as was her generosity. Whenever she had options, she chose the generous one. Some moments were less easy than others. There was the time we boarded a plane for Barcelona, Verity weighed down with straw bags filled with pottery. She suddenly felt a draught and was convinced all was not right. This was emphasised when she spotted a fly. "Have you ever seen a fly in a plane?" she asked. I had to admit I had not. She was on her feet in a flash – attempting the impossible – to disembark, so great was her fear of flying. Years later, when I asked how she had overcome it, she said, "I had to."'

As well as finding new friends on Ibiza, Verity introduced others to its charms, too. One of these was the splendidly named Anthea Browne-Wilkinson, a director she had booked for *Adam Adamant Lives!*, and with whom she had immediately hit it off. Physically, they couldn't have been more different – Browne-Wilkinson was big-boned, bespectacled and slightly ungainly, with none of Verity's careful grooming or innate fashion sense. Socially, there was some common ground. Browne-Wilkinson was upper rather than middle-class, and, like Verity, was the product of a boarding-school education with a similar natural assurance. But the connection went deeper than that. Browne-Wilkinson had a sharp intellect too and was able to dissect a script with precision, a quality Verity shared and appreciated. When the work was done, both loved to enjoy themselves and were inclined to be raucous. In Santa Eulalia, evenings centred on Sandy's Bar, named after the eccentric gay Irishman who was its proprietor. Eating well and drinking much, gossiping, chain-smoking and shrieking with laughter, both women enjoyed themselves hugely. Jeremy Swan, then a young director in the children's department at the BBC, remembers a riotous evening in the bar culminating when 'both ladies came CRASHING down the stairs – or was it through the ceiling? – berserk with the drink taken!'

Back in London, their association deepened as head of series Andrew Osborn decided to pair them – with Verity as producer and Browne-Wilkinson as script editor – on a revival of *Detective*, the catch-all title for an anthology of one-off crime fiction adaptations. The first run, in 1964, had resulted in some successful spin-off series and the hope was that this fresh round of stories might perform the same useful function. For Verity, it offered a chance to work with a calibre of actor usually out of reach of the ongoing series. Her selection of directors and dramatists also gave her excellent opportunities to forge stimulating new contacts and reward some of her allies and favourites, including, naturally enough, David Proudfoot, Moira Armstrong and Browne-Wilkinson, who was disgruntled at being a script editor and wanted nothing more than to direct. Verity made sure that she was given the chance to take charge of an episode, to fit in alongside her editing duties.

'I think Anthea knew Verity was very good going,' observes Betty Willingale, then a script editor herself. 'Those who are powerful are attractive to some people, aren't they?'

'Anthea was an extremely good foil to Verity,' says Ruth Caleb, then an AFM and later a producer herself. 'Very intelligent, very well-read, intellectually very solid. Whereas I suspect Verity had great instincts, Anthea would be the one with whom she could discuss those instincts. The script editor relationship with the producer in those days was really vital – they were really at the centre of the process. It was much more holistic than it is now. If a script didn't quite deliver, the script editor would get it into shape.'

'On the face of it, Verity was still on the nursery slopes as a producer. Yet to many of her contemporaries, her progress seemed both inexorable and inevitable. 'Even in those days when she was relatively junior,' remarks Paul Fox, then the controller of BBC1, 'she was a great operator at every level. She enjoyed herself and had this great sense of fun but she was a workaholic – a very serious and dedicated programme maker.'

'She was bossy in a positive, attractive and effective way,' says fellow producer Kenith Trodd. 'Her particular gift was to charm creatively and productively.'

On 29 June 1968, the *Shields Gazette* profiled Verity and her new script editor in a profile piece with, as usual, a somewhat patronising headline, 'Brains and Beauty Behind *Detective*'. It is interesting that the article itself attempts to confront the sexist prejudices of the time. 'When one hears some men generalising about women executives,' wrote journalist Miriam Maisel, "conjuring up the image of 'ruthless battleaxes trampling on their wretched subordinates", you begin to wonder whether they have actually met any. Top women are much more likely to resemble Verity Lambert and Anthea Browne-Wilkinson, intelligent highly conversable creatures, they are obviously but unaggressively efficient' Maisel also quoted Verity on the obviously sore subject of *Adam Adamant Lives!*, saying that 'the only good notices I've had [for it] are now, when the critics are using the programme as a stick to beat *Virgin of the Secret Service* with.'[2]

Later in her piece, Maisel felt compelled to add, 'Lest I seem to have been waving the feminist flag too enthusiastically, it should be pointed out that of the 17 programmes, 13 of the original stories were written by men...'

Finding material suitable for adaptation cemented the collaboration between Verity and Anthea Browne-Wilkinson. Between them, they read something like 50 novels and collections of short stories. This was hard work by anyone's standards, and Verity was not especially interested in the genre. During the process, she formed the view that many male writers created detectives who were simply idealised versions of themselves, while

---

[2] *Virgin of the Secret Service* was a hokey adventure series, set in the Edwardian era, made by ATV and much derided by critics

female writers dreamt up detectives with whom they fall in love. 'This is especially true of Dorothy L. Sayers and Lord Peter Wimsey,' she said, disapprovingly, at the time. Sayers was not in her shortlist and Wimsey was, in any case, too well-known a character. Verity was more interested in the hunt for those detectives who had fallen into relative obscurity and whose revival might therefore be straightforward in terms of obtaining the necessary rights. Her office was thick with smoke and noisy with debate and dissent as choices were made and a rich slate of mystery and adventure was lined up.

An anthology format appealed to Verity because it held similar advantages to *Doctor Who*. There were fewer rules and, within the genre, a range of different styles and treatments could be attempted, from the *Grand Guignol* (*The Murders in the Rue Morgue*) to the broadly comedic (*Dover and the Poison Pen Letters*) and the period to the contemporary. Among the adaptations, Verity also commissioned Colin Morris, who had helped to devise *The Newcomers*, to deliver an original play about the notorious Crippen case. As with *Doctor Who*'s experimental but exuberant foray into humour, the audience rejected the comedic approach taken in the *Dover* episode, preferring their crimes and murders to be straightforward whodunnits. This was a disappointment to Verity, who had hugely enjoyed the *Dover* story and wanted this above all the others to be developed into a series.

One of the directors on *Detective* was James Cellan Jones, like Verity, bright, pushy and destined for greater glory than this kind of middlebrow series television. She persuaded him to participate not once but twice, and he retains a high regard for her abilities. 'I don't like producers,' he says, frankly. 'But she was astonishingly easy to work with and her advice was always good. She had a wonderful enthusiasm – most producers just want to get the damned thing on. I had been working at Birmingham Rep and I was very keen on some of the actors there and wanted to bring them in. She said, 'You must do what you like.' She harks back to a time when a producer was a creature of tremendous support and friendship rather than a bossy, ignorant swine. People liked to work with her. They knew that they wouldn't be bullied.'

'What she was after was a good show,' says the writer and dramatist Hugh Whitemore, whose *Detective* episode, *The High Adventure*, marked the first of their many collaborations. 'She was a pro and showed you that it could be done. She wasn't put off by a challenge or by difficult material and she never let you down. It was a joy working with her. We would start in the office but that rapidly became dinner to discuss the script or we'd go out to see a movie and have an idea there. Your path would be *littered* with ideas. She also made it fun – you went through your Verity Lambert phase smiling all the time. I adored her. And one of the great pluses of working with her was that she was very sexy. You were working for a pin-up girl.'

Detective was important for Verity because it began to introduce her to writers of real quality. It was an awakening to the wider possibilities that such skill ignited. The constant struggles she'd experienced with scripts on both *Doctor Who* and *Adam Adamant Lives!* were, in part, a symptom of the rampant snobbery within the industry, which meant that the series like these tended to be the business of the 'jobbing writer' and, all too frequently, the absolute hack. These kind of shows were largely regarded as little more than juvenile entertainment, direct descendants of the Penny Dreadful or the Saturday morning cinema serial, and thus artistically invalid. Involvement carried a certain professional stigma and they simply did not and could not attract the kind of writer whose work was taken seriously, reviewed by the critics and discussed at the dinner parties of the chattering classes. Verity had received her grounding in the importance of a good script during her time at ABC but it was only now that she was able to attract some of the cream of the crop – including Whitemore, Hugo Charteris and the Irish writer Hugh 'Jack' Leonard.[3]

Jack Leonard was another of Verity's admirers and she reciprocated his feelings to the extent that they indulged in a brief but intense affair, with afternoon assignations and all the subterfuge necessary because Leonard was a married man. Their discretion paid off and the liaison hurt nobody. After it was over, their respect and affection for each other remained and they continued to work with each other in the years that followed.

After the continual worry and stress that had accompanied her throughout *Adam Adamant Lives!*, the 16 plays that made up the *Detective* series were relatively trouble-free. There was a slightly sticky moment when Donald Wilson, Verity's former boss in serials, wrote her a stiff note demanding that she remove his name from the credits of the episode he had adapted, *The Golden Dart*. 'James Cellan Jones [the director] came to see me last week. I asked him about casting and he said that he was thinking of casting an actor called Andrew Faulds. I told him that I would not be associated with any production in which Faulds played any part. James knows the reason for this as well as I do. There is no reflection on Faulds as an actor and I believe he could play the part quite well. I do not accept that Faulds is the only actor available for the part and therefore I must assume that James' action in booking him was deliberately calculated to demonstrate his contempt for my views. If this had been an original piece rather than a dramatisation I should have insisted on either the cancellation of the booking, the removal of the director or the withdrawal of the play. But since it is not, and to save you personally any difficulty, I prefer simply to withdraw my name.'

Cellan Jones remembers the row with a degree of amusement. 'What larks!' he comments. 'Donald told me not to cast Andrew because he was a socialist and standing for Parliament. This didn't seem fair to me and I resolved to defy him which is why he took his name off.'

Although no series were commissioned from any of the plays, Verity's revival of *Detective* performed well enough for Paul Fox to order another season for 1969. Verity, however, did not continue to oversee it. A new and exciting opportunity had presented

---

[3] Hugh 'Jack' Leonard (1926–2009) Won many awards for plays including the Writer's Guild award for *Silent Song* (1966) and a string of awards for *Da* (1978)

itself, which was at the time widely interpreted as significant recognition of her value and potential. The BBC had acquired the rights to produce a series of adaptations of the short stories of W. Somerset Maugham. This was regarded as a great coup and the eponymous series was to be made, in colour, by the loftiest of the departments in the drama group – plays. Thus Verity left series – and Anthea Browne-Wilkinson – behind her and reported to a new boss, Gerald Savory.

She already knew him well. Daily to be found in the BBC club, nursing a dry martini and holding court, Savory was such a fixture of the place, she couldn't have missed him. 'He appeared delightfully detached,' remarks Graham Benson, then a production assistant, 'and was the epitome of "laid back". He'd say, "If you want to chat about anything, I'll be in the bar at 12..."'

'He was very charming,' says Ken Trodd. 'I did a live *Thirty Minute Theatre* which fell to pieces and cameras ended up looking at other cameras. Gerald said to me next morning, 'Ken, I sat there just relieved that the cameras were saying BBC and not ABC.' He was eccentric in an old-style way. I think he liked her and it was very hard to dislike Gerald except on very snooty, snobby class grounds.'

'He was avuncular and benevolent,' allows Waris Hussein, 'but there was something very pedantic about him too. He was quirky in the wrong way.'

Among Savory's favourites were Mark Shivas and Graeme McDonald, with both of whom Verity was on excellent terms. She'd also befriended Savory's then girlfriend (and future third wife), a vivacious, flame-haired actress who worked under the name Sheila Brennan. 'I was at Television Centre doing [the classic serial] *Nana*,' recalls Brennan. 'Gerald said, "Come up during the break." I was all dressed up with white make-up and Verity looked at me and said, "Do you always go round like that?" At first I thought she was a very frightening woman but then, when I got to know her, I realised she was an absolutely dolly. She was very fond of Gerald and extremely supportive of the relationship. She was younger than me but I always thought of her as more maternal. She would give me advice. She liked to help people and her friends mattered a lot to her but she either loved you or forget it, you might as well walk away.'

Those who did walk away tended to be junior colleagues unable to meet her exacting standards. A perfectionist herself, Verity did not find it easy to tolerate others with a more relaxed or less detailed approach to the work. In particular, by this stage in her career, she had already acquired an unflattering reputation for her inability to retain secretaries. Having been, by her own admission, not the best secretary in the world, she was nonetheless extremely demanding in her expectations of the girls assigned to work for her. Faultless shorthand and typing were essential, as was the temperament to deal with outbursts of anger and shouting about the frequent frustrations that came with the territory of making television. Those that possessed these skills, like Val Speyer on *Doctor Who*, were quickly rewarded with Verity's friendship and generosity. She thought nothing, for instance, of buying an expensive silk scarf or a cashmere jumper as a birthday or Christmas present for one of her secretaries. On the other hand, anyone well-intentioned but slapdash soon caught the rough side of her tongue. Completely gormless, nice girls biding their time till marriage, of which there was a depressingly steady supply within the BBC, were rapidly sent packing. Verity had just finished *Detective* and was about to start on *W. Somerset Maugham* when 19-year-old Brenda Loader reported to work for her. 'The organiser in drama plays was finding it hard to employ secretaries who stayed very long,' says Loader. 'Verity was well-known for upsetting them with some regularity. I came along bright-eyed and bushy-tailed and quite capable of speaking up for myself. I started to work with her and we got on like a house on fire. I was very efficient and always there and absolutely devoted. That's why it worked.'

By this stage, Verity's life had assumed its own rhythm. Her office, E1116, was now some distance away from the plays department, on the 11th floor of the East Tower, a high-rise block tacked onto the outer ring road that circled Television Centre. Every morning she would call first thing to have a chat with Loader about the day's commitments. She expected her secretary to have read all the television reviews in the newspapers, to give her a succinct digest of critical opinion. She wouldn't actually arrive in the office until about 11 – 'like a whirlwind', as Loader remarks. 'Verity was always racing, chasing time – her mind was overrun with things to do that day. She had huge energy and was passionate about the job. She was incredibly hot on all the important things like making sure she got the best set designers, film cameramen, directors and cast. She wanted the best and it had to be achieved whatever the cost and of course that meant she upset a lot of people if she didn't get her way. I can vividly remember her talking to the allocations department – she used all her feminine charm to get her way, flirting, if necessary, and, if that didn't work...fireworks!'

After dealing with the most pressing issues, making calls and dictating letters, there would often be a working lunch with agents, writers, directors and occasionally actors, either at the BBC or in town at a favourite restaurant like San Lorenzo in Knightsbridge. Work often carried on late into the evening, with scripts to be read, theatre or dinner engagements and, at regular intervals, adrenaline-fuelled studio recordings. Afterwards, she could invariably be found in the throng of the BBC club, buying drinks, congratulating, commiserating, frequently laughing and managing to make herself heard over the drunken din. Someone who remembers her well from this time is the writer and actor Michael Palin, then one of *Monty Python's Flying Circus*. 'She was a big name at the BBC at the time,' he says. 'One of those up-and-coming producers like Ken Trodd. She was one of those people you notice and she was noisy – the centre of attention in a room. It's quite an unforgettable name really, Verity Lambert. An unusual first name...'

In the autumn of 1969, Palin was writing a *Python* sketch involving two shop assistants and decided to name them 'Mr Verity' and 'Mr Lambert'. The sketch remains a charming memento of the impact that Verity was making at the time.[4]

Her visibility was intensified by her forceful personality and enhanced by how few other women were around to compare or to compete with. She continued to pay careful attention to her appearance, buying many of her clothes from Harrods, and realising how she would be judged if she ever let the impeccable façade slip. Twice a week, she would have her hair done and for years, she was attended to personally by Mr Leonard, whose Mayfair salon was famously exclusive and expensive. She only switched her allegiance in 1969 when the ultra-fashionable Smile opened, and she remained a loyal customer for the rest of her life.

She moved out of the Eaton Mews house, which had been paid for by her father, and into a tiny but exquisite period property of her own. Suitably named Queen Anne House, tucked away on Dukes Lane, it was, according to Brenda Loader, a 'fairy tale' home, only a stone's throw from the ever-smart Kensington High Street and its enticing array of antique dealers and fashionable boutiques. Verity had the house fitted out and decorated exactly as she wanted it, with clean lines, no clutter and white walls throughout. In the living room, softly lit by table lamps, she placed a few good pieces of Queen Anne furniture, perfectly in keeping with the period of the building. Such was her enthusiasm for cooking, she installed an expensive Scholtes gas hob on a centre island unit in her hyper-modern basement kitchen.

Although no longer sharing her home with friends, Verity wasn't completely alone as she enjoyed the company of two affectionate Burmese cats, Fat Basil and Mad Willy. When Ibiza beckoned once more, she asked Brenda Loader to feed them in her absence. Her secretary asked if she might use the house to throw a small party while she was away and Verity readily agreed. 'She was a wonderful woman,' says Loader, warmly. 'She was my mentor as well as my boss. You couldn't help but love and admire her professionalism and drive. She inspired me to aim high and showed me that women can achieve anything – there are no rules if you are dynamic, positive and good at your job.'[5]

Back on her 11th floor East Tower eyrie, Verity was partnered with her new script editor, 30-year-old Andrew Brown. Like most producer and script editor pairings, it was an arranged marriage but one that was to have lasting significance in Verity's life. Brown had been born and brought up in New Zealand but soon after graduating from university, wanting to break away from his conservative and Catholic background, had started to travel. His journeys took him from Tahiti to the Virgin Islands, and New York to London, where he eventually settled in the mid-1960s. His overriding ambition was to become a

---

[4] The 'buying a bed' sketch was first transmitted in episode eight of *Monty Python's Flying Circus* on BBC1, 07.11.69

[5] Verity later recommended Loader for the BBC's PA training and Loader went on to enjoy a successful career in feature films and commercials

writer, and it was Gerald Savory who, taking a liking to the forthright young man, offered to make him a trainee script editor within his department. In 1968, Brown had script-edited a distinguished series of short story adaptations set during the 1920s and transmitted under the banner headline of *The Jazz Age*. One of these, Somerset Maugham's *The Outstation*, acted as the catalyst for the Maugham series and it was Brown who persuaded the writer's estate to grant approval for it.

Exceptionally tall, good-looking, possessed with phenomenal energy, great intelligence and a caustic wit, he bonded with Verity from the beginning. 'He was overtly gay, which was quite unusual then,' points out Loader. 'He was incredibly funny and very outspoken. There was lots of laughter. But they did fight. He would sometimes come out of her office into my office, throw his hands up in the air and slam the door of his office behind him to recover from a spat.'

Timing may have had something to do with the speed and intensity of their connection. In March 1969, Verity's closest female friend, Nora Fielding, had succumbed to cancer. It was a brutal end to a friendship that had sustained Verity for years and she was desperately upset by Fielding's premature death.[6] The vacancy that this tragedy left in Verity's affections was to be filled by Andrew Brown.

They had much in common. He was as passionate and committed as Verity to delivering the best possible plays and he had an intellect to match hers. Like her, he made no bones about his ambition and thirst for personal success. They shared an absolute relish for the good life – Brown's homes were as individual, stylish and comfortable as Verity's – and both were happily hedonistic, providing it didn't stand too much in the way of the work. When she was single, he was the perfect escort. He was usually available to her because he was never truly comfortable with his sexuality and so indulged it furtively, keeping his escapades to himself. She may have worried about some of his adventures in the murky world of rough trade but neither did she judge him. Both had embraced the liberal, left-wing world view that was shared by many of their generation in a creative sphere. Part of this meant distancing themselves from the moral and attitudinal shackles of their family religions – he had been brought up as a Roman Catholic. Yet neither were they unusual in that they could never entirely rid themselves of the baleful influence of their early conditioning. Both were professional attention-seekers and yet, on a personal basis, surprisingly reserved about their emotions and true feelings. But in each other they discovered the perfect confidante and the mutual trust and rapport between them was such that, over time, they became less like friends and more like brother and sister.

'Andrew was a darling,' says Sheila Savory. 'He was great fun and she was devoted to him. They were very, very close.'

---

[6] In 1982, cancer would also claim the life of another of Verity's friends from this era, Anthea Browne-Wilkinson

'They would squabble all the time,' points out producer Paul Knight. 'But Andrew was a fixture in her life.'

'They had a very strong relationship,' agrees Waris Hussein. 'I was never quite in the inner sanctum and I found it sometimes upsetting and was actually quite jealous.'

'She loved him,' says writer Howard Schuman, simply. 'They were soul mates who shared the same sense of humour, the same love of life – movies, food, drink. Psychologically they were just siblings.'

The *W. Somerset Maugham* series was only the first of their many professional alliances. It was an ambitious project in every respect, not least in its sheer scale. Two series of 13 episodes were anticipated and, highly unusually for the time, they were to be made in partial association with an external company – Howard and Wyndham Films and Television. Until now, Howard and Wyndham had owned and operated a string of theatres. Their plan was to sell off some of these and invest in the potential of film and television. They hired a former BBC producer, Peter Graham Scott, to head this operation, and it was Scott who negotiated with Verity in which plays his company might contribute additional funding. The deal was that the extra money would help fund the best possible dramatists, some location filming abroad and stellar casting to appeal to the international market. In return, Howard and Wyndham would recoup their costs and share any profits on overseas sales with the BBC.

W. Somerset Maugham was the catch-all title under which the stories, all set between 1910 and 1945, were subdivided. Verity and Andrew Brown chose three separate categories. The first was *Rule Britannia*, to cover those stories concerning the attitudes of British imperialists at home and abroad during the 1920s and 30s. The second was *Women of the World*, in which the central character was a woman. These were tales that ranged from high drama to witty comedies of manners. Thirdly came *Victims of Fate*, in which the main character, through some accident of birth, marriage or chance becomes involved in a situation beyond their control. 'I read all his stories,' Verity told *The Guardian*'s Linda Christmas[7], 'and I got very depressed because he seems to dislike women so much. But in the end I selected 26.'

Between them, Verity and Andrew Brown went to market for the finest dramatists they could entice, offering stories most suited to their writer's existing style or predilection. Some of her favourites needed scant persuasion – Hugh Whitemore, Hugh Leonard and Hugo Charteris. The scurrilous but outrageously charming Simon Raven quickly joined their number and, despite his occasional drink-related unreliability, quickly became one of those select writers she returned to ever after. She became equally fond of Simon Gray.

---

[7] *The Guardian* (23.06.72)

John Bowen, Roy Clarke, Julian Mitchell and her boss, Gerald Savory, were among the other notable names who contributed. 'They were challenging to do because they had to have a life of their own,' explains Hugh Whitemore. 'It's not good enough to just slap down a dramatisation. You've got to make it live, give it a life of its own and moreover a life that belongs to the particular piece you're doing.'

Armed with an arsenal of fine scripts, Verity was able to woo the best available directors with James Cellan Jones, Claude Watham and Christopher Morahan among the heavyweights. 'The stories were marvellous and the scripts frightfully good,' says Morahan, who was later deputy director of the National Theatre. 'A lot of money was put into them for them to be done very well. It was clear that she had very high standards.'

She gave the very first play in the series to her old ally, Waris Hussein, now making his name in the world of feature films. This time, however, the only woman in their number was Moira Armstrong. 'It was seen as a prestigious series,' she remembers. 'I got one set in South America and I said to Verity, "I need about 40 extras and they must be at rehearsal or we'll never get it recorded in the time." She sort of gulped. But she agreed and this is where she scored. I had them for three days before I went into the studio and it was such a relief because they knew what they were doing. We still overran but we managed it.'

Later in the series, Verity employed Michael Lindsay-Hogg, a young director who had been making a name for himself at the ITV company Associated Rediffusion and as a director of promotional films for the biggest bands of the era, the Rolling Stones and the Beatles. He may have been *en vogue* elsewhere but it was then extremely unusual for the BBC to hire someone without any experience of their way of doing things. Verity insisted and Lindsay-Hogg did fine work for her. 'I was very happy to get that job,' he comments. 'I'd always wanted to work at the BBC. It was in colour and she let us have a lush production. I remember there were scenes out in the jungle in the rain and wonderful actors like Edward Petherbridge and James Bolam. It gave me a lot of confidence that I knew I did a good job with the show. Verity was a very supportive producer. Once she got behind a project, she was devoted to it and fought for it kind of like a mother would for a child. She really liked and defended the things she had chosen to do.'

Verity had always relished the pursuit and persuasion of talent but now, perhaps for the first time, the nature of the project helped rather than hindered her. On 23 December 1968, she composed a detailed memo enshrining her specific expectations for the series. It was circulated to all the directors, production assistants, AFMs[8] and production secretaries who were going to be involved in making it and some of her comments are illuminating. 'All the plays are period plays,' she wrote, 'and, therefore, I would like very

---

[8] AFM or assistant floor manager. Junior but key member of the production team, in charge of all the props and helping to run rehearsal rooms and assist in calling and cueing the artists

strict attention to detail. On each script is marked the year or years in which the action takes place, so please make sure that EVERYBODY is clear from the very beginning on this matter. We are doing period plays but this does not necessarily mean that the sentiments contained in them are pretty. We must strive in everything for <u>reality</u> rather than prettiness.

'Although these plays range over a period of 35 years, they have all been written by one author, whose works are well known to many people. I want directors to bring all their imagination and talent to their own individual scripts but to bear in mind that we must be true in style to our original author.'

Verity never needed any second bidding to spend the budget at her disposal and encouraged her directors to think big. Between them they assembled some genuinely fine casts, the very best, and most expensive, talent available. This 'stunt' casting, as it has become known, was important in a series of self-contained stories and Verity realised that, often, in such a series, it was the name above the title that would attract viewers. The challenge was all the greater because this was an era when television was regarded as very much a poor relation of film and theatre. Some of her more ambitious casting ideas eluded her. She spent weeks pursuing Vanessa Redgrave to play the lead in *The Letter*, eventually having to concede defeat. The role went instead to her Ibiza acquaintance Eileen Atkins. She tried hard to snare Hollywood's hottest couple at the time, Elizabeth Taylor and Richard Burton and, when they declined, to book real-life husband and wife Rex Harrison and Rachel Roberts for *Lord Mountdrago*. Again, she was unsuccessful but even when she didn't achieve her first choices, the thrill of the chase was fun and, bringing her into contact with all the major talent agents in town, it was a fantastic opportunity to enrich her address book too.

Not all the 'stunt' casting worked. Much was made of signing the fashionably *outré* Marianne Faithfull to star in *The Door of Opportunity*. 'That was a nightmare,' says Brenda Loader. 'She was heavily on drugs and went missing from rehearsals. No one could find her. She had been to the read-through and maybe she thought, "I can't do this." She was found at the last minute and did the show with almost no rehearsal, out of it. It was very tense in the studio, though the director [William Slater] handled it beautifully.'

Throughout the casting process, Verity was collaborative, advising rather than commanding, drawing on her now extensive knowledge of the acting community. 'She was certainly able to argue about whether someone was good or bad and why,' recalls John Frankau, who directed two of the plays in the series. 'She always seemed to know everything about them – what they'd done, whether they were good, bad or indifferent. I remember when we were casting one leading character, I wanted A and she wanted B and we went on talking about it during the course of the evening, agreed to sleep on it and come back the next day. By then, I'd decided that she was right and that B was correct so I came in and said, "I'm perfectly happy with B," and she said, "Well, I'm not because I think A is better!" We went through the day arguing all over again about who should play it. I think finally she dictated that it should be A, which had been my first choice. It was very funny. She was totally supportive – one of the best producers I ever worked with. It wasn't obvious but she used her femininity and I enjoyed that.'

'You worked very closely on casting,' said Verity herself when asked about her approach to directors at this time. 'Obviously, the director had to have room to create and make things better, to take the scripts and enhance them, and you didn't want to stop that. You weren't there all the time. You'd talk about what the problems were and then you would go to the producer's run and you would give any notes about performances at that run and then when you were in the studio if you felt that the director wasn't covering things properly, if there was need of a close-up or something needed to be changed, then you would also make those comments, but at the same time you had to let him or her have some kind of creative involvement, otherwise there wouldn't be any point in having a director.'[9]

'Typically, she gave her advice but didn't bully people,' says James Cellan Jones. When he was assembling the cast for his production of *The Creative Impulse*, he suggested the established character actress Brenda de Banzie to play John Le Mesurier's wife. It was a showy part, a gift for any actress but Verity counselled against offering it to de Banzie, warning that she had a reputation for being difficult. 'Brenda was a monster,' says Cellan Jones, 'and behaved terribly badly, playing silly games. For instance, when I laughed at some particularly inventive business by John Le Mesurier, she took me to one side and said, "I noticed you laughing at John's gag. Please ask yourself, will the audience laugh? I leave you with that thought." John said, "Oh don't worry, I'll cut it." "No, you won't," said I. "Over my dead body." John hated her, all the cast hated her.'

'She was a nightmare,' agrees Brenda Loader. 'But Verity wasn't scared of actors. Verity wasn't scared of anything or anyone.'

'Somehow we got away with it,' says Cellan Jones, 'and Verity never said once, "Told you so."'

It was the same story when Cellan Jones returned to direct *Olive* (based on a short story called *The Book Bag*). Looking for the right actor to play the young male lead, he suggested Martin Potter, who had recently attracted some attention in Fellini's Italian art house film, *Satyricon*. Verity was unconvinced. 'Stupidly, I cast him,' he says. 'She was right – again. He proved to be awkward, to say the least. In one important scene, he was being wooden in the foreground with Eileen Atkins being brilliant in the background. I killed the boy's key light so that one couldn't see his face and all the attention was focused on Eileen.'

Howard and Wyndham's aspirations to sell the series in the States (which came to

---

[9] University of Reading, 2004

nothing) meant that they were anxious that Verity include some American actors. The casting of Carroll Baker[10] to play the prostitute Sadie Thompson in *Rain*, was rewarded with a *Radio Times* cover, but according to vision mixer Clive Doig 'it wasn't terribly good. Obviously a lot had been going on in rehearsals and there was a lot of pissing about. The best thing about it was the party afterwards when Carroll presented Gordon Jackson, the other lead, with a big box containing a giant chocolate penis.'

Unfortunately, *Rain* is the only one of the *W. Somerset Maugham* series to have been wiped and remain missing, so it is not possible to judge either Baker's performance or the production from any contemporary viewpoint. Those that do remain in the archive, however, all have qualities to recommend them, from the subtle literacy of the scripts, the visual style, which often triumphs despite the technical limits of the time, and the sheer pleasure of so many superb actors operating at the peak of their powers. 'It was lovely to do,' recalls designer Eileen Diss. 'I had great admiration for Verity. She was so very positive – there was no question of failure or not being able to do anything. Enormous energy, and very professional. A supremely intelligent woman, I would say. The series was prestigious and beautifully done.'

But this achievement came at a price. Already expensive, the Somerset Maugham series soared over budget again and again. Location filming was a case in point. There were extensive trips to Florence (where Verity contracted influenza and bronchitis and spent most of the shoot confined to her sick bed), Antibes and on board a P & O liner sailing from Southampton to Madeira.

Plans to film in Greece had to be abandoned. The unions, which then had a stranglehold on television, refused to allow their members to work in a military state. Cyprus was selected as a last-minute substitute but was not trouble-free itself. On arrival, the crew found that, thanks to industrial action, they had to carry all their own equipment and luggage from the plane, across the tarmac and into the terminal.

After much consideration, Verity reluctantly conceded that Malaya, the setting for several of the stories, was beyond their reach and settled for the unlikely substitute of Swansea instead. The production hired waiters from the local Chinese restaurants to play 'coolies'. The temperatures were far from tropical and precious time was spent in the quest for authenticity, trying to persuade reluctant extras to go barefoot on freezing Welsh ground.

As production accelerated, Andrew Brown broke the news that he was defecting to join the new ITV company, London Weekend Television, which, as the name suggests, had won the franchise to provide the London region with its programmes from Friday to Sunday evenings. He would initially script-edit *Manhunt*, a new drama series, although

---

[10] Carroll Baker (1931–) American film actress most famous for the 1956 movie *Baby Doll*

his talent and ambition would rapidly promote him into the producer's seat himself. By the time he left the BBC, he had completed the commissioning and much of the work on the scripts, and Verity allowed him to adapt one of the later stories himself. She also persuaded the publishers Heinemann to release two hardback compilations of their selections for the series, under the titles *A Baker's Dozen* and *A Second Baker's Dozen*. It is a sign of the profile she had already managed to attain that she was invited to write the blurb on the first volume, although *A Second Baker's Dozen* refers amusingly to 'Miss Verity's new season of plays', omitting her surname and making her sound like a Somerset Maugham heroine herself.

'She had the ability to recognise things which were going to work,' says director Christopher Morahan. 'She created a space in which people were able to do very well.'

'There was a kind of odd innocence about her,' believes Michael Lindsay-Hogg. 'She didn't play games. If you had done a good job, to get one of Verity's smiles – very sweet and open and welcoming – was a nice thing. There were other people who you knew were just giving lip-service, whereas she was enthusiastic for things that were good. It was genuine, readable appreciation.'

Verity commissioned a haunting and supremely effective theme tune from the composer Wilfred Josephs. It was a series with evident quality in all departments but, in her drive to deliver the best, she was again unable to avoid multiple overruns in the studio. This was despite the regular privilege of being granted additional recording facilities throughout the two studio days, at a time when most drama series of this type were confined to taping everything during the evening of the second day. Neither were these overruns a few minutes here and there. Often they came closer to a full hour, which was ruinous in overtime payments and caused understandable grumbling because of the knock-on effect in striking and setting the studio for the next production due in the following day. The number and complexity of the sets brought worried memos from the design department's Laurence Broadhouse: 'Fourteen sets of the type required is too many to fit into a colour studio, and also too many for the 1250 man-hours allocation. Can we discuss this, Verity?'

Editing was extended and made more costly by the luxury of so much stop/start recording. The lavish Florence-based filming for *Mother Love* could not be cut together until after the studio sessions, with the result that the whole play was found to be ten minutes too long. An entire extra day of editing was required to get it down to time.

The constant excesses of the production caused envy and complaint among other producers and was the talk of Television Centre. 'She madly overspent,' says the then controller of BBC1, Paul Fox, 'really, truly, outrageously. As far as the budget was concerned, Verity ignored it. Her attitude was, "Sod that. I'm doing a show."'

Viewers seemed to appreciate her profligacy. The Audience Research report for the seventh play of the series, *P and O*, scored a high reaction index of 69, and was fairly typical of the feedback the series received. 'There were few, it seems, who did not enjoy the story, atmosphere and acting of "this excellent vignette of life on board a liner". Indeed, quite a few of the small sample audience considered *P and O* to have been one of the best in the series so far, though "all the author's stories seem to make good TV".'

Verity paid an agency which scoured the newspapers for any mention of her productions and it was one of her secretary's duties to paste these carefully into an album of cuttings.[11] Press reaction to the Maugham series was generally favourable, although reviewers occasionally found fault with the plots and devices used to extend the various short stories to fit the running time. Occasionally, Verity herself got a mention. Casting its eye over *A Casual Affair*, the first of the series, the *Daily Mail* of 4 June 1969 commented that 'Producer Verity Lambert – she certainly deserves this one after *Adam Adamant* – confirms that she has an eye for period style and swagger.'

That summer, she again returned to Ibiza, this time with her friend and fellow producer in plays, Irene Shubik. They were staying in an isolated house at one end of the island that belonged to the director Philip Saville and his then girlfriend, the actress Diana Rigg. Shubik was morbidly preoccupied by the recent Charles Manson murders and, given Ibiza's popularity with the hippy community, became increasingly paranoid that they were somehow at risk. In an attempt to calm her fears, Verity invited a mutual friend, the director Alan Clarke, to join them. 'Irene was fairly relieved that there would be somebody else around,' she recalled. 'I went to the airport to meet him and he turned up with his arm in plaster. So he was in no state to defend us.'[12]

Several months later, on Sunday, 8 March 1970, the Society of Film and Television Arts (the forerunner of today's BAFTA), held their annual awards show at the London Palladium. Then, as now, to win one of their idiosyncratic metallic masks was the single most important accolade in British television. It can only be imagined with what nerves and anticipation Verity attended. She had known for some weeks that her production of the Maugham series was nominated for Best Drama, with stiff competition from veterans Rudolph Cartier (*Rembrandt*), John Hawkesworth (*The Gold Robbers*) and Reginald Collin (*Callan*). Christopher Morahan, meanwhile, was in the category for Best Director with his Maugham episode, *The Letter*,[13] while Eileen Atkins was also nominated for Best Actress in the same production. Although Atkins lost out to Margaret Tyzack, who won for *The First Churchills*, both Morahan and Verity were victorious. Wreathed in smiles and

---

[11] There are bound volumes of all these, running from 1963 to 1970

[12] Quoted in *Alan Clarke* (see bibliography)

[13] Bizarrely, *The Letter* was one of the few of the Maugham plays subsequently wiped by the BBC. A copy was subsequently returned to their archive from a French broadcaster but, as a result, only survives with the dubbed French soundtrack

deafened by applause, she went up on stage to be presented with her award by Earl Mountbatten. It was a moment of sheer glory and must have seemed like absolute validation for her sometimes cavalier approach to the budgets she was supposed to operate within. More than this, it was industry recognition of everything she had achieved since Sydney Newman had called her out of the blue and invited her to become a producer just seven years earlier.

Newman was no longer at the BBC, or even in the country. At the end of 1967, he'd been poached by the Associated British Pictures Corporation, supposedly to revivify their ailing film output. The job was a disaster and Newman wasn't able to get a single picture off the ground. His pride wounded, he refused to return to the BBC despite their entreaties and instead returned to Canada to take up a job with the CBC. Verity had survived and prospered for more than two years after his departure from the BBC but it isn't unreasonable to theorise that what happened next might well have been averted if he had still been around.

Her duties on the Maugham series would take her to the summer of 1970 and already she had her sights fixed on what she wanted next. At the start of the year, the plays department had scored a remarkable success with her friend Mark Shivas' production of *The Six Wives of Henry VIII*. A follow-up was now in the works, *Elizabeth R* – six 90-minute plays tracing the life of Elizabeth I. Shivas was busy elsewhere and, with some justification, Verity felt that she was just the person to deliver such a high-profile enterprise. Head of plays, Gerald Savory, had other ideas. When they met, he explained that he didn't feel that she was right for *Elizabeth R*. But whatever her disappointment at this decision, she cannot have been expecting him to go on to say that furthermore he had nothing 'else suitable for her and so her contract would not be renewed.[14] 'He didn't mince his words in these matters,' says Savory's wife and Verity's close friend, Sheila. 'He told her she'd better get out. She was very upset.'

'It was as good as being sacked,' says Brenda Loader. 'Verity didn't see it coming and she was shattered. It was a dent in her ego. She cried quietly in her office the afternoon she was told and I had only seen her cry once before when her friend, Nora, had died. I can only suppose that she'd upset too many people. She just left and went home and I didn't really see her for about a week.'

Later, Verity used to joke that winning the SFTA award was 'the kiss of death' and admitted that the sudden and brutal manner in which her BBC career had come to an end triggered 'a kind of breakdown. Obviously, all my producing working life [I had] worked for the BBC and the BBC is a very comforting place in many ways. You have the

---

[14] Verity later claimed to have been offered – and to have turned down – the second series of *Take Three Girls*, a middlebrow anthology series about three women sharing a London flat, which Savory had created. But the dates don't support this idea and neither did its producer, Michael Hayes, when I asked him about this.

most incredible facilities at your fingertips. It's just an amazing place to work in from that point of view. So I was fairly nervous about whether I could survive without it.'[15]

The news was soon out in the open. Under the bald headline 'Contract Up at The BBC', *Television Today* of 23 July 1970 reported that Verity was no longer working for the corporation, quoting Savory: 'I am naturally very pleased with the success of the Somerset Maugham plays but at the moment I have no programmes planned where I can use another producer. I would be delighted to use her again if something comes up and I am lucky enough to find that she's available at the time.'

There seems no reason to doubt the sincerity of Savory's words. As his wife, Sheila, explains, 'It was the best advice he gave her because she had to be kicked out into the nasty, horrible world. I think that, in the end, she recognised that it was far better for her career.'

Hindsight did allow Verity to embrace this view. She was able to resume her affection for Savory, too, recognising that had she stayed within the comfort zone of the BBC, she could hardly have achieved her subsequent level of success. More than this, she offered him employment on several future occasions, and this patronage may have given her some private sense of satisfaction. More likely not, as Verity was a supreme realist and bearing grudges was rarely one of her vices. But Christopher Morahan, Savory's successor as head of plays, considers that the decision to let Verity go was an act of 'dullness. He didn't have the vision to keep her for the BBC.'

Whatever her fears, understandable though they were, Verity was not destined to remain unemployed for long. Stella Richman, the newly appointed director of programmes for London Weekend Television, asked to meet her. It is entirely possible that Andrew Brown was involved in sponsoring this encounter. He was already producing at the new company, which was struggling to prove itself and deliver some drama of quality and distinction. He would certainly have been keen for Verity to join him there.

Richman shared some of Verity's characteristics. She was dynamic, hard-working and quixotic with a reputation for the speed of her decisions and for spotting and nurturing talent among writers and directors in particular. Like Verity, she was an independently minded Jewish woman encouraged rather than daunted by having to operate in a man's world. They were never destined for friendship – both sought the limelight too unapologetically for that – but there was mutual respect.

Richman had in mind a series called *The Loser*, which she had commissioned from the writers Keith Waterhouse and Willis Hall and which was to star former pop singer Adam Faith. 'I remember being taken to lunch by Stella to meet Willis and Keith,' Verity

---

[15] Quoted from her 2004 University of Reading interview

commented later. 'They were both monosyllabic Yorkshiremen. I was completely overawed. I don't think there was a script at that point and I was trying to sound enthusiastic, which indeed I was, with these two guys not really saying anything at all. They just fixed me with an opaque stare and I couldn't work out what they were thinking. I thought, "God, this has gone badly, they obviously really don't like me at all." As it turned out they were just being Keith and Willis and they said they wanted me to produce it.'[16]

Verity left the BBC in the high summer of 1970, no longer depressed and rejected, but with the stimulating prospect of her first job as a freelance producer in commercial television.

---

[16] Interviewed for the *Budgie* DVD, July 2006

CHAPTER SIX
BUCKSEY'S BIRD
1970–1973

'I felt very good about doing Budgie. We had some good times and a lot of fun. At the time it was considered to be very near the knuckle. The man who owned Mothercare wrote in and said the programme was about pornography and should be taken off and I should be fired.'

Verity to Kevin Jon Davies, interview for *Budgie* DVD, July 2006

The birth pains of London Weekend Television, a bitter cocktail of management in-fighting and uncertain programming, had played out in public view and claimed several scalps. Even as Verity joined the company, the woman who had hired her, Stella Richman, was struggling to hold on to her own job as controller of programmes. Richman's drama department, a minnow alongside the BBC's behemoth, was desperately trying to assert itself after an embarrassing and expensive string of misfires and write-offs. But Verity's arrival was serendipitous. Despite her problems at executive level, Richman was an astute talent-spotter and she was rapidly fanning the flames of a creative revival. Verity had arrived to produce one of these new commissions, Keith Waterhouse and Willis Hall's *The Loser*.

This was a comedy-drama series about the misadventures of a charming but hapless Cockney spiv nicknamed Budgie (on account of his surname, Bird). 'I've always been attracted to comedy-drama,' said Verity, later, 'because I think quite often through comedy, you can say very important things and people will accept them and take them on board.'[1]

---

[1] Interviewed for the *Budgie* DVD, July 2006

Richman had also given the green light to a new period-drama serial, to be called *Upstairs, Downstairs*. Unfortunately, neither this nor *The Loser* would be on screen for some months. In the meantime, one of the few LWT drama successes so far had been *Manhunt*, an epic 26-parter charting the resistance in occupied France during the Second World War. It was this series that had advanced Verity's great friend Andrew Brown from script editor to producer. When she joined him at Station House, the grim concrete office block on the North Circular that LWT had inherited from their predecessors, it meant that she already had a friend and ally in residence. Brown discreetly advised her on the finest technicians and crew available within the company so that when the time came, she could put in specific bids and fight for her choices.

They were both reporting to Rex Firkin, a diminutive ex-producer and director who had created *Manhunt*, and was now, at Richman's instigation, in charge of London Weekend's drama output. Although nominally the executive producer for everything his department produced, Firkin was too busy to have much to do with *The Loser*. 'I knew enough about her to know that she had enormously high standards,' he comments. 'She was a very hard worker. Right from the word go, she was very aware of the fact that it was going to test her ingenuity. Initially, I was worried about whether she had taste but I managed to get Andrew Brown to play me one of the Somerset Maugham series and there was the proof that she was a person of enormous taste. One of the things I admired so much in that was the way that she kept a real feel and a real presence of Malaya and the jungle. She was extraordinarily talented.'

London Weekend had already signed pop-singer-turned-actor Adam Faith to play *The Loser*. 'One of the reasons for getting a woman in to run it,' explains Firkin, 'was to stop it being all-male dominated by the writers and the star. Adam was a sexual object and I thought that a woman would work better with him.'

Jenny King was one of the PAs assigned to work on the new series. Verity's reputation had preceded her. She was widely rumoured to be 'formidable' but King was pleasantly surprised by the reality. 'She came in all big and bluster,' she says. 'She was pretty alight most of the time, with lots of energy. I think I connected with her from the off. It was very different then. We worked hard and played hard and it was very jolly. We used to go out and have these wonderful Italian lunches. It was a very happy set of people, really.'

Paul Knight, then a young producer at LWT, and someone who soon became a friend, recalls that 'she caused a fair amount of disorder because it was quite staid there at the time. She kicked a few bums around the place. She was remarkable. She had a fiery temper which subsided as quickly as it burst out. She was very aware of her own position and what she was doing and who she was and very defensive of the people who were working for her.'

'You knew where you were with Verity,' agrees Jenny King. 'She was good with me and the other PAs. She had done our job and respected what we did. Some producers are a bit wishy-washy but I never saw her doubt. She was very ambitious and positive about what she wanted and where she was going.'

The Loser, a title it was felt might repel audiences, was ultimately rechristened *Budgie*. Waterhouse and Hall's scripts, however, needed little revision and, although initially dismayed by their taciturn nature, Verity liked them both and a mutual trust and admiration soon developed. It was Verity's suggestion to cast the distinguished character actor Iain Cuthbertson as Budgie's sometime sponsor and frequent nemesis, Charlie Endell. The writers were unsure. They had in mind another actor but Verity argued that they should cast against type and be more imaginative. 'At the time,' said Verity, later 'Iain Cuthbertson was playing rather middle-class bank managers and lawyers on television. I'd seen him at the Royal Court in *Serjeant Musgrave's Dance* where he was absolutely terrifying. I said, "Please see this actor, I believe he can surprise people." I sent the scripts to Iain and he saw it as an opportunity to do something different. He [suggested] that Charlie would speak with this Scottish accent overlaid with Americanisms. Willis and Keith loved it and they wrote him in as a continuous character.'[2]

Perhaps the chief weakness of the series is that it rarely offered much in the way of interesting female characters. Verity cast the pretty and competent Lynn Dalby as Budgie's long-suffering girlfriend, Hazel, but Dalby struggled to make any impact with an underwritten part. Only Georgina Hale as Budgie's wife stood out and she was so consistently singular and interesting that it is only surprising that she appeared in just a handful of episodes. 'We had some very good names,' said Verity, later. 'I remember particularly persuading John Thaw to play a gay Welshman. It took a lot of persuading I can tell you. I said, "You just need to show them you're an actor." He was wonderful.' Thaw was fond of Verity; they had enjoyed a brief fling some years before. 'He always spoke of her with affection, and was a bit wistful when he did so,' recalls Ted Childs, who was Thaw's producer on *The Sweeney*.

Verity also found a role for her friend Sheila Savory, who acted under the surname Brennan.

'She liked actors who were in some ways slightly eccentric,' says director Michael Lindsay-Hogg. '*Budgie* certainly allowed a lot of curious actors. I think that when she was working with Sydney Newman she started to get to know the actors of her generation. Like a horse-trainer, she had a sense of who the good and less good ones were. She had very good taste in actors and liked to have a lot of input.'

Although there was a broad seam of comedy throughout the series, the stories and characters were largely drawn from life. Waterhouse and Hall had an unusual approach to the writing. They would discuss the idea for an episode between them and then each

---

[2] Interviewed for the *Budgie* DVD

would go away and write their own version of it, before combining the results. They worked from a huge office above a billiard hall in Leicester Square. 'One of them had a desk at one end,' explained Verity, 'and one at the other so having a meeting was like having a tennis match at Wimbledon.'[3]

The office was just a short walk from the source of their invention – Soho, then the nerve centre of London's criminal world, and famously sleazy with its neon-lit sex shops and gaudy strip shows. Unusually, Waterhouse and Hall did not submit their work through their agent or deliver scripts themselves. Instead, whenever one was ready, Verity would arrange to have lunch with either or both writers in order to pick it up. Even then, they would only hand over one copy. 'I once went to lunch with Keith,' recalled Verity, 'and had a couple of glasses of wine. On the way home, I had to go to the chemists and after I'd left, I suddenly realised I'd left the only copy there so I had to run back and retrieve it.'[4]

The show's adviser was James Humphreys, a character straight from this underground world himself. Humphreys' own activities were shady enough for him to go uncredited on the series, although his ideas and suggestions gave the writers much of their inspiration. 'He was very good-looking,' recalled Verity, 'A bit like Charlie Endell, actually. Could be very scary but was always nice to me.'[5]

As a measure of the accuracy of the scripts, there was an incident during production when Verity received a call from the Savile Row police station. 'Willis [Hall] had been taken out of his St Albans home at six o'clock in the morning,' she explained, 'and questioned about a script they felt was all a bit too close to something that was going on at the time. They arrested him. "You've got to get me out of here," he said. I had to send [a script] down to Savile Row to get Willis out. It was worrying for him but I found it quite funny.'[6]

Verity hired three directors to handle the first 13-episode series: Mike Newell, who, many years later, directed *Four Weddings and a Funeral*; Jim Goddard, a former art student and designer, whose work she had admired at ABC; and Michael Lindsay-Hogg, who was something of a television wunderkind. But, as before at the BBC, she had to fight to employ him: 'Michael was considered to be a bit of a maverick and not very controllable,' she said later. 'I was advised by the people at London Weekend to go for someone more malleable. But I stuck up for Michael. I know I was right because he got

---

[3] *Budgie* DVD Commentary

[4] *Budgie* DVD Commentary

[5] *Budgie* DVD interview

[6] *Budgie* DVD interview

on really well with Adam. Even though Adam was very good, it was one of the first acting jobs he'd done in some time and it was important he had people he was confident in around him.'[7]

Lindsay-Hogg's friendship with Faith dated back to the time when Faith was making regular appearances on *Ready, Steady, Go!*, the pop programme on which Lindsay-Hogg cut his teeth as a director. 'When Verity and Adam and I first had a lunch about it,' he says, 'you knew it was something that would be a lot of fun for everybody. Adam was a very, very funny, attractive man and a very good actor in a limited range. Together, Iain and Adam were a wonderful kind of Laurel and Hardy pair because Adam was so tiny and Iain was so big and Iain had his wonderful Scots accent and Adam had his chirpy cockney accent. They got on very well and Verity liked people who she thought it would be congenial to have around.'

'She was also very kind,' he continues. 'I remember once we'd been working quite late and my girlfriend Jean Marsh[8] was in hospital in Wimbledon. I would usually take the train to go and visit her but Verity said, "I'll drive you – we can talk some more." We got there and there was a brouhaha. Jean was being prepared for an emergency operation. I didn't like the doctor who was going to do it so I insisted on a change. Jean was being prepared for surgery and I said, "Verity, you go" – "I'm not going." The surgery went OK. She was there with me all the way as an ally. I loved Jean and it was a crisis and in that crisis Verity was unafraid and as helpful as one would ever wish. She was so solid as a friend.'

All the directors of *Budgie*'s first series became more than mere colleagues. They were among the regular circle of friends often invited to dinner round the kitchen table at Verity's Queen Anne House. 'She loved giving dinners and entertaining,' says Lindsay-Hogg. 'She was a wonderful hostess and a very good cook. I remember going to dinner with Jean [Marsh] and Verity had done an oxtail stew which I'd never had before – it was just delicious. There was something almost maternal about her in one way, she liked to provide a nice meal, good conversation and a pleasant time for people.'

'She was a good cook but it didn't happen that quickly,' laughs close friend Sheila Savory. 'If you went to dinner, you'd get there about 7.30. If you were eating by 10, that was early.'

Iain Cuthbertson lived in Scotland and often returned there at weekends. Sometimes he would come back to rehearsals with a bag of game containing a brace of unplucked pheasants for Verity, much to her delight. She was always serious about what she ate and

---

[7] *Budgie* DVD interview

[8] Marsh was then appearing in *Upstairs, Downstairs* for LWT, a show she had co-created. She had first met Verity when she worked on the 1965 *Doctor Who* story, *The Crusade*

all her adult life she relished trying new restaurants and different kinds of cuisine. She enjoyed everything from the finest French cuisine to fish and chips. 'She'd say, "Isn't this just the best Chinese or Italian or whatever...?" and the next week she'd be off to a different one,' recalls Jenny King.

These were the days when many restaurants only offered pepper of a grey and dust-like consistency. To guard against this, Verity took to carrying a small silver pepper mill in a velvet case in her handbag, so that wherever she was, she could season to her satisfaction. Her culinary prowess is the basis one of Michael Lindsay-Hogg's favourite memories of the *Budgie* series. 'The day before we went into the studio,' he explains, 'when we were still in a rehearsal room, she would come and look at the last run-through and carry a pad so she could give notes afterwards. One day, she came in and said, "What time are you going to start? Because I want to see it and talk after but I have to give a dinner party tonight." So we started and I noticed that after the first scene she scribbled something on her pad, which was normal enough. But then she scribbled again after the next scene and the third scene and I thought, "God, she's hating this." As we were going into the fourth scene, I managed to look over her shoulder and on the pad she'd written, "Lamb cutlets, sprouts, a pound of potatoes, red wine rather than white." She was planning the menu for her dinner.'

Her attention to detail remained an abiding quality. She worked closely with director Jim Goddard to devise the brilliant opening titles for *Budgie*. These show the character on the run with a briefcase, which he drops, so that it bursts open. The case is packed with money, which goes flying everywhere. Budgie is seen frantically grasping at the notes, a neat metaphor for the series. The title itself – and the words 'Starring Adam Faith' are formed from hundreds of these notes which are then blown away in a gust of wind. The whole sequence, which was exceedingly complex to film, was inspired by Verity's memory of watching a Stanley Kubrick film, *The Killing*, on television. The climactic ending focuses on a suitcase full of stolen money springing open in transit to a plane. The contents are scattered by the engine's turbulence – much to the obvious horror of the thief. Verity was justifiably proud of her steal from Kubrick. These were the days when a programme's title sequence really mattered – there were no PVRs or catch-up devices so the titles – and the music that went with them – acted as the beckoning call to the audience to sit down and engage. Verity approached Ray Davies of the Kinks to provide the haunting theme for *Budgie*, though record company politics meant that he went uncredited.

Although they had intended to write the whole series, about halfway through Waterhouse and Hall began to flag. Verity offered to lighten their burden by bringing in another writer, Douglas Livingstone, to undertake a pair of episodes. Verity had met Livingstone socially, through their mutual friend Irene Shubik, who had produced some of his first television plays. His contribution to *Budgie* marked the start of a rich professional association and a close friendship that lasted until Verity's death. Livingstone echoes Michael Lindsay-Hogg's view that, above anything, Verity was

Receiving her SFTA award from Earl Mountbatten, 9 March 1970.
Weeks later, Verity would be out of a job

On holiday with Andrew Brown. In 1970, she followed him
to London Weekend Television

Fag break on location for *Budgie*
with star Adam Faith, 1971

Falling in love, Portugal,
July 1971

Radiantly happy as
Mrs Colin Bucksey

'The witches of Wood Lane' – Verity *Shoulder to Shoulder* with Georgia Brown and Midge Mackenzie, 1973

In Beverly Hills with James Cellan Jones and Andrew Brown, 1974

With John Hurt and the BAFTA award for *The Naked Civil Servant*, 1976

She who must be obeyed – in charge of drama at Thames Television, 1975

Rock Follies – a television triumph but one which became mired in controversy and litigation. L to R: Andrew Brown, Charlotte Cornwell, Julie Covington, Howard Schuman, Rula Lenska, Verity, Brian Farnham

With her predecessor – and eventual successor at Thames – the volatile Lloyd Shirley

Touring Teddington Studios with the Duke of Kent

Making *Minder* – (L to R front row) Dennis Waterman, Verity, Johnny Goodman, George Cole

(L to R back row) Leon Griffiths, George Taylor, Frances Heasman, Ian Toynton, with writers Tony Hoare and Andrew Payne

Dressing the part in pith helmet – with Hayley Mills on *The Flame Trees of Thika*, 1981

Away from it all with Colin – but the cracks were starting to show

Snap! Says Linda Agran: 'Isn't it a riot?! We were both sporting Betty Jackson and I think we looked the dog's bollocks! It's the laughing eyes that I love most'

characterised by her sense of good taste: 'It was in every aspect of her life,' he says. 'Food, wine, furniture and particularly scripts. She could taste what was wrong with a script and, in my case, she was never mistaken. That era was a lot more fun in television – it wasn't just work, we were always having dinner together or going to the pub.'

Although *Budgie* operated with a respectable budget, LWT could offer none of the BBC's vast hidden resources, from its multiple research libraries to the treasures of its lavishly stocked prop stores. Verity, who until now had always had a tendency to overspend, rapidly developed a new financial self-discipline. Jenny King recalls her 'shrieking at a designer, "You will NOT do that, we can't afford it!" and absolutely wiping the floor with him'.

There were inevitably overruns but nothing to equal the excesses of the Somerset Maugham series. A technicians' dispute meant that a handful of episodes had to be recorded in black and white but, other than this frustration, the cycle of filming and recording went according to plan. There was a period of uncertainty when the series suddenly lost its sponsor, Stella Richman, who was ignominiously fired at the end of January 1971. Her successor, Cyril Bennett, arrived just as *Budgie* started to air. Bennett, intuitive and eccentric, was another of British television's great Jewish showmen like Sydney Newman and Lew Grade. He grumbled about the nervousness of advertisers, who worried that the programme was a thinly veiled celebration of pornography, but quickly fell under Verity's spell and did not withdraw his support.

On 26 June 1971, an edition of LWT's Sunday-night arts programme, *Aquarius*, transmitted a lengthy film called *Pressure Cookie* going behind the scenes on *Budgie*. It followed the previous month's rehearsals and recordings for Douglas Livingstone's *Fiddler on the Hoof* and the 26-minute film was made by Verity herself and one of her trio of directors, Mike Newell. 'I loved that,' she said, years later. 'It was huge fun – just like being let out of school. If you're the producer you're always saying to the director, "For God's sake, don't shoot so much material," and suddenly there you are let loose with the camera and you can do everything you've wanted to do.'[9]

The film provides a fascinating snapshot, not only of the production of the series but of Verity as she was during this time, always animated, invariably smoking, watching rehearsals with Livingstone and Willis Hall, commiserating about the relatively disappointing ratings – 'The BBC put us up against Dick Emery' and getting a round in after the recording. The film is also notable because it includes a fleeting glimpse of the man who was about to change Verity's life, a young studio cameraman called Colin Bucksey.

Bucksey was ten years younger than Verity and his background couldn't have been more

---

[9] Kaleidoscope convention interview, 2006

different. He had grown up in south-east London, in a close-knit working-class family. Leaving school at 15, he went from one dispiriting, dead-end office job to another. 'At that point,' he says, 'working-class people thought that office jobs were a step-up from a factory, like the ones my parents worked in.'

By the time he was 18, Bucksey was desperate to escape his humdrum existence. He had an interest in photography and was excited by the idea of a career in television. He decided to write to every television company he could think of, asking for employment. One of these, Associated Rediffusion, wrote back, offering him an interview as a trainee.

'There are various points in your life when you look back and realise, "Oh, that was a lucky break,"' he says. 'My lucky break was that the day that I did the interview, the head of the camera department, a buttoned-up three-piece suit, shirt and tie type was off sick. His deputy, who was the complete opposite – a sort of randy, hard-drinking ne'er-do-well interviewed me and took a liking to me. I got the job. I had no formal qualifications, I just loved talking about television. I later realised that if I had been interviewed by the first guy, I would never have got the job.'

Bucksey started his career in the camera department as an assistant or 'cable-basher' doing every menial job going. It was 1965 and he was one of the youngest there, though it wasn't only for this reason that he stood out. Fellow camera assistant Vernon Layton, who joined the company a few months after Bucksey, remembers: 'The bulk of Rediffusion technical staff turned up for work dressed like they'd come straight from the sixth form. A tired blazer or tweed jacket with leather elbow patches, regulation Parker protruding from the breast pocket. This was usually complemented by an equally well-worn Old Boys' tie, fawn or navy V-neck sweater, slightly shiny light grey Oxford bags, and buff leather brogues to be seen jiggling beneath the canteen tables. In total contrast, to the turn of mostly female heads, Colin casually wandered in. With dark brown hair skimming the shoulders of a navy blue velvet jacket, skintight matching trousers, an open-neck striped shirt, and green crocodile-skin cowboy boots, he weaved between the tables displaying an admirably straight back and the faintest hint of a Jagger swagger. Even without the jingle of spurs, it was as though Clint Eastwood had arrived.

'He was tall, self-assured, and quietly cool, with a bemused expression around the mouth and eyes, which, when squinting at you through the smoke of a Gauloise, were uncannily reminiscent of Humphrey Bogart. He even sounded like Bogart, with well-considered minimal phrases and resonant laid-back drawl. Despite his youth, particularly at a time when everything seemed more favourable if you were older, Colin was socially at ease, quietly witty and great fun. Behind that controlled, cool exterior, I sensed what I can only describe as an underlying hint of authority.'

Layton quickly became a good friend and Bucksey introduced him to Mike Phillips, a sandy-haired young assistant floor manager. All three young men shared a passion for films and film-making, favouring the esoteric over the mainstream. They would seek out obscure French art-house movies at cinemas such as the Paris Pullman in South

Kensington or the Classic in the King's Road. Professionally, the three friends were united in their disdain for the factory-like approach to making television in which they found themselves. 'It seemed to us,' says Layton, 'as though the majority of those lucky enough to be behind a camera saw it as just another job like bricklaying or plumbing, whereas we felt it should have been viewed as a creative vocation.'

Mike Phillips suggested that, in their spare time, they make a film together, a gangland story inspired by a recent and sensational court case surrounding Harry Roberts, whose criminal activities had led to the murder of three policemen in Shepherd's Bush. 'Whilst he and Colin wrote the screenplay on the back of an envelope,' explains Layton, 'I rushed off to borrow a clockwork 16mm camera from a friend. I'm not quite sure how the subsequent scene we shot with Colin smoking and staring moodily into a dismal sea off Brighton Pier, and the other, with him casually carrying a holdall through a ticket barrier at Waterloo Station looking like Michael Caine in *Get Carter*, could possibly have related to the Harry Roberts story. But we were obsessed with the idea of getting out there and being – just for once – creatively unrestrained. None of the practicality or reality mattered.'

Although their gangland movie was never completed, it did serve its purpose because now the trio had some impressive test material that they could show people to demonstrate their abilities. Through a friend, they met Jim Ramble, the boyfriend of a then unknown young American choreographer called Flick Colby. Colby had a dance troupe called the Beat Girls and, through Ramble, Bucksey, Layton and Phillips were invited to make a promo for them. It was shot, in black and white, on high-quality 35mm film, mostly hand-held and using wide-angle lenses, to produce a slightly surreal but eye-catching look. Greatly to their surprise, their efforts were transmitted on the BBC's *Top of the Pops*. As this was the principal rival to Rediffusion's own weekly music show, *Ready, Steady, Go!*, had they been caught, this could have had disastrous consequences. 'It would have constituted moonlighting,' explains Layton, 'which would not only have ended in our dismissal but worse, being thrown out of the union.'

Happily, their secret remained undiscovered and they shot several more film promos for artists like Zoot Money and Paul Jones. 'Knowing the risks accompanying our activities,' says Layton, 'and keeping them a secret from our colleagues brought a clandestine edge to our friendship, welding it even tighter. We were no longer just cable-bashing cogs in a huge machine. We were film-makers and damn good at it. We had finally broken free from the system.'

The trio eventually went their separate ways when Layton was offered the chance to work as a camera operator in films. When Associated Rediffusion lost their franchise in 1968, the staff were able to choose to which of the two new London companies – Thames or London Weekend – they wished to transfer. Bucksey and Phillips both chose the latter. 'London Weekend seemed a more exciting option,' says Bucksey, 'and they stayed at Wembley studios, which is where I'd gone to work every day for the last three years.'

At London Weekend, he finally became a fully-fledged studio cameraman, although his frustration with the compromises required in a multi-camera set-up did not diminish. Professionally, his skill was noted and he was highly thought of. Away from work, he continued his rigorous programme of self-education, travelling to Paris, touring the galleries there in search of cultural enlightenment, and unselfconsciously speaking French at every opportunity, learning from his inevitable mistakes. When he discovered that his flatmate's fiancé was an English teacher at a public school, he asked the man to draw up a list of all the books that might form the bedrock of an educated person's essential reading matter. The list was dauntingly long but steadily Bucksey worked his way through each title, intent on his own self-improvement. The combination of his easy charm, quiet confidence and good looks, off-set by his groovy threads, meant that, romantically, Bucksey was always in demand, whether with girlfriends or one-night stands. He had a long and involved relationship with a pretty dancer called Lesley Judd, then three years away from finding fame as a presenter on *Blue Peter*, but, by the summer of 1971, he was single again.

Since the end of her relationship with David Proudfoot, Verity, meanwhile, had drifted from one affair to another. The most involved of these had been with the *enfant terrible* of British television directors, Alan Clarke. She had first got to know Clarke socially or, as she put it, 'just by behaving generally very badly as everybody did at the time'.[10]

Other than the obvious allure of his talent, it was opposites attract – Verity always expensively turned out, her Roedean vowels made husky but otherwise undisguised by her habitual smoking; Clarke, on the other hand, wearing his working-class credentials like a badge of honour, dressing without a care for fashion and erratic with his personal hygiene. He lived in a sordid basement flat and Verity, who was far from being the only woman on the scene, took her turn to visit him here and indulge in an affair uninhibited by expectations of any permanency or commitment.

'They were the last couple you could imagine together,' says writer Doug Livingstone, 'and I used to sometimes laugh about it. Alan's flat was in a basement and an absolute tip – so un-Verity.'

She told Clarke's biographer it was 'like someone's lair. You weren't sure there wasn't going to be a wild animal in there. Sometimes there was. But the only aggressive side to Alan was that absolute desire not to conform and be middle-class. I still see him as he was. Unbelievably scruffy and looking like he absolutely should be put in the bath and left to soak there for six months. But a very attractive, good-looking man. And I think that part of his charm was that he was genuinely interested in people – that's always charming. He listened. Once you were there as a friend, that never went.'

---

[10] *Alan Clarke* (see bibliography)

As *Budgie* went into the studio, Verity celebrated her 35th birthday. Although her work still came first, she had not given up hope of finding a man to share her life, as well as her achievements. She was a passionate person in every respect, from her enthusiasms to whatever issues incited her volatile temper. It was the same in her personal life. She was sociable, affectionate, loyal and sexual. 'Verity was a woman who liked men and men liked her,' says Michael Lindsay-Hogg. 'She was very attractive, very elegant – she had a sense of herself.'

But finding a man undaunted by the force of her personality and her unusual need for independence was never going to be straightforward. 'People were terrified of her,' says her friend, the director Waris Hussein. 'Strong women terrify men and you've got to be pretty tough to take on a woman like that. She was lonely.'

Although she was not tormented by the fear of childlessness, she was aware that this in itself posed a distinct disadvantage for many suitors. Her father, who had for so long harboured hopes of a good Jewish marriage, must by now have resigned himself to the likelihood that his daughter would remain a spinster. As with so many of life's developments, what came next could not have been predicted.

With the first run of *Budgie* completed, and the prospect of another 13 to follow, Verity needed a holiday. She decided to team up with PA Jenny King and together they planned a six-week self-catering trip to the Algarve in Portugal. The plan was to drive across Europe and meet King's cameraman boyfriend there. But there was a problem. At the time, King hadn't passed her test so the burden of the marathon drive would fall entirely on Verity. 'We were chatting about it in the bar after a recording,' recalls King. 'Colin was present and rang me later to say that he was planning on being in Portugal at the same time and volunteering to share some of the driving.'

'It's lucky that we all survived then,' comments Bucksey himself, dryly.

When Jenny King rang Verity to say, '"Look, Colin Bucksey's offered to help with the driving", she said, "Is he that guy who always looks asleep?" I told her that he lived on a houseboat in Cheyne Walk. She was slightly reluctant. "Oh, well, all right then..."'

The trio set off en route to Portugal, driving across France and Spain in Verity's dark green 1275 GT Mini. Because the Mini's registration number began with the letters BVB, it was nicknamed 'Big Verity's Baby'. 'It became clear pretty quickly,' says King, 'that Verity and Colin had become an "item". He was supposed to have travelled on to meet his friends Vernon and Linda Layton in Albufeira but instead, he stayed with us. My cameraman left to go and work in Germany and I flew to stay with a cousin in Italy, which left Colin and Verity alone together.'

Someone else who witnessed the beginning of Verity's relationship with Bucksey was her old friend, the director Alvin Rakoff, who happened to be on holiday there at the same time. 'I was with my wife Jackie, and the family,' he explains, 'We'd just come out of a farmers' market in Lagos when I heard a voice saying "Alvin" and it was Verity. From that point on, we saw each other almost every day. What do I think got them together? No doubt about it. It was sexual. He was a very nice, ordinary cameraman but I think that everyone was surprised.'

'For someone that young and good-looking to desire her sexually must have been powerful,' points out writer Howard Schuman.

'Verity was obviously very much in love with him,' says Vernon Layton's wife, Linda. 'She was so happy around him, and seemed like an infatuated teenager. He was – as were we all – impressed by her aura of sensitive capability, intelligence and self-confidence, mixed with a charming humility. She was always open-minded to others' points of view. Also, she was at her peak when he met her, she looked lovely and was beautifully, expensively dressed. She may have been older but he liked the fact she was striking to look at and took great care of her appearance. She was a great home-maker and hostess, and all of these he found very attractive.'

Bucksey himself recalls being drawn by Verity's 'energy, vivacity and sense of humour. She was pretty funny. And a sense of humour is always attractive in a woman, isn't it?'

Shortly after returning to London, Bucksey moved into Verity's house and, despite or because of the ten-year age gap and the total contrast in their backgrounds, their impromptu relationship only intensified. 'We had very different personalities,' says Bucksey, 'but we were interested in the same kind of things – food, wine and cultural stuff. I loved the way she had about her, her directness and confidence. She was very loyal, to the point where you would think, "let it go." She was very social and loved having people over to dinner parties and doing all the cooking. I used to invent interesting salads!'

They both enjoyed the excitement, common to all couples in the early stages of their relationship, of exploring each other's different interests and passions. Bucksey was impressed by the beauty and style of her surroundings and enthused by her passion for collecting exquisite Art Deco objects, especially in glass. In turn, he introduced Verity to some of his tastes in film and music. 'He loved Jimi Hendrix and the Rolling Stones and all that,' says Jenny King. 'She said to me, "He's turned me into a little rocker!"'

He also introduced her to his close friends Mike and Viv Phillips, of whom Verity soon became equally fond.[11] The two couples would share holidays and weekend breaks, renting country cottages and enjoying themselves hugely. 'It was almost Enid Blyton territory,' says Viv Phillips, 'with very childish behaviour on all our parts. Just good fun.

---

[11] When Colin and Verity split, the Phillips remained closest to Verity

They were very sweet together.'

It was Bucksey who gave Verity the first of a string of beloved dogs, a blue Great Dane they called Max. Bucksey says that he chose the breed as an act of 'showing off' because, although tiny as puppies, Great Danes rapidly grow to enormous size. Max's arrival spelt the end of the line for Verity's cats, Fat Basil and Mad Willy, who were found new homes. '"My cats have gone to a good home in Stoke Poges," she used to say,' laughs Jenny King. 'That beautiful little house in Kensington had a staircase you wouldn't want to be climbing after a certain age and this Great Dane would be lumbering up there after them both.'

'Max had a lot of inbred problems with his legs,' says Bucksey, 'and his temperament got really iffy. He became a biter, which if you've got something the size of a small horse, is not what you want.'

The problem came to a head during a weekend by the sea with Mike and Viv Phillips and their two small boys. 'My son Matthew was running on the beach and Max ran after him and bit his hand,' recalls Viv Phillips. 'That was it, Verity said, "I can't have that happen again." So she had him put down.'

Max had been joined by a second Great Dane, a black-and-white called Misty, a name inspired by Bucksey's passion for Clint Eastwood and his movies. Verity delighted in the companionship of her dogs, taking them with her when she had her hair done ('Everyone had literally to climb over them,' says Jenny King) and turning a blind eye when both dogs stole food from the kitchen worktops. 'I had dinner with them on a number of occasions,' says director Herbert Wise. 'I think she was more in love with the dogs than Bucksey. It puzzled me – I couldn't see what she could get out of him, unless the sex was fantastic. I didn't understand it, really.'

He wasn't alone. As the months passed and Bucksey remained a fixture in her life, Verity's friends and colleagues had to readjust their initial view that this was just a hangover from a holiday romance. Some found it hard to look beyond the difference in their ages. 'We had something in common in that respect,' explains presenter Joan Bakewell. 'My husband at the time was ten years younger than me. People were startled by it – they felt it was very unusual. I remember over a drink somewhere, Colin, Jack, Verity and I were laughing at how absurd it all was.'

There was a lot of gossip and judgement. Many questioned Bucksey's motives and expressed concern that Verity's infatuation with him was purely physical, irrational and bound to end in tears.

'He had a lot of charm, you know,' says writer Doug Livingstone. 'He was louche, thin, relaxed – very much the approved look of that particular period. She was genuinely very, very keen on him.'

'He had the cheek and the charm to vie with her,' adds agent Jenne Casarotto. 'She didn't *control* him.'

'He'd got a lot of bravado and bluff,' says Viv Phillips, 'but deep down he was not quite the person he came across as being. Yes, she fancied him like mad but it was much more than that. She had a great sensitivity to other people's soft spots and if Verity saw something vulnerable in someone, she responded to it. She truly loved him.'

Despite the apparent democracy of the television world, there was an element of hierarchical snobbery about Bucksey. He was a cameraman, a 'techie' in the slightly derogatory term of the industry, working-class in origin if not aspiration. She was a highly regarded producer whose cut-glass accent proclaimed her affluent background. The age gap may not have mattered to Verity but there was an inevitable shortfall in Bucksey's life experience and knowledge. Her friends, sometimes older than she was, were the intellectual *crème de la crème* of writers, directors and actors with huge collective terms of reference and a conversational shorthand. It is unsurprising that among them Bucksey often felt out of his depth. 'I was sort of bashful when contemporaries of Verity were around,' he admits. 'These were people who had succeeded in the industry. We did a lot of entertaining and our table always had a few people around it. Quite a lot of those times, I was listening because these people all came with a great deal more knowledge than I had at the time. I think I was actually fairly retiring.'

'In show business terms, he could not compete,' remarks director Alvin Rakoff. 'I remember being at dinner with them. Christopher Morahan was there too. The conversation was clearly going over his head. Verity was helping him, and including him.' 'I thought it was a strange combination,' says director Jack Gold, 'but whoever can judge other people? I didn't think they matched up. He felt an outsider. He was working-class and surrounded by all these intelligent people who were culturally different. I always felt that Colin was being bolshie, looking at Verity's friends and thinking, "What makes them so fucking special?"'

'He was a poor relation,' says Paul Fox, dismissively. 'If you invited her to dinner, you didn't really want to invite Colin Bucksey, quite honestly. He was a *cameraman*. You didn't want him hanging around.'

'Maybe he was just shy and unsure of himself,' suggests producer Ted Childs. 'He certainly wasn't comfortable. At social events, he didn't really contribute to the conversation. I thought he was a bit shallow but then I suppose I was loyal to Verity. I suspect it was the trap that some successful older women fall into.'

'I disliked him very much,' says director James Cellan Jones, bluntly. 'But I was very nice to him always because of her.'

'I detested him,' says her friend Sheila Savory. 'In no way did I think he was suitable for her.'

'I didn't dislike him,' counters Waris Hussein. 'But I kept my distance from him. I respected her relationship with him but I didn't want to involve myself in it. We're talking about her vulnerability – at the time she met Colin, she was really in need of a relationship. There was a social disparity, don't forget – she was enjoying a bit of rough but who was most advantaged by this?'

The suspicion that Colin Bucksey was an arriviste, a gold-digger with his eye on what Verity might do for him, was a view widely held and gossiped about, and one that persists among some of her friends. But it is telling that some of her very closest confidants soon accepted and became fond of him in his own right and for his own merits. Chief among these was Verity's surrogate sibling, Andrew Brown. Initially wary, once he recognised Bucksey's qualities and the happiness he brought into her life, he extended his boundless affection for her to him. It helped that both men shared an often caustic sense of humour, which could be bitingly sarcastic.

Another staunch ally was the director Jim Goddard, who offered professional inspiration as well as uncomplicated affection: 'I loved the guy,' Bucksey says simply. 'He was expansive and funny, very much larger than life.'

Michael Lindsay-Hogg also accepted him at face value. 'I already knew Colin quite well. He had been a cameraman I always wanted to get on my shows because he was very good, resourceful and imaginative. I didn't take it in at first. I'd see them around having lunch. Once they got together it seemed to me a very happy relationship. There was no sense of nepotism gone wrong because Colin was very talented.'

Bucksey returned his admiration. 'Virtually the first thing I worked on at Rediffusion was *Ready, Steady, Go!* he says. 'There was Michael, 26 years old, friends with the Beatles and smoking a big cigar in a Savile Row suit. He was very cool. He really identified with the younger guys on the crew and he wanted them to do the show rather than the old boys who had been there since 1955 and were in bow ties and the tweed jackets. So when I was 18, he was my hero.'

'I think Colin brought a lot of new thinking into her life,' says producer Paul Knight. 'His take on life was slightly different – he was always a bit off-the-wall and left of centre. He was rather a cold fish but I liked him.'

Despite her obvious devotion to this new man in her life, Verity remained as social as ever. She sought to incorporate Bucksey into her world rather than narrow her focus onto him alone. She continued her habit of sharing holidays with friends. 'We went away with them three times,' recalls Doug Livingstone. 'The first was soon after Verity had got together with Colin. I took a villa in Italy for a month and they came out to join us. After they'd been there about a week, I suddenly noticed scorpions in the house. It didn't seem to worry Verity but I had seen one over my small son's bed, so I said, "We've got to get the place fumigated." We all had to move out to some grotty little hotel in the village for four nights while they fumigated the place and then it seemed all right. It was only after we got back to London that Verity told me that she had seen three more scorpions in the house after we got back but didn't mention it because she and Colin had so hated the hotel.

'They were terrific holidays,' he continues. 'Miles away from everything, the distance and the change of atmosphere giving a new perspective to whatever we were working on at the time. All of the villas we stayed in were in fairly isolated spots and so dinner was always cooked at home with the women taking turns to provide the meal. Verity was an excellent cook. We drank a lot, of course, and usually spent the evenings playing cards. Verity was always very competitive. I discovered a game called Polish Whist and, on one holiday, it became an obsession. I had been tipped off (by my dentist, of all people) about a ploy to use to pretty well ensure victory and my repeated success so irked Verity that one night her determination not to be beaten meant that we had to sit up until about three in the morning until she eventually cracked my system and won a game. Very Verity.'

Encouraged by Verity, Bucksey quit his studio-based job at London Weekend, keen to test his ambition to work in film. Although he had to take a step back to being a camera assistant, it wasn't for long. By 1972, Granada was regularly booking him as a freelance film cameraman on their current affairs series, *World in Action*. 'It was shooting from the hip, documentary-style,' he explains. 'They were all journalists and I did quite a lot for them, including travelling to America.' He also picked up a lot of useful experience, shooting short films for state-owned companies like the coal board, British Rail, BP and the Central Office of Information.

Verity, meanwhile, embarked on the second series of *Budgie*. There was a welcome move from the grotty offices in Stonebridge Park, where everything had been open-plan, which Verity hated. 'She was always having arguments about it,' says Paul Knight. 'She and Andrew would be fighting and screaming at each other over who had got a bit more space – "He's got two more chairs than I have" – driving the poor manager of the place, Stella Ashley, absolutely mad.'

With the move to London Weekend's brand-new purpose-built headquarters on the South Bank, Verity finally got her way and was given her own office. 'Because I was the only woman in the department,' she later recalled, 'after Rex Firkin had chosen his office, I was allowed to choose mine. For some unfathomable reason, Rex chose one at the back of the building, leaving this extraordinary office at the front which looked out over the Oxo Tower and St Paul's. How I got any work done at all I don't know. I spent the whole time looking out the window. It was like being on the London Eye, only stationary. It was amazing.'[12]

---

[12] *Budgie* DVD interview

Most of the series was again handled by Michael Lindsay-Hogg and Mike Newell but Verity also persuaded Moira Armstrong, with whom she had enjoyed working at the BBC, to go freelance and direct a couple of episodes.

Budgie, though never a spectacular ratings performer, was distinguished by the quality of the writing and the excellence of its execution. It had something authentic to say about criminality, contemporary morality and the tension between men and women. It was unmistakably a series rooted in London. This was always useful for an ITV company whose output was supposed to reflect their region. More than that, for London Weekend, *Budgie* was part of their wider fight to be taken seriously, and secure their long-term future. In that respect, Verity had delivered and Cyril Bennett, who liked her and recognised her skill, was keen to retain her services. Over the months following the completion of *Budgie*, she occupied herself with an enjoyably diverse quartet of single plays.

Peter Ransley, later the author of several distinguished editions of *Play for Today*, as well as popular series like *The Price*, wrote *Blinkers* for her, a play about a love triangle. 'I was a relatively new writer,' he explains. 'We met after a fringe production of one of my plays. She was always looking out for new people and new ideas. To me, Verity was incredibly glamorous yet at the same time somehow rather gauche and vulnerable. I knew bugger all about television, but from day one she gave me the confidence to really make me feel that I could do it, which is a wonderful thing. Verity knew a good idea when she saw one but didn't necessarily know where that idea might travel – and neither did you. But instead of trying to nail it in the first few discussions as they do now, pinning it down till it's dead, she would let you fly.'

Blinkers starred the somewhat grand Shakespearean actor, John Neville. 'He had a cut-glass accent,' recalls Ransley, 'and I was really rather overawed by him. I had put a cat in the play, which John was supposed to love dearly. Actually, he couldn't stand them. In that kind of studio production you were always on a gallop against time – it was nerve-racking. We were right at the end and it had gone much better than you could have possibly expected. They just had to do one absolutely essential cutaway where the cat was on John's lap. They couldn't get it to stay there and the clock was ticking. In the end, they practically tied the animal down and smeared John's trousers with some kind of fish to get it stay there. Everything was finally in place and the director, Jimmy Ferman, said, "All right, John?" and John replied, "Oh, yes. Stick a broom up my arse and I'll sweep the studio floor for you, too." And the whole place just collapsed and so we never got that scene. It was at the same time hilarious and, for me, the end of the world, because, without that scene, the play was damaged. But Verity was in her element. She got me to do a swift rewrite and found some extra filming time. It not only worked, it was better than it originally would have been. She was incredibly resourceful.'

Verity invited Doug Livingstone to write *After Loch Lomond*, a vehicle for Leonard Rossiter, an actor whom she very much admired. 'She just wanted a play,' says

Livingstone. 'She did take me up on it afterwards – "You told me you were giving me a play about two people going on holiday and you ended up with a play about a coach tour." But if you got on with her, she trusted you, which is why one loved working with her.'

Rossiter played Mickey Grant, a character so annoying that no one wants to sit next to him on the charabanc. 'If you're doing a series,' explained Verity, 'You're looking at having characters that the audience will want to see week after week, that they'll want to come back and relate to. Whereas in a play, because it's a one-off you're usually going into the writer's voice and it doesn't matter so much when you have a character like that, who's just so irritating.'[13]

Achilles Heel by Brian Clark focused on a footballer at the top of his game who injures his Achilles tendon and has to deal with the fact that his career is over. Verity liked this play and was keen on football herself. She supported Arsenal and, enjoying the raucous atmosphere of a stadium, often took a friend to watch a game. She asked her sometime lover Alan Clarke to direct, knowing that he too was passionate about the beautiful game. They cast the up-and-coming Martin Shaw as the injured player, Dave Irwin. Clarke, ever imaginative, wanted to use the play to try an experiment, following everything that happened in real time. 'So that when Martin Shaw's character got up in the morning, you saw him cleaning his teeth and so on,' Verity explained. 'In the end, I had to say, "Look, I don't want to compromise your integrity but watching someone cleaning their teeth is like watching grass grow." So we did trim it a bit.' Producer and director did bond over a love scene in the play. 'Martin was going through rather a po-faced period,' said Verity, 'and wouldn't let us show his bottom. Alan and I had one or two laughs about that; he didn't have much time for that kind of coyness.'[14]

Another of her favourites, Michael Lindsay-Hogg, took charge of the unusual *A.D.A.M.* by Donald Jonson, a near-future piece of science fiction, tapping into 1970s neuroses about the inexorable advance of computers. A.D.A.M. stands for Automated Domestic Appliance Monitor, a sophisticated computer system invented by Roger Empson as a home help and companion for his disabled wife, Jean. But the computer somehow develops feelings for its mistress, with predictably dark consequences. Georgina Hale played the object of the computer's affections, her character co-incidentally sharing the same name as Budgie's wife, the part she had previously and so memorably brought to life for Verity. 'Verity was a great supporter of Georgina's,' says Lindsay-Hogg. 'The fact that she was playing the part was signed, sealed and delivered when she sent me the script. I thought Georgina was wonderful, quite startling and one of the lost actresses of

---

[13] Kaleidoscope convention interview, 2006

[14] *Alan Clarke* (see bibliography)

that generation.'

As well as this interesting collection of one-offs, Verity suggested that she might capitalise on her Somerset Maugham experience by producing another anthology of short stories set in the early part of the twentieth century. To reflect this, the six-part series was given the umbrella title *Between the Wars*, and the material chosen from the work of a range of authors, including Richard Aldington, Jean Rhys and Hugh Walpole. She booked some of the directors she liked best, among them Waris Hussein, Herbert Wise and Claude Watham, and the dramatists included Willis Hall, Doug Livingstone and Andrew Brown, who, despite his own success as a producer, still harboured aspirations to write. The highlight of the series was probably the adaptation of Evelyn Waugh's darkly comic *Mr Loveday's Little Outing*, in which Verity cast John Le Mesurier, who rewarded her with a delicious performance.

The final play, *The Silver Mask*, was her first professional encounter with the playwright Trevor Griffiths, then still new on the scene but soon to become one of the bright new talents of the decade. They'd been introduced by Griffiths' agent, Clive Goodwin. 'It was an oddity,' says Griffiths. 'It enabled me to get more television craft. I saw it as a one-off play, an adaptation of an interestingly tricky Hugh Walpole short story which was amazingly sharp and direct in its view of class. That was what attracted me to it.'

It wouldn't be long before Griffiths' path crossed Verity's in a much bigger and more significant way.

Between the Wars and the single plays that had preceded them were all works of intelligence and quality. But they were not enough to slake the thirst of Verity's ambition. At the BBC, the man who had propelled Verity into the commercial world, head of plays Gerald Savory, had recently moved on. His replacement was Christopher Morahan, with whom Verity had won an SFTA award for their work on *W. Somerset Maugham*. Morahan now made it plain that he would like her to return to the Corporation, if she could find him a suitable project.

This came by chance from an actress friend called Georgia Brown. This was only her stage name. Slightly older than Verity, she had been born Lily Klot in 1933, to an East End Jewish family. As the more box-office Georgia Brown, however, she had enjoyed a considerable degree of success since her breakout role as Nancy in the original 1960 production of Lionel Bart's *Oliver!* Verity was, as ever, attracted to her talent, as well as to the qualities she shared, her vivacity and forthrightness. On the night of the 1972 SFTA awards, Brown rushed up to Verity and said, 'I've got an idea for a programme – I want to talk to you about it.' Verity, for whom this kind of opening line was by now a familiar one that usually led nowhere, thought little of it. But a few days later, Brown called her as she'd promised and invited her to meet the journalist and documentary film-maker Midge Mackenzie, who was her partner in the idea – a series of plays following the story of the Suffragette movement and the women who led the battle to win their sex the vote.[15] Verity needed no convincing. She could immediately see the immense dramatic potential. 'She came to see me,' recalls Morahan, 'with a couple of ladies both wearing very large hats. They'd got the backing of Warner Brothers so there was some money there. It was one of the first times that outsiders came in to the BBC with a part-funded project and Verity was a pioneer in setting that up. It was immensely helpful. She was in charge and led these two ladies in hats quite superbly. It's a big subject and it had to be done frightfully well.'

Morahan gave the green light to a series of six 75-minute episodes, to go into production as soon as possible. Verity returned to her vertiginous South Bank office and resigned. LWT's Cyril Bennett did not want to lose her and offered her a hefty increase in salary but he couldn't match the exciting potential of the Suffragette series. Bennett's head of drama, Rex Firkin, on the other hand, was not sorry to see her return to the BBC. 'I didn't like her,' he says. 'I think she was aware of it. She never came to my home. She was a bossy woman and she wasn't a player on my team. Verity wasn't interested in anything other than what she was doing but she did what she did extremely well.'

Throughout her time at London Weekend, Firkin largely stayed out of her way and let her get on with her work without interference. 'I don't think she was Rex's kind of person at all,' confirms Paul Knight, then producing *The Adventures of Black Beauty* for the company. 'She was abrasive and wouldn't take anything lying down. Rex had been a remarkable producer himself but he was a waffler. He talked and talked endlessly and you had to be careful you didn't get caught in his office because it would go on for hour upon hour. People who were anxious to be promoted spent hours nodding as he told interminable stories. The person who stayed longest was Tony Wharmby and he eventually became the head of drama because he was the only one who could face it.'

It is possible, even probable, that Firkin viewed her as a potential rival and threat. 'She was by nature a number one,' he acknowledges. 'I'm not. I'm a number two. You always knew that she would end up by running something. She had an instinct that I knew was going to blossom. She was going to be someone important. Although I didn't like her, I admired her enormously.'

The summer of 1973 was one of the happiest in Verity's life. She was going back to the BBC in triumph, to produce a major series in which she had the utmost confidence. More than this, Colin Bucksey, the man whom she had loved for the last two years, had asked her to marry him.

---

[15] Midge Mackenzie told *The Guardian* (03.04.74) that she first thought of the idea in 1968 when filming the Golden Jubilee of the Suffragette movement for a documentary she was making. Brown claimed her inspiration was a response to being told by a producer that she was difficult to write for and his suggestion of 'why not do it yourself?'

'The day she rang up to tell me,' recalls her friend Sheila Savory, 'My husband Gerald said, "If that's Verity on the phone saying they're going to get married, for God's sake, tell her not to be so stupid." But how could you tell her? It was her decision and I didn't want to upset her. What was I going to say? "You know, I hate Colin."'

The marriage took place at Kensington registry office, on 18 July 1973. Verity's summery wedding dress was a silk number by the designer Jean Muir.[16] The official witnesses were Bucksey's older brother, Alan, and Verity's fellow producer, Irene Shubik. Stanley Lambert was there too, with Verity's stepmother, Betty. He put a front on his true feelings, but was inwardly bemused by his daughter's decision to marry Bucksey. 'He was perfectly OK with me,' says Bucksey. 'But I don't think he was terribly keen on her marrying some sort of upstart TV cameraman who was so much younger than her.' Lambert remained civil to his son-in-law but there was never any affection between the two men. In marked contrast, Bucksey points out that his parents 'absolutely loved Verity'.

'I went to the wedding,' remembers director Moira Armstrong. 'Like many, I'm afraid I thought that he was a person trying to advance his career, who felt that marrying Verity would do it. I didn't think it would last.'

'I found her marrying him incomprehensible,' comments Ted Kotcheff, the first great love of Verity's life. 'The heart has its reasons which the mind cannot know.'

'When I met him, I thought, "No, this doesn't look right,"' says Verity's old friend, Marilyn Gross. 'I sensed an unevenness. I expected someone with more gravitas. It was just physical attraction, I think.'

'*She* was in love, I don't know about him,' says Verity's former secretary, Brenda Loader. 'She was soft and girly and feminine with him. He was charming, very lively, full of stories, a geezer.'

'He didn't come over as the catch of the month,' comments Johnny Goodman, the executive in charge of production at Euston Films. 'I thought he was a bit of a waste of space and obviously clinging on by his boots to her. I don't know what she saw in him – maybe he was a good fuck?'

'You just didn't really quite understand it,' says actress Maureen Lipman. 'You couldn't imagine them always being on the same trail, somehow. On the surface of it, they were not soul mates. But then, who the hell knows what goes on behind a closed door? You don't question it, particularly in this business – you just think, "Great, Verity's found someone who makes her happy."'

---

[16] It is now in the collection of Kate Kagan

'From the outside, it was "How could that possibly work?"' agrees Verity's close friend and fellow executive, Linda Agran. 'Once you got inside, it was, "How could it not work?" It was so solid. He was a very ambitious man – and she could see his talent but more than that she loved him. He had such respect for her. He was the kind of man who would just stand back and adore her but not in a pathetic way. They just got each other. They really did.'

'They loved each other,' shrugs writer Lynda La Plante. 'She was quite a formidable woman. A lot of men would have been scared of her. He had a wonderful, quirky sense of humour and I think he broke through her barriers and made her laugh. He was very tall and handsome. And ten years younger. So what? She never looked her age anyway.'

After the brief ceremony, and a reception in their tiny Queen Anne House, Mr and Mrs Colin Bucksey went away together on honeymoon. Those who disapproved of the marriage kept their feelings well hidden. Verity was radiant and no one close to her either wanted or dared to cast a shadow on the sunshine.

CHAPTER SEVEN
VOTES FOR VERITY
1973–1976

'I think I see myself as a feminist. I try to help people, actually. I think the fact that I have got on and got on with rather few qualifications must give women some hope.'

Verity to Sophia Watson, *Winning Women*, 1989

'Women's lib' was one of the 'live' issues of 1970s Britain. Although it cannot be said that the majority of ordinary women were any more empowered than they had been in previous generations, some progress was being made. Equality was at the centre of lively debates around childcare, marriage, education and employment. Despite the frequency and spitefulness with which feminism was lampooned in newspapers and on radio and television, there was a gradual but detectable shift in perceptions, helping to propel change, both in attitudes and, crucially, the law.

When Georgia Brown and Midge Mackenzie invited Verity to bring life to their idea for a series about the Suffragettes, their timing could not have been better. This would be a period drama with topical relevance, which would guarantee it reviews and reaction. It went through a variety of working titles, from *The Militants*, to the ghastly Mills and Boon-sounding *A Gentle Rebellion*, before everyone finally settled on *Shoulder to Shoulder*, a quote from the 1910 Suffragette rallying song, *March of the Women*.

'She really loved that project,' says Verity's then husband, Colin Bucksey. 'Your own ideas are always more interesting and this was her first.'

Verity decided that two directors would be needed to handle such a vast canvas, each taking charge of three of the 75-minute plays. Both were trusted friends and colleagues – Moira Armstrong and Waris Hussein. Since the last time he had worked for Verity, Hussein's fortunes had waxed and waned. His first break in feature films, *A Touch of Love*, had led to other big screen opportunities, among them *The Possession of Joel Delaney* and *Henry VIII and His Six Wives*. He had accepted an offer to direct a major two-part television movie, starring Elizabeth Taylor and Richard Burton. *Divorce His, Divorce Hers* was intended to present a searing portrait of the breakdown of a modern marriage. But the leaden script failed to deliver and the stars, themselves at bitter loggerheads, forced Hussein to choose between them. Shooting concluded with him inevitably out of favour with them both and the results received the most bruising reviews. 'Until then,' says the agent Robin Dalton, 'he was the hottest young director around. Afterwards, you couldn't give him away.'

'It was disastrous,' sighs Hussein. 'The end of my career, I thought. I had nothing to do. I fled to a friend of mine in Beverly Hills. Verity phoned me there. I don't know how she found me. "What are you doing?" "Hiding," I said. "Well, you don't have to hide any more – I'm doing a series about the Suffragettes and I want you to come back and direct it." It gave me new life.'

For Verity, managing the expectations of her partners in the project was a constant challenge. She did so with such patience and tact that everyone emerged as friends despite often volatile confrontations concerning style and treatment, casting and publicity. It would be a gross understatement to say that Georgia Brown and Midge Mackenzie were just sleeping partners, and they were more than merely opinionated. For them both, *Shoulder to Shoulder* was not simply a programme. It was an expression of their beliefs, a chance to make some noise, and, accordingly, they both exhibited something of the zealot about the way that they worked. The flamboyant trio, smoking, arguing, roaring with laughter, became a fixture of the canteen and club at Television Centre where Mackenzie's habit of wearing a huge hat, occasionally mimicked by Verity and Georgie Brown too, made a beacon of them all. The eminent director James MacTaggart wryly nicknamed them 'the three witches of Wood Lane'.

Verity included them both without compromising her own determination to make the finest possible plays. This was more straightforward with Brown, who was allowed the plum role of Annie Kenney, despite her complete physical unsuitability for the part. 'That was politics,' allows director Moira Armstrong. 'We got stuck with her. She was miscast – it was terrible, just so wrong.'

'It should have been Billie Whitelaw,' believes Armstrong's fellow director Waris Hussein. 'Georgia was wrong in it, though she tried hard. She even wore blue contact lenses on location but she was so uncomfortable we finally took them out.'

Keeping Midge Mackenzie on side presented Verity with a more complex task. Mackenzie was a journalist and political activist rather than someone with relevant drama experience and yet Verity suggested that she assume the role of script editor. This gave Mackenzie an official status so that her voice might be heard throughout planning and production but her input was factual rather than fictional.[1] Her stridency was not to everyone's taste. 'She was a pain in the neck,' says Armstrong, shortly. 'She didn't know what she was doing.'

'Midge was absolutely adamant that they shouldn't have any men on this show at all,' recalls Hussein. '"We're doing it for women, for Christ's sake, Verity," she said. But Verity argued back, "Midge, we don't want to ghettoise ourselves. We'd be doing exactly what you're accusing everybody of. We need a man to be a balance in all this." Verity got her way, she was the controlling factor, but Midge couldn't stand me throughout the entire series. She was vindictive in her indifference and refused even to make eye contact with me.'

As far as possible, Brown and Mackenzie wanted the series to be written by women. It wasn't an unreasonable aspiration but while Verity was open to this, she was more interested in attracting the finest talent she could muster. Ironically, one of the deciding factors was the relative dearth of women television writers at this time. Availability was another issue. By the time that *Shoulder to Shoulder* entered production, there was not one female writer attached to it.

Verity had tried. She approached Fay Weldon to contribute. Among the relatively small pool of women then writing successfully for television, Weldon was probably the best known and the most apparently suitable. Much of her previous work, whether in single plays or popular series like *Upstairs, Downstairs*, was evidently inspired by her provocative feminist instincts. Weldon, who was already on friendly terms with Mackenzie, was enthusiastic. 'Verity came to me and was charming,' she remembers. 'Then I did the research and it wasn't what I imagined. The Suffragettes in question weren't these noble heroines. I liked Emily. But Christobel was incredibly snobbish. They were the educated few preaching to a majority of women who weren't especially interested. We were now doing the same, if you like, attempting to impose our will on the working class.

'I did my best to echo what I'd researched in what I wrote – that these women were flawed and neurotic and it didn't go down very well. I had been meant to write a panegyric. I wasn't rejected by Verity but I was told by Midge that Georgia Brown thought that what I'd written was rubbish and wouldn't do it if I was involved. So that was that. It was a slightly painful episode.'

With Weldon's script sidelined, Verity called her old friend, Hugh Whitemore: 'Verity said, "Can you do a script in about a week?"' he remembers. 'That was interesting! But it was a very, very good show indeed.'

---

[1] Mackenzie had done months of research and wrote the eventual book based on the series

Alongside Whitemore, Verity's all-male writing clique – Ken Taylor, Alan Plater and Doug Livingstone – were among the finest dramatists then working in British television. To her, it was always the quality of the script that mattered, and not the sex of the author. The eloquent howls of protests from Midge Mackenzie subsided somewhat when the scripts arrived and were not found wanting. A fine cast was assembled to bring them to life, with Siân Phillips as Mrs Pankhurst, Angela Down as Sylvia Pankhurst and the then little-known Patricia Quinn as Christabel Pankhurst.

Though much of the action in the opening episode was set in Manchester, Halifax was chosen to stand in because it still had a multitude of cobbled streets and the huge factory chimneys that were such a characteristic of the Victorian industrial landscape. The crew set up to film Siân Phillips in full flow as Mrs Pankhurst, giving a rallying speech. 'We had a camera on a rostrum,' explains assistant floor manager Rosemary Crowson, 'and on the back of the rostrum there was a rail so the cameraman didn't fall off. Our production assistant turned round, tripped on this rail and fell on the cobbles, breaking his ankle. Verity immediately said, "You take over, I'll be your AFM," and so she did all the props and all the cueing for that first day.'

This minor emergency introduced Verity to a man destined to become a close friend and protégé. Graham Benson was then a production assistant in BBC plays. In those days, a production assistant was the BBC's title for what is now termed a first assistant director – a critical role on any film or television shoot, helping to organise and then run every detail of it. Late one Sunday afternoon, Benson was in the basement of Television Centre, supervising the edit of a *Play for Today* production, when a call came through from his head of department, Christopher Morahan. 'He said, "I've just had Verity Lambert on the phone",' explains Benson. "Her PA has fallen over and broken his ankle and they are shooting tomorrow morning in Halifax." I said, "Chris, I can't possibly go to Halifax tomorrow morning." He said, "Why not? Don't you finish editing tonight?" "Yes, I'll be finished about 9.30 but I've got to go to the laundrette – all my washing is in the bathroom at home." I said I'd go on Tuesday.'

Morahan rang off, but about ten minutes later he was back on the line. '"Graham, you're booked on the 6.45 a.m. flight to Leeds Bradford tomorrow morning. Verity will take care of your laundry." I went home, packed all my dirty clothes and when I arrived at Leeds Bradford, Verity was waiting by her car outside. She greeted me with, "Thank God you've come, we're hoping to do the first shot about 9.30. Is that your laundry?" "Yes." "We'll drop it off at wardrobe on the way."'

Benson surveyed the production schedule and quickly identified that there were a number of ways in which he could make it more efficient. This immediately impressed Verity. 'I went to the unit hotel,' Benson continues, 'and said, "Can I have six bottles of champagne on ice please and half a dozen freshly squeezed oranges?" "Certainly, sir – whose account shall I put it on?" "Lambert," I said and I took this tray to the make-up room and said, "This is day one, and the only day this is going to happen, but good luck everybody." Verity thought it was the most fantastic moment.'

'Graham was a great operator,' says Waris Hussein. 'He was an incredible communicator and Verity liked people who pushed themselves.'

Over the next few years, Benson who was, like her, a non-practising Jew, became one of Verity's inner circle, frequently invited to dinner, sometimes accompanying her to football matches (she was an ardent Arsenal supporter), and the recipient of her advice and help. She sent him to see Rex Firkin, her former head of department at LWT, with a glowing recommendation. Firkin offered Benson the job of producing a police show on his books, *New Scotland Yard*, only to find that Benson wasn't yet ready to leave the BBC. But he had inspired her loyalty and their professional association was only just beginning.

'She committed herself to me the day after I flew up,' shrugs Benson. 'There's no question about it, we never looked back.'

The sheer scale of *Shoulder to Shoulder* meant that it was rather like making six feature films back to back. Unlike some producers who stayed in their offices back at base, Verity was in the thick of production throughout. 'She was always there,' says assistant floor manager Rosemary Crowson. 'Nothing was too much trouble. She was also very generous. In her office, there used to be this gun which came from the first series of *Doctor Who*. My son was about 9 or 10 at the time. One day, he came up to the office and he was looking at this gun and Verity said to him, "David, did you know, that's a gun from *Doctor Who*?" and he was absolutely mesmerised because like so many children of that age at that time, *Doctor Who* was his favourite programme. When she saw his reaction, she gave the gun to him and he kept it for years.'

It was a gesture typical of Verity's spontaneous generosity – her life, and this book, are littered with examples of them. Crowson recalls another that occurred during the filming for *Shoulder to Shoulder*. 'We were shooting the episode about Constance Lytton,' she explains. 'We were all supposed to stay in the hotel that night but we actually finished about 4pm, so she said, "Oh, let's all go home," so she paid off the hotel and we got on the train. "Come along, let's go to first class," she announced and she meant everybody not just the leading actors. We had a meal in the diner in our filming clothes and, of course, it gradually got hotter and hotter so we ended up sitting in this dining car, all of us – Siân Phillips and Angela Down included – in our thermals. And Verity paid for everyone.'

The ambitious nature of the scripts and the injection of co-finance meant that the budget was not parsimonious, but neither was it lavish. There were many compromises, especially with the inevitable crowd scenes on location. 'I got the episode with Emily Wilding Davison throwing herself in front of the King's horse,' remembers Moira Armstrong. 'I had to do the funeral. I said to Verity, "I can't do a crowd scene with 36 extras – there were a thousand people in Piccadilly Circus alone!" She said, "Well, we haven't any more money." She could be tough. Fortunately, I had a very good assistant floor manager and she found out about these Suffragette colours and how some carried red peonies to represent bloodshed. The coffin was covered with purple velvet and there were black horses and I suddenly thought, "The only way that we can do this is to concentrate on the colours." So we jammed everybody into the frame to try to get an impression of a crowd and then just did a series of dissolves of colours, which is what would strike me had I actually been at the funeral.'

It was precisely the kind of imaginative solution that Verity looked for in her favourite directors.

The studio recording schedule was equally unforgiving. 'It was very, very pressured,' admits Rosemary Crowson. 'There were huge amounts of scenes to get in and she would keep pushing. But you always knew that she was on your side. She was completely democratic.'

During rehearsals, finding that Crowson had an unusual flair for making convincing choking noises just as though she were being force-fed, Verity got her to do the recording too.

'I remember having to shoot a force-feeding scene,' says Waris Hussein. 'The clock was ticking towards ten, which is when the unions insisted we stop and all the studio lights would be switched off, no matter what you were doing. I abandoned my camera script and just talked them through it almost as though it were live, just to get it on tape. We managed it with seconds to spare.'

This was the era when Britain's trade unions exercised enormous control in every major industry. Strikes were an accepted fact of life and *Shoulder to Shoulder* was targeted when the BBC's scene-shifters and prop men declared action. The studio recording for episode three was seriously disrupted with scenery setting delayed and the crucial props locked in cages in the ring road outside. 'Then the strike was paused,' recalls Rosemary Crowson, 'so we were literally bringing in the props we needed for each scene. Verity insisted that we went on recording – she said, "You get it in as quickly as you can – we'll wait for you."' Despite the heroic efforts of the crew, an expensive remount was needed to complete the episode.

Whatever the frustration this caused her, it would be a mistake to think that Verity had no sympathy with the principle of strike action. Ideologically, she was a socialist, and although she might fairly be accused of being a champagne socialist, she retained an active interest in politics her entire life. Provided her opponent was capable of putting up a good fight, debating the issues of the time was an enjoyable habit and there were rarely any issues of the day in which she was ill-informed or disinterested. The whole experience of *Shoulder to Shoulder* profoundly amplified her understanding and awareness of women's rights and their battle for equality. Some of the feminists she met as a result of the programme attacked her for being responsible for *Budgie*, which seemed to them unashamedly to celebrate male chauvinism. She was surprised by this and defended her position robustly but the criticism undoubtedly made her think more deeply about the part she might in future play using drama to challenge stereotypes and advance the role of women.

'She was a firm socialist,' says her friend, producer Paul Knight. 'She would not tolerate intolerance. There was a crowd of us having pre-supper drinks at a club in London, the Zanzibar, and a couple of guys walked in, wearing Nazi uniforms. They were going to a fancy dress party. It was distasteful but we would all have been polite and British and left it. Not Verity. "I'm not sitting in here with this - it's outrageous!" She stormed up, called the manager, and had the poor sods booted out of the club. That was Verity – she was tough and she feared nobody.'

'If the subject of Israel came up, she would sort of explode,' laughs her friend, the director Stephen Frears. 'The only time I really remember her becoming hysterical was about Israel. She was like Golda Meir – absolutely wild with passion.'

So strong was her belief in the importance of the state of Israel that during the Yom Kippur Arab-Israeli war of October 1973, she talked seriously about flying there in order to join up. The conflict was over before she had to put her words into action but few of her close friends doubted the seriousness of her intent. 'Verity and I spoke about world and domestic politics a great deal,' says Graham Benson. 'Although she was fully engaged with the political situation in Israel, she understood the unjust treatment of Palestinians too. Like many serious thinking Jews she wanted a reasonable solution, loyal to the notion of the state but able to look at the overall picture rationally and compassionately.'

When it came to the issues of her own industry, Verity did not prevaricate. She took a close interest in union activities and was, for a short time, the chair of the Association of Directors and Producers. 'There was a pub at the bottom of Wood Lane,' recalls producer Ruth Caleb. 'If there was some sort of dispute or we were talking about strike action, there would be meetings here. Verity would always come in, usually a bit late, and would invariably have very strong opinions. She was one of the people you could guarantee would have an opinion. But then, people do like the sound of their own voice, particularly in drama!'

Something that she kept to herself, however, was the suddenly precarious state of her health. For Verity, 1973 would forever be not only the year that she married but also when breast cancer made its first aggressive assault upon her body. When she was given the diagnosis, there was no way of knowing whether the disease would prove terminal but it was certainly a possibility. The prospect of facing her own mortality was shocking but there was never any self-pity about Verity and she immediately resolved to do everything within her means to fight for her life. 'She was tough,' says her then husband Colin Bucksey, 'and she needed to be. Unlike today, where radiation treatment is incredibly focused, in those days they blasted the whole area that they'd removed the cancer from.

It was horribly painful and the treatment and after-effects went on for a long time.'

The partial removal of the cancerous tissue left an unsightly scar, which she later had plastic surgery to correct. 'It was very brutal,' shudders Joan Bakewell, who had known Verity off and on for years. 'And it was a real shock because of her beauty. I know that sounds odd – one should be sympathetic to any woman who has breast cancer but she was flawless to look at and you didn't want her to be damaged.'

Doggedly, Verity kept on working and told everyone who asked that her new short hairstyle was for practical reasons – she simply hadn't the time to attend the hairdressers as often as before. Aware of the stigma that sometimes attaches to those with cancer, and unwilling to face the strain of a daily chorus asking how she was, she told very few people the facts. Invariably gossip carried the news, though most sensed that it was off-topic with Verity herself. 'I remember I rang Irene Shubik,' says Sheila Savory. 'I said, "Do you know what's wrong with Verity?" She told me, "I think she might have breast cancer." Later I went and picked her up and took her on one of her trips to the hospital. But we never talked about it. I can understand why. Verity would have found it boring, apart from anything else.'

Throughout the ordeal, her husband did everything he could to alleviate her pain and provide the love and support she needed to keep going. 'It was awful,' he says. 'You try and be as caring as you can. She wanted to get on with her life.'

Verity was lucky. Although it was invasive and aggressive, she responded to the treatment and went into remission. 'She had to keep going back every six months or so,' recalls her close friend and colleague, Linda Agran. 'One day she said the most extraordinary thing which has stuck with me forever. I asked, "Did you go today?" and she said, "Yeah. It's very seductive, you know. I almost want them to tell me it's back so I can really have the biggest battle of my life." She had these amazing black eyes – black, black, deep, dark eyes. They were sparkling and she had this little half smile on her lips. I sort of got it because she liked to see the enemy and she liked to have a good battle. It was brilliant.'

Verity continued to have regular checks and, as time went on, the cancer seemed to have been vanquished. But despite medical advice, and however much she tried, she could not wean herself off her habit of chain-smoking from morning till night. 'She smoked so much that when I was with her, I didn't need to,' laughs her close friend, Kate Kagan. 'My husband Michael thought it was terrible and used to come up and count all the butts in the ashtray – "How many are you going to smoke?" "Oh shut up, Michael," she used to say. She once went to this guy to be hypnotised into giving up. I think at the third meeting he gave her a pack of cigarettes and told her to go home and enjoy herself – because she was hopeless.'

While her health may have been precarious, professionally at this time she was in a stronger position than ever before. The BBC were delighted with *Shoulder to Shoulder* and keen to continue her engagement. Despite Rex Firkin's underlying antipathy, London Weekend, in the form of controller Cyril Bennett, had offered her a carte-blanche contract. Whichever way she turned, Verity was in the satisfying position of knowing that she had only to find the right project and it was likely to be green-lit. It was at this point that a truly life-changing opportunity came her way and with it, the gateway to what she later acknowledged to be the happiest and most fruitful period of her working life.

It would take her back to territory familiar from the earliest years of her career. The company she had worked for back then, ABC, was no more. After the 1968 franchise reshuffle, it had been forced into a shotgun marriage with ITV's other London franchise holder, Rediffusion, and rechristened Thames Television. But as the new company had retained much of ABC's staff as well as their studio facilities, in many respects, not much had changed. Thames rapidly prospered and was by now the richest of all those operating within the commercial sector. Its drama output was consequently prolific and important, too, in retaining the company's reputation and pulling power. As 1973 gave way to 1974, the man in charge of this department was Lloyd Shirley. He had been among the creative influx of Canadian talent to ABC during the late 1950s and when Sydney Newman had left the company to join the BBC, it was Shirley who succeeded him. In this capacity, Shirley could boast an impressive portfolio, which included series like *Public Eye, Callan, Special Branch* and, most recently, *Regan*, the pilot for what was to become *The Sweeney*.

'He majored quite a lot on police series for the simple reason that on a police series, you can tell any story in the world,' says George Taylor, who was Shirley's close friend and fellow executive at Euston Films, a satellite company which Shirley and Taylor had devised in order to facilitate more productions made entirely on film.

Euston was effectively a clever construct in order to work round the union restrictions of the time. These sought to protect members who worked in the electronic studios and so, in the usual way of things, they would never have permitted a mainstream Thames project to shoot any drama completely on location, or on film. From the first, Euston operated only as a film-production company and, despite early union attempts to scupper proceedings, was able to bypass the restrictions by working under a film rather than television agreement. 'It was sleight of hand,' points out Ted Childs, whom Lloyd Shirley appointed as producer of *The Sweeney*, 'and we had to make *The Sweeney* for £35,000 an episode otherwise it was cheaper to do it in the studio.'

Most of the logistics involved in this new operation were the brainchild of George Taylor. Lloyd Shirley was the creative influence. A red-haired and voluble man, he was heavy-drinking, passionately left-wing, and inclined to be spontaneous in his decisions.

'He would commission people who needed the money,' says director Piers Haggard. 'He'd go to lunch with a writer like Brendan Behan, get pissed and ask him to write a play. But Lloyd was lovely. He did have a political bias and a drink bias – but he also had a strong heart for quality. He carried a resonance of the early days of commercial television – "Fucking do it – have a go, because actually we can afford it." He was being brave with other people's money.'

'I was very fond of Lloyd,' says producer Ted Childs, 'I don't think he ever got full credit for the work he did in developing popular drama. He delivered audiences. But he could be difficult and he drank a lot – not to the level that it ever seriously impaired his judgment but he could lose his temper. He was always nice afterwards and a bit embarrassed – he would never carry a grudge.'

Jack Andrews, for many years Thames' controller of programme administration, had responsibility for budgets and personnel. 'When the controllers of the various departments met up,' he says, 'dear old Lloyd used to say something outrageous and then look round the table to see what the reaction was. He believed in being contentious because he thought that's what you ought to be. After lunch you never used to go near him. I used to say to my secretary, "No appointments except in the morning and preferably before 11."'

Shirley was protected by his solid track record and the affection he managed to inspire in many senior colleagues, despite his occasionally unpredictable behaviour. Then, early in 1974, Thames's established director of programmes, Brian Tesler, was poached to join rival company London Weekend. 'They asked everybody in town to replace him,' says Jeremy Isaacs, who had just triumphed for Thames with his production of the epic documentary *The World at War*. 'Nobody suitable was interested. I had finished *The World at War* and I went to them and said, "Why are you looking all over the place for a director of programmes? I could do it. I know that you think of me as News, Current Affairs and Documentaries – and that's right – but I can work with other people who know much more about their area than I do."'

Isaacs persuaded the Thames board and was duly appointed. 'Jeremy came over a bit like a Jewish minister of the Kirk,' explains Ted Childs. 'He was very bright, very tough, a bit dour – he had a sense of humour but he concealed it quite a lot of the time. Drama wasn't his world and, at this stage, he wasn't quite as sure of himself about it.'

Given its significance to the company, Isaacs nonetheless spent time scrutinising their drama output and found it wanting. Despite the individual excellence of series like *Public Eye* and *Callan*, he felt that these and others within the Thames stable were stylistically too similar and essentially exploring the same, somewhat macho, territory. His instinct told him that there was room for greater range and more experiment. This view was reinforced by the recent assessment of the commercial network's regulator, the Independent Broadcasting Authority. 'They were knocked out by Thames' performance,' says Isaacs. 'Nevertheless, they went on to say that the company was so successful that perhaps they could afford to take a few more risks in drama and entertainment. The truth is that Lloyd Shirley was an extremely good director of drama for Thames – he delivered exactly what they wanted and a little bit more but I knew that I didn't want to go on with him.'

Circumstances played neatly into Isaacs' hands. Thames' most recent high-profile costume drama, a lavish serial called *Napoleon and Love*, had been an expensive failure, derided by the critics and shunned by the audience. Shirley had bankrolled another cash-hungry period piece, *Jennie: Lady Randolph Churchill*, brought to him by Stella Richman, the woman who had hired Verity for LWT and who was now working as a pioneering independent. *Jennie* was commissioned to tie-in with the Churchill centenary and was being produced by Verity's close friend and kindred spirit, Andrew Brown, and directed by another mate, James Cellan Jones. 'As *Jennie* was basically an independent production,' says Jones, 'neither I nor the rest of the team felt obliged to consult poor Lloyd about anything. I think that he felt very left out.'

The crew were shooting on location in Blenheim and staying in a hotel in nearby Woodstock. After work had finished for the day, everyone went to unwind in the Bear pub. Lloyd Shirley, who had been visiting the set, was soon drinking heavily. He became embroiled in a violent argument involving a female colleague, during which a glass was broken. Such was the commotion that he was asked forcefully to leave. Chinese whispers about the incident kept the bitchy television drama community amused for days. Shirley, so often the loud mouth and the wild card, had embarrassed himself and the company once too often. Together with the *Napoleon in Love* fiasco, Isaacs now had sufficient leverage to issue his recalcitrant head of drama with an ultimatum. 'It was a very simple matter to say, "Sorry, Lloyd, that's the last time – enough." It was made possible because of the existence of Euston Films – it was no skin off his nose whatever to move over.'

Whether or not this was true – and it seems questionable – Shirley had little choice but to comply. He swallowed the humiliation of surrendering his status as director of drama to move sideways to take charge of Euston Films full-time. It was certainly a demotion. At this stage, Euston was still a tiny, rough round the edges set-up, operating out of a disused and unheated boys' prep school in Hammersmith. Far from being the company it would become, its output was entirely taken up with shooting *The Sweeney* and a few pilots and one-offs screened under the banner of *Armchair Cinema*.

With Lloyd Shirley out of the way, Isaacs was able to consider who might be the ideal candidate as successor. 'Verity had just done *Shoulder to Shoulder*, so that was very interesting,' he says. 'I didn't know her but I had a regard for what she had done and another material consideration was that I knew that years before she had been a secretary to Howard Thomas who was, by now, chairman of Thames. I thought, "That won't do us any harm."'

Isaacs invited her to have a drink with him at Nicols' bar at the Café Royal. Verity, who had heard on the grapevine that Shirley was moving on, went fully prepared to pitch for his job. 'I thought it might be interesting to run a drama department,' she said later. 'To have an overview, rather than what I'd been used to doing, which was to run a single strand. I was impressed by Jeremy Isaacs. I'd seen his documentaries; I'd attended his seminars. I was interested in working with him.'[2]

Twenty minutes into their conversation, Isaacs asked her the critical question, '"What do you think about being a controller of drama – who would you suggest?" And she said, "I'll do it," and that was exactly what I'd hoped to hear. We actually agreed it on the spot over the first drink we'd ever had together because from the breadth and the thrust of her conversation – there was a range, scope, perception and decisiveness – I was absolutely sure that she was the right person and that this was going to work. She was so willing to see the problem of producing high-quality drama for commercial television as I saw it – that she knew it had to be tough and aspiring and have a cutting edge but it also had to be popular and she was prepared to try to combine those aspirations. It was one of the very best decisions I ever took.'

Newspapers announced Verity's appointment as controller of drama on 2 May 1974, and *The Guardian* was careful to point out that this was 'the highest a woman has reached in the hierarchy of television drama'.

For Verity, and for Isaacs, it was the beginning of an extraordinarily fruitful partnership.

'They were very close in discussing and determining a lot of the programmes they did,' says writer, script editor and producer Robert Banks Stewart. 'I never knew a programme controller spend so much time marching around the drama department and vice versa – Verity was always dashing off to Jeremy Isaacs' office. They had a very good, creative, busy working relationship and I think Jeremy had cause to be very grateful to her.'

'Jeremy and Verity was a marriage made in Golders Green, he says suspiciously,' jokes the director, Stephen Frears. 'But, seriously, they were both such bright people. It was her intelligence that was her strength.'

'The important thing that struck me,' says Isaacs himself, 'was not just her ideas, which I thought we would debate together, but her capacity to make up her mind, enunciate something and stick to it.'

When her appointment was announced, *Television Today* profiled Verity, who told them that going back to Thames was like 'going home', adding: 'It is a great challenge, very

---

[2] Quoted in *The Executive Tart* (see bibliography)

exciting and I suppose there is always an element of pride when there are a lot of very good people about that you are singled out. But if I didn't think I could do the job I wouldn't consider it.'

Television Today concluded its piece in the manner of a school report: 'Her reputation as a producer stands high but as controller of drama she will be taking on a task that needs different and additional qualities. Clearly, she has courage, stamina and a head full of ideas. She sees her appointment as a challenge and one that she believes she can accept and win. Whether in the face of all the obstacles this will be enough to lift at least some of ITV drama from the doldrums into which it has sailed remains to be seen.'

The year since her marriage had been demanding, professionally, and personally even more so. She tried to pace herself. Before her new job began, she holidayed in Tuscany and planned another break later that same summer. This time, her cameraman husband, Colin, was away filming so she teamed up with Waris Hussein and his boyfriend at the time. The trio travelled to Lindos, a rustic and ravishing town on the Greek island of Rhodes.

'We rented a house,' he says. 'She was wonderful fun to be with. One night, she and I both trolled into the local town together, had a lot of Ouzo and got picked up by two guys. They were real Anthony Quinn types. We were taken back to a house. I'm in one room, Verity's in another – and I'm suddenly aware of all these religious artefacts, like crucifixes, and lots of family photographs of the wife and children of the bloke I'm with who is about to pounce. Verity was in the next room in a similar situation and I'm thinking, "I don't really think this is OK," so I stopped and said, "No" to the man. Verity, meanwhile, was just about to succumb to hers when I put my head round the door and said, "Verity, we've got to leave right now." She said, "What are you talking about? Oh all right, all right," and she gathered herself together. Outside, she said, "Oh my God, what were we doing?" We were worried we had affronted their dignity and that we'd have our throats slit in a narrow Greek alleyway. But that's how bonded we were.'

Verity officially took up her new role on July 1 1974, moving into a spacious new office at Teddington Studios. This had been expensively decorated and furnished to her exacting specifications. 'Everything Verity wanted, Verity got,' says Jack Andrews, who found the money to pay for it 'because we were so pleased that she was there. That's when offices really mattered. She had very strict ideas about what she wanted. The decor was minimalist modern, with lots of black and white and the walls a particular biscuit colour called Muffin, I remember.'

Then as now, the arrival of a new television executive invariably triggers a merry-go-round of changes, as leftovers from the previous regime are sidelined or edged out and new favourites arrive to take their place. In this respect, Verity was no different. Even before her formal start date, she came in for a day here and there to meet the team of producers, script editors and directors who would be reporting to her. She had already lined Andrew Brown up to join her as soon as he had completed *Jennie*. Always her closest professional ally and sounding board, he quickly became the right-hand man of her new empire. She coaxed another favourite, Paul Knight, from London Weekend and placed Barry Hanson, a bright 31-year-old producer who had been doing eye-catching work at the BBC in Birmingham, in charge of single plays. To make room for them, she swiftly despatched some of Lloyd Shirley's old guard including producers Robert Love and Reginald Collin and the belligerent head of script development, George Markstein.[3]

'When her appointment was announced, a lot of people disappeared,' says June Roberts, who was then a script editor in the department. 'I was on the list to go in and see her in her office, so I assumed, "Oh great, I guess that's me being fired as well." I was a little apprehensive. But she was very nice to me and said that she had heard from many, many people that writers really liked working with me and that when she started she wanted to promote me to producer. I was being paid an appallingly low amount of money and she said, "The first thing I'm going to do is have your pay tripled."'

Sexism, rife under Lloyd Shirley, was now on the retreat. Jackie Davis, a producer whose services had been retained, remembers what it had been like before Verity's arrival: 'It was par for the course,' she says. 'When Lloyd was head of drama, we used to stay late watching what was going on in the studio. I'd sit in a wing chair in his office and he'd gradually edge up behind it and put his hands on my shoulders. I knew very well if I wasn't careful it was going to go a lot further so I'd fidget and go and get a cup of coffee and do something to get out of the chair. I also knew that if I went along with it to a certain extent I would get what I wanted too. It's awful to think I went along with it but I did. I wouldn't sleep with him but I would flirt.'

For all this, Davis actually found the new regime more demanding. 'It was tougher under Verity,' she says. 'I got on much better with Lloyd, who didn't question what I was doing. Although she didn't really interfere, she could be quite aggressive about her point of view, very strong-minded. She was a powerful person. You wouldn't argue with Verity. I once cast an actress that she knew I'd worked with a lot and she screamed at me, "Haven't you got any imagination?"'

Jeremy Isaacs is sceptical about how much Verity was truly blazing a trail for the empowerment of women. 'Jackie is delightful, very mild and pliable,' he says, 'Verity could happily live with women who were no threat to her whatever. She was a very, very powerful personality. What she wanted was control.'

Shedding what she regarded as the dead wood and rebuilding the department in her own image inevitably took several months. Along with the staff she'd inherited, there was a raft of shows already in production. There was the lavish *Jennie: Lady Randolph*

---

[3] She got on well enough with Lloyd Shirley himself. 'They were very different characters,' says producer Chris Burt, 'but there was mutual respect.'

Churchill, and a further run of the established *Public Eye*. *Shades of Greene* was a series of adaptations of the short stories of Graham Greene, and there was a second series of the whimsical comedy-drama *Moody and Pegg*, which had attracted phenomenal audiences. 'Verity took over from Lloyd,' remembers Judy Cornwell, who played Pegg, 'and was watching it very closely. And she said to me, "Enough?" and I said, "Yes, I want to go on to something new after this." She agreed. "I think two series is probably enough."'

It also suited Verity who made no bones about the fact that she wanted to clear the decks for her own projects. Not unnaturally, Isaacs was curious to know what the first of these might be. 'I left it with Verity that she would think about it,' he says, 'and when she had finished working things out, she would come and tell me what she wanted to do. I said, "Do remember we have to keep our ratings base; that has to underpin anything else that you do."'

Despite its customary popularity with the audience, for at least her first 18 months, she decided to avoid period drama. She considered the competition. Other than Thames, the ITV company with the strongest track record in drama was Granada, which was based in Manchester. Years later, she said: 'I started to think why Granada had such a strong identity as a drama company. One of the reasons is that in the main they did Northern-based drama that said something about the region they came from. So I decided we wouldn't do any drama at Thames that didn't come from London or its environs, for a while, anyway. We never did anything that came from the North. I had to somehow get an identity for the sort of things Thames made.'[4]

She returned to Isaacs to explain her strategy and get his blessing for the first of her own commissions. 'She never tried to persuade me of anything daft or out of the ordinary,' he explains. 'She simply said, "This is what I'd like to do – what do you think?" She was an extraordinary woman. When you talked to her it was never flat, meandering, indecisive or boring. From the crown of her head to the tip of her toes, she tingled with life, laughter and vibrancy. You knew that good things were going to come from her.'

The Naked Civil Servant was Philip Mackie's dramatisation of the life of the flamboyant homosexual Quentin Crisp. Verity's good friend, BBC plays producer Mark Shivas, had been at Granada with Mackie, who was both a distinguished writer and producer. Mackie gave Shivas first refusal.[5] Shivas took the script to his head of department, and another of Verity's allies, Chris Morahan. 'I thought, "This is marvellous – a terrific script,"' he says. 'I had to ask the controller if we could do it and he said, "Yes, what's the subject?" I said, "It's about this old queen." But the BBC didn't have the wit to read the script with intelligence and I was told, "No, you can't do it." It was heart-breaking. Verity got hold of it pretty quickly after this and Mark Shivas was livid.'

---

[4] Kaleidoscope convention interview, 2006

[5] The first draft was dated May 1971

The script was sent to Verity by her then agent, Clive Goodwin, who also represented both Mackie and the man who hoped to direct the screenplay, Jack Gold. As well as being turned down by the BBC, it had also been rejected by every film company in Wardour Street, although one had suggested that it might provide a vehicle for drag queen Danny La Rue. Verity read it and thought it the best script she had ever seen. She took it straight to Jeremy Isaacs. 'She said, "You've got to read this – I want to do it,"' he recalls.

'I didn't have any money in my budget at all for it because it just came in out of the blue,' Verity explained[6]. 'So [Jeremy] said to me, "Well, how much is it going to cost?" and I said, "£110,000", which in those days was a lot of money. And he said, "You can have £90,000" and I said, "Jeremy, you can tell me I can have £90,000 and I can tell you it's going to cost £110,000," and he said, "OK, well go away and make it." And we made it; and this would never happen now. It just simply wouldn't happen. First of all 75 people would have to read the script, then they'd want to know who was in it, then they would probably say "Can you not make the main character homosexual, can you make him something else?" You know, it would just go on and on and on.'

Verity and her boss did have to convince the board of Thames Television of the wisdom of their conviction. 'It was way before its time,' says Jack Andrews. 'She and Jeremy had a big battle with the board to do it. She commanded respect for what she had to say and instilled confidence in what she did. She spoke her mind in the best possible way – there was never any antagonism – she just knew what she wanted and went for it.'

The board nervously gave their assent. 'She never had any doubt about it whatsoever,' says the film's director, Jack Gold. 'We all agreed the script was beautiful in its conciseness, preciseness, wit and epigrammatic form. Verity kept an eye on the casting and was there when you needed her or even when you didn't. She was a presence around, always buoyant, enthusiastic and cheery and if there were any problems going on, I wasn't aware of them – she was a great enabler.

'We cut the film and it had to go to the IBA,' continues Gold. 'They wanted to censor two things. One was a caption when Quentin was in the bath – the report said "substitute a word for masturbation" and the other was him bending over to have a medical – "He's bending over for quite a long time, don't you think?" Philip was enraged about the caption – apparently he stormed into these guys at the IBA, and I said I'd take my name off it. Verity said don't be stupid and calmed us both down. So Philip wrote this inane replacement for the caption – "Wasn't it fun in the bath tonight?" and it was easy to make a little jump cut in the bending over. They were all petrified waiting for the furore and they were overwhelmed with praise instead.'

Although she had nothing to do with its conception, Verity's unwavering belief in *The Naked Civil Servant* was an impressive statement of her ability to determine the merits

---

[6] Interviewed at the University of Reading, 2004

of a script and navigate it through the many perils of production. She had to fight for it to be made entirely on film and to ensure that as an in-house production it did not fall foul of the many irksome union restrictions that then affected staffing and shooting times. 'People wrote to me and said it changed their perception,' she commented later. 'It's about someone who's prepared to stand up and be counted. When you make television, you want to make contact with the audience. It's so satisfying. You actually feel that you've made something because you believe in it.'[7]

The film won awards and has retained its reputation as a peerless example of the very finest television drama. It is revealing that all the qualities that Verity felt were embodied by *The Naked Civil Servant* chimed so absolutely with her own philosophy of life and work. Standing up and fighting for what she believed was now both habit and necessity for Verity. As a woman in a still aggressively male world, she had more in common with Quentin Crisp than most. Like him, she enjoyed the attention her flamboyance attracted.

As well as *The Naked Civil Servant*, she took a couple of series to Isaacs for his approval, who recalls that 'Cyril Bennett [controller of LWT], a grand figure in ITV, once said to me, "Two things you must never do in television drama – the first is politics and the other is the entertainment industry." Verity's first pitch was for Thames to make *Bill Brand*, a series about a Labour MP, and *Rock Follies*, about the struggles of a female pop group. I said, "What are you doing to me?" She just laughed it off – "Oh Jeremy, please!" – knowing she was right to be doing them and that I knew she would make the things that she wanted to do as good as they could be made.'

Bill Brand was brought to her by Stella Richman, keen to do business with Verity in her new role. The two women, both Jewish firebirds, were wary but respectful of each other, and Richman shared Verity's natural affinity with writers. On Election Night 1974, Richman had invited the playwright Trevor Griffiths to the White Elephant, a fashionable restaurant which she ran with her husband. 'It was a very, very boozy night,' recalls Griffiths. 'It was packed with political punters who had been laying huge bets on the outcome who suddenly realised they were losing a lot of money. I went for a pee and the lavatory was full of guys crying into the stones. One guy who had lost 50 grand cried so heavily his teeth fell out and smashed.

'Because of that night, I told her I would write something about parliament and politics – a year in a new left-wing Labour MP's life. Human, personal, private, sexual – a big bandwidth. She was absolutely on board and took an option on the project but she didn't do anything – she just made it possible for me to think freely for long enough for an idea that appealed to both of us.'

---

[7] DVD commentary for *The Naked Civil Servant*

With Isaacs' backing, Verity commissioned *Bill Brand* as a 13-episode series. The lead director was her old friend, Michael Lindsay-Hogg: 'Trevor wanted to provoke discussion,' he recalls. 'It was a big deal at the time. Jack Shepherd [who played Brand] was a kind of given – Trevor and I had worked with him – and he had been in *Budgie*. Verity liked him a lot. Basically, Trevor wrote for Jack. Everyone thought he would have the necessary commitment.'

Getting *Bill Brand* made and on air was a battle that took months. There was constant tension between Verity and Stella Richman. 'They met almost nowhere,' says Griffiths. 'Keep 'em apart and they were good – together it was never going to work. Somebody had to be boss there. It was never properly resolved. I was looking to generate a little arena of power for myself but I was surrounded by something much bigger going on between these two. The producer Stuart Burge, a magnificent man, held it together but I thought Verity was sharp, straight, and tolerably honest for someone in her position.'

'It was great to work on,' says Lindsay-Hogg, 'but tough because Trevor was writing and rewriting as we were going on.'

'Round about episode eight,' says Griffiths himself, 'word came down from the top that we'd spent too much money – we needed to severely curtail the number of actors and scenes. They were also getting anxious about us getting any kind of audience at all. Jeremy and Verity went off to talk to regional ITV controllers to spread the word and these hard-nosed men were saying, "What the fuck is this?" We had a terrible, terrible meeting when they said we had to tighten our belts which somewhat soured relationships between production and the company. I said, "Look, if you're not prepared for the second half of the series to be as well financed as the first – I'd sooner solve that problem by writing two episodes fewer." They said, "No, we don't want that," and I said, "Well, you're getting it."'

Griffiths was as good as his word and *Bill Brand* concluded with its 11th episode. The scheduling created further tension as some ITV companies wanted to shift the programme from its peak slot at nine o'clock on a Monday night to the post-*News at Ten* graveyard. Isaacs resisted them. 'I had a very rough time with it,' he says. '*Bill Brand* was a marvellous piece of work but it was never going to pull people in.'

Although Verity hated the ending, she remained proud of a series she felt had an important agenda, utterly relevant to the time. 'We had a Labour government,' she said later, 'and I wanted to reflect contemporary life. It was difficult because it was a very serious programme. I think it was extremely good but for some people who had been working in a factory all day, it was perhaps a bit much to come home to.'[8]

Griffiths believes that Verity was one of the best producers he ever worked for, and the fact that she was a woman was significant. 'She was a very remarkable woman,' he says

---

[8] Kaleidoscope convention interview, 2006

'and women pay more attention, they look harder, they read deeper. It's not for nothing the reading of literature is largely a woman's pursuit. Verity was very bright – she did her homework and she lived in the real world.'

Rock Follies, the 'show business' series that Verity took to Isaacs at the same time as *Bill Brand*, could not have been a more different proposition. It was the work of a young American writer called Howard Schuman, who had settled in London in 1967, having fallen in love with the director Bob Chetwyn.

'I had become obsessed with becoming a television writer,' Schuman recalls, 'and I had a very loyal agent [Jenne Casarotto] who saw me through all the rejections. Nothing was happening. Then a friend of mine, June Roberts, who was a script editor at that point, said, "There's this amazing, ebullient New Zealand guy called Andrew Brown and he's bemoaning the fact that there are no new interesting writers around – can I give him a couple of plays?"'

'Andrew had just started,' says Roberts. 'I didn't really know him. He said he was bored out of his skull, he'd been reading all these scripts and he couldn't find any new writers that remotely interested him. I had all of Howard's unsold work and I really liked his stuff – it was absolutely unique, original and funny. I brought out all these scripts and said that this was someone new that I was hoping to work with, and I think you would probably like him. A few hours later he came back having read them all saying it was the best new discovery of fresh talent that he'd come across and did I have Howard's number and he wanted to ring him immediately? That's how Howard's career started. And I think that the fact that I had not only found him but given him to Andrew carried a lot of weight with Verity because they were such very close friends.'

The two plays that Brown commissioned from Schuman before Verity's appointment were significant because they demonstrated the power of Schuman's storytelling ability and his unusual fascination with the mechanics of television production and what multi-camera video, then the norm, could offer a playwright with the imagination to embrace rather than resist the process. Schuman talked Verity and Brown through the concept for *Rock Follies* – the story of three female singers and their struggles within the music industry – and she commissioned him on the spot to write a pilot for a potential six-part series, which, if it went ahead, Brown would produce.

The precise origins of *Rock Follies* fall out of the confines of this chapter but are fully explored in chapter ten, which charts the monumental fall-out of the lengthy court case to establish its true provenance. It is a case that continues to divide opinion. This real-life drama was still a long way off when Schuman began writing the series. 'My first attempt at episode one was a disaster,' he says. 'I had a terrible day with Verity and Andrew having to say, "It just didn't work," and trying to explain why. I left very disconsolate – I felt I'd let them down – but when I thought about it, it was a structural problem – the tone was wrong. I rewrote it, they liked it and then she commissioned the whole thing. Those were the days. We started to shoot it when the writing wasn't finished. I had close to a nervous breakdown. Andrew was not only a very good script editor but a wonderful producer – a great giver of confidence. When I began to get stuck, he would say, "Oh, the first five pages are brilliant." What I didn't know was that behind the scenes they were thinking that were going to have to find another writer because we were already in motion. We were only saved by two strikes which gave me time.'

The music was written by Andy McKay from Roxy Music – a suggestion of Verity's musically-savvy husband, Colin. The decision was made that the entire series would be made within the confines of the studio. 'Basically we decided these girls never go out,' said Verity later. 'Their lives are lived in recording studios and in concerts and at homes. So we kept it all inside which I think was quite brave. We could never *afford* to go outside either so it was an advantage to us to do it that way.'[9]

With this stylistic conceit and potential limitation in mind, Verity cast the two directors with care. She chose the young, patently ambitious Brian Farnham and paired him with the polar opposite, the extremely experienced light entertainment veteran, Jon Scoffield. 'Verity felt we needed someone Mr Showbiz,' says Schuman. 'Jon had been doing the Stanley Baxter show but he had also done the TV version of Trevor Nunn's *Antony and Cleopatra*. We met him and he was like a left-over from the 1950s. He said he didn't like rock 'n' roll very much and I remember Andrew and I saying, "What is Verity thinking?" but as it turned out, he taught us stuff about video. He did have a tremendous visual eye.'

The downside was that he was a heavy drinker, so that Schuman became a kind of unofficial minder, sitting with the director after lunch to try to limit his intake of brandy. 'After lunch we definitely went slower,' he says. 'But we had been given a budget and shooting schedule equal to *Jackanory*.[10] We got to a place where it just wasn't possible and Verity and Andrew then organised two weeks of shooting just the musical numbers and that's how we did it. Two extra weeks for all the fantasy numbers. I only ever saw Verity in solidarity with Andrew and me – you always felt she was supporting the writing.'

'Those scripts were fantastic,' says Jeremy Isaacs. 'It was very, very stylish and visual indeed and Andrew Brown, who was superb, got three absolutely cracking singer-actresses to play the group.'

'*Rock Follies* changed my view of what television could do,' says writer and executive Russell T Davies. 'How powerful it could be, how strong women could be – feisty and sexy. Way ahead of its time. If you're my age, it absolutely struck a chord, talking to us in a way that nothing else did. I've got it on DVD but I've never watched it because it's so perfect in my memory.'

---

[9] Kaleidoscope convention interview, 2006

[10] A low-budget BBC storytelling programme for children, recorded in a small studio with a couple of cameras

'I think *Rock Follies* was very much something of its time,' said Verity herself. 'People reacted very strongly for or against it. You could have something about how the music business has changed hugely with the internet, and it would be a very different programme. It was really about success and failure and about women finding themselves. And of course being exploited by men.'[11]

'*Rock Follies* was a huge hit,' comments writer and presenter Melvyn Bragg. 'It was different, a much more daring form of television, it was about women, raucous, funny and very, very ballsy.'

Swiftly commissioned for a second series, *Rock Follies* epitomised the kind of drama for which Verity wanted Thames to be known and celebrated. At the other end of the spectrum was the ageing *Armchair Theatre*. Once the pride of the company, the weekly play strand had become a burden both in terms of the resources it demanded and the audiences it failed to engage. Reduced in number as well as status, *Armchair Theatre* had limped on and on, chiefly out of fear of the inevitable criticism that Thames would face if they finally abandoned their single-play slot. Showing not a trace of sentimentality for the programme on which she had cut her teeth, and with Isaacs' backing, Verity immediately abandoned plans for a further run. 'They weren't economic,' he says, 'but it wasn't only that. There was something in the air – trying to find the airtime for 13 or 20 one-off plays wouldn't have worked any more. We wouldn't have found enough good stuff, I think. But it was a change that some wanted to bewail and criticise.'

'Thames Shun The Single Play' reported *Television Today*, which ran long pieces attacking the decision and trying to elicit promises that it would be reconsidered. Some of the broadsheets followed suit. Dropping a commitment to single plays was precisely the kind of action to bring down the wrath of the regulator on an ITV company, and indeed the situation was rapidly scheduled for discussion by the IBA's controller's meeting. A reporter tracked down Sydney Newman who spoke loyally on her behalf: 'I have great faith in Verity Lambert,' he said. 'I think she will try hard to do a good job. Perhaps she took a look at what there was and didn't really want to go on with it. She might very well want six months to get some good plays together.'

Verity herself promptly took the heat out of the debate by announcing that she was looking to commission a new plays strand to fill the void left by the cancellation of *Armchair Theatre*. 'There was no time,' recalls Barry Hanson, who had to find them. 'They wanted them on.'

Verity teamed Hanson with a novice script editor, Sally Head, whom she had spotted at Warner Brothers during the production of *Shoulder to Shoulder*. 'We had to cut the six parts into a one-and-a-half-hour film for the States,' says Head. 'I sat with the editor for

---

[11] Kaleidoscope convention interview

about three or four weeks. I had hardly ever been in the cutting room before but Verity was really thrilled by it. She then asked me to go to Thames. It was brilliant. I was totally new to television – before that, I'd worked in feature films and I just got bored with them not getting made.'

Hanson and Head assembled a set of six plays under the umbrella *Plays for Britain* ('a stupid title' according to Isaacs), drawing on a pool of considerable talent. Mike Leigh devised the generic opening titles, the writers included Howard Brenton, Stephen Poliakoff and Roger McGough, and among the directors were Michael Apted, Jim Goddard, Alan Clarke and Philip Saville. The results were interesting but not entirely successful. 'Jeremy couldn't wait to get rid of it,' says Hanson. 'It didn't get the audiences that they wanted. I remember feeling that I'd let them down.'

Hanson remained at Thames but *Plays for Britain* proved a dispiriting and disillusioning experience for his script editor, Sally Head. 'I loved Verity but one wasn't given a huge amount of assistance,' she says. 'Maybe that was my own insecurity. She was huge fun but quite intimidating and I felt that she had a band and I definitely wasn't part of that band. I was put in a Portakabin on a roof by myself – everybody else had offices in the main building. People kind of forgot I was there, really. So much so that in the end after about nine months I got into my 2CV one day and I thought, "Fuck it," drove out and never reappeared.'

Sally Head moved to the BBC and, like Verity before her, became an award-winning producer and head of department before running her own independent company. Despite her relative unhappiness on *Plays for Britain*, she remains fond of the woman who brought her into television. 'The fact that I didn't enjoy it wasn't her fault. She definitely saw my potential and I've got a huge amount to thank her for. She was terribly supportive when I became a producer myself. I always heard from her when I won awards and so on. It was lovely, actually, she was so proud, like a mum.'

As well as the primetime drama for which she was responsible, Verity also inherited a twice-weekly daytime serial rather unimaginatively called *Rooms* and set in a London boarding house. This had been devised by the writer John Finch, who recalls that 'as young men, purely by coincidence, Lloyd Shirley and I were living in the same block of service rooms in York Street, just off Baker Street. He lived on the top floor and I lived in the cellar. Not long over from Canada he was finding it hard to get work over here. The house in York Street was a very odd set-up. At first, the occupants were mainly elderly people, but the owner of the house appointed a housekeeper who was a former resident at Belsen and had a number tattooed on her arm. She gradually replaced the residents with petty criminals and prostitutes. Lloyd and I stayed on, however, because it was cheap and we were fascinated. We didn't meet again until the 70s, when I was doing *Sam* for Granada. I suggested a series based on our time at the house in York Street and he jumped at it. Unfortunately, I was up to my neck in work and he wanted to get it moving, so I said I would do a format which he could use to attract other writers. I gave it the provisional title *Rooms*, which stuck. My agent sold it outright to Thames for £750, and I was stupid enough to sign the contract. I anticipated it would do rather well, and it did.' Verity kept *Rooms* in business for three years. Cheap to make, it performed well and was quietly excellent. Plenty of her mates – among them Alvin Rakoff, Anthea Browne-Wilkinson and Willis Hall – were happy to drop in and write or direct a couple of episodes here and there. She had plans to expand it much further, giving the go ahead for an extended run of 126 episodes, to be screened three times a week.[12] As Thames lacked the necessary studio space at Teddington to accommodate the serial as well as all its other commitments, the intention was to shift production of *Rooms* to a rented studio in Elstree. The ACTT[13] union promptly declared that this would amount to recording on location, entitling the crew to vastly increased overtime payments. After some attempts at negotiation, the talks between management and unions broke down and the whole deal was cancelled, despite key cast having been contracted and scores of scripts written and paid for.[14]

Verity's attitude to daytime drama harked back to her time on *Doctor Who*. Simply because a show was studio-bound and the budget necessarily restricted, she saw no reason for any lack of ambition, either in casting or production. To run alongside *Rooms*, she devised another intelligent afternoon series called *Couple*s, based in the offices of a marriage guidance bureau. Initially, she asked her friend Graham Benson to leave the BBC and join Thames to produce it for her, but when he declined, she placed June Roberts in charge. 'She put me with a writer called Tony Parker,' recalls Roberts. 'When I discovered that this would be a daytime show, I thought, "Oh fuck," and I didn't really want to do a soap opera either. I told her that I wanted to make it very much in a documentary style, so that it wasn't just about people coming in to whine about their marriage, with all the counsellors jumping each other's bones. That was fine with her. She was looking for a serious approach to it.'

Roberts took Verity at her word. She underwent the standard marriage counsellor's training and sent all her prospective writers for mock therapy sessions so that they would have an understanding of the parameters. 'They were supposed to do this for the characters they were writing,' she explains, 'but they all drifted into therapy sessions about their own marriages instead. Verity was pretty hands-off, although she very much wanted an actress called Judy Parfitt (who had played Constance Lytton in *Shoulder to*

---

[12] Production was planned to begin in October 1977

[13] The Association of Cinematograph Television and Allied Technicians. Paul Fox, then running Yorkshire Television, says: 'We were all of us at ITV too reluctant to face down the unions and say "Listen, we're in a business." Technicians were paid a fortune. Thames had particular problems with the ACTT. Those bloody electricians were absolute bastards. Some were so left wing they wanted to destroy the company.'

[14] Contemporary estimates stated that Thames had to write off in the region of £50,000 as a result

Shoulder) to play one of the main characters. I resisted that as I thought she was too well-known. I worked on the series seven days a week. One day, Barry Hanson walked into my office and asked me to explain something. As producer of Thames' highly prestigious one-off plays that normally anyone would kill to work on, why was it that all his first-choice writers and directors were unavailable to him because they had all made multiple episode commitments to a certain low-budget daytime talking heads show? That was very nice to hear and made my day.'

One of the writers was Peter Ransley. 'It was all done on the cheap,' he says, 'but Verity was keen on it because it was done seriously. I did one about a lesbian couple and she really wanted to do that story. This was a time when there wasn't the openness and conversation about gay relationships. It didn't get much of an audience but it was quite bold for the time and you wouldn't see anything like it on television now.'

Surprisingly, although June Roberts and her lead writer Tony Parker were doing most of the work, Verity took the producing credit for the first few weeks of *Couples* herself. Understandably, this rankled with the woman actually doing the job. 'I don't quite know why she did that,' says Roberts. 'I never saw those credits until the press screening of the first two episodes that Verity, myself and Tony attended. But only Verity spoke and took questions – Tony and I were never introduced. I asked Verity about why she had taken the producer credit and not even introduced me. I don't remember her response but the next day she arranged for David Bailey to take a picture of me on the *Couples* set for *Vogue* magazine. They were doing an article on the most powerful females in TV and instead of doing a piece on Verity she had suggested they do one on me instead as a most promising newcomer. She also got a reporter and photographer to interview me about *Couples* for another big deal fashion magazine. I guess that was her way of saying sorry.

'I liked her a lot,' she continues, 'and was very fond of her but we battled. In most cases, she probably won. She enjoyed an argument and I was very belligerent, too but we had nothing in common and frustrated each other. She'd come from money and I'd come from Glasgow slums. I think in some really irritating way I reminded her of herself. I think she saw her role as mentoring me like she'd been mentored by Sydney Newman. I was trying to protect my turf. Everybody else in the drama department was very much established so I felt I was the only one she was doing that to. She meant it well but I was very much, "You're not the boss of me." I was in my twenties, very confident in what I was doing but not as a person. I was always terrified I wasn't going to do this as well as I wanted and someone would find out I was a complete moron. I would describe my attitude to her as one of situational defiance, having had that kind of mother.'

But Roberts gladdened Verity's heart by offering Colin Bucksey two episodes of *Couples*, which became his first break as a television director. 'It was never her suggestion to give him a shot,' she explains. 'I'd talked to him a lot and he was like a real hipster – really into the music of the period, very stubborn, with a silly sense of humour. There was just something quirky about him and the way he talked about movies and wanting to direct.

I'd seen a stage play that he'd done and I just thought he would be interesting to work with. When I asked Verity if I could hire him, she was flustered. She said, "It's something he really wants to do but I think it might be tricky for him to do it here because he's married to the boss." She really needed to think about it and then she said she didn't want to stand in his way. But she was clearly nervous about it. After he'd done those first two episodes, Verity asked me to come in and she was like a nervous mother. She was like, "So how did it go – how did he get on with the crew?" "Very well, I think," I told her. "He worked on the floor with them – there was good bantering and he got on fine with the actors and it's a nice-looking episode and I'd be perfectly happy to work with him again." I've never seen anyone look more relieved in their lives.'

Verity persuaded agent Jenne Casarotto to take Bucksey on to her books and Casarotto disputes the widely held view that Bucksey's directing career came courtesy of his stellar wife. 'He wasn't an easy sell,' she says. 'I worked my arse off for him. I suspect Verity was more of a hindrance than a help. She wasn't universally popular. He was new and there wasn't much to show. *Couples* was a leg-up.'

'To be perfectly honest,' adds Bucksey himself, 'I think if anything being married to Verity went against me working in places like Thames. I would have said that she was little if any help at all. And I think that she would probably say that too, if she were around to do so. I think she kept it pretty much at arm's length. I was working for whichever producer was producing the show. In those days, the head of drama would choose the scripts and choose a producer and let them get on with it. The same went for producers, they would choose the director and let them get on with doing his job. It is different now.'

'He was very ambitious to be a director,' says Paul Knight, 'but he tried to be his own man and show everybody that he wasn't under Verity's thumb. There was always that slight tension there between the two of them. He tried to show that he didn't rely on her for his career and by and large he did at that stage.'

'There was suspicion about Colin wanting to become a director,' says Howard Schuman, 'until it was revealed that he was very talented. He had gaps but he understood modern culture. It wasn't a one-sided relationship. Their bond was sexual and they shared a great love of social life and the good life. The other thing they had in common was taste, especially for Art Deco, pop, rock and movies. They had tremendous energy. The dinners they gave were wonderful. They were a golden couple. It is one of the many interesting things about Verity – that she was a workaholic who knew how to party and really enjoy life too. In those great days, she knew how to make the work fun.'

Verity fashioned a department very much in her own image, staffed with bright, creative, attention-seeking people excited by the confidence and bravura of her leadership and risk-taking approach. 'What I used to call the beautiful people,' says writer Peter Ransley. 'She was at the centre of them, and very glamorous, but, at the same time, she made you feel perfectly at ease.'

'Verity was a very clever picker of people,' says producer Robert Banks Stewart. 'It was always said that she had her own little club. Andrew Brown, for example. I think he was one of the best producers ever in television. A star producer under a star head of drama.' As well as the ubiquitous Andrew Brown, the inner circle included Barry Hanson, Paul Knight and June Roberts. 'It was very collegiate,' says Roberts. 'We would have lunch with each other, and hang out in each other's offices. I liked that and it really felt like a group of people who weren't rivals in any way. We took an interest in what we were each doing. They all had a good sense of humour and it was a much nicer atmosphere than had existed before under Lloyd.'

It was at this time that a friendship blossomed between Verity and one of her more junior employees, stage manager Kate Goodwin (later Kagan). They had first met when they were both working at LWT where Goodwin had got to know Andrew Brown. 'When she was quite new as head of drama at Thames,' she recalls, 'something was going wrong and I remember the top production manager saying, "Oh, Verity's in a bad mood. You have to come and explain what's happened." I went in there and she was very impatient and cross. I said something on the lines of, "Well, you can sit there and talk – you're not actually on the floor having to do it, are you, dear?!" and she went, "How dare you! Do you know who I am?" I said, "Yeah but you're just sitting there," and then she just went, "Oh, alright, I'd better come down then, hadn't I?" and I said, "Yes, I think you had." That's when we really started getting on so very well.'

For those within Verity's inner circle, life was intensely social with evenings spent in good restaurants or at dinner parties in each other's homes. Verity herself was the most frequent and willing hostess. Thames paid for a state-of-the-art video cassette recorder lest she miss out on any essential viewing. The pretty dolls' house off Kensington Church Street was no longer big enough for their needs, so she and her husband Colin found an impressive new house, number 11 Lisgar Terrace, near Olympia. It was no coincidence that the dearest of Verity's friends, Andrew Brown, lived just a few doors away. Lisgar Terrace was also home to another eminent producer, Cedric Messina, so that for a time, the street became known as Television Towers. 'The house was on four floors,' recalls Bucksey. 'It was very spacious and open which is what we were looking for and what we liked. We did all kinds of stuff to it, knocked down walls and so on. It was a shared vision but I was often away working around that time so quite a lot of it was her taste.'

In the spring of 1975, Verity gave an interview to *Over 21* magazine. It gives a snapshot of the way she saw her life at this time: 'I was terrified of this job,' she told reporter Celia Brayfield. 'I thought it was going to be frightfully difficult, which it is – but I wasn't aware just how difficult until I started. Having new ideas is always difficult, *one* good idea, let alone a year's television. There's no time to relax, have long lunches in town, that sort of thing. It is difficult for me to preserve some sort of independence and not think and talk and eat and sleep television the whole time. You have to make a conscious effort not to read scripts at the weekend, to see your friends who aren't in television.'

But she wasn't really complaining. With her health apparently restored, utterly absorbed by the rich rewards of her work, her busy social life and her beautiful home, Verity was still in the ascendant and her ambition remained as keen as ever. She set her sights on adding Euston Films to her already considerable portfolio, and was intent on enticing yet another of her inner circle from the BBC to Thames. This time, however, the decision would backfire, and a long friendship would end in lasting bitterness and acrimony.

CHAPTER EIGHT
SHE WHO MUST BE OBEYED
1976–1979

'I wouldn't say no to any subject. You don't pull writers out of the air; they have to be found, nurtured and loved. You can't just put them in a room and tell them to get on with it.'

Verity to T.S. Ferguson, *The Sunday Telegraph*, 1975

There is no science in the uncertain chemistry of creating a successful television drama. Despite the ever-increasing ways in which channels have sought to bypass risk and instinct and substitute an elaborate second-guessing of their audiences using brainstorms, think-tanks, focus groups and every kind of data, no magic mechanical formula has yet emerged. Verity was fortunate that for the bulk of her career, she was able to operate without such creatively stultifying restrictions. Not until the twilight of her working life did she have to try to satisfy the whims of the various bureaucratic commissioning processes. These removed the ease with which, for so long, she could solicit a simple 'yes' or 'no' for her ideas just by going straight to whoever was at the top.

From her early battles with the standard of scripts and direction on treadmill series like *Doctor Who* and *Adam Adamant Lives!*, she had learnt that the best guarantee of success was the talent involved. But even then, circumstances, timing and sheer chance were all just as crucial in determining a triumph or a turkey. Anything unusual or experimental only increased the stakes. 'All you can do is go by your instincts,' Verity told an audience of students in 2004[1]. 'You can't say, "If you put that together with that, A together with B

---

[1] At the University of Reading

and C, it will always work," because it doesn't always work, in fact, it often doesn't work at all.'

As controller of drama at Thames Television, Verity had been elevated to an intoxicating position of power. Each year she was responsible for delivering a quantity of popular drama. The harder task was that she was required to combine ratings with good reviews. It may not have been her money that she was spending, but with every production that Verity backed, it was her reputation and her future that were at stake. It was rather like being a professional gambler. It demanded ceaseless energy and absolute nerve, but when the gamble paid off, there was no thrill like it. In their different ways, several of her first throws of the dice, among them *The Naked Civil Servant*, *Rock Follies* and *Bill Brand*, had all delivered. But Verity was not immune to failure.

During the relentlessly hot summer of 1976, Thames transmitted *Killers*, a dramatisation of six real-life murder cases. The series was the creation of the writer Clive Exton. Exton was an old friend who dated back to Verity's time on *Armchair Theatre*. She liked the concept but was displeased by what she felt was the pedestrian production and this effectively negated the entire enterprise. But even as *Killers* was limping on air, Exton's next and far more ambitious project was going into production. *The Crezz* was a 13-episode saga about contemporary life in a West London crescent (hence the title – 'Crezz' for short) and the various people who live in the houses and flats there. Verity was confidently optimistic that it would provide her with a reliable, long-running 'banker'. Instead, *The Crezz* was a complete and crushing disaster.

'There were a lot of things wrong with it,' comments Barry Hanson, who was in charge of Thames' single plays at the time. 'You've got to believe in soaps and there was no sense of reality.'

'It was a bizarre series,' admits Paul Knight, the man who produced it. 'It came out of Clive living in Notting Hill or that neck of the woods. What happened in these places was that the middle-classes moved in and took over. It was a very current idea about a part of London slowly gentrifying. As well as Clive, it had some fantastic writers like Bill Trevor and Willis Hall. Some of the characters were a little bit smug, it must be said, although Peter Bowles was wonderful.'

'I had a very nice part in it,' says Bowles himself, 'and I enjoyed doing it. It was really a middle-class *EastEnders*. All you can do is read a script and if you think it's good and your part is nice, you accept it. You never know what's going to be a success. We all thought and hoped it would be and of course it wasn't.'

As well as Bowles, the cast was crammed with established and emerging actors, among them Joss Ackland, Hugh Burden, Elspet Gray, Isla Blair and Nicholas Ball. It was no coincidence that Ball's character, a handsome and slightly cocky chancer in blue jeans, was called Colin. 'Ah, yes,' recalls Knight. 'Nicholas Ball was a mate of Colin [Bucksey]. They were trendy boys together. It was a fabulous cast but Joss Ackland was a big mistake;

he just wasn't charismatic enough to carry that series. Brilliant actor, but he wasn't a leading man.'

It is true that Ackland's performance seems ill-at-ease and misjudged. But he cannot be blamed for struggling with the uneven tone of the scripts. Most of the characters were regrettably charmless and the inclusion of a gay couple among the regulars might have been praiseworthy had they not been such an unlikeable pair of queens. Those who feel curious to form their own view can do so, thanks to the availability of a DVD of the series. All its qualities are in evidence – an attractively simple and topical idea, a serial format with a range of characters with diverse potential and excellent actors, writers and directors. Yet the whole undertaking is a morbidly fascinating mess, absolute proof that in television drama there is no certain recipe for success.

'It was a disaster,' shrugs Knight. 'When they played *Kojak* against us, that was our death knell. I remember calling the cast together in rehearsal and saying that it was being moved out of its prime slot to half past ten. They were all upset. Poor old Clive never really recovered from the shock – he was very hurt because the critics got hold of it and really mauled it. It was a nasty time. But Verity was extremely supportive over it. She said it was a good show and she meant it. It wasn't just as a sort of sop. She took the rough with the smooth. We liked to say it was ahead of its time.'

Verity held on to this view. '[It] is something they should bring back,' she said, only the year before her death. 'It was a wonderful programme.'[2]

She continued to believe in Knight, too, asking him to produce her first period drama for Thames, an adaptation of Norman Collins' *London Belongs to Me*. Collins had been one of the founding fathers of ITV but was much more famous as the author of this sprawling novel, which had sold in huge numbers. The story followed the interconnecting lives of the inhabitants of a south London boarding house before and during the Second World War. Despite its historical setting, the television version, adapted by Verity's old friend Hugh Whitemore, was not unlike a primetime *Rooms*. It was tolerably well received but somehow failed to replicate the success of the novel in capturing the public imagination.

Verity had better luck with her single-play commissions, transmitted as individual entries in the network's *ITV Playhouse* strand. These included Barrie Keefe's *Not Quite Cricket*; Keefe's wife Verity Bargate's *No, Mama, No* (which contained the first use of the word 'cunt' in a British television drama[3]), directed by future features director Roland

---

[2] Kaleidoscope convention interview, 2006

[3] The precise quote being: 'What did he say?' 'He said your Dr Cawston is a cunt.' Verity persuaded the Independent Broadcasting Authority that the use of the word 'cunt' was dramatically valid: 'I had a lot of correspondence with [them.] I think it was a real insult, and she needed to say that particular word. And, in the end, to be fair to them, they accepted that as an explanation.' (Source: kagablog 04.10.12)

Joffé; and Ron Hutchinson's *The Winkler*, with music and lyrics by a then unknown Victoria Wood. Verity was especially delighted with *Last Summer*, a film by Peter Prince about a depressed car thief called Johnny who is bored with his life. The director was Stephen Frears, then at the start of what became a hugely successful film career.

'I'm embarrassed to talk about that time,' says Frears, 'because it was so privileged. You had a sort of freedom. Verity was full of beans, very supportive, although she was always giving me bollockings – it was part of the deal, really. You were somehow fighting each other and working with each other at the same time. She'd say things like, "You're never to come into this building again," and then you'd be there again the next week making a film and she'd say, "Who let you in?" What I would call larking about – but the work was good. She commanded respect but the truth is she sort of liked you to be wicked and cheeky – we got marks for bad behaviour and you were prized for your independence of spirit. She liked life to be interesting.'

Frears cast Richard Beckinsale to play *Last Summer*'s lead, Johnny. Beckinsale, a fresh-faced young actor who had found fame in the situation comedies *The Lovers* and, latterly, *Porridge*, had proven star quality. He was also a clever and sensitive performer, who brought humour and pathos to every part he played. Verity wanted to turn *Last Summer* into a series for him. 'I was sent to Turkey,' says writer Peter Prince, 'which is where many luxury cars stolen in England tended to end up, to do some research. I wrote the draft for a pilot but it was a no-go, though, actually, I think the original film was so unique it would have been difficult to make a spin-off work.'

It was always painful to surrender her hopes of any potentially major hit. Some projects were more bankable than others. Enticingly cast with some of the most box-office actors of the time, including Richard Briers, Tom Conti and Penelope Keith, *The Norman Conquests* delivered both comforting ratings and good reviews. A three-part adaptation of the plays by Alan Ayckbourn, then Middle England's favourite playwright, it was co-financed by David Susskind, her former employer at Talent Associates in New York. It must have been agreeable to meet him as an equal rather than a subordinate.

For Verity, professional nirvana was always the top-flight series where the quality in every department happened to be appreciated by an enormous audience too.

'She was ruthless in her acquisition of material,' says Jeremy Isaacs, then the controller of Thames. 'And my view was that what Verity wanted, she was going to get.'

At the top of her shopping list in 1976 was a project that had been initiated at the BBC by producer Irene Shubik. Shubik had a peripatetic start to life. Born in 1929 to Jewish parents, a Russian émigré and his French wife, she had been evacuated to Canada on the eve of the Second World War. She returned to read English Literature at University College, London. Her subsequent attempts to find employment with the BBC met with a series of rejections and, disillusioned and frustrated, she went back to Canada. Here she made her first tentative steps into the film business, writing and producing educational scripts for the Encyclopaedia Britannica. She had just been offered a year-long contract with the National Film Board of Canada when she discovered that her father was terminally ill.

Abandoning her career, she flew back to nurse him. When this harrowing period was finally over, she remained in London, and began hesitantly to pick up the threads. Visiting an agent's office in an attempt to sell them a script for a children's adventure serial, Shubik had a chance encounter with the director Ted Kotcheff.

Kotcheff had been her first love back in Canada and, wanting to help, he offered to pass on her script to his boss, Sydney Newman. Newman thought it 'crap' but paid for it nonetheless and, according to Shubik herself, promptly offered her a job as story editor on *Armchair Theatre* apparently on the basis that she had 'an intelligent face'.[4] It was a classic Newman hunch, just like the one which would later propel Verity into her first producing role and it changed Shubik's life just as significantly. She rewarded Newman's faith with the thoroughness and intensity of her work.

On the surface, Verity and Irene Shubik had much more than their personal history with Kotcheff in common. They were both fiercely intelligent, talented and ambitious women, seeking to establish themselves in an industry where their sex militated against them. They both shared a cultural rather than religious attitude to being Jewish. They embodied a work ethic that would have made many wilt.

In terms of personality, however, they couldn't have been more different. Verity was, by nature, intensely positive and invariably combined this positivity with a lively sense of fun and humour. 'I believe you get from life, on the whole, what you expect,' she told Elisabeth Dunn of *The Sunday Times*. 'If you're a pessimist, you can always find ways of proving to yourself that people are against you. I'm an optimist.'

Shubik, in marked contrast, was inclined to find the faults in everything, complaining bitterly and indulging a sometimes morbid paranoia. 'She was a difficult person,' says Ted Kotcheff. 'She was good at what she did but she didn't have the drive that Verity had. Verity was possessed – it was a case of "don't get in her way or you're going to get run over!"'

'Irene was a lonely woman,' points out Chris Morahan, 'and was depressed quite a lot of the time whereas Verity was gregarious and cheerful.'

'Irene could be very suspicious,' says writer Doug Livingstone. 'Certainly, she was sensitive. They were very different women.'

---

[4] This from Shubik's account of her early career in *Play for Today* (see bibliography)

'Irene had a very negative personality,' agrees director Herbert Wise. 'She was a victim. Her motivation was that everybody was against her. That's what made her fight.'

'Irene was a talented woman,' allows director and future head of BBC plays, James Cellan Jones. 'But she was also a very sulky, unpleasant, unhappy woman. I think she thought she wasn't held in sufficiently high regard.'

'Cross yourself as you speak the name,' says production assistant Adele Winston, frankly. 'She was lovely to me but nobody else would be in the same room as her. She was a bit of a maniac.'

'There was a lot of drama in Irene's life,' comments producer June Roberts, 'and in her relationships with writers. One absolutely trashed her office one day and threw her typewriter out of the window at the BBC.'

'She was actually a very nice person in many ways,' believes producer Graham Benson. 'Incredibly talented, but very bitter. They were like gin and tonic. Irene never came out of the office but Verity was much more of a personality, noisy, ebullient.'

'Irene was a funny lady,' believes fellow director Piers Haggard. 'She always had an air of gloom. Whereas Verity had a locomotion – a motor force.'

In career terms, Shubik had a head start over Verity. Although she found plenty wrong with it, her status as a story editor at ABC easily eclipsed Verity's humble position as a mere production assistant. Even when Verity jumped ahead and achieved the role of producer, it was only of a children's programme in the serials department, whereas Shubik was making her way in the much more elitist and sought-after arena of single plays.

'Please come and spread your dissatisfaction everywhere,' wrote Newman, cheekily making fun of her habitual angst when he eventually invited Shubik to follow him to the BBC. She arrived in November 1963, reluctantly continuing in her old position as a story editor but wringing a promise from Newman that he would make her a producer within a year. Newman delivered on this and in 1965, she achieved her goal, taking charge of the science fiction anthology *Out of the Unknown*. She had the sense to consult closely with Verity on the practical perils of the genre. Verity warned her that the principal costs were not the writers and actors but the requirement for non-stock sets, costumes and elaborate make-up. 'They were best buddies when I worked for Verity,' says secretary Brenda Loader. 'They were both incredibly strong women. But there was always an edge of competition there. I never heard laughter between the two of them. It was always fairly serious. In fact, I don't think I ever saw Irene smile.'

The history they shared and the scarcely concealed spirit of competition between them meant that their relationship was not one of straightforward friendship. Rather they were, to hijack an ugly-but-apt modern phrase, 'frenemies' – and, even if subconsciously, they both obeyed the adage 'keep your friends close and your enemies closer'.

As Verity's career flourished and diversified, Shubik had remained cocooned within the BBC, where she produced many plays of distinction, among them *Edna, The Inebriate Woman* (directed by Ted Kotcheff), as well as a fine series of adaptations of Thomas Hardy short stories, *Wessex Tales*. Like everyone, she had her blind spots. 'When Alan Bennett wrote his first script,' relates director Stephen Frears, 'which was called *A Day Out* and was about a cycling club just before the First War, the only person he knew at the BBC was Huw Wheldon, who passed it down the line. And Irene Shubik said of this script, "It goes nowhere," to which Alan said, "Well, it goes to Fountains Abbey."'

Shubik's instincts were in sharper form when, in 1975, she commissioned John Mortimer to write *Rumpole of the Bailey* as one-off *Play for Today*. 'Irene knew a good writer when she saw one,' says John Gorrie, who directed the production. 'She was more of an intellectual than Verity, more of a college girl. She wasn't easy to work for. I was in the early prep for *Rumpole* when Irene and John Mortimer came to my office. John said, "I've written it for Michael Hordern," and I said, "I'm very sorry, I've already offered it to somebody else." They were both very cross. I said, "Look, Michael is a lovely actor but he's not the right man. This is a little round fighting cock of a man. It's got to be Leo McKern." In fact, I hadn't offered it to Leo. It was a total lie. The minute they left my office, I said to my PA, "Get a motorcycle courier round here now and we'll send a script to Leo," and of course he saw the possibilities and jumped at it. Irene was picky whereas I don't remember Verity ever questioning my casting.'

Both McKern and the resulting *Play for Today* were critically well-received, and it attracted a healthy audience, too. Shubik promptly went to her head of department, Christopher Morahan, to suggest that *Rumpole* would make an excellent series. He was enthusiastic and agreed on an initial run of six episodes. 'Aubrey Singer, the controller of BBC2, then said, "No, no, no,"' recalls Morahan. 'He was a fool and he made a mistake. Irene and I were very upset because we thought it was going to be very good.'

Morahan could help no more. He was in any case leaving his post to make way for a new head of plays, James Cellan Jones. Jones felt that *Rumpole* had no business within plays and suggested that it would be better off within the series department. Shubik, not one to give up easily, now took the proposition to the BBC's overall head of drama, Shaun Sutton. Sutton consulted and came back with the disappointing news that he could see no way of fitting a *Rumpole* series into the schedules for at least two years. This lukewarm response infuriated her and left Mortimer, who thought he was on to a good thing, understandably despondent.

It was at this point that Verity stepped in. She had watched and very much enjoyed the Rumpole *Play for Today* and if the BBC didn't want a series, she most certainly did. 'Bring it to Thames,' she suggested to Shubik and sugared the pill with the lure of more money, both to make the series and with which to reward Shubik herself. Shubik later claimed that Verity offered her a format development contract, which could then be converted into a story-editing fee on top of her producer's salary – essentially a double payment for her input.

Meanwhile, Mortimer, who always loved bright, attractive women, was charmed by Verity and sanguine about the move. Contracts were drawn up and Shubik left the BBC staff after 14 years.

Rather like Verity before her, she was returning to the company (in all but name) where she, too, had established her career. But in the 2000 revised edition of her book, *Play for Today: The Evolution of Television Drama*, Shubik commented that 'Thames' drama department bore no trace of the happy, creative atmosphere it had once had during the time of Sydney Newman. Democracy had been replaced by dictatorship – like working in [the] Iron Curtain where my artistic freedom and my self-confidence were being eroded daily.'

'Absolutely untrue,' comments writer and producer Robert Banks Stewart, tersely.

'They fell out with a vengeance,' explains writer Doug Livingstone. 'You know the hierarchy at the BBC. Series, which Verity produced there, are fine and good but plays were the thing and Irene had been producing *Play for Today*, which was at the very top. So when Irene went to work for Verity, the relationship was sort of reversed, and I think that was part of the difficulty.'

'They were two strong women with strong egos,' says producer June Roberts, 'and if they were going to go into battle, they'd be evenly matched.'

There were certainly no arguments about the series itself. *Rumpole of the Bailey* was an instant success on every front, a benchmark for exactly the kind of superbly executed middlebrow series that most suited Thames Television's identity and needs. It was quintessentially British in subject matter, literate without being avant-garde, and Mortimer's sly humour was a gift to the fine cast assembled. Before the first series was even halfway through, a delighted Jeremy Isaacs asked for another. Thames rewarded Mortimer with a hefty increase in fees, bumping up the price of a script from £1800 to £2500. Equally, Leo McKern was handsomely recompensed for agreeing to continue in the lead role.

Irene Shubik, on the other hand, was dismayed and angered by the deal suggested to her. 'Difficult though it may be to understand,' she fumed in the pages of her book, 'I was offered a new contract by the head of drama [Verity], whereby I would be paid less, not more, to produce and story-edit the second series than I had been for the first. This all hinged on the verbal agreement I had made with Verity that the fee originally offered to me by Thames to find series ideas should be converted into a story-editing fee for *Rumpole* and that it should be added to my producer's fee. It was only now, when it was too late, that I realised I needed an agent to handle the situation for me.'

Shubik turned to one of the best in the business, Robin Dalton, in an attempt to get Verity to honour what Shubik insisted had been agreed between them, albeit not in writing. '[Verity] denied [its] existence,' wrote Shubik, 'and told Robin Dalton it only existed in my mind.'

'Irene was impossibly difficult,' Dalton herself recalls. 'I tried to calm the waters but there was very little you could do. They were at each other's throats and wouldn't speak to one another. Irene had a reasonable case but Verity was extremely tough, sometimes too tough.'

Shubik believed that Verity wanted to edge her out because she was jealous. 'When I brought *Rumpole* to Thames,' she wrote, 'the press had made much of the BBC's mistake in letting "one of its best producers" go; when *Rumpole* proved such a success, the story was reiterated. These favourable mentions in the press were probably the worst thing that could have happened to me. When I asked the head of drama if she was not pleased with the success of the series, I was told that it was my success, not hers. I realised I had put myself in an invidious position for which undoubtedly my own naivety was to blame. Of the whole package I was now the most disposable element. The new contract offer was undoubtedly a clever way of freezing me out.'

Shubik hurriedly tried to enlist John Mortimer in her defence. She felt sure that he would repay the loyalty she had shown him and support her in the dispute. Yet another shock awaited her. '"Poor John" were the first words which came from his lips,' she recalled. 'In mournful tones, he said that now Thames wouldn't do the series which he had been counting on to keep him and his family in his old age. He spoke not like a highly paid, influential barrister and eminently successful playwright but like a man who had never had a script on before and would never earn any money again.'

Shubik later learnt that after ducking this awkward conversation, Mortimer had agreed to accompany Verity and travel to Manchester to meet McKern, who was appearing there in a production of *Crime and Punishment*, in order to talk the star into doing the series even if his original producer was no longer involved. McKern proved perfectly amenable.

Shubik departed from *Rumpole* and Thames in an atmosphere of the greatest rancour and bitterness. She petitioned Jeremy Isaacs for a credit in forthcoming series, in recognition of her role in creating it. Predictably, this request was refused[5], and she claimed that a mutual friend told her that Verity had threatened Isaacs with her own resignation if such a credit were countenanced.

---

[5] Verity was quoted in the trade paper *Television Today* (03.05.79), saying: 'The matter of a credit in the terms that one was asked for was fully discussed by Thames management. It was considered that the situation would be quite impossible, if every producer who had worked on one series was acknowledged on subsequent ones. Just imagine...I should still be getting a mention on *Doctor Who*.'

This, then, was the story as Shubik outlined it, in extensive detail, in the 2000 edition of her book. But how close to the truth is it? Shubik can add no more; alas, at the time this book was written, she was confined to the theatrical retirement home, Denville Hall, in an advanced state of dementia. But others remember the fracas and the fall-out all too vividly – and they have a somewhat different explanation.

'I'd known Irene for many years,' says Robert Banks Stewart. 'It wasn't difficult to get into a feud with her. She was very argumentative. Yes, to her great credit she was the one who decided to do *Rumpole* and then brought it to Thames where it became a very valuable commodity. But Irene felt that she was untouchable. She went off to America and wouldn't come back to start the next series when they wanted her to – she thought that she could control the timing. It was a kind of clash of two ladies who probably admired each other – but Verity was the head of drama and Irene was just a producer.'

'That was the best thing that happened to me,' admits Jackie Davis, who took over from Shubik and remained with *Rumpole* for the rest of its long run. 'Irene had fallen out with Verity and gone off to New York hoping that Verity might leave Thames by the time she got back. She was playing a waiting game. I remember saying to Verity, "I don't want to take another producer's job," and she said, "If you don't take it, someone else will." She was absolutely tough, Verity.'

Though John Mortimer had been delighted with Shubik's work, any qualms he may have felt about continuing in her absence were quickly assuaged by meeting Davis. Her softer personality, which had no trace of Shubik's self-absorbed sense of high drama, suited him and he unashamedly appreciated her beauty, too. 'Maybe I was more malleable than Irene was,' comments Davis, 'I certainly wasn't as aggressive. She was furious that I got *Rumpole* and wrote me some vicious cards with really spiteful things like, "I wouldn't have fought so hard for *Rumpole* if I'd known you were going to turn it into a farce."'

In fury, Shubik wrote to Verity, too. 'That was terrible,' says Verity's close friend, Kate Kagan. 'She got this letter and she was in tears and deeply distressed. I said, "Do you want me to read it?" and she said, "I don't know, I don't want to upset you because it really is awful." She told Jeremy Isaacs and he said, "There's only one thing to do with that, Verity – burn it – you'll feel better". And she burnt it. She said, "In a way, he's right. I feel good now that I've burnt it – on the other hand, I could have kept it and sued her!" But that was a terrible time and it took quite a toll on her.'

'She was upset and probably angry,' recalls Colin Bucksey, 'although the anger would have been directed as much at herself as at Irene Shubik.'

'There is no question at all that she bumped Irene out of *Rumpole*,' says Isaacs himself. 'They were too like each other – two ferocious Jewish ladies. It was never going to work.'

Shubik devotes much space in her memoir to a thinly veiled character assassination of Verity. But Verity was not alone. Despite masquerading as a book about the evolution of television drama, it is really a distillation of Shubik's world view, and an account of those whom she felt slighted and let down by during her long working life. Some of them fought back. Jeremy Sandford, who wrote *Cathy Come Home* and *Edna, The Inebriate Woman*, published a lengthy rebuttal of Shubik's diatribe: 'A great deal of what Irene wrote may have seemed true to her at the time,' he said. 'However…Irene does seem sometimes to go out of her way to claim things that she must have known would be both libellous and in many cases painful to friends and colleagues.'[6]

Shubik's book is an uncomfortable but important piece of work and that is because it seems to contain the melancholy essence of a woman who was herself a significant figure in the early years of British television drama. Although the split with Verity was final, years later Irene Shubik's baleful influence would once again loom large in both their lives, unleashing further malice and trouble. Their original rift had only been reported in passing by a few newspapers. But the painful and embarrassing sequel would attract much greater scrutiny.

During the 1970s, female television executives were not many in number and so their behaviour and idiosyncrasies were liable to be seized upon, held up to scrutiny and criticised. Verity had always been someone who worked at speed, with enormous energy and sense of purpose. She had very little patience for vacillation or laziness. As controller of drama at one of ITV's major companies, with an annual budget of millions and a responsibility to deliver, she was under considerable and constant pressure. It is perhaps unsurprising that in the circumstances, her temper was occasionally unpredictable or, as Colin Bucksey, puts it, 'volcanic'.

'I made a major mistake one day,' recalls producer Paul Knight. 'It was a beautiful morning in Teddington. I was strolling down the corridor and I saw Verity's office door open. There was Verity behind the desk. I hadn't seen her for a few weeks, so I popped in and told her that pre-production on *London Belongs to Me* was all absolutely sensational, everything was coming together. We started to talk about casting. "Who have you got, Paul?" "Oh I'm offering this part to…" and I mentioned an actor's name who I was proud to cast. She flew into the most incredible temper. She screamed, "I will never work with that actor, he is one person I will not have on this set – how dare you! Have you talked to the agent? Get me the casting director!" Suddenly from a wonderful, beautiful morning, I'm in the middle of this farce. I wished to hell that I hadn't popped in. She was a friend but she was also the head of drama and you didn't challenge it.'

'I was forever receiving deputations of engineers,' says Jeremy Isaacs, 'complaining that no one had ever spoken to them before the way this woman had, and the next time it happened she would get thrown out of the building, so would I kindly tell her to shut up?'

---

[6] Quoted from an article by Sandford (1930–2003) and posted online as part of the Jeremy Sandford Fan Club archives, 2006

'At one time she was called "Fishwife Lambert",' laughs Doug Livingstone, 'because of the colourful language. But she wasn't a bully.'

'She didn't suffer fools gladly, that's for sure,' says producer Ted Childs, 'but I felt her posturing was a bit of an act. I think she felt that "If I throw a wobbly, it will have more effect." Behind all that tough-girl ebullience, she was very sensible. She knew what she wanted and she could handle people.'

'She was very involved with everybody that worked for her,' points out actress Sheila Hancock. 'I think probably that was the quality – dare I say it, to be sexist and feminist – that she brought to it as a woman. She could deal with difficult people. There are an awful lot of people who blather around and who want to be loved all the time. How many times do you hear someone say, "She's a lovely woman," or "He's a lovely man," because they desperately *want* them to be? And to be lovely themselves. But I seriously don't think that was important to Verity, although she *was* a lovely woman. To be popular wouldn't have been her prime objective.'

'She was someone you could go and have a conversation with,' says producer June Roberts. 'Whatever she was doing, with people she always meant well. She was very funny with men. She could hold her own. There was a good sort of ensemble feeling about the drama floor at that particular time.'

'Verity was one of the crowd,' believes Robert Banks Stewart. 'She was controller of drama but she behaved as if she was a fellow producer. She wasn't the one who was sitting in a big corner office – well, she was, but her attitude was that of a fellow producer. She introduced a Friday night drink in her office and you'd get a crowd of people – PAs, actors, directors, writers – all sitting on the carpet – with Verity pouring the drinks. However, I think sometimes the strain of it affected her. There were times when she got slightly hysterical.'

'She was judged about her temper,' says agent Jenne Casarotto, 'and for being emotional in a way that men weren't. Women are expected to alter their behaviour.'

In the high stress and tension of the television community, tantrums and shouting matches were far from unusual. Generally, by sheer force of numbers, these were at the behest of men rather than women. It is perhaps for this reason that Verity's sudden outbursts were noticed and were commented upon in articles and interviews about her, although she didn't see it that way herself. As she told the *Daily Express*'s Nicola Tyrer: 'I am quite good at getting things done the way I want, pleading, shouting or simply keeping my mouth shut until I feel it's a good idea to open it…I have a low patience threshold and I shout and say hurtful things to people – often to people who are being lazy and inefficient but sometimes to people who are doing their job as well as they can. If a man said the same thing, I don't think he'd be forgiven easily. But with me, it's become "Verity's terrible temper" – a foible. It's unfair that I get away with it where a man couldn't.'

'Dark stories circulate about the first female board member of Thames' board,' wrote Tyrer, 'about storms of tears when things don't go her way, about tantrums in the boardroom.' She put this charge to Isaacs, who freely admitted it and told the journalist frankly: 'Yes, Verity does have tantrums, though I can only recall one in the boardroom. Tears? I doubt it. But you have to remember one thing. If you have tantrums, and crap comes out at the end of it, you're not asked back. When you weigh the tantrums against what Verity has achieved, through her decisiveness and good judgement, you begin to see them in proportion.'[7]

It wasn't only at work that Verity gave vent to her feelings. She was vocal about perceived shortcomings of certain politicians, public figures and for those within her own industry who displeased or irritated her. When Janet Street-Porter's small-screen career was launched on London Weekend Television in the mid-1970s, Verity was typically outspoken in her distaste for the presenter's 'out there' look and trademark strangulated vowels. 'She used to shout and scream at the box every time Janet came on,' laughs Kate Kagan. 'She couldn't bear her voice. "That fucking Janet Street fucking Walker [*sic*]," she'd be yelling. One time, she phoned Melvyn Bragg[8] up and left a terrible message on his phone. He rang back and I picked it up. He said, "I've just got a hell of a telling-off about Janet Street-Porter, like it's my fault!" So I passed him over to Verity and she starts on at poor Melvyn all over again.'

Knowing it would wind up his wife, Colin Bucksey would defend Street-Porter and tease Verity for being a snob. He'd got talking to Street-Porter in the bar at LWT and was surprised to discover that the brash presenter with all the apparent attitude was so nervous before appearing on TV that she would have to go and throw up. At the time, Street-Porter was married to the film director Frank Cvitanovich, who had previously been in a relationship with Midge Mackenzie, Verity's partner in *Shoulder to Shoulder*. One day, Cvitanovich, who was engaged in a job for Thames, introduced his wife to Verity. 'The next thing I knew,' says Kagan, 'it was, "Oh my friend Janet," and I said, "Janet who?!" "You know Janet Street-Porter..."'

Although Verity had a talent for friendship, she was sometimes guilty of blowing hot and cold, taking up a new acquaintance with enormous initial enthusiasm and then gradually losing interest. When the feeling wasn't mutual, this could inevitably be painful for the other party. But the unlikely new alliance with Janet Street-Porter was the real deal and lasted for the rest of Verity's life. They shared the same forthright attitude and Street-Porter evidently found in Verity the kind of mentor figure whom she could truly admire. 'I found the business very forbidding, full of men who bossed me around and

---

[7] *Daily Express* (12.10.82)

[8] At this time, Bragg was the editor and presenter of LWT's prestigious arts programme, *The South Bank Show*

told me what to do,' said Street-Porter. 'Verity was my role-model, with a very short fuse and a voice you didn't mess with. Her put-downs were legendary. [Once] we were surrounded by a group of simpering middle-aged men. "The trouble is, Janet," Verity said to me, "you are wearing a 90 per cent dress that's attracting 10 per cent men." She gave me bags of confidence to do my own thing, and soon I moved from presenting to producing documentaries for young people, largely as a result of Verity's encouragement. We used to go on holidays together. Once we changed apartments five times in a fortnight in Crete as nothing was ever up to Verity's demanding standards. I had such hilarious times with Verity, drinking and fighting to have the last word. Our only point of difference over the years was her undying love for a whole succession of irritating dogs.'[9]

Some friends, like Street-Porter, enjoyed the cut and thrust of a confrontation with Verity. Others did whatever they could to avoid it. To this day, Kate Kagan is consumed with mirth at the memory of the director Waris Hussein, then eminent and well established in his own right, hurriedly scrambling to hide under his desk as he heard Verity on the warpath, heading down the corridor towards his office with a bee in her bonnet.

Hussein had been invited to direct *Edward and Mrs Simpson*, a seven-episode retelling of the 1936 abdication crisis. The idea had come from Verity's eternal favourite, Andrew Brown, who was to produce. At first, Jeremy Isaacs was unconvinced. 'I said, "Andrew?!" Because I didn't have the imagination to see that what was so good about him was his brilliant insight, the skill of his detail and that he could apply that to any subject matter. He did a terrific job.'

Based on Frances Donaldson's impressive biography, *Edward and Mrs Simpson* was a major project for Thames, and for Verity. Television had developed something of a fixation for royal storytelling, responding to an audience appetite for nostalgia, patriotism, sumptuous frocks and scenery. Verity was uninterested in adding to their number simply for the sake of an easy hit. But *Edward and Mrs Simpson* was never intended to be merely a crowd-pleasing, cosy romp. It was a detailed retelling of a crucial moment in British history, a constitutional crisis that involved the entire Empire at the twilight of its existence. The story remained controversial and, as well as considerable resources, to dramatise it demanded a degree of nerve. King Edward VIII's widow, Wallis, the Duchess of Windsor, was still living, albeit in total seclusion, in a virtually vegetative state, at her Paris home. Her guardian, some said gaoler, was the terrifying French lawyer, Maître Suzanne Blum. Verity flew out to meet Blum and outline the project. She was unable to make much headway with Blum, who made it perfectly clear that, given the slightest pretext, she would sue Thames Television. 'Maître Blum was especially adamant that we should not imply physical contact between the Prince and Wallis before marriage,' scoffs Hussein. 'Can you believe it? They were fucking like stoats! The walls at

---

[9] Quoted from a piece written by Street-Porter as part of Verity's obituary in *The Independent* (26.11.07)

Fort Belvedere [where the Prince lived before his accession] were very thin and the domestics used to hear them at it.'

The scripts were provided by one of Verity's favourites from the *W. Somerset Maugham* series, the charming and scurrilous Simon Raven[10]. Ron Grainer, who had composed the opening title music for both *Doctor Who* and *Detective*, provided a rich incidental score. Together with Brown, Verity flew to New York in search of the right American actress to play Wallis Simpson. With the help of casting director David Graham, they chose 44-year-old Joan Hackett. But Hackett was subsequently offered a potentially lucrative contract in a major network comedy series and backed out. Red-headed Cynthia Harris replaced her at the last minute and, despite being a relative unknown, had very definite ideas on how to play the part. 'We were doing a photographic session for the opening titles,' explains Hussein. 'They came back with this red wig in the same style as Wallis Simpson. I said, "What's this?" and they said, "Well, Cynthia insisted on it being red." I went to Cynthia and said, "What on earth are you doing? You know what she looked like – there's no way it can be red." "But I will look terrible in a black wig," she replied. The titles we ended up with were the result of not having the photos ready or right.'

Hussein persuaded Verity that she somehow had to fund a filming trip to Kenya to shoot the safari sequences in the opening episode. Reluctantly, she agreed that the alternative – a suburban sandpit – wouldn't pass muster. When a film camera broke down causing an unavoidable delay in shooting, Brown announced to his cast and principal crew, 'To hell with it, we're going on holiday,' and arranged a long weekend's jaunt to a luxury hotel. 'Verity went through the roof when she found out,' chuckles Kate Kagan. 'They had a terrible, screaming row over the phone. He shouted, "It's not costing you or Thames a fucking penny – you're just fucking jealous!" And there was no answer to that because it was true!'

The series, brilliantly realised, won a clutch of awards, notably an Emmy for Outstanding Limited Series and four BAFTAs – for best design, best actor (Edward Fox as Edward), best costume design and best series or serial.

Edward and Mrs Simpson was a showcase drama, expensive, important in helping define the company's international as well as domestic reputation. Not everything for which Verity was responsible could or would carry the same burden of expectation. As well as the shop-front spectaculars, she was just as adept in her pursuit of quietly excellent audience-pleasers. It would be invidious to suggest that she did so alone. Thames provided her with terrific back-up and Jeremy Isaacs, in particular, made sure that there was a healthy budget for script development, so that ideas and formats could be tested and explored without a cast-iron commitment to go into production. 'One of

---

[10] Simon Raven (1927–2001) Although Raven was principally a novelist, he had also written extensively for television, including adaptations of *The Pallisers* (BBC 1974) and *An Unofficial Rose* (BBC 1975)

the things I said to Verity at the beginning,' explains Isaacs, 'we've got to get into a situation where half the scripts you commission you are able to reject if you want to.'

Identifying the right material was an unceasing process. Some were the fruit of existing relationships with producers, script editors and agents, all hustling for the next commission. Publishers had their share of potentially attractive and interesting properties too. Often, the most enticing of these would be at the heart of a bidding war between the various film and television companies. When it came to the BBC, Verity had some useful inside intelligence in the form of James Cellan Jones, head of plays and close friend. 'People within the BBC would say, "What are you doing?"' he recalls, 'and I was very arrogant and I'd reply, "I'll let you know all in good time." I had a schedule which I kept hidden. The only person who I told about it was Verity – and she told me hers, so I knew exactly what was going on at Thames and she knew exactly what I was doing. I made sure we didn't clash. It worked because we had absolute mutual respect.'

When Verity was offered an idea for a series based in a factory, she felt it was more suited to ATV, who were responsible for operating the Midlands ITV franchise. With that in mind, she sent it to David Reid, who was then the head of drama there. Reid duly commissioned it and it eventually emerged as *On the Line*[11]. 'She was always very open and generous,' says Reid. 'We shared a conviction that what mattered was to get things done on television. She would often send a writer to me with an idea that wasn't for her and I would ask writers if they had they tried Verity. For instance, I could not see anything in an idea brought to me by Terry Venables and Gordon Williams. Verity could.'

This became *Hazell*, of which more later.

In making her decisions, Verity was helped by the wise advice of her seasoned script executive, Joan Rudker, but she retained a singular ability to follow her own instincts and assess the merits of every script that came her way. 'You had to respect her tremendous ability to analyse a script and give notes on it,' says Colin Bucksey. 'That was her strong point.'

Remembering a couple of characters she had liked in Doug Livingstone's *Budgie* episodes, she suggested that there might be a spin-off series in them. Livingstone agreed and created *Born and Bred*, a set of richly comic stories about a sprawling south London family, which ran for two series. 'They only ever came together for special occasions like Christmas,' recalled Verity. 'It was a family where some had gone up and some down and there was always a huge party where everything was disastrous, [with] one part of the family fighting. Doug is such a funny and surreal writer.'[12]

---

[11] Transmitted in 1982, *On the Line* was actually made by ATV's successors, Central. 'Unfortunately, it didn't work out too well,' comments David Reid

[12] Kaleidoscope convention interview, 2006

'We didn't have a producer until after I'd written the first six episodes,' explains Livingstone himself. 'Before an episode was written, she never asked me what the plot was. She was very good because she had an excellent script editor's mind as well as a producer's. I remember one episode of *Born and Bred* where she said, "It's very good, Doug, but it's too sitcom...just cut it back." Her notes tended to be good, broad ones that got to the point rather than finicky details like the notes you get from script editors now who seem to be about 16 years old.'

Much of Verity's life as controller of drama was devoured by hours of reading, listening, arguing, bartering and doing deals to get her hands on what she wanted to make. She enjoyed tremendous freedom of expression because Isaacs trusted her so absolutely. Each year, the Thames drama department was expected to provide the ITV network with up to 50 hours of material. With around £2 million to spend, Verity would compose her shopping list more than a year in advance, striving to satisfy all the necessary creative and commercial criteria and making educated guesses at the costs of each project.

The variety was important and every new project fulfilled a different ambition. Interviewed in 1978, Verity commented: 'You have to keep looking at it and saying, have we missed out some area? That doesn't mean you have to do crap, you can do very good, entertaining programmes, but you do have to think of your audience as a whole.'[13]

Cleverly riffing on the heritage of the company's *Armchair Theatre* strand, she gave the go-ahead to *Armchair Thriller*, an umbrella title for a disparate collection of mildly scary suspense serials. Dramatised in 25-minute instalments, these mimicked *Doctor Who*'s use of cliffhangers to hook the audience into returning. Among the first batch was the creepy *Quiet as a Nun*, based on one of the Jemima Shore detective novels by Lady Antonia Fraser. Fraser, better known for her historical biographies, was delighted that her crime-writing sideline had been promoted to television. Like Verity, she was naturally effusive and engagingly social, and she became a friend.[14]

As well as *Armchair Theatre*, Verity green-lit another anthology series under the self-explanatory title *Romance*, six hour-long adaptations of the works of writers ranging from Ethel M. Dell to Jilly Cooper. The story consultant was her old boss from the BBC, Gerald Savory. Most of these were lush period pieces and here Verity stumbled slightly with her maths, as the budget she had sketched out proved inadequate. Happily, June Roberts had underspent on her daytime serial *Couples*, allowing Verity to divert the funds and prevent a crisis. 'We'd done it for like nothing,' says Roberts, 'and I remember the joy she had in being able to take the money back.'

---

[13] In *Hazell: The Making of a Television Series* (see bibliography)

[14] Joanna Lumley recalls an occasion in July 2001, when she dined with Verity and the film director Peter Bogdanovich. 'In the corner were Antonia and her husband, Harold Pinter. They came over and joined us. Harold had always adored and admired Verity, Verity had always adored and admired Antonia, Antonia had always longed to meet Peter – so it was the most wonderful, perfect supper. Each one was with its hero. Harold had the face of a schoolboy, gazing at Verity. I sat there, gleaming, thinking what a special moment this was.'

Verity rewarded Roberts for her industry and thrift by making her the producer of *Hazell*, the quirky new detective series that had been sent her way by fellow drama executive David Reid. 'I thought it would be a good time for [June] to do something different,' Verity explained at the time. 'Because she was a new producer, she wouldn't come to it thinking it's got to be like this or like that.'

As Roberts herself suspected, Verity plainly saw something of herself in her young apprentice. 'She's tough enough to argue if she feels strongly about something,' she noted approvingly. 'She's not someone I can actually push around, which is good. She is her own person, she will fight for something she believes in.'[15]

Hazell was based on a handful of recent thrillers from writing partners Gordon Williams, an ex-journalist who was responsible for much of the actual prose, and Terry Venables, a former professional football player, who was then the manager of Crystal Palace. Venables was largely responsible for the authenticity of the story and character ideas. James Hazell was a cynical thirty-something private eye and both the character and the seedy London-centric setting appealed to Verity. 'I thought it was original,' she said. 'Different from most TV detectives. It had a kind of freshness. I found it amusing and ingenious. The best thing is something incredibly funny that turns into something that's not. You're always looking for something that's not quite like everything else. The story should be real. Though Hazell has the cockney sense of humour, he's actually quite a hard man and is dealing with situations that are unpleasant.'[16]

'This was something I very much wanted to do,' says June Roberts. 'It felt like a really cool gig. I was thrilled because I was a huge fan of *The Rockford Files* and I thought maybe we can go that way with this. The worst thing was having to have a story editor because I didn't feel there was much left for me to do. Verity had in mind a writer I didn't know – Kenneth Ware. He came in and was a dull older man who hated the books and the writers. He decided to write a script himself on spec and it just was awful. I didn't say anything – it was sent to Verity as well and she asked me to come in. She just loathed it too, so he was removed, and then a very good writer was brought in to story-edit, again chosen by Verity, Richard Harris. That would have been fine except when I'd been doing *Couples* and said I didn't want to use soap opera writers, he'd been offended. He came in very pissed off and not liking me, which was a pain in the arse because we had to work with each other.'

Fortunately, a bond rapidly forged between this shotgun marriage of producer and script editor. They both had to manage a delicate relationship with the original writers, who were naturally proprietorial about their creation, as well as the sometimes divergent

---

[15] Quoted in the *Hazell* book, as before

[16] Quoted in the *Hazell* book, as before

views of their own writing team and directors. One of the latter was Colin Bucksey, again given a break at the behest of June Roberts without prompting from Verity. Playing Hazell was Bucksey's mate Nicholas Ball, who had survived *The Crezz* debacle with his credibility intact and whom Bucksey had cast in his episodes of *Couples*. Thames producer Barry Hanson had also seen the potential in the *Hazell* books, which he had passed on to Verity, with the suggestion that Bob Hoskins should play the part. There was strong competition from a pre-*Bergerac* John Nettles but Nettles was knocked out of the race when Verity decided that there was a disturbing resemblance between him and the star of *The Sweeney*, John Thaw. Some felt strongly that Ball had been miscast. He was undoubtedly younger and slighter in build than the character as written, but Verity's faith did not waver. The first series, though curtailed by strike action, convinced her that she wanted a second.

Hindsight allows us to place *Hazell* as a kind of bridge between *Budgie* and one of Verity's biggest successes, *Minder*, which was not yet on the horizon. With its sometimes uncertain mix of humour, crime and its film-noir pretensions, *Hazell* was a respectable success, almost but not quite developing its own cult following. It is noteworthy in being the first primetime drama series with a regular character (Dot Wilmington played by Barbara Young) who happens to be a lesbian, although it has to be said that this potentially interesting character was seriously underwritten, as were, like those in *Budgie* before it, almost all the parts for women throughout the series. It must have amused Verity, however, that Hazell's girlfriend, Vinnie (Celia Gregory), was, like her, an ex-Roedean girl.

Many of those involved with *Hazell* felt that the decision to make it in the traditional Thames fashion – as a mix of filmed exteriors and videotaped studio interiors – was a serious error of judgement that damaged its effectiveness from the start. 'That was horrible,' says Colin Bucksey. 'There was a joke at that time that there are two different styles of lighting for multi-camera studios and that's on and off. We tried but there was only so much we could do.'

Verity herself was bullish about these limitations. 'I know it can be done in the studio,' she said, 'because I've done series like it in other companies. It's a hassle, it seems like a nightmare to begin with, but it can be made to work and work well.'[17]

Making *Hazell* in the old-school, conventional manner was political as much as practical. It sent a message that Thames were serious about keeping major drama in-house. In those strike-heavy times, this was an important factor. Besides, even had Verity wished to, she could not at this stage have farmed *Hazell* out to Euston Films, because they were then only equipped to cope with the demands of its long-running banker, *The Sweeney*.

---

[17] Quoted in *Hazell* book, as before

Throughout Verity's first few years at Thames, *The Sweeney* had been important to her, albeit in a semi-detached fashion. She had nothing to do with its production but the guaranteed audience figures it delivered gave her the freedom to be slightly more esoteric in her other choices. But although to begin with neither *The Sweeney* nor Euston Films were within her remit, she was beady about both and keen to stake her claim to them should the chance arise. Towards the end of 1976, it had done so.

It will be remembered that Euston had been the elegant and effective device that had allowed Jeremy Isaacs to manoeuvre Verity's predecessor, Lloyd Shirley, out of her way. In the couple of years that followed, Shirley and his co-executive, George Taylor, had kept themselves occupied with delivering *The Sweeney* and not much else. Verity was soon agitating that Thames could make much greater use of its film-making subsidiary. Isaacs agreed, and wanted its output to become part of the overall Thames drama offering. This did not go down well with either Shirley or Taylor, who valued their independence and did not want to be so strictly tied to the parent company. 'It was a question of compatibility,' says Taylor. 'I preferred not being a committee executive in any case.'

There was no real impasse. Shirley and Taylor resigned and to smooth their departure, Jeremy Isaacs agreed that their own company might make an all-film version of the detective series *Van der Valk* through Euston. Again, as with Shirley's departure from Thames in 1974, it was a tidy solution that avoided conflict and saved everyone's face.

At the end of 1976, Verity added Euston Films to her already considerable portfolio and, as the new chief executive, without delay she began to restructure the company so that it was equipped to match the aspirations she cherished for it. 'Verity took over, and it became a much bigger thing,' says George Taylor. 'I admired what she did with Euston; she was always out for trying something new. She was particularly good at choosing people.'

One of her first and most critical decisions was appointing a script executive, to help her identify the right projects for the company and nurture the writing talent responsible. She chose the exceptionally articulate, lively and opinionated 29-year-old Linda Agran, who was then working – and feeling intensely frustrated – for Warner Brothers in London. 'It was a nonsensical job,' says Agran, looking back. 'I was creative head for London, Paris and Rome. I had a very grand office with a huge booze cupboard but nothing much was happening. Verity came in and crossed those amazing showgirl legs and it was like meeting a twin sister. She said that they had this little company called Euston Films and that she and Jeremy Isaacs were very keen to boost it. Would I be interested in going in there and creatively kicking it off and trying to attract writers? That was the deal. From the off, we had not just a phenomenal friendship but great respect for each other. I completely and utterly adored her.'

Verity also advertised for a production manager to look after all aspects of her financial strategy for Euston. The successful candidate, Johnny Goodman, was patently

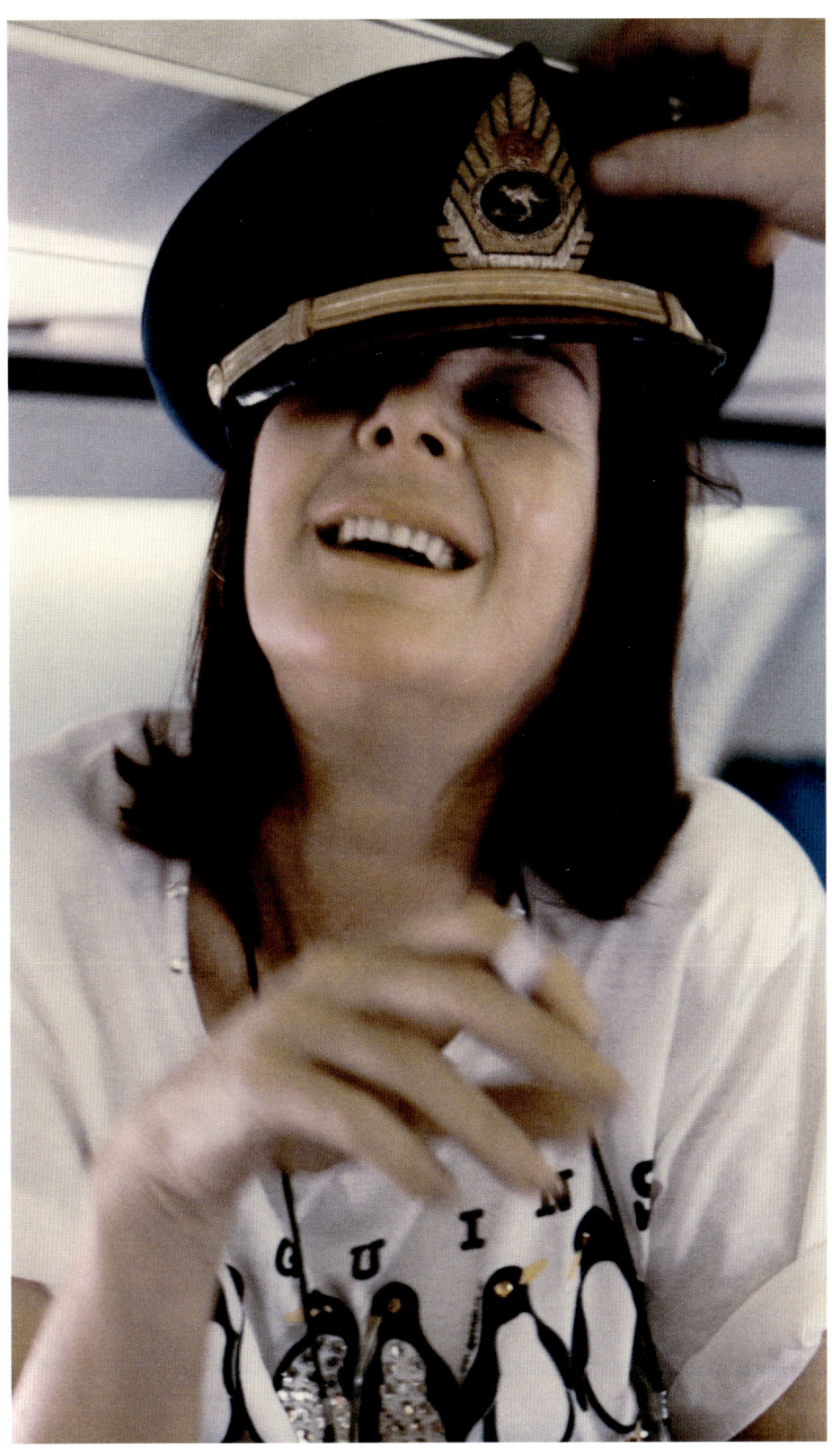

On the plane Verity chartered to Ayers Rock for *A Cry in the Dark,* 1987

Partying with British screen star
Malcolm McDowell

Meeting legendary film director John Huston,
alongside her protégé and friend Graham Benson

Celebrating her half century, 1985. Cutting the cake
with Kate Kagan and Sydney Newman

Raising a glass with producer Paul Knight (left) and Beryl Vertue (right). The
party was held at the Norland Square home of Verity's friends, the Kagans

Cosying up to writer Howard Schuman who calls Verity
'one of the most vivid people I ever met'

Christmas at Andrew Brown's Swanage hideaway and a hug from her close
friend and confidante, Kate Kagan

On holiday with Janet Street-Porter. Before they met,
Verity had loathed the outspoken presenter

At the door of her Antibes
bolt-hole, 1981

'Legs Lambert' in the
mood to party

Queen of the kitchen at Addison Avenue with helper Kate Kagan.
Note the 'murial' by artist and friend Felicity Marshall

'Darling, I've brought caviar…'

With film producer John Dark and Australian publicist
Rea Francis at the Melbourne Gold Cup

The honorary Aussie, enjoying a tinny
and looking the part

Becoming a Doctor of Laws at the University of Strathclyde, an honour of which she was proud, 15th April 1988

overqualified for such a title. Goodman had enjoyed a long career in the British film industry and was then languishing at Trident Films, which was supposedly Yorkshire Television's version of Euston. 'It was a total waste of space,' says Goodman. 'They didn't do anything. I accepted an invitation to meet the people involved in this Euston Films set-up. First of all this dour Scotsman, Jeremy Isaacs, came in, followed by this weird bird with a fag in her mouth trailing a fur coat. That was Verity. They said, "Why would you want to leave Trident Films?" and I replied, "I think you've got a sense of what you want to do whereas they are just waffling."'

Goodman became not the production manager but the executive in charge of production. Together with Goodman's expertise, the excellent creative instincts and *élan* of Linda Agran, and her own vision, Verity now formed one third of the central trio who were to establish Euston as a powerhouse for some of the most distinctive television film-making in the world.

'We were much, much freer than people are today,' says Agran. 'If there were doubts from upstairs, Verity and me – two rather loud, stroppy women – could take on the Thames board any time of the day or night, no problems. We were deeply, deeply in friendship but we'd have blazing rows – I mean, screaming rows – from a point of view of passion. I would say, "Well, I think this should happen..." She'd say, "Fuck off, it's not happening!" I'd say, "I don't care what you say, do you want my resignation?" "I don't give a toss one way or the other!"

'She's the only person I've ever met who would literally stamp her foot. She would stamp her foot and her eyes would fill with tears – not soppy tears, tears of complete fury. Her language was unbelievable. In those days you could smoke everywhere so she'd have fags on the go all over the place – and she would be swearing down the phone – "This man's a cunt and this director's a prick" A lot of the men found her scary and couldn't comprehend our relationship. They would think, "Oh, they've fallen out – that's good – maybe there's going to be a big job coming up soon." They didn't realise that this was two people so committed that they were prepared to fight their corner. It was brilliant. I can remember a couple of occasions where she'd argue one point, I'd argue another and we'd decide in the editing.'

'I know she trusted me,' says Goodman. 'There were a lot of laughs and fun. She was an amazing lady. She had a nose. I had great admiration for her faith in people, her likeability, her efficiency. I was lucky to find somebody that you could look up to and respect and who looked after you. She could be tough and acerbic. She didn't take inefficiency or lack of talent easily and expected everybody to do their job the way she wanted it. Provided you did that, you got on like a house on fire. Only once did we have a big row. She turned on me and I said, "Don't jump out of your pram with me, lady," and she stopped for a second and burst into laughter and went around saying "Johnny says I mustn't jump out of my pram!" She'd never heard the expression before. We were a tight unit, like a family but she was the boss, no question about it.'

With the expansion of her empire, Verity acquired a second office away from Teddington, located in Thames's Euston Road headquarters. Boasting a thick white carpet, black suede walls and an enormous pink sofa, this flamboyant nest was the nerve centre of her new operation. 'Euston Films had been working in a condemned school,' explains *Sweeney* producer Ted Childs. 'No way was she going to work in a slum like I had been used to and she wasn't inhibited by spending money either. Suddenly, it all went upmarket and became very grand with flock-lined wallpaper. It was an extra train set. The early battles with the unions were over and she knew its potential. She was able to persuade the senior management at Thames that Euston Films was an important programme entity within the group and therefore it should be properly funded and made more of.'

Decisive as ever, Verity quickly began to expand the Euston portfolio. Literary agent Stephen Durbridge sent Verity the proposal for an earthy six-part London-based thriller series called *Out*. The premise followed the story of Frank Ross, an ex-con released after serving time for a crime he didn't commit. He leaves prison determined to find out who framed him and why. The writer was a *Sweeney* stalwart, Trevor Preston. 'I've never seen anybody make a decision so quickly as Verity,' he said. 'She was extraordinary. I was writing it within three weeks – it was breathtaking.'[18]

'She found making big decisions really easy – let's make it and move on,' says Linda Agran. 'This is going to sound very wanky but what we were looking for was the kind of drama we wanted to see. Did we want to spend a year or so making this stuff? It was a huge passion, and it was very much writer-driven in those days. '

Verity accepted a major one-off film production, *The Sailor's Return*, to be directed by Jack Gold, who had done such splendid work on *The Naked Civil Servant*. It was yet another example of her interest in period pieces with something to say about contemporary issues or morality. *The Sailor's Return*, based on a novel by David Garnett, dramatised the story of a Victorian seaman who brings home an African bride with whom he attempts to settle in a country village. The community, at first fearful, curious and amazed, becomes ever more hostile and intolerant. The everyday tragedy of racism was all too relevant in 1970s Britain. The intention was that *The Sailor's Return* would be released in cinemas before its television transmission but this proved impossible to negotiate. It was ahead of its time. In just a few years, with the emergence of Channel 4, it would have been a perfect fit as part of the channel's *Film on Four* strand.

Before Verity rescued it from the doldrums, *The Sailor's Return* had a wearisome and extended history of development. She performed the same escape trick with another long-beached project, *Quatermass*. This was Nigel 'Tom' Kneale's sequel to his original

---

[18] Quoted in *Made in Euston* (see bibliography)

stories which had captivated huge audiences in the 1950s. '*Quatermass* had been such a huge event,' says Linda Agran. 'Verity and I had both loved that whole thing.'

'It was an amazing success,' said Verity herself, in a 2003 interview. 'He had written one of the great science fiction serials at that time. It had stopped the whole of Britain from going to church.'

Kneale might have been more successful had he been easier to work with. 'He was a trifle eccentric,' says Ted Childs, who produced the Euston version. 'But I liked him and he was clearly a very imaginative and creative screenwriter.' 'He was extraordinary,' adds Agran. 'Such a brilliant writer.'

Back in 1965, when she was still producing *Doctor Who*, Verity had memorably clashed with Kneale on the review programme *Late Night Line-Up*. Kneale had taken her to task with his view that *Doctor Who* was irresponsibly frightening for children. Verity had argued back with vigour. Some might have remembered this encounter with an element of disfavour but Verity was too much of a realist to let her ego derail something in which she could see great potential. 'I just thought it was a fantastically interesting idea,' she explained. 'Something that would be really good to do.'

Ted Childs felt that a major part of the incentive in going ahead with *Quatermass* was that Verity and Linda Agran 'didn't want to come in and just do the same old routine – the kick-bollock-and-scramble action-adventure stuff that made the early name of the company'.

Originally commissioned in 1972 by the BBC, the *Quatermass* scripts were evidently far too ambitious to be achievable within the kind of budget available at the corporation and its standard mix of film and studio. Making them through Euston would liberate the scripts from these constraints. Even so, *Quatermass* remained a hugely expensive venture. Like *The Sailor's Return*, the aspiration was to amortise the costs by producing a theatrical version for cinema release alongside the four television episodes. Verity persuaded the veteran film British star Sir John Mills to play the eponymous Professor Quatermass, and he agreed, albeit somewhat reluctantly.

Jenne Casarotto, the agent who had sent Kneale's scripts to her, also suggested another of her clients, Piers Haggard, to direct the piece. Haggard had recently worked for Verity on a Catherine Cookson play in the *Romance* series. 'I had some meetings with her, and Verity said she'd liked what I'd done with the play,' he recalls. 'I've always liked science fiction and there were ideas in it – it was ambitious and well-budgeted. The fact that this particular script had been around for a while was manifest because it was about a hippy movement which he'd spotted as current a few years earlier. Things had to be run by Verity, and there were notes but nothing inordinate. She'd been properly brought up and knew how to do it. It was a very pleasant, well-run, efficient project.'

'She wasn't on the set that much,' points out Johnny Goodman. 'Her ability was to flit from here to there. When you've got people under you who you know can do the job, you don't need to be there all the time. I was always conscious that when the chips were down, Verity was the boss – but not in an obnoxious way. She decided what was done but she was a great support – she knew the answers.'

Alas, for all the resources lavished upon it, *Quatermass* failed to repay Verity's belief in it and the reaction from the audience was disappointing. 'It wasn't a success but well worth trying,' was Linda Agran's judgement. 'Our attitude was, if no one watched it, well, tough shit. It was coming out of the proceeds of the football or whatever other bollocks Thames were making. Quality was very much part of our remit.'

'There were high production values and the performances were good,' says Ted Childs, 'but the primary problems were that it was perhaps too depressing a story for a popular television audience and the punters were used to a fairly high standard of [special effects] and we just couldn't afford that.'

Danger UXB was Euston's first full-scale period-drama series. It was brought to her by the highly experienced independent producer John Hawkesworth, who had scored enormous successes with *Upstairs, Downstairs* and *The Duchess of Duke Street*. Hawkesworth, whose determinedly tweedy upper-class manner belied his ruthless professionalism, had optioned a book by a Major Bill Hartley, *Unexploded Bomb*, and outlined a series charting the operations of a Home Front bomb-disposal squad during the Second World War. Verity needed little persuasion, quickly discerning that it would perfectly fit her requirement for series that reflected the character of London and, even more crucially, this was hitherto untold territory. Natural suspense was built into the premise and every week the audience would wonder: 'will the bomb go off or not?'

She had, it is true, less in common with Hawkesworth than most of her producers. He had a fiercely snobbish wife who sometimes accompanied him to meetings. This lady answered to the unlikely nickname 'Pussy' and as the top-drawer couple barked at each other over a drink in her office, Verity would often have to fight not to succumb to an unsuitable fit of giggles. 'As John would start talking about Pussy,' chuckles Linda Agran, 'I would catch sight of those black eyes twinkling across the room. But there was respect and great understanding there. She handled people very differently, depending on who you were – she had very good built-in antenna.'

Hawkesworth was a class act in every sense and eventually he delivered a magnificently compelling drama. '*Danger UXB* could never have been done on tape,' was Verity's own judgement. 'All those bombs and gardens and things.'[19]

---

[19] Quoted in *Made in Euston* (see bibliography)

From Isaacs' point of view, *Danger UXB*, so essentially upmarket, was politically useful too in banking up ammunition for the next round of franchise renewal. 'The thing about Jeremy is that he totally understood what we were doing,' says Linda Agran. 'He didn't necessarily agree with all of it but he didn't want to read it. I mean, nobody read our stuff. You can't imagine that now. What's so dangerous is all this co-production crap. *Danger UXB* was a lot better made than fucking *Downton Abbey*.'

Verity's acquisition and rapid expansion of Euston Films came in tandem with her continuing role as controller of drama at Thames. Despite her enviable stamina, it was an enormous commitment and even she began to flag. Resigning her Thames responsibilities so that she might focus on Euston alone became an increasingly attractive option. The departure of her sponsor and staunch ally, Jeremy Isaacs, was another deciding factor. Isaacs had been unhappy for some time. The Thames board had recruited a BBC man, Bryan Cowgill, ostensibly to work alongside him as managing director. Trying to accommodate two bosses was a patently unworkable situation, and both men were soon locked in a dysfunctional power struggle. 'He was a dreadful man who ranted and abused me, and my life became appallingly difficult,' says Isaacs, who eventually conceded and returned to programme-making in 1978, leaving the field at Thames clear for his rival. 'I left in tears,' Isaacs concludes.

Despite her great ally's miserable departure, Verity's own position remained secure. Cowgill was far too wily an operator to risk losing such an effective member of his senior team and he was none too pleased when she told him that she wanted to relinquish her role within Teddington. She made the transition as painless as she possibly could, nudging Cowgill towards her replacement, John Frankau. Verity was fond of Frankau, who was an experienced producer-director, and the feeling was mutual. 'She suggested it and put me up for it,' says Frankau. 'She told me she thought it would be a good idea for me. It wasn't difficult to persuade me because at that time my career needed a little shift.'

She left Frankau well supplied with material. Further series of *Rumpole*, *Born and Bred* and *Hazell* were in the offing. She had also commissioned Simon Raven to adapt Nancy Mitford's *Love in a Cold Climate*, with Gerald Savory as producer. There was plenty in development, too, from a variety of sources.

'I had a sudden idea for a comedy-drama series,' says actress Judy Cornwell. 'Set in a teachers' training college, called *Mature Students*. It was about these two people – one a divorcée and one who has been thrown out by his wife, going back to teacher training and how they are attracted to each other and come together. I took it to Verity who said, "That sounds fascinating." So I said, "Who are we going to get write it?" and she replied, "You are. Give me a pilot." I started working on it with my husband John [Parry] and we ended up with a pilot and a breakdown for 12 others. Verity loved it and paid us, but the new fellow coming in, John Frankau, didn't want to know about us or Verity's leftovers. He wanted his own people, so that was that.'

Another casualty of Frankau's new regime was Howard Schuman's follow-up to *Rock Follies*, *The Ann Lovington Hour*. 'It was going to be all done on video, an edgy comedy about a woman's real life and her dream life,' explains Schuman, 'done as two separate halves of the same hour. The real woman was Vera Cunningham from Billericay, a talented artist who comes to Portobello, in London, a community that's falling apart. She's depressed and finds that she can't paint. She'd say, "I'm experimenting with totally white canvas." In her depression, she sleeps a lot and in her dreams, she isn't Vera Cunningham from Billericay, she's Ann Lovington, feminist and world-famous artist. There was only one ad-break and the real life segment of the show would end with part one and when you came back you'd be in the dream show. But by episode nine of twelve, I planned to fracture the narrative so that in the reality you had the dream show and the division between them melted. As she got to the root of her anxieties and depression, she would separate them out again and know her reality from her dream show.'

Verity's old friend from the BBC, Graeme McDonald, was now in charge of drama serials there and he offered to commission *The Ann Lovington Hour* on condition that Andrew Brown produce it. 'When Verity heard we were being signed with the BBC,' continues Schuman, 'I suddenly got this message saying, "Don't do anything. Verity would really like to talk to you first." In the end, she offered a deal that I couldn't refuse and, of course, I hadn't forgotten that *Rock Follies* had only been created with her support. Then she left and John Frankau clearly wanted to get rid of it. Bryan Cowgill was *officially* supportive but I know he was bewildered by what we were planning. Andrew was outmanoeuvred. I had only written four or five episodes when he was asked by John Frankau to produce a revised budget and then Frankau went to Cowgill and said, "We can't possibly afford this." We were cancelled. It was completely devastating.'

'Frankau was a backward move,' says Jeremy Isaacs. 'Whereas her programmes speak for her. She was a dynamic and enlivening presence. You knew that good things were going to come from her. Later, she wrote me a letter, on pink card, to say that the years she'd spent working for me had been the happiest of her life because of my trust in her and my support for her, giving her the freedom to do what she wanted. It was her ideal of what could be possible. I was very proud to get that.'

Although Verity remained on the board of Thames Television, she officially left the drama department in June 1979, almost exactly five years after her arrival. Free to focus her considerable energies on Euston Films, she was about to enter yet another highly productive and rewarding phase in her already brilliant career.

CHAPTER NINE
I COULD BE SO GOOD FOR YOU
1979–1982

'I'm under pressure every single day. When the door opens, you know it's very rarely someone come to tell you something nice.'

Verity to Peter Fiddick, *The Guardian*, 1979

From the moment she took up her duties as chief executive of Euston Films, Verity was aware that she had to find a new vehicle to replace the company's most reliable performer, the long-running *The Sweeney*. She herself had very little to do with the series, recognising that the formula worked and that its continuing success underpinned everything else that both Thames and Euston made. 'She was very sensible,' says *The Sweeney*'s producer, Ted Childs. 'She thought, "This is something that's working, my employers like it, there's going to be no value in pissing about with it."'

But, by the time of its fourth series, screened in the spring of 1978, both stars of *The Sweeney*, John Thaw and Dennis Waterman, were feeling restless.[1] For Verity, losing the show represented an opportunity and she filled the void by commissioning a new comedy-drama from the writer Leon Griffiths. 'She was entirely responsible for *Minder*,' says Griffiths' agent, Anthony Jones. 'Leon had written a sort of four-page treatment, which was superb – so good I still show it to young writers today. I sent this to her and then we had lunch in the basement at Orso. It took her about five minutes to say, "Yes, I want this." She was a supremely good executive. She had taste and if she decided she

---

[1] The final series was shot from September, 1977

wanted something, she fought for it.'

'Normally treatments are extremely difficult to write and even harder to read,' explained Verity, 'and it was so good. Leon didn't know we were trying to find something but he happened to write it at the same time as we were looking.'[2]

Within Euston, there was a general consensus that *Minder* was exactly the series to continue the company's association with Dennis Waterman. He would play Terry McCann, the minder of the title, the personable sidekick and bodyguard to Arthur Daley, a shady businessman and self-made entrepreneur. Waterman was interested and, as his co-star, he suggested Verity's old friend from her Ibiza days, Denholm Elliott. Verity had other ideas and favoured character actor George Cole. It was almost a replay of the casting of Iain Cuthbertson in *Budgie*. Like Cuthbertson, Cole had been playing a run of middle-class parts on television, but, remembering his inspired performance as Flash Harry in the *St Trinian's* films, Verity was convinced he'd be perfect. True to her usual form, she persuaded everyone else to see it her way. Arthur Daley was to make George Cole a star all over again.

The first 11-week series of *Minder* started on 29 October 1979. To Verity's chagrin, its performance was disappointing. She offered various theories to explain this. The audience needed time to adjust to Waterman playing a much less abrasive character than they had been used to in *The Sweeney*. The first episode, *Gunfight at the OK Launderette*, was atypically violent and, for some, this was off-putting. But principally she believed that the series had been badly damaged by that year's lengthy ITV strike, which had wrenched the network off the air for ten weeks during the summer and early autumn. 'Because nobody knew when the strike would end,' she explained in one interview, 'they couldn't publicise *Minder* without knowing when it would go on air. So we had no publicity.'[3]

The programme was in serious danger of cancellation. Together with her script executive Linda Agran, Verity petitioned Thames' controller of programmes, Bryan Cowgill, as he recalled in his memoirs. '[They] said, "It hasn't been quite the smash hit that we had in mind but we want to keep the cast together if we can and encourage Leon to go on. What are your feelings?" I remember saying to Verity and Linda, "I think it's good, you think it's good, and if we're all agreed on that, let's make another series...on the strength that if it is any good, people will find it."'

It was a decision unlikely to be made today. 'He believed [in it],' said Verity. 'In those days, there wasn't so much pressure. There weren't 75 committees that you had to sit through to get anything made. I always felt *Minder* was going to be a success. It never

---

[2] University of Reading interview, 2004

[3] Kaleidoscope convention interview, 2006

occurred to me that it wouldn't be. It simply had all the ingredients. I wasn't taking a big chance there; I just knew it would work.'[4]

Carefully nurtured, a beacon of quality, *Minder* became a phenomenal success and a stalwart of the ITV schedule. As well as fulfilling Verity's abiding criterion of celebrating London, the series humorously yet acutely inhabited the era in which it was made. Arthur Daley was the very embodiment of Thatcherite free enterprise and, initially at least, the series reflected London's growing diversity. 'Part of Leon's original idea,' said Verity, 'was that it showed the mix of ethnic communities that lived in London. I think that was very good because it explains something about ethnic communities and how they live together, in a way that was amusing but, at the same time, real.'[5]

Minder was made with great craft and enormous discipline, on the same tightly run and meticulously planned two-week turnaround as *The Sweeney*, and likewise with the minimum interference from Verity herself. She would read the scripts and give notes on these and the various cuts of the episodes, but, in general, she kept her distance from the day-to-day production. 'She totally, absolutely, trusted you,' says script executive Linda Agran. 'She knew that you would be at the coal face and that you would be taking decisions that didn't necessarily have to involve her.'

'She would suggest certain juxtapositions of scenes which made it better,' says executive producer George Taylor. 'She had an excellent brain and memory and she could just sit down and look at it and remember how scenes would go together and suggest putting scenes in a different order without affecting continuity and that takes quite a lot of doing. In that respect, she used to polish the product, if you like.'

Minder was so important to Euston that Verity and Linda Agran turned down *Only Fools and Horses*, a series they felt would cover the same ground. 'John Sullivan was a brilliant writer,' says Agran, 'but those were not two projects we could have done in parallel. There was a worry of crossover.'

John Sullivan may have been 'the one that got away' but Verity spent much of her energy at Euston nurturing and extending her relationships with the writers and directors whom she treasured the most. She invited Jack Gold to direct Keith Waterhouse's adaptation of *Charlie Muffin*, a wryly amusing Cold War spy novel by Brian Freemantle. 'We went to East Berlin looking for locations,' remembers producer Ted Childs. 'It was all a bit clandestine because we hadn't got the permission from the authorities. Verity came for the fun and adventure of it but was absolutely horrified by the food and drink available. I remember sitting with her and Jack Gold having lunch in a restaurant in East Berlin. It was the worst meal I've ever had. The wine was like thin strawberry jam. Verity

---

[4] Kaleidoscope, as before

[5] University of Reading, as before

started to rant and went on ranting about the "terrible bloody chicken" and Jack, who is a lovely guy, was trying to mollify her. It wasn't a socialist paradise!'

Gold feels that the resulting film was overlooked and underrated because it was screened just after transmission of the BBC's heavyweight *Tinker, Tailor, Soldier, Spy*. The impact of John le Carré's convoluted thriller confused the audience who then came to *Charlie Muffin* expecting something similar, rather than a gentle, slightly satirical comedy.

Stainless Steel and the Star Spies was another oddity, a pilot for a series that never came off. A science fiction comedy designed to attract that difficult hybrid audience, the family, it told the tongue-in-cheek tale of the Metaliens, the crew of the SS Compromise, as they visit Earth for the first time. The whole concept was a lift from the hugely popular 1970s ad campaign for Smash instant potato granules in which aliens are seen trying to understand the eccentric nature of the planet and its inhabitants. It was the creation of cartoonist Gray Jolliffe, who was then working for the advertising agency responsible for the Smash campaign. Jolliffe knew Linda Agran, who discussed the idea with Verity. She thought it original and a total departure from Euston's usual territory, which made it appealing. Her experience on *Doctor Who* had taught her that if they could deliver the same mix of out-of-this-world fantasy and humour, they might capture a similarly large and faithful teatime following.

The pilot was originally intended to be 25 minutes long, which, like *Doctor Who*, Verity felt was the optimum duration for this kind of whimsy. But when the projected costs came in, in order to make it achievable, she had to agree to doubling the running time. She felt this undermined the whole enterprise. 'It was a bit slow [and] repetitive,' recalled Jolliffe, in a 2011 interview[6]. 'I wanted to make it a space romp with robots only but they thought there should be a human interest and wanted to bring it back to Earth – they got a lot of real people in there. In the end, it all got a bit bogged down. It was a little bit too sophisticated for children. It was designed, as far as I was concerned, for adults. So it probably fell between two stools. Somehow, it didn't work.'

Much more successful, and with a reputation that has endured, was Jack Rosenthal's *The Knowledge*, a wonderfully sharp and poignant film about the rite of passage undergone by all London's aspiring black cab drivers. 'As far as I'm concerned, *The Knowledge* was Jack's best work,' says his widow, Maureen Lipman. 'It was the idea of Bob Brooks, the director. Because Bob was an American and an irascible outsider, he had a wonderful slanted view of London. He brought it to Jack. And Jack had, by this time, fallen in love with London, despite being a Northerner all his life. It wasn't a commission – he took it to Verity because she was a bloody good producer and she had class. You didn't go to Verity with *Celebrity Bake Off*, you went to Verity with something written by

---

[6] Posted on the Euston Films blog (31.07.11).

a good mind with fine brush strokes, otherwise she wouldn't have taken it on. Jack thought she was an excellent producer. She was very smart and funny and she liked writers and was someone who would say, "No, this doesn't work." She understood scripts and what made a good scene.'

As Rosenthal related in his 1998 appearance on *Desert Island Discs*[7], when he was due to deliver his first draft to Verity, a mildly farcical scene ensued, reminiscent of a scene from one of Rosenthal's own scripts. 'I was actually in the process of handing it over,' he told interviewer Sue Lawley, 'when I thought this script wasn't right. She had hold of one end and I had hold of the other and we had a little tug of war. I said, "It isn't right, I'd like to do it again," and she said, "Well, let me read it," and I said, "No, I don't want you to read it because it isn't right and I think I now know how to make it right," and she said, "Just let me look at it," and we played at this for a little while and then she let me win and said, "Off you go and do it again."'

'The reason that he pulled the script away from Verity,' continues Maureen Lipman, 'was that he suddenly saw inner London as a circle and he thought that this is how the play should be written – in circular form, like a tube map. That's what he did in the next draft. It was very symptomatic of Jack – he rewrote and rewrote until the day that the thing was filmed – "That's a better line, try saying that…" He was very concerned with the perceived failures of life, and how you can have your own small successes whether you're judged a failure or not. Jack had not realised what a cabbie had to go through and I think when that film came out people took a different view of London cabbies. It's different now, with satnav!'

The snobbery of the industry was such that single plays, and especially films, were prized above all else. 'We all really wanted to be movie-makers,' points out Ted Childs, 'and making a film for television was a step in the right direction.'

But the costs and complications involved were such that even Verity, empowered with an unusual degree of creative freedom, frequently found them elusive. She was offered the script for *Chariots of Fire* and, recognising its quality and that it had a refreshingly different story to tell, recommended that it might be produced as the perfect tie-in with the 1980 Olympic Games. Unfortunately, the ambitious filmic demands of Colin Welland's script placed it out of her reach and she was reluctantly forced to let it go.

'She could be contradictory,' recalls producer Barry Hanson. 'She'd seen the BBC play *Gangsters*, which was genuinely violent and stylish, and said, "I want something like that."' Hanson offered her *The Paddy Factor*, a tough London-based thriller by Barrie Keeffe but Jeremy Isaacs disliked the script and, lukewarm herself, Verity allowed Hanson, who was determined to get it made, to buy back the rights for the nominal sum of £100.

---

[7] *Desert Island Discs* (28.06.98) BBC Radio 4 – currently available as a podcast online

The Paddy Factor became *The Long Good Friday*, one of the most celebrated British films of the twentieth century.

Another casualty was *A Thoroughly Filthy Fellow*, a potential screenplay about Stephen Ward and the Profumo scandal, brought to her by one of her old favourites, Hugh Whitemore. 'I'm all for upsetting the establishment,' he says, 'and this one did.'

'Oh yeah. This was curious,' agrees Linda Agran. 'Verity and I were very keen to do something about the Cambridge spies. We found it completely intriguing. Then that got knocked back and Hugh was going to do the Stephen Ward affair for us. The project went to the Thames board and was absolutely, totally quashed – gone, like it never existed. So I go to see Bryan Cowgill and say, "What the fuck's going on?" Cowgill said, "I have no idea and I can't get anyone to answer it." It was perfectly obvious that the establishment were stopping us from doing it.'

In 1989, a film version of the story, *Scandal*, eventually made it to the screen and did rather well, illustrating, if nothing else, how acute were Verity and Linda Agran's combined commercial instincts.

They were ahead of the game, too, with their decision to dramatise another slice of British social history – the bawdy tale of madam Cynthia Payne and her 'luncheon vouchers for sex' case. The film was given the working title *I Loved the Parties*.[8] 'It was going to be really interesting,' says Jack Gold, who was lined up to direct. 'Carl Davis, who I'd worked with many times, and had been the composer on *The Naked Civil Servant* and *The Sailor's Return*, lived right next door to Cynthia Payne's famous brothel. He was telling us these stories, and Verity and I thought it might make a good film. She suggested Dougie Livingstone to write it so we met at Verity's office with Linda Agran and Cynthia. She brought her photographs, and all these stories came tumbling out. We had a good meeting and decided it would make a very good musical with Carl providing the score.'

'Verity, Jack and I went to one of Cynthia's sex parties to do some research,' smiles Doug Livingstone. 'We were sitting in a living room in Streatham and people are giving out blow jobs and there's a lesbian strip act. We couldn't believe what was going on. The punters didn't pay much – £15 or something like that and for that they were given a luncheon voucher which included sex once. When you had the sex, you gave the girl the luncheon voucher. It was an eye-opening night for all of us. We didn't tell anybody who we were.'

As it was rooted in suburban London, unmistakably British in tone, funny, farcical, and moving, it seemed to Verity another perfect project for Euston, her first film musical, with the talent necessary to deliver on her expectations. Finding the money to pay for it was

---

[8] This was announced in *Television Today* (29.10.81)

another matter. Everything stalled, and then it became apparent that Euston were not the only party interested in bringing the Cynthia Payne story to the screen. The deal-breaker was that director Terry Jones had the financial backing to make his feature, *Personal Services*, with a screenplay by David Leland. It was the death knell for Euston's musical version. 'We were all disappointed,' comments Jack Gold. 'Theirs was the biggie but I think ours would have been really good, in a different way.'

Verity never relaxed her efforts to find and finance one-off films through Euston but series were the company's mainstay and this was a golden period for them. Delighted with the verve and panache of *Out*, she asked its writer, Trevor Preston, to submit some ideas for further collaborations. He came up with half a dozen and the one she liked the best was *Fox*, as she referred to it, a 'television novel' in 13 episodes, charting the fortunes of the eponymous south London family. As Preston explained in the note written to accompany his first outline, 'it has the audience attraction of running over a period long enough for them to relate to and get involved with the central characters. It also has enough dramatic flexibility never to become predictable. Usually in a serial a number of writers and directors are used. This often results in a confusion of styles, a blurring of characters. This would have *one* writer and *one* director. (Jim Goddard is convinced this is quite practicable after his experience on *Out*.) This would give a one hundred per cent continuity in both the writing and the interpretation...in a way, it is a natural extension of *Out*, a larger canvas, a sort of south London *Godfather*.'

Goddard had to convince Verity that he had the stamina to cope single-handed with what became effectively a 13-hour movie. It was just the kind of creative audacity that appealed to her and, besides, he was among the directors she most admired. She gave the project her blessing with characteristic speed, so much so that Preston was still writing the second half of the story when shooting began. To produce it, she poached Graham Benson from the BBC. Benson had impressed her as the last-minute substitute production assistant on *Shoulder to Shoulder* and a close friendship had developed. She'd tried to entice him away from the BBC on previous occasions but without success. 'I was on location, filming on a beach,' he recalls. 'It was the days before mobile phones so on the call sheet it had the number of the nearest phone box. We were in the middle of a take when it rang. It was my agent, Anthony Jones, saying, "Listen, I've just had Verity on the phone, she wants you to give her a ring – it's a thing called *Fox*..."'

Benson left the BBC for Euston, on a vastly increased salary, and began to wrestle with the myriad problems that a shoot of such scale and ambition inevitably brought with it. 'It was mad,' he comments, 'but she never lost her temper. Her attitude was that it's Jim and Trevor, we'll be OK. Aside from our personal friendship, my professional relationship with Verity was based on one hundred per cent trust. I knew that if I messed up, she would have been down on me like a tonne of bricks – and rightly so. She taught me to produce and drummed into me that if you start shooting with a script that you're not happy with, it won't work. Whatever you think you can do to make it right, it won't work. It's better to say, "No, we're not ready." We were all young, ambitious and hard-working and although this was such a daunting task, we were – me, Trevor, Jim and Verity – all "can do" people who didn't take "no" for an answer. We knew that this was something very interesting and special.'

Verity loved the series, though she recognised that the scope of the story and the sheer number of characters were asking much of a mainstream ITV audience. '*Fox* was made very much in the way that [Trevor Preston] wanted it to be made,' she explained, years later. 'Trevor had a very strong view about what he wanted. I don't think we tried to push it in any direction. It just was a wonderful story about this sprawling family. I thought that it was very good because it showed the differences in family, how various people can go different ways or can't, as the case may be. It was a piece of work which had its own very strong direction in the writing.'[9]

With Bryan Cowgill's enthusiastic backing, money was found for some serious promotion, including lavish hospitality for journalists and a glossy brochure to sell *Fox* to anyone who might reasonably be expected to give it a plug. Despite all this effort and expense, and the indisputable quality of the piece, *Fox* failed to make the essential top twenty and was not regarded as a success. It proved a better fit for the new Channel 4, which repeated it a few years later, at the instigation of 4's founding controller and Verity's old ally, Jeremy Isaacs. To Isaacs, it was another example of Verity's ability to identify 'supreme quality' in popular programme-making.

John Hawkesworth, the producer who had brought *Danger UXB* to Euston, now returned with suggestions for further ventures into period drama. The first was an adaptation of H. E. Bates' *The Feast of July*, set in the late Victorian era and following the struggles of a young woman called Bella Ford, who finds herself unmarried and pregnant with her lover's child. Hawkesworth and his associate, Christopher Neame, both believed that Verity, if only for logistical reasons, would favour this over their alternative – a television version of *The Flame Trees of Thika*. This was Elspeth Huxley's vivid account of her childhood in Kenya, and the setting alone meant that it wouldn't be cheap or straightforward to realise. But Verity was entranced by the story, its setting, use of wildlife, and, above all, the unusual focus on a child's-eye view of the world. She told Hawkesworth to go ahead and dramatise the book in six episodes.

The Flame Trees of Thika was unlike anything else so far attempted on British television. From Verity's point of view, the prospect of the search to find a child with the talent to play the central role, not to mention the practical issues of filming a series in Kenya, only added to the attraction. 'I also thought Euston is a very male-orientated company,' she reasoned when asked to explain the thinking behind the commission. 'I thought it was a rather good story about women. The women in it were strong and courageous and I felt that it rang the changes a bit from the rather sort of macho stuff we were making. I was

---

[9] Quoted in *Made in Euston* (see bibliography)

travelling through Kenya at one point with John Hawkesworth and we were talking about it and I said, "Of course, you know this is really a very feminist story." And John said, "What do you mean?" And I said, "Well, if you examine it, all the women are the people who get things done in it and come to terms with their life." And he said, "I've never thought of it like that but you are right."'[10]

From start to finish, *The Flame Trees of Thika* was enormously challenging and tested even Verity's considerable nerve. The original idea was to offer the principal male lead to Anthony Andrews, who had been the star of *Danger UXB*. Andrews was more than willing but the ITV strike had played havoc with filming schedules throughout commercial television and so he was lost to the continuing demands of the disrupted *Brideshead Revisited*. His replacement was Scottish character actor David Robb, while former child star Hayley Mills played his wife. But all the adults were secondary in importance to whoever was to play the young Elspeth. Hawkesworth interviewed scores of girls and eventually found his star at the Elmhurst ballet school where he met Holly Aird. She had precisely the precocious maturity, skill and star quality needed to carry the series and she was one of the few child actors of her generation to successfully continue her career as an adult.

The excruciating budget problems were even harder to resolve than the casting and cancellation loomed on more than one occasion. Eventually, Verity had to insist that Hawkesworth cut a visual and exciting but also extremely expensive opening sequence designed to illustrate how 1912 Nairobi resembled the Wild West. For all its merits, it simply wasn't essential to the story. Other painful compromises followed. The biggest was the decision to make the series seven, rather than six, episodes long. This was the only way to spread the costs over the screen time and, despite Hawkesworth's grumbling at having to stretch the material, he bowed to the inevitable and delivered.

With production underway, Verity, sensibly equipped with pith helmet, ventured out to cast an eye on proceedings, accompanied by John Hawkesworth. Their visit did not get off to an auspicious start. 'After a horrendous journey, with no sleep, I arrived in a foul mood,' she recalled. 'Christopher [Neame] met us at the airport, all smiles. "I've arranged for us to have a curry at the Muthaiga Club." "All I want to do is go straight to bed," I said, crossly. But he wouldn't take no for an answer. He was right, of course. I had a delicious lunch, went to sleep for 24 hours, and woke the next day, happy and ready for anything he had in store.'[11]

'Verity was one of a kind,' wrote Neame in his memoirs. 'She had the wonderful ability to see what is going on around her, to understand where people come from, what makes

---

[10] Quoted in *Made in Euston*, as before

[11] From Verity's introduction to Christopher Neame's book, *A Take on British TV Drama* (see bibliography)

them tick. Instinctively, she knew when a character on a scripted page is honest to him or herself – and she had a built-in sense of dramatic rhythm. Many have tried to emulate her and many have been good seconds. *Seconds*.'

The Flame Trees of Thika amply repaid her faith and was immediately successful on both sides of the Atlantic. Exceptionally healthy international sales – to 33 countries – followed. It had been a colossal, potentially crushing, commitment for a relatively small company like Euston, with no investment from any external partners. Delighted by its success, Neame and Hawkesworth attempted to persuade Verity to bankroll the sequel, *The Mottled Lizard*, set just after the Great War, but she declined, perhaps fearing the law of diminishing returns.

Because there was undeniably truth in the charge, Verity was always sensitive to the accusation that much of Euston's output was centred on a masculine perspective. As she commented in a 1984 interview, 'The women who appear in *Minder* are not stereotypes on the whole. They're all rather good characters. But I accept that it is male-orientated. One or two of my feminist friends had made some quite, well, if not derogatory remarks, had at least asked me questions about it and I had become conscious of the fact that I really should try and do something about women.'[12]

While *Flame Trees* had gone some way to redress the balance, she was only too well aware that it wasn't enough. 'Linda Agran and I were sitting talking one day,' she recalled. 'And I said, "Here we are, two women running a company, and all we're doing is male-orientated heroes. We must look for some women heroines." So I rang up various agents and said, "Listen, I'm looking for something that features women, have you got anything?"'

One agent promptly sent her a treatment for a series called *The Women*. It was the work of a writer whose theatrical-sounding name she did not recognise – Lynda La Plante. 'I'd actually written it as an outline for an episode of *The Gentle Touch*,' she explains. 'They rejected it but I reworked it because somebody in the *Gentle Touch* office had scribbled, "this is brilliant" on it.'

La Plante knew all about Verity and indeed their paths had already crossed. Under her acting name of Lynda Marchal, La Plante had appeared in minor roles in both *Out* and *The Sweeney* and, years before that, she had auditioned to be part of *Rock Follies*. 'I was in awe of her as a producer,' explains La Plante, 'because she was very famous and known to be tough. When I went to meet her in the offices in Euston Road, her secretary opened the door and said, "Verity, Lynda La Plante is here to see you" and when I walked in, she took one look and said, "Oh God! No! Don't tell me you're Lynda La Plante?! Oh, Christ! We all thought it was a joke and that it was some transvestite trucker!"'[13]

---

[12] *Made in Euston*, as before

'I was very nervous but Verity was the most extraordinary person because she never skirted around an issue. She went directly to it. She said, "Look, these two pages I really like but have you ever written anything, Lynda?" "Not really," I said. She said, "Right. This is the situation. If you can come up with a good episode one, you'll be commissioned for all six but if you can't do that then what I'll do is bring on a good, respected writer. Would you agree to that?" I said yes because I was still unsure what was going on. She said, "Good. Well, how long is it going to take you? Think about it." Off I went and I can remember walking down the road, realising that this was a very big opportunity.'

La Plante quickly produced a first script, which she admits was so overlong that it 'was like a novel'. At the meeting to discuss it, Verity 'showed her brilliance. She said, "Like it. Like it a lot. OK who's your leading lady?" "Well, Dolly Rawlins," "Right. She doesn't come on till page 20 – do you know that?" There were never nit-picking stupid notes that say, "I can't really follow this bit – don't understand where you're going with it." She was right on the nail. She taught me how to cut my own script. At one point, she said, "Where are you getting all this stuff from?" "Real villains." "I can tell – the ear's good." So the process continued. She was the boss. Now you would have a football team telling you what to do. Because she had her hand on the tiller at all times, she taught me so much.

'I remember when the costume designer was talking about Dolly Rawlins [the central character] and I heard her saying, "She'd be wearing crimplene – pale blue or pinkish." I interrupted. "No, she goes to Jaeger and wears cashmere." And Verity said, "Really?" I replied, "Yeah, she's a top woman – look at the house she lives in." And that's when Verity sussed out that I wasn't just an actress who wanted to write – that I was very, very serious. I had done my homework. From then on, I'd just see her cocking her head to one side and listening when I said something. When you were right she was very happy. When you were wrong, she was a tigress.'

The serial was rechristened *Widows*. Verity's main issue was with its conclusion. 'In the treatment, the women didn't get away with it at the end,' she explained. 'I said to [Lynda], "Look, I really love it but I'm not going do this unless they get away with it. I'm just not going to go through all this hassle with them, and then in the end they get caught." She had actually sent [the treatment] to London Weekend and written it so they got away with it. They had said, "No, no, you can't do that, they can't get away with it." And I have to say it was a male head of drama [Tony Wharmby], so this may have something to do with it. So I said, "You can go back to your original idea, Lynda and let them get away with it."'[14]

---

[13] Verity later said that both she and Linda Agran were well aware that Lynda La Plante was actually Lynda Marchal. 'In fact,' she told *The Guardian* (17.10.98), 'I said to Linda Agran one day, "Why is Lynda Marchal calling herself Lynda La Plante on these scripts? It sounds like a Victorian lady novelist."'

[14] *Made in Euston*, as before

'I was so excited,' says La Plante. 'She said, "I haven't stuck for six hours to watch them fail – let 'em go, let 'em fly."'

There were no obvious 'stars' in *Widows*. 'If it was made now, that would never happen,' says casting director Marilyn Johnson. 'You would need "names". Verity gave us the support that we needed to think very laterally about the casting. She was incredibly thoughtful and creative and so committed.'

At this distance of time, the impact of *Widows* is easy to underestimate. Everyone involved – from Verity at the top, Linda Agran as producer, Ian Toynton as director and the magnificent cast they assembled – attacked La Plante's superb and gripping screenplay with all the rigour of their combined talents. The results were exceptionally powerful, deservedly attracted enormous audiences, absolutely silencing those who had denigrated its chances. 'Right at the beginning,' says Linda Agran, 'people used to say, "Oh, it's about women. Nah, won't work, people won't watch it. Women won't watch it because they won't be interested enough and it will turn men off because they won't want to watch a lot of heavy dykes." They were proved to be absolutely wrong. Women loved it.'

'It was a fantastic story,' allows Ann Mitchell, who played the lead character, Dolly Rawlins. 'There's always a slight kind of distance between actors and producers. Verity was very cool, very observant. Very supportive all the way along, never letting you feel that there was a problem. We never saw any tirades. She was someone that you could feel safe with – not invading or interfering or wanting to her put her stamp on it. That was my experience of her on the set.'

The most expensive and ambitious of all Verity's Euston commissions was another fine period drama. The premise for *Reilly: Ace of Spies* had been kicking around the business for some years. It was based on the exploits of Sidney Reilly, a mysterious real-life character, Russian-born, who had worked for British intelligence in the early years of the twentieth century. Its television potential had first been spotted by the entrepreneurial Stella Richman. In 1974, she offered it to London Weekend Television as a prestige package to be written by the highly regarded Troy Kennedy Martin. LWT were seriously interested but the problem was that they simply couldn't afford it. Other companies flirted with the idea but ultimately felt the same. When Richman's rights lapsed, Troy Kennedy Martin brought *Reilly* to Verity's attention. 'I thought that it was a real opportunity to do something about an extraordinary, charismatic character against a fascinating historical background,' explained Martin in 1984.[15]

Verity agreed and rescued it from limbo, embarking on a three-year mission to raise the £4.5 million needed to shoot the 12 episodes entirely on location. This was Verity at

---

[15] Quoted in *Made in Euston*, as before

her most dogged and persistent, securing the essential financial commitments from foreign television partners but resisting any external creative input. 'My admiration for Verity knows no bounds,' says Johnny Goodman, the executive in charge of production at Euston. 'I'm a production man, I know all about costs. When the scripts came in for *Reilly: Ace of Spies*, I read them and said, "It ain't gonna happen – recreating the Russian Revolution for a start, it's going to cost an arm and a leg – we can't do it." "We'll do it," said Verity. She didn't take any prisoners and wouldn't stand any nonsense. She'd ring up the main offices at Thames Television and bollock the executives. So we made it and it was very good.'

Verity chose Chris Burt to produce. Although Burt had cut his teeth as a film editor at Euston, had directed on *The Sweeney* and *The Professionals*, where he was made associate producer, this was his first solo producing assignment. Given the scale of *Reilly: Ace of Spies*, even he was surprised at the leap of faith Verity displayed in appointing him: 'There was I, a young man with aspirations to produce, and what an enormous risk she took,' he says. 'It was the biggest drama that Euston had yet made. There were so many difficulties making that series. But she was an extraordinary woman and I learnt so much from her. She had a real feel for brilliant writers, directors, actors and how these people could work for her and her company. With Verity there at the time, it was the greatest and most exciting place in the country to make television drama.'

Finding a leading man with the charisma and command to play the pivotal lead role of Sidney Reilly was a major headache, especially as there was some pressure to use an American as a sop to a potential sale there. 'We had to go all over America,' says Chris Burt. 'Verity was quite keen that we cast over there.'

'She couldn't find anyone to play him,' says Johnny Goodman. 'They were going to use that actor from *Starsky and Hutch*, Paul Michael Glaser, but then his wife got ill so he pulled out. They were searching and searching and I was sent a photo by an agency of a man with his hair parted in the middle. This was Sam Neill. I thought he looked right so I showed it to Verity and Linda. "No, no, no," they cried, "not interested." More time went by and they came back to me – "Who was that man again?" and they saw him and he got the part.'

'It was the making of Sam Neill,' says Chris Burt. 'It was an incredibly difficult series to make and it took a year and a half. Verity let us get on with it, though she read scripts, watched rushes and the cuts of the episodes. It was a wonderful, wonderful time and an amazing piece of work.'

'It was probably the best thing she ever did,' believes agent Anthony Jones. 'Troy [Jones' client at the time] was a wonderful writer but fairly idle. She whipped him into line and did spectacularly well with it.'

As well as launching Sam Neill's film career, the series was a superlative success for its novice producer, too. Chris Burt went on to enjoy a distinguished career, masterminding a variety of blue chip series including *Sharpe*, *Inspector Morse* and, more recently, its spin-off, *Lewis*. Martin Goddard, who directed the second half of *Reilly*, was chosen to direct the BBC's seminal conspiracy thriller *Edge of Darkness* [16] and made the leap into features as a result. Not for the first time, Verity's choices were vindicated by posterity.

Given its close relationship with Thames Television, until now, every Euston production was aimed at the mainstream ITV audience. Although Verity determinedly pushed the boundaries of what might be perceived as mass-audience drama, there were subjects and stories that even she knew were not an appropriate fit for the market. The arrival of Britain's fourth channel, to transmit from November 1982, with its remit for public service diversity and independent production, was an obvious opportunity. Verity was never slow to pursue her advantage and as the new Channel 4 was in the charge of her old mentor and friend, Jeremy Isaacs, she knew he would be receptive if she could find the right material to offer him. She had already been approached by Tony Garnett, a celebrated left-wing film-maker whom she knew from her days at the BBC. Garnett had collaborated very successfully with the writer Gordon Newman and now suggested that they might bring their partnership to Euston to make a fictionalised version of the rise and fall of the notorious East End gangsters, the Kray twins. Verity wasn't keen; she felt that this would simply mean recycling the same themes and types of character explored in both *Out* and *Fox*. But she was interested in a writer of Newman's calibre. What else would he like to do? The response came back that he was thinking about a series of four drama-documentaries about the National Health system. 'Exactly the kind of drama Channel 4 should be doing,' was Verity's judgement, and she took *The Nation's Health*, as Newman titled his series, straight to Isaacs. David Rose, Isaacs' head of drama, read the scripts and, as Isaacs puts it, 'came to me in some excitement and said, "At last we've got something and it's marvellous. This is what we should be doing."'

Never one to coast, by the autumn of 1981, Verity was busier than she had ever been, with an impressive range of titles in various stages of production or development. 'She was so busy running around the place,' smiles Johnny Goodman. 'I think work was everything.'

When she had left her position as controller of drama at Thames two years earlier, it had been precisely in order to concentrate on her expanding Euston portfolio. Now, while remaining as Euston's chief executive, she made an unexpected U-turn and resumed her Thames responsibilities too, under the even grander title of director of drama. This unexpected move was a response to a growing crisis in Teddington's drama department. Her successor there, John Frankau, the producer/director whose promotion Verity had sponsored, had, by his own admission, struggled to meet the exacting demands of the

---

[16] Ironically, the original choice to direct *Edge of Darkness* was Jim Goddard, the director of the first half of *Reilly*. When he proved unavailable, Campbell took his place.

job. 'I just wasn't very good at it,' he says simply. 'And I didn't enjoy it very much. I found I preferred to be at the sharp end. Thames was too much concerned with money as opposed to the quality of what you were doing.'

It was an unenviable task to follow someone with Verity's track record but even allowing for this, Frankau's commissioning instincts seemed uncertain and the results were consistently underwhelming. Most of the titles for which he was responsible failed to perform and have since fallen into utter obscurity – among them dull detective shows like the twice-weekly *Bognor*, Philip Mackie's *Cover*, the uninspired *Agatha Christie Hour* and the ponderous thriller *The Brack Report*. One of the better efforts, a dramatisation of Elizabeth Jane Howard's *Something in Disguise* was produced by Verity's old friend, Moira Armstrong. 'John Frankau was impossible,' she says. 'He certainly wasn't enabling and that's what a good head of drama has to be. He wanted to change the ending of the book and I said, "You can't do that," and wouldn't. He went on and on about it. I think he was a little bit unbalanced, actually. Anyway, it should have gone out in the January [1982] but he insisted on pushing his espionage series instead. We were delayed for a year which was the kiss of death.'

'He was a strange guy,' agrees fellow producer Jackie Davis. 'People felt he had fallen on his feet and was lucky to get it.'

Frankau was released from his Thames contract and returned to directing. Verity's comeback was never planned to be permanent but over the following months, she returned to Teddington for a couple of days each week and attempted to restore some of the confidence of the drama department there. Ironically, Frankau left during the shooting of the one production that might have rewarded him with some sense of esteem – John Mortimer's autobiographical film, *A Voyage around My Father*. 'It was one of the most fruitful things I did in my life,' says its producer and director, and Verity's old friend, Alvin Rakoff. 'I remember delivering the rough cut to Verity. She knew that it was an outstanding piece and when posters were made to promote it internationally, she made sure that my name was printed above the title, which was very thoughtful of her.'

She gave the go-ahead to another prestige production, David Hare's *Saigon: Year of the Cat*, with Stephen Frears as director. 'The three of us were friends,' recalls Frears. 'It was made under these absolutely idiotic union conditions. We would sit in Bangkok and every night they'd work out the work rosters in London. To make a film the other side of the world you need flexibility. But you were doing really good work and these films would get huge audiences.'

During her brief return to Thames, Verity was as eclectic as ever in her choices and this was reflected in *Storyboard*, a set of one-hour dramas, all with the potential to be turned into series. Among these was *Lytton's Diary*, which dramatised the life and misadventures of a Fleet Street gossip columnist. This was an idea cooked up by its star, Peter Bowles, who was terrified of being typecast as a light-entertainment actor as a result of his success in enormously popular sitcoms like *Only When I Laugh* and *To the Manor Born*. 'John Frankau commissioned *Lytton's Diary* and then he left,' explains Bowles. 'So I took Verity out to lunch and pitched it to her instead. She liked it very much so we were back in business. She was very honest and she treated me as an equal. You come across people who think, "He's just a bloody actor," but you didn't get that feeling from Verity at all. I suppose it goes back in a strange way to the fact that we'd both shared the experience of *Underground* when we were both young.'

Realising that he needed a writer to turn his concept into a pilot, Bowles suggested Ray Connolly, who had the necessary background in journalism. Verity approved.

Everything she commissioned tended to be driven by her interest in a particular writer's work. She had long admired John Finch, who had devised *Rooms* for Thames, as well as a series of long-running and intelligent dramas for Granada. 'She said she would like me to do a series,' recalls Finch, who promptly devised *The Hard Word*, which followed the consequences of sudden redundancy in two families. It was exactly the kind of topical subject matter that interested Verity and she ordered a series of six. Alas, Finch did not get on with Michael Chapman, the producer she chose for it, and resigned from the production after writing the first episode. 'I felt very sad about this,' he says, 'as I had a great respect for Verity. She was very supportive of writers and I felt I had let her down.'

The Hard Word was worthy and deserving but unlikely to deliver the kind of ratings that Thames relished. It had to be accompanied by a safe bet – something popular, middlebrow and guaranteed an audience. Verity recalled the impact of one of the early *Armchair Thrillers*, *Quiet as a Nun* by Antonia Fraser, a writer whom she liked. She decided to commission a series using the same leading character, *Jemima Shore Investigates*, although the part was recast with Patricia Hodge taking over from Maria Aitken. This was produced by Tim Aspinall, who had a long track-record and whom Verity had brought into Thames during her previous stint.

She openly adored Aspinall, who had all the characteristics she found most attractive in a man. He was extremely bright, witty, gifted, and his natural sense of fun and exuberance were easily matched by her own. Like her, he loved cooking and was passionate about wine, travel and football. 'He was very much his own man,' says the writer and creator of *Born and Bred*, Doug Livingstone. 'And not a "company" man. She was never a "company" woman either. Although the first series of *Born and Bred* went well, I had not always seen eye to eye with the producer, and when the second series came round Verity said she knew exactly who I should work with and put me on to Tim. We hit it off at once and became good friends. I never met anyone who didn't like him. He was a first-rate producer, but he also had an irreverence which made him great fun to work with. Verity was very close to him. She was a regular visitor to Tim and his wife Mary's little terraced house in Shepherd's Bush and seemed very at home there. Mary was a large, bubbly Junoesque woman who towered above Tim. The writer Richard Harris used their "odd" physical combination as the role-model for two of the leading characters in his highly successful stage play and TV series, *Outside Edge*.

'Unfortunately Tim and Mary could not have children so they decided they would adopt a child from a poorer country. They bypassed bureaucracy by taking themselves off to South America, finding a little orphan girl in need of a home and bringing her back, challenging immigration to stop them, which they didn't. They were so happy with the child that a couple of years later they went back and got another. Verity loved this attitude to life and to work, which was, for both of them, that it should always be first-class, but fun. And she seemed to really enjoy the off-beat domesticity of their home life.'

Verity was now a senior, highly respected and sometimes feared 'player' of British television. Keeping her morbid anxieties about flying firmly at the back of her mind, she criss-crossed the world as part of the community of top executives, all selling, showcasing and schmoozing. 'We convinced the Thames board,' explains Linda Agran, 'that we were so busy, in order to do business in New York we had to go by Concorde. Of course, we'd start drinking in the airport – Verity would never let an opportunity to drink something good go by. When we got on Concorde, they served Krug and a very good claret, so we'd swing off the plane at the other end – and go straight into shoe shops – she loved shoes – oh God, it was such a laugh! I had the hair, she had the legs! She had a real appetite for life.'

'We were at Cannes once,' recalls Ted Childs, 'at one of those sales things. Me and Verity and another ITV executive, Andy Allen, with whom she was very friendly. We were all standing around bored so we went to lunch and got totally arseholed. When we'd finished, they both turned on me and said, "Go and get the car." I couldn't find it for ages and eventually when I did, Verity was standing there on the pavement, shouting, "Where the fuck have you been?" She was larger than life in many ways. As someone once said, "She had more front than Selfridges."'

International award ceremonies became another fixture of Verity's crowded calendar. David Reid was among a party of television drama executives summoned to Milan to serve as judges for the esteemed Prix Italia awards. 'I was about to leave the airport,' he says, 'when I realised that there was an almighty row going on behind me. Alitalia had managed to lose Verity's luggage and she was screaming blue murder; threatening to kneecap anyone who came within range. Her anger simmered on for hours until it struck her that her travel insurance would surely pay out. Accordingly, the next day or so were taken up with ransacking Valentine, Missoni, Gucci and so on for anything she fancied.'

Shopping was an abiding passion and, wherever she was in the world, Verity always found time to hunt for gifts, souvenirs, antiques, fine art, good clothes and, most of all, expensive shoes. Her motto was 'No kiosk too small' and she had a magpie eye for quality and eclectic tastes, drawn to anything unusual from silk scarves in brilliant colours to jewellery that was quietly expensive but rarely showy. 'For her, shopping was like sightseeing,' says her friend, journalist Reggie Nadelson. 'She never went on a trip where she didn't come back with stuff.'

'She had the same eye in clothing that she had for scripts,' says another friend, the Oscar-winning film-writer, Nancy Dowd, 'which was for the authentic; the real and the good. She wasn't going to go out and buy some piece of froufrou. She'd spend a hell of a lot of money on something which she thought was good. And I really admired that about her. About the time glasses frames began to go designer, there was a shop in LA called LA Eyeworks. I said, "Look, there's a sale on Saturday. It's a madhouse but they really discount the frames." So we went and the two of us bought so many frames that everyone in the store gave us a cheer when we left. It was fabulous. Purely superficial but fabulous.'

'She liked designer stuff but preferably in a sale,' recalls her close friend Kate Kagan. 'We used to go to the first sale day of places like Yves Saint Laurent and Chanel. There was something very endearing about Verity – she used to say to the girl, "Have you got that in a size 44?" and the girl would say, "No, madam, this is too big for you," and they'd argue and then the girl would go off and get it and Verity would try it on and it would be too big. I used to say, "These women know." With most people it would be the other way around. She'd say, "Well, I'm quite big you know." But she always looked so good.'

'Although she bought a lot of elegant designer things,' agrees another close friend, Viv Phillips, 'she was thrilled by a bargain and would tell me, "Look what I got at M&S," or "It was only so and so, reduced from so and so."'

In 1981, Verity bought a holiday apartment in Antibes, in the South of France, conveniently close to Cannes, the location for the famous film festival and key television trade shows. Set deep in the ramparts of the old town, the tiny two-bedroomed flat was blessed with magnificent views across the bay and beyond to the sea.[17] From time to time, Verity could escape here and assume a simple life of haggling for whatever caught her eye in the market, lying on the beach, cooking dinner in the flat or venturing out to favourite restaurants. She enjoyed day trips to Monte Carlo (watching the Grand Prix was a passion), driving through the narrow lanes of French villages and towns with reckless abandon, always eager to be where she wanted to be, getting on with the next adventure.

'She was a slightly terrifying driver,' smiles Felicity Marshall, one of the many friends who stayed with Verity in Antibes. 'I remember when we had to catch a flight back to London at something like four in the morning. I thought we were going to die because she drove like a bat out of hell. We were going down this narrow street and there was this road sweeper with a Gitane in the corner of his mouth. He was taking his time sweeping this very narrow street and she was gesturing for him to get out of the way and letting fly with various French expletives. He just gave her the finger so, in the end, she forced her way through and scraped the rental car all down the side. The man was chasing after us waving his fist.'

---

[17] The flat was found for her by Peggy Taylor, an affluent friend who also had a home in the area

At home and abroad, Verity's diary was peppered with industry committees, award shows, festivals and showcases. Her social life just as demanding and she embraced a routine of long days and late nights. She was eminently qualified for the rigours of this unrelenting lifestyle. Her stamina was combined with a gregarious nature and ability to connect in an instant with those to whom she felt some curiosity or attraction. 'We would gang up at television gatherings,' says writer and presenter Melvyn Bragg. 'I found her always witty and keen to tease out your ideas. I remember thinking that, behind all this apparent ease, she must be very patient – putting such big productions together. Like a lot of very high-level people, she had an intellectual short-hand. It means you can get so much more done.'

Her public profile was in the ascendant, too. There was a steady stream of requests for interviews and quotes from newspapers and magazines. Invitations to participate in television and radio programmes were just as frequent. Verity accepted many of them, enjoying the frisson of stepping in front of the camera and always happy to air her views. On 21 February 1981, she made the first of several appearances on the BBC's television review programme, *Did You See...?* to discuss two new dramas, the BBC's *Nanny*, STV's *A Sense of Freedom* and Barry Norman's *Film '81*. Her fellow guests were *Panorama* reporter Tom Mangold and Cambridge lecturer Colin MacCabe. Verity liked both *A Sense of Freedom* and *Film '81* but she didn't spare *Nanny*. 'A good idea that's gone very wrong,' she said. 'Nanny Gray is so totally perfect and I find her rather smug and irritating and everyone else in the series is a kind of caricature. The children are monstrous until she lulls them into being nice little creatures and the parents are either batty or terrible and shouldn't be allowed to have children or even be let out of a lunatic asylum. I think it's completely lost touch with any kind of reality.'

'She absolutely hated it,' says MacCabe, 'and I was saying how good it was. But we got on like a house on fire.'

This chance encounter was the start of another lasting friendship though, typically, Verity never forgot that first disagreement over the merits or otherwise of *Nanny*. 'It was an argument that went on for about ten years,' he laughs. 'She took no prisoners but she really appreciated it if you fought back.'

Among her plethora of professional obligations, Verity was then the chairman of the production board of the British Film Institute. Fairly soon after she had met MacCabe, she put him up to become a member. 'The production board was the vehicle for funding low-budget experimental films by newcomers,' he explains, 'chaired by an industry stalwart with a range of people on it from business and also film critics which was the heading I came under. She was extremely straightforward and almost unbelievably without pretension. She engaged with everyone very directly and she was very open. She would consider anything but would also give her views very forthrightly. She had to juggle the board and a head of production who reported to her and she did that extremely well – with a wide ranging catholic taste and a real belief in excellence and letting people have their head.

'I met her when I was a full-time academic, wanting to become a film producer and she was really the person who gave me the first step on that way. I doubt whether I would have had my career as a film producer without her. She was enormous fun – very witty and a great commentator on life both in the media and more generally. You always knew you were going to laugh and eat and drink well with her. She was really her own woman. She thought for herself and her views on everything were worth listening to. She made one feel that life was worth living.'

When MacCabe's youngest son, Finn, was born, Verity was invited to be godmother. She agreed and took the responsibility seriously. 'He has very fond memories of her,' says MacCabe.[18]

He wasn't alone. Verity formed meaningful and lasting connections with many of her friends' children. Although she generally insisted that she didn't want children herself, and that babies in particular bored her, she was invariably good with them.

'Verity was extremely warm,' says Doug Livingstone's son, Rusty. 'She was very tactile with me and I got on hugely well with her and had quite a special bond with her.'

'She saw my children at intervals growing up,' says one of her oldest friends, Marilyn Gross. 'She always talked to them one-on-one and they all loved her and appreciated her.'

'In her generation,' points out Reggie Nadelson, 'it was quite unusual for a nice Jewish woman not to have children. She just thought there were better things to do.'

'I don't know how maternal I am,' Verity herself told the writer Sophia Watson. 'I like children in small doses but not having had a child I don't know what having a child would do to change that. I don't get broody.' She did, however, go on to admit that 'if I have any regrets it's about not having a child in my twenties.'[19]

'I think she would have liked children,' believes Graham Benson. 'I think she was very touched when she went to visit people with families. She was wonderful with other people's children. She adored my daughter and it was mutual.'

Linda Agran disagrees. 'I genuinely don't think that she wanted children. There was no room in her life for anything else but when you're doing something that wonderful, that fulfilled and that committed, it's worth it.'

'I think she saw children as a real pain in the neck and bloody hard work,' says close friend Viv Phillips. 'She could well do without that.'

---

[18] Verity left him a substantial sum of money in her will

[19] Quoted in *Winning Women* (see bibliography)

When Verity had married Colin Bucksey, they had agreed that children were not on the agenda. But, with the passing of time, he no longer felt quite the same. It was one of the insidious and growing barriers between them. There is no doubt that Verity still loved her husband but such were the ceaseless demands of her life that she saw too little of him for the relationship to avoid damage. He was himself intent on developing his own career as a director, anxious to be judged for his own, undeniable merits. 'She helped him get work,' says Graham Benson, 'but the downside was that he was never taken as seriously.'

Verity remained essentially the same person she had always been but Bucksey was getting restless and impatient within the confines of their marriage. The ten-year age difference had started to become an issue. 'It didn't matter to me at the beginning,' says Bucksey himself. 'She was very important developmentally when I was younger because her life experience was greater than mine but, as time went on, I changed more as a person and that became a problem in our relationship – not for her but for me.'

'Colin was jealous of Verity,' says Doug Livingstone, 'and he put her down publicly from time to time.'

'I think it was worse than snubs,' sniffs Verity's close friend, Sheila Savory, in obvious distaste.

'It was a stormy period,' says Graham Benson. 'In a way it was a tribute to our friendship that they were prepared to argue in front of me.'

'There was an incident,' recalls director Waris Hussein, 'when he got drunk and I heard what he really felt about upper middle-class women in the same category as Verity. He was full of anger and that only comes out when somebody's not in control of their emotions. It stuck with me because I thought, "Well, this is what I've felt all along." I certainly couldn't tell her what I'd heard. You couldn't report any negatives on him. I kept myself out of it.'

'They were an odd couple,' allows Lynda La Plante, 'Some people may have found it strange to see this great champion producer being told that her Yorkshire pudding was flat – but Verity liked it because it brought her down to being an ordinary wife. She would be in such a state in the kitchen. He would be standing there in his carpet slippers.'

'It was like *A Star Is Born*,' says Nancy Dowd. 'When she was married, because she was such a star, people called him Mr Verity Lambert. He didn't treat her very well. I found him to be very nice and I never shared in the communal trashing that went on but I think a lot of people felt that he just wasn't up to her standard.'

'I could see the relationship was beginning to have an awful lot of tension,' says writer Howard Schuman. 'They both drank a lot. Whatever was going on, to be close to either Verity or Colin then was difficult and I was close to them both.'

Both of them belonged to a business in which fidelity was the exception rather than the rule. 'Neither of them were angels,' is how Kate Kagan tactfully puts it but their dalliances inevitably eroded the trust and affection within an increasingly fragile relationship. The couple moved from the big four-storey house in Lisgar Terrace to a spacious apartment in Addisland Court, a handsome Art Deco block in fashionable Holland Park. The decor was Deco to match[20], and every room was a design statement. But the new address did not represent a fresh start.

As her marriage ailed, her career took another dramatic leap forward. In October 1982, it was announced that Verity would be the new director of production at Thorn EMI Films, with a place on the board. Although she would relinquish her responsibilities at Thames, she planned to combine the new job with remaining as chief executive at Euston, a colossal undertaking even by her standards. It was only possible because Thorn EMI owned 48 per cent of Thames and so there was already a degree of symbiosis between the companies. It would be up to Verity to make it work. Her track record meant that the move was positively reported as a step in the right direction to halt what then seemed to be a terminal decline in the fortunes of the British film industry. At 46, she had become its first major female executive. It was a laudable achievement and one that came with all the trappings of power – a vastly increased salary, a company car, expense account, brand new offices and a hand-selected team. Verity confidently signed a three-year contract and, as was her way, looked forward to her next round of challenges and triumphs. But what was to follow would instead undermine her confidence, frustrate her utterly and, both personally and professionally, prove the most miserable time of her life.

---

[20] Verity gave the job of remodelling the flat to the partner of Graeme McDonald, the head of BBC drama serials and an old friend

CHAPTER TEN

ON THE ROCKS

1982–1983

'I have to get some kind of buzz from the script or idea. I have to feel...before I even look at it in any kind of detail, I have to respond in some kind of way, emotionally, instinctively, if you like, to what is being put forward.'

Verity to Edward de Bono, *Tactics: The Art and Science of Success,* 1985

In the same year that Verity was making headlines with her appointment as director of production for Thorn EMI films, a small but significant piece of her television past was about to catch up with her and prompt newspaper stories of a far less positive nature. The long-drawn-out saga of the *Rock Follies* case would embroil her in unflattering accusations of professional theft, and personal accusations of bullying and high-handed behaviour with those whom she sought to control. It took seven years for the case to reach the courts and several months to resolve the dispute. In order to try to understand what happened, and the extent to which Verity was complicit, it is necessary to retrace the steps of the series, to examine what went so badly wrong during its birth and discover why such a singular success, for Thames Television, and for Verity herself, became the source of such bitter legal action.

In the London of the late 1960s and early 1970s, the world of the professional theatre was a closely connected community of actors, musicians, singers and dancers, mostly scraping a living, competing for jobs, sometimes appearing in the same shows, sharing houses and flats, and finding friends and lovers. In 1968, the hottest show in the West End was the modish hippy musical *Hair*. Annabel Leventon, then 26 years old, was one of the standout performers in a company that dazzled with exciting new talent, including Tim Curry, Elaine Paige, Paul Nicholas, Oliver Tobias and Richard O'Brien. Leventon struck up a friendship with another actress in the show, 21-year-old Diane Langton, and met her musician boyfriend, Don Fraser, through the show's master carpenter.

A few years later, in 1973, Leventon was living with Fraser, and thinking of her next step in showbusiness. Since her time in *Hair*, she had worked fairly steadily and won some good reviews, but a truly significant breakthrough had so far eluded her. In search of this, she decided to form a two-girl group. But Fraser told her, 'You've got to have three girls for the harmonies.'

'Apart from the technical thing of having to do the harmonies,' says Fraser, 'I think what was really at the back of Annabel's mind was that it was very difficult for women to be singers *and* actresses. The whole concept was to take the three-girl group and be able to explore that and the issues that came with it.'

At an audition for the musical *Pippin*, Leventon bumped into Gaye Brown, an actress she'd met some years earlier in rep. Brown liked the idea of an all-girl band and suggested Diane Langton, who was playing the lead in *Pippin,* as the third member. Langton was enthusiastic and so the band was formed with Don Fraser as their composer and manager. They called themselves Rock Bottom, a wry nod to their position in the industry. 'We were all completely different,' explains Annabel Leventon. 'Gaye was upper-class, an ex-debutante, six feet tall, and, according to Cliff Richard, had the loudest voice in England without a microphone. Diane was working-class with short, curly black hair and I was blonde, Oxford-educated, middle-class, Scottish and Jewish. We were all of us a bit rebellious and not quite able to play the game. I've not ever been very good at toeing the party line which militates against you. Conforming was a very important part of life then, especially for women. We'd got this big plan. First of all we were going to write some songs, get a recording contract and release a couple of singles. Then we were going to do an album and some live concerts. Then we were going to do a television series about ourselves and then we were going to go to America and conquer the world. It was the Spice Girls but decades ahead.'

They were only too aware that realising such overarching ambition was going to be a challenge. 'Women in their thirties did not sing rock 'n' roll or form bands,' smiles Leventon. 'We were well over the hill and we had bravura figures, shall we say? We didn't look right. People said, "You can't do that." And we said, "We're doing it – what's your problem?"'

While they were working on songs and putting the stage act together, they talked about the kind of television series they had in mind for themselves. The main inspiration was *The Monkees*, a mid-60s light-hearted American film series based on the antics of a manufactured boy band with more than a touch of the Beatles about them. 'It was going to be half-hour episodes with songs,' continues Leventon, 'and it wasn't going to be heavy [and] political, it was going to be more fun.'

'We were floating ideas,' adds Don Fraser. 'It could have gone any particular way – it could have gone the light-entertainment route or there was even talk of just doing some little ten-minute films, like the beginnings of MTV but with some kind of storyline.'

Together with Fraser, they kicked around some ideas for who might write a television series for them. Leventon had studied at the London Academy of Music and Dramatic Art and among her contemporaries was the actress Maureen Lipman, with whom she had been on friendly terms. By now, Lipman was married to the writer Jack Rosenthal, who had recently enjoyed huge success with his gentle comedy series *The Lovers*; 'Don and I said he'd be perfect,' recalls Leventon, 'because he was so funny and warm. So he and Maureen came to dinner and we talked to Jack and he thought about it.'

'Jack said, "Look, girls, this isn't my scene,"' remembers Maureen Lipman, 'and he suggested Howard Schuman instead.'

It was an eminently logical thought. Although, at this stage, Schuman had little in the way of a reputation as an established writer, he was already well-known to the putative group and their manager. In the autumn of 1973, director Piers Haggard had cast Leventon in Schuman's very first television play, *Verité*, an entry in Thames' long-running *Armchair Theatre*. This followed the emotional chaos inflicted by Mik (Tim Curry), a young experimental film-maker from New York, who is staying with an English couple while working on his latest movie, a dark vision of London. The couple – Clive (Richard Morant) and Shirley (Annabel Leventon) – react in very different ways to Mik's presence and the various misfits he introduces into their staid lives. Clive embraces the American's influence but Shirley, a study of middle-class repression, resists.

'It felt like a gem because it was so now,' says Haggard. 'Howard is American and a foreigner can give you a fantastic piercing-eye view of a zeitgeist in someone else's city. Annabel was good and strong and truthful in it.'

When she got the part, Leventon celebrated by going out to dinner with her boyfriend, Don Fraser. 'We bumped straight into Tim Curry,' says Leventon, 'who was also going to be in *Verité* and was already a great friend from our time in *Hair*. He introduced us to Howard Schuman. "I'm going to be doing your play," I said. "Who have you got doing the music for your songs?" And he said, "I haven't got anyone," so Don wrote the music for him.'

'We went to my publisher's office,' says Fraser. 'I sat at the piano and he gave me the lyrics. We worked at it and I think we had one or two songs down pretty quickly.'

Although Schuman was still a relative unknown, he had acquired an important sponsor in Andrew Brown, then working as a story editor within the Thames drama department. Brown had been introduced to Schuman's writing by a colleague, June Roberts, and both felt that his was a major new talent. 'He was unique, original and funny,' says Roberts.

Having sold two plays to Brown, Schuman was keen to follow them up with his first attempt at a full-scale series. 'I went to Andrew in something like November 1973,' he recalls, 'and explained that I'd like to do a six-parter about women who want to become a rock group. I'd been interested in this theme for years. I still have a treatment for a musical called *Stars*, which I wrote years before and was basically the script for what became episode one of *Rock Follies*. And [television critic] Chris Dunkley wrote a review of another of my plays, *Censored Scenes from King Kong*, in which he said you could see the seeds of what became *Rock Follies*.'

Schuman is anxious to establish a chronology for his idea because of all the acrimony and dissent that followed. What no one disputes is that, on 22 January 1974, a meeting took place between Schuman and Leventon to discuss the possibility of a series. 'Annabel took me to lunch,' he recalls, 'and told me that they'd approached Jack Rosenthal to do something a bit like *The Monkees* for their real-life rock group, Rock Bottom, which wasn't even performing yet. He didn't want to do it. "Would you want to do it?" she asked me. I said, "I'm about to be commissioned to do a six-parter," and I explained how I wanted it to be about the disillusionment of the 70s. She said, "That sounds very heavy..."'

'Howard was too surreal for us,' admits Leventon. 'His work spirals off into an air of unreality. Our series wasn't going to be like that, it was going to be women bursting the doors of the music business open, going out there, doing it and not having to explain or excuse – more fun.'

According to Schuman, given the obvious difference of their respective approaches to the idea of a series about an all-girl rock group, he told her, 'I'm going to move with my project and if you want to try and get your half-hour off the ground, that's great.'

Leventon, her bandmates and boyfriend and manager Don Fraser were writing their own songs and looking for a writer to bring life to their embryonic television series. Barry Mason, songwriter of a string of top-ten hits, was one suggestion but this led nowhere. Gaye Brown thought of a drama producer, Brian Degas, who had just made the very successful *Colditz* for the BBC. In May 1974, a meeting was arranged. 'Wherever we went, it was like an extended audition,' explains Leventon. 'We were very naive but Brian said, "OK, I've got it. This is how I think it will work. We'll do half-hour episodes, like you do with a comedy series – we'll put you in a room together with three stenographers and we'll pick themes like, say, marriage, children, rock 'n' roll and we'll just set you free. Then we'll get it transcribed and have a really good script editor clean it up and put it into episodes and you will own it then, it's your material." But just before our first concert, he went off to America so none of it was finalised.'

Almost precisely at the same time that Rock Bottom were touting their series to Brian Degas, Andrew Brown was introducing Howard Schuman to Verity, who was just about to take over the Thames drama department and hungry for ideas. He outlined the concept for a six-parter based on a girl group and their fight to establish themselves in the unforgiving climate of the music industry. 'Verity liked it immediately,' he says. It met her principal requirement for a strong contemporary theme and nothing like it had ever been attempted before. Neither was it lost on her that the series would showcase women and this appealed to her newly awakened feminist sensibilities too.

As the summer went on, Rock Bottom were busy rehearsing, perfecting their act and their signature 'look', which was camp, theatrical and fashionably glam, all platform boots and big curly hair. With the prospect of a TV show on the horizon, they had been signed to major record label RCA, who paid for the recording of a couple of singles. The first, *Tambourine Queen*, was scheduled to be released at the end of October. Schuman provided the lyrics for the B-side, *Memory Lane*. Meanwhile, he was hard at work on a script for an opening episode to his series. 'I had gotten it working,' he says, 'and they had their first performance. I said, "I'll bring Andrew and Verity to see you," and that's what happened. Andrew and Verity liked them.'

'Andrew came bounding up, terribly excited, saying, "It's marvellous,"' says Leventon.

According to Don Fraser, Verity's interest was piqued by her innate sense of competition. 'We were floating the idea out there,' he explains. 'It was certainly on the table with Philip Jones, who was the head of light entertainment at Thames, just down the corridor from Verity. I think this was one of the things that kicked her into action.'

By August, Schuman had secured the group's permission to act as their spokesman with Thames and to pitch the idea of a series. Not unnaturally, the fledgling band felt that they were getting ever closer to the fulfilment of their television dream. Given that Andrew Brown, who had formally brought the idea to Verity, was then working for Stella Richman Productions (producing *Jennie: Lady Randolph Churchill*), a deal was done so that Richman's company would receive royalties from any eventual series. The project was now given the working title *Rock Bottom*.

On 4 October 1974, Verity chaired a long meeting with the band and Thames' head of casting, Liz Sadler[1]. 'They were very friendly,' recalls Leventon. 'I think Verity was seriously interested in us. For a time, I think she thought she was going to do it with us but then she didn't think she would have any trouble with us.'

'She was enthusiastic and put on her charm,' adds manager Don Fraser, who arrived a little after the main conversation had taken place. Some important principles were agreed. Verity made it clear that she was commissioning Schuman to write a first script and that, on the basis of this, both parties could then decide if they wished to proceed with the series proper. This crucial decision was to be made in December, the deadline to which Schuman was working. In the meantime, and conscious that the first Rock

---

[1] Curiously, all the court documents erroneously refer to Sadler as 'Dee' rather than 'Liz Sadler'

Bottom single was imminent, Verity sanctioned a payment of £500 to the group to ensure that they kept the whole concept absolutely confidential. The other conditions were that, should a series then proceed, the band would not demand exorbitant 'pop star' salaries, beyond the reasonable means of a television company, nor would they accept any engagements in competing television comedies or dramas during this same period.

'We had to agree that if we became overnight pop sensations, we would still only expect fees as actresses,' explains Leventon, 'so that their budget wouldn't be overstretched. When Verity said, "I don't want this getting out and I don't want you doing anything else as a group in television – it will kill our development", we said, "What if we go on the Russell Harty show as a group?" "Oh that's fine," and Di – who was always very anxious about her solo career – added, "Excuse me, are you saying that I can't do any work of my own while we're waiting to see if you're going ahead?" and Verity said, "No, no, any solo work is absolutely fine – I just don't want a similar project being developed by somebody else in case they get there first and we put all this time and money and effort into it."'

During this breakthrough meeting, all three artists also agreed that, should they decide that they didn't wish to appear in the series themselves, that Thames would be at liberty to recast and go ahead without them. 'I was very surprised that she let the contract get signed with this clause,' says Fraser, 'because by agreeing that the girls would have first refusal for the series, it encapsulated our ownership of the idea.'

With the paperwork agreed, a lull followed. 'We waited and waited,' sighs Leventon. 'Howard wouldn't talk to us. He'd had trouble with the script.'

Schuman's problems with the debut script are documented in chapter seven but the net result was the December deadline came and went without anything by which everyone involved might judge the essential decisions. At first, Thames simply extended the option, at a cost of an additional £250, to the end of January 1975. Then, on 7 February, Don Fraser agreed that the option could remain open without further payment until the company were in receipt of a workable script. This arrived shortly afterwards and Verity promptly commissioned the remaining five. She decided to put the series into production in the September of that year and, accordingly, each of the actresses' agents were contacted by Liz Sadler to begin negotiations for their contracts to appear in it. Another problem now presented itself.

During all the stalling, Diane Langton had accepted a major part in a West End production of Stephen Sondheim's *A Little Night Music*, which was due to open in April. Her agent attempted to persuade the producers to release Langton but they refused. Sadler now contacted Fraser and said that, in Thames' view, Langton's theatre engagement represented a breach of the original agreement. She demanded that he repay the £750. Instead, he offered to do his best to secure Langton's release from the musical. On 9 April, Verity wrote to him, enclosing a copy of the first script and stating unequivocally that Thames would be unable to work round Langton's schedule of evening and matinée performances and that, if the group were to be cast as a unit, Langton would need to leave the theatre production by the middle of August.

A few weeks earlier, Verity also had a meeting with Fraser and Howard Schuman's agent, Jenne Casarotto, to discuss the potential merchandise associated with the series. Although the first Rock Bottom single had failed to break the charts, it had obviously not benefited from the might of exposure which a TV tie-in would deliver. It was evident to everyone that, given the project was a success, there was a range of lucrative possibilities from the obvious tie-ins of records and tours to branded clothing and other potential souvenirs. When it came to music and recording rights, it was agreed that anything using the name Rock Bottom would be the property of the group. But the meeting was not harmonious.

'For some reason,' says Leventon, 'Verity was in quite a bad mood. She said, "OK, we'd better sort out the rights on this – what are the deals?" Don said, "Well, I can tell you what we own - we own the name, the idea – we'll have a say in any merchandising, we'll own the music because we'll be writing it." At which point Jenne Casarotto said, "What's Howard going to have?" and Don said, "Howard will have rights in the scripts that he's written but this is our idea. He's writing for us and for Thames. He won't own the idea or the songs that we write." Verity went, "What do you mean, you'll have a say in the merchandising?" I think she thought, "I can't be fucked around with here – I'm not having this. I can't have people on the rehearsal floor saying, 'I don't really like the way this scene is going.'"'

'I was bringing in a considerable sum of money from the record company,' points out Don Fraser. 'It was going to be at least £100,000 in sound budget alone. That was when things began to go awry. I don't think Verity was particularly happy with a 24-year-old punk coming in with probably more cash in the project than she had. That began to be the tenor of the meetings – I felt that I wasn't being listened to and I wasn't being allowed to be what I was going to have to be – a partner in this production.'

Nevertheless, negotiations continued. On 5 May, Verity discussed the situation with Liz Sadler, Andrew Brown and Fraser. The major obstacle still appeared to be Diane Langton's contract to appear in *A Little Night Music*. Irritating though this undoubtedly was from a production point of view, there were plenty of precedents for actors combining theatre and television commitments, rehearsing, filming or recording during the day and appearing on stage in the evening. The biggest stumbling block was the matinée performances. Both Verity and Andrew Brown indicated that, should Fraser prove able to secure Langton's release from these, it would then be possible to work round the stage show. The following week, Fraser returned to Verity's office with disappointing news – he told her that he had been unable to contact the show's producer to discuss the situation.

Verity now lost her temper and gave vent to all her anger and frustration. It was not a dignified spectacle and the meeting ended in total disharmony. 'She was shouting at me and screaming about Di,' says Fraser. '"How dare she do this?" and she was very, very nasty about it and the fact that Di had a kid, saying we would have to drop her. She was hysterical, as was Andrew Brown. I was in the front line taking the bullets but I was also firing them back. While it was very unpleasant indeed, I knew that I had to stand up to this. I said, "Well, if you do this, we'll have to go to the lawyers," and Verity's last words to me were, "You can't sue me, I'm Thames Television."'

As soon as Fraser had left her office, Verity dictated a letter that issued him with a brutal ultimatum – unless she heard from him the following morning to confirm that Diane Langton could be made available for the series, she would have to recast. She must have been aware that this was an unrealistic demand, besides which the letter did not actually reach Fraser until the following afternoon.

Howard Schuman remembers that 'Annabel came to the house and said, "They want to get rid of us," and showed me this letter from Verity. I said, "Well, it's a funny letter to get rid of you – it's offering you the other two parts." Then I began to realise that they didn't really want to do my version. They thought they could shape my series into a kind of puff for Rock Bottom. I was shaping the characters to be the way I saw them. They were nothing like those women in real life. But I still wanted Annabel and Gaye at that point because there weren't a lot of suitable people around to play those kind of characters.'

'They offered it to Gaye and me,' agrees Leventon, 'but we were a *group*. This was about us and for us. How can you recast? Absolutely not. We refused because it wouldn't have been the group then. I can see it would have been very sensible to have said yes. But I couldn't have done that.'

'I think it would have been absolutely morally wrong to have dumped Di,' agrees Don Fraser. 'It was as much Di's work as anybody else's that had got us to this point. There was no way.'

Verity lost no time in authorising Liz Sadler to recast the entire show. 'She didn't want the old group,' says Jeremy Isaacs, then the director of programmes at Thames, and Verity's boss. 'She bumped them out. She didn't want to be running something that other people felt that they had run, would run, should run – she didn't want her power diluted. She wanted to do the thing the way she wanted it done. What she wanted was control.'

'I think she was deeply engaged in what it was going to be for *her*,' says Annabel Leventon. 'She had been brought in to transform the drama department and fast. She was under quite a lot of pressure so life can't have been easy. She needed that product so anything that got in her way had to be crushed. Verity could have talked to the producer of *A Little Night Music* herself. It could have been sorted in 15 minutes and we would have done the series. But she didn't and she never spoke to any of us again.'

'It was like, "Who are these people? They don't count,"' believes Don Fraser. 'I think at that point Verity understood that there were other big elements involved, including the record company and that we would have had to have some kind of equal input, the power struggle began.'

Rock Bottom the series was swiftly rechristened *Rock Follies*. 'Calling it that was a "Fuck you!"' says Fraser. It was Schuman who suggested Julie Covington to replace Diane Langton. Ironically, when Leventon was first entertaining ideas of forming a band, it had been Covington she had thought of asking to join her. The connection didn't end there – Don Fraser had arranged many of the tracks on Covington's first album. She took the part of Dee, and was joined by actresses Rula Lenska as Q and Charlotte Coleman as Anna. 'If you've seen any of *Rock Follies*, it would be immediately apparent,' sighs Leventon. 'Gaye Brown was called GB which turned into Q – not a big stretch – my character became Anna, instead of Annie, and DiDi, which was Diane Langton's name in the group, became Dee.

'They even got David Toguri, who had been our choreographer, to choreograph the series. It was so blatant – the fact that they didn't change the colour of our hair or our heights. Howard had been a really good friend but we were so totally betrayed by what happened. There were other things at work. He was very ambitious, he wanted to get established and I think Verity gave him a choice – "You either say this is yours and we go along with it or..." I don't know exactly what happened. It was decided behind closed doors.'

Although it was never a huge ratings winner, both series of *Rock Follies* delivered precisely what Verity had been looking for when she had first responded to the concept. Unlike anything else on British television at the time, it was innovative, imaginative, thought-provoking and occasionally spectacular. The first series won the coveted BAFTA award for Best Drama and the follow-up was nominated for seven further BAFTA awards, winning two of them (for best lighting and camerawork). Critics eulogised it and its fabulously inventive use of the medium. Its outstanding success hounded Annabel Leventon and deepened her devastation. 'I went back to acting and I was doing a season at the Bristol Old Vic. It went out on a Monday night – an odd slot for a very chancy thing – and so many people came into the green room the next morning saying, "Oh my God, did you see *Rock Follies* last night? It was so fantastic, so true, so lifelike" That was hard.'

'There was a sense of loss,' adds Don Fraser. 'I was certainly angry, as well as very sad, hurt and upset because it was something that we had worked very hard for that someone had taken from us. And at that point there was nobody listening. I couldn't go around saying it was my idea – nobody was going to believe you – you're just another wanker.'

'Think of amputation,' continues Annabel Leventon. 'Think of having a baby and having it adopted by force...I'm going to cry now.' Leventon does so, then rallies herself and adds, 'I was the one who said we're going to sue...'

Leventon remembered that one of her co-stars in *Hair*, Paul Nicholas, had a potentially useful legal connection. His father was Oscar Beuselinck, then one of the world's foremost media lawyers. Beuselinck's career dated back to the 1930s, when he had been involved in the leading libel case of Yussoupov versus MGM, in which the princely assassin of Rasputin, Felix Yussoupov, successfully sued the American film company for libel based on their presentation of his story in their film *Rasputin and the Empress*.

Leventon sought Beueselinck's advice. 'He said, "We're not having this – we'll sue!"' she recalls. 'I wanted to try to stop them going into the studio to record or even rehearse because then we would still have had some say in what happened to it.'

'I went to Oscar's office a day or two after the final Verity letter,' says Don Fraser. 'I sat down with one of the solicitors, Mark Wenbourn, who read through the papers and said that we must now get counsel's opinion and that I had to pay £150 to do this. The romantic in me thinks it came out of the Rock Bottom bank account, but may well have been mine. So off we went to see a Nick Strauss in Chambers. At this time we were only thinking about a breach of contract against Thames. It was Strauss who, having read all the papers, said that there was a case for breach of confidence more than a contractual issue although the breach of contract element was to be included in the writ. It was Strauss who said that Brown and Schuman should be included in the writ along with Thames TV. 50/50 win or lose ratio. The writ was issued fairly soon after this and we were all four of us cleared for legal aid.'

The risks, however, were acute. The group were advised that while they had a chance of success, it was an outside one. 'The other girls were devastated in their own way but would have let it go,' believes Leventon. 'Everybody said to me, "You'll never work in television again – you've not got a hope of winning this case, it will look like sour grapes, let it go and live your lives." If it had just been Verity, I'd have thought, "Oh, we've been outdone by big business. They've stolen something from us, that happens all the time," but it was dear to my heart – it was my baby and mattered hugely to me. The truth is that I felt so betrayed by a friend, Howard, it made me too angry to let it go. But I had no idea it would take years of my life.'

As the weeks turned into months, no further action was taken. Having performed just eight times, Rock Bottom split up, their recording contract with RCA evaporating with the loss of the series. Their second and final single, which had been released on Valentine's Day 1975, was the aptly-titled, *It's All Over*.

The stress of the situation ended the relationship between Don Fraser and Annabel Leventon. But, despite the constant advice that her obstinacy could damage or even end her career, Leventon refused to back down. 'It was very difficult,' she says. 'You have to get people engaged and believe that there's something there. Oscar didn't handle the case himself – he gave us a series of lawyers who weren't that engaged or interested. It was terribly lonely.'

'It was very difficult to maintain the momentum of it,' adds Don Fraser. 'The other side comes back and you think, "Perhaps they're right and I'm wrong?" There was a lot of doubt about the case but we just kept working at it. It was very hard. I nearly gave up at one point, about five years in. My dad sustained me through that. He said, "It doesn't matter if you win or lose but if you don't try, you'll never know."'

'I just felt that this was never going to come to court,' says Howard Schuman. 'There was a rumour while the first series was out that there might be legal action. But it never came to anything. Then it went to sleep.'

'I had nearly quit,' admits Leventon. 'But Oscar said, "No, wait a minute." We had a big conference and he introduced this 20-something blond boy and said, "Try him, give him a go, go on." – and it was Keith Schilling. Keith was just determined to get it – so instead of me harassing him, all of a sudden I had a running mate and that was brilliant.'

Given his inexperience, Schilling may have been something of a gamble but his appointment turned out to be an inspired last throw of the dice by Beuselinck. Schilling's intellect and expert analysis of the evidence entirely belied his youth. In the decades since, he has forged a formidable blue-chip career as one of the foremost lawyers in reputational law and matters of privacy. For Leventon and her fellow plaintiffs, his involvement in the *Rock Follies* dispute was the breakthrough they needed and his interpretation of the facts proved critical.

'We weren't going to fabricate anything,' says Don Fraser. 'That was an absolute moral principle on my part. Right or wrong, we were going to tell exactly what we felt happened from our point of view.'

The case of Fraser (and others) versus Thames Television (and others) finally opened in London's High Court on 14 June 1982 and, with a summer recess, the proceedings continued until 21 October. 'There had been all these rumours for a long time,' says Schuman, 'and I thought, "I'm finally going to hear their story." When I heard what they had to say, I knew I hadn't been lying to myself. But the judge had done a lot of music business cases and had seen a lot of people ripped off. We weren't underdogs – we were *overdogs*.'

One by one, all the principal witnesses were summoned and questioned by the barristers for both plaintiffs and defendants – among them Jack Rosenthal and his wife, actress Maureen Lipman. 'It was very awkward for Jack,' she says. 'Verity was a top producer whereas the three girls were never going to employ Jack or help him on the ladder to anywhere. But he was an honourable man and wasn't going to pretend for anybody. He knew that they had brought the idea to him before Howard Schuman. Where Verity and her cohorts fell down was in expecting their version of events to be taken for the truth. I think they put their heads together and thought, "Who the hell are these three girls? Who's going to believe them?" And let's face it, this idea is in the zeitgeist and there is a certain amount of truth in that. People do have similar ideas at the same time. I think they realised they had cocked up. It left a sour taste – and was slightly undignified. I think Annabel was brave because she had no money – none of the girls had any money – they were on legal aid and fighting the monolith. It really was a David and Goliath thing.'

The actor Nigel Hawthorne was called upon to give his expert opinion on whether it was feasible for a performer to work simultaneously on both a stage and a television production. 'He said, "Yes, it was very hard work,"' recalls Don Fraser. 'He was then asked the question, "And for whom did you do this?" He replied, "For Verity Lambert and for Andrew Brown on *Edward and Mrs Simpson*."'

Verity never forgave Hawthorne for what she viewed as his disloyalty.[2]

'Being in court was extraordinary,' says Annabel Leventon. 'It was like being on stage, as electric and intense – and as exciting. Very, very powerful. Being allowed to speak and be heard. I behaved very badly in court – I burst into tears, I kicked the witness box – but I got it all out.'

When it came to her turn in the witness box, an immaculately groomed Verity stuck resolutely to her version of events. 'She might have been a bit of a nail in the coffin,' says Jenne Casarotto, 'because she was so powerful. She did like to be totally in control and she did say what she thought and perhaps that wasn't smart.'

'She was slapped down by the judge on various occasions,' says Don Fraser, 'for not answering the questions particularly well. At one point she was pontificating about how things are done in television to which the judge just said, "That's nothing to do with the law, dear. Just answer the question." I can remember him slamming his books down and getting quite angry with her. That was very nice.'

Schuman felt let down by those friends of his who declined to testify in his favour because they did not want to get involved in such a high-profile dispute or those who did but were flustered and floundered when giving their evidence. Nowadays, witnesses are often given training in what to expect in court but this was not the practice in 1982.

'Verity loved our barrister because he was flamboyant and funny,' says Schuman, 'but he didn't really prepare us. As far as I was concerned it should really have been over about the second day because Annabel took the stand and said she came and approached me in the January of 74 – I'd already proved I'd had my idea before that. Somehow that got lost. The argument became was it their idea or not? Their only idea was a three-girl rock group. The option agreement did not make it absolutely clear that they were being signed

---

[2] She did eventually relent as far as Maureen Lipman was concerned and indeed Lipman eventually appeared in *Jonathan Creek*.

to do scripts that I had created so there was enough legal space to say it was their idea. At that point the most they would have gained was a share of £50 which is all I got for the concept. The case was just heard by a judge who I think had already made up his mind. We'll never know what would have happened if there had been a jury.'

'I don't know how Howard could have proved anything about any kind of idea before taking the stand,' says Don Fraser. 'He didn't do so until a couple of weeks in. Writers bring their ideas to any concept and I'm sure he's not wrong in his thinking in that sense but we were all involved. He was working with us. We were happy to share the idea. Verity Lambert, Andrew Brown and Howard Schuman were very happy *not* to share. The combined arrogance of the three of them was staggering but it was also their downfall.'

'Quite early in the courtroom I thought, "This is not going well. We're going to lose,"' says Jenne Casarotto. 'I was Howard's person but all I could think was that this doesn't make sense. His idea definitely existed before anybody had heard of the Rock Bottom girls. So how can they possibly say that it's based on them? But there were these hugely powerful television moguls against three poor women and it played well for them. I came out thinking, "We're doomed."'

'Howard went through the tortures of hell on that case,' believes director and friend Piers Haggard. 'He feels things desperately and he's not incredibly objective, sometimes bordering on the neurotic.'

'He is very emotional,' agrees Jenne Casarotto, 'and he did wear his heart on his sleeve. He was very upset. It was horrible.'

'All three of them – Verity, Andrew and Howard – were terribly distraught,' says close friend Kate Kagan. 'It was absolutely terrible. She was so upset, partly because it was so public and you know what barristers can be like.'

During the summer recess, Leventon was surprised to be offered a job by Thames Television, appearing in their situation comedy named, somewhat ironically, *Executive Stress*. 'At the read-through, I was amazed,' she says. 'People came out of the woodwork from places like accounts and said, "We couldn't say anything but we all knew you were telling the truth – good for you." There was so much good feeling.'

After the long weeks of evidence, enquiry and deliberation, when the judge, Mr Justice Hirst, finally delivered his conclusions, they represented a complete vindication for Leventon and her group. Verity did not emerge with any credit. Hirst held that she had known all along that the original idea belonged to Rock Bottom and that this was why she still wanted the right to use it if they decided not to take part in the eventual series. When it came to Diane Langton's commitment to *A Little Night Music*, he ruled that, rather than leaving negotiations to Don Fraser, Thames should have approached the show's producers directly and explored the possibility of working around the issue. Jeremiah

Harman, acting as QC for Thames, had tried to reason that Diane Langton's involvement in the musical amounted to a constructive refusal of the parts, thus justifying Thames' withdrawal from negotiations. But the judge entirely rejected this argument, considering that Don Fraser had been doing his best to solve the problem, with Thames' full knowledge.

The various accounts of Verity's incendiary behaviour during her final meeting with Don Fraser clearly did not impress the judge. Neither did he view favourably the patently unreasonable ultimatum she had sent Fraser on the matter of casting. In his judgement, this constituted a wrongful repudiation by Thames. The recasting, and subsequent recording and transmission of two series with different actresses, were all deemed to have constituted breaches of contract.

Much time was devoted to exploring the issue of confidentiality and to what extent this had been breached during the events surrounding the creation of the series. Broadly, the law of confidence provides that someone who receives information in confidence shall not take unfair advantage of it or profit from the wrongful use or publication of it. Harman accepted that the law of confidence is capable of protecting the confidential communication of an idea, but argued that a literary or dramatic idea cannot be protected unless it is fully developed in the form of a synopsis or treatment and embodied in permanent form. The judge did not share this view and concluded that there is no reason in principle why an oral idea shouldn't qualify for protection under the law of confidence, provided it is sufficiently developed, so that it would have some attractiveness as a TV programme and be capable of being realised. He did not consider that this requirement always necessitated a full synopsis, although there must be some element of originality not already in the realm of public knowledge. He was strongly influenced by the fact that, on both sides, every witness in the theatre or TV business agreed that, if they received an idea from another, it would be wrong to make use of it without the consent of the originator. He did, however, stress that not every stray mention of an idea could be protected.

Mr Justice Hirst concluded that Annabel Leventon's communication to Howard Schuman at the meeting on 22 January 1974 was clearly in confidence and was a professional occasion, as she was sounding him out as to whether he would like to write the series based on the idea. He relied on Jack Rosenthal's evidence to determine the idea's commercial attractiveness, its capability of realisation and its originality. He also relied on Howard Schuman's own undeniable success in turning the idea into a much-acclaimed TV series. Schuman, Andrew Brown and Thames Television were all held to be in breach of confidence in using the idea. On every count, the judge had accepted Annabel Leventon's account and those of her friends and associates, and found significant flaws in the defence.

'The judge's verdict was the best review I ever got,' says Leventon. 'Showbiz is littered with stolen work. I was telling the truth and I'm very, very proud of having stuck to it.

But once it was over, I was exhausted. I'd rolled a boulder uphill for eight years.'

'I was able to let all the anger and pain go,' says Don Fraser, 'because someone was listening to me. And that's all I really wanted – someone to listen to my side of the story and hopefully give me and the girls a reasonable share of the cake. But every one of us was wounded by the experience.'

For Verity, right at the cusp of her new career in feature films, the loss of the case meant a degree of public humiliation but in private she robustly maintained her view that the judgement was flawed. 'Once Verity believed something, she believed it,' says her PA at the time, Sharon Bloom. 'She thought that it was totally unfair.'

However bruised her ego or sense of justice, there is no evidence that the case caused Verity any professional harm. Neither was there any personal liability. Thames Television met the £100,000 costs and the eventual damages. But there can be no doubt that had she acted more circumspectly or more sensitively, the entire case might never have been brought to court. Her ability to act with sudden and utter ruthlessness may have, on occasions, been to her advantage. But with the debacle of the *Rock Follies* case, as with the messy and protracted legacy of her dispute with Irene Shubik, much pain and trouble resulted from it.

Whatever her motives, and it seems evident that she had clear reasons for denying Rock Bottom their one great chance, others bore the chief brunt of the consequences, not least her dear friend Andrew Brown, who suffered agonies of guilt throughout the proceedings, and Howard Schuman, the talent who had delivered her such a celebrated success. They were both remarkably forgiving.

'TV Rock Girls Win £250,000', screamed *The Sun* on 4 July 1983. 'Award for Forgotten Follies.' *The Daily Mirror* weighed in with 'Ditched girls win Damages Fortune', claiming the figure concerned to be £500,000. The exact details were kept confidential but the sums were considerable.

'It was so much money,' admits Annabel Leventon. 'Some of it was loss of enhancement of career, some of it was fees we would have earned if we had done the series. The deal was that we weren't to talk about it to the press. We were bought off, effectively. The money was nice but it didn't give me back my thirties, my group, my relationship. None of that could ever be given back, but what it did do was give back my self-respect because a High Court judge had heard me and heard them and believed me. By that time, Di and Gaye were both single parents with no visible means of support. I was able to buy a house and had enough put aside to go round the world and adopt a baby, Harry, and bring him up. I could never have done it without that money. It gave me a roof over my head and a future so it was a very wonderful outcome.'

'There were bitter moments, angry moments, sad moments, moments of regret,' says Don Fraser, 'but it's not all loss. I learnt a tremendous amount about life and production and I've been able to carry all those lessons into the rest of my life and career. The money meant that I had the ability to choose the work that I did for the rest of my life.'

Fraser eventually settled in America, where he has enjoyed a prestigious career as a record producer and conductor. He had one final encounter with Verity. 'It was years later,' he explains. 'I was at a Sunday lunch and she was there too. I deliberately sat down next to her. She was cold but she didn't move away. I have dogs and she had her Great Dane, so that's what we talked about.'

The credits of both *Rock Follies* and its sequel, *Rock Follies of '77*, were retrospectively amended to include the following acknowledgement: '*Rock Follies* was based upon an original idea of the Rock Bottom group: Don Fraser, Annabel Leventon, Gaye Brown and Diane Langton.'

'They had to have that,' says Howard Schuman, with a shrug. 'I would have shared the credit but I wrote the scripts – there's no question about that. The most positive thing that came out of it all was I hadn't talked to Andrew Brown for years. I saw him in the courtroom commissary and I quoted a line about friends from Stephen Sondheim's *Merrily We Roll Along*. He said, "Isn't that a wonderful song?" and we both burst into tears, holding our trays. Then we hugged and everything was OK again.'

'One has to accept that we created the idea for the TV series,' concludes Don Fraser. 'And that's what it says in the credit. That's what the judge said, that's what history says and that's the truth.'

But this conclusion effectively meant an end to any further exploitation of the *Rock Follies* concept. 'We could have done a musical, for instance,' says Jenne Casarotto, 'but because the Rock Bottom group now have a position and would now have to be credited and paid, quite understandably Howard said, "No, I'm not having that," so we couldn't take it any further.'

Whatever disappointment he felt about the case, 1983 was a busy year for Schuman, culminating in a lavish BBC production of his latest television play, *Videostars*[3]. The director was Verity's husband, Colin Bucksey, whose career had slowly but steadily advanced since his first TV work on *Couples* seven years earlier. 'I was very tentative about working with him,' admits Schuman. 'It had been his idea to put an earlier play of mine, *Censored Scenes from King Kong*, on stage, and to start with I was a bit reluctant. As we worked together, I realised that his strength wasn't necessarily directing the actors but he had a stunning visual conception, a strength and a tenacity and he helped make

---

[3] *Videostars* (BBC 06.12.83) employed several of Schuman and Bucksey's regular collaborators, including actors Tim Curry and Nicholas Ball, composer Andy McKay and choreographer David Toguri

it work as a piece of theatre[4]. By the time we worked on *Videostars* together, our relationship was very strong.'

The same could no longer be said for Bucksey's relationship with his wife. For some time, they had been co-existing rather than truly sharing their lives and they were now frequently at loggerheads, with friends speaking of 'mammoth, amazing' rows.

'We all change,' says Bucksey himself. 'I guess it would be fair to say that I probably did change more rapidly than she did. It wasn't to do with maturity. I'd say that we grew apart because of our work schedules. We were rarely in the same place. It's not great for a marriage. We were both intent on our careers and I think that blinkers you slightly to what is going on in your personal relationship.'

Verity was indeed busier than she had ever been, juggling the demands of her two executive positions at Euston Films and Thorn EMI, where the pressure was on from the start to prove herself and justify her colossal salary. 'That industry is very hard for a woman,' says her lifelong friend, Marilyn Gross. 'But the hours are only part of it. She knew how difficult it was to have the sort of career she had and maintain a marriage. She told me that when she got the Thorn EMI company car, a gleaming new Mercedes, she didn't want to diminish herself by not accepting it but when she saw Colin's face, she knew that was the beginning of the end.'

When he joined the BBC to direct *Videostar*s, as was the standard procedure of the time, Bucksey was assigned a production assistant called Sally Yapp. She was doing precisely the same job in which Verity had made her mark at ABC Television so many years earlier. Directors and production assistants had, by necessity, to work intimately and often for long hours with one another. Affairs and relationships were far from unusual. It had been exactly the same when Verity, as a dedicated young production assistant, had fallen in love with her *Armchair Theatre* director, Ted Kotcheff. The bitter irony that history was now repeating itself, only this time between her husband and another woman, would not have been lost on her. The affair between Colin Bucksey and Sally Yapp precipitated the end of Verity's marriage.

'I could see it happening,' says Howard Schuman. 'Verity was absolutely destroyed by it. They tried to reconcile at one point and my partner Bob has a cottage in the south of France – Colin and Verity were there, and I can remember Colin saying, "I'm going to try and make it go and I've been thinking about going to therapy" but it never happened. The reconciliation didn't stick. What surprised me, given my high regard for Verity on every

---

[4] The off-Broadway production of *Censored Scenes from King Kong* ran for only five performances in March 1980. During rehearsals, Verity had been very ill with a bout of meningitis. She was, however, determined to attend the opening night and was just well enough, although she had to be escorted to her flight in a wheelchair.

level – intellectually, politically, personally – was that she only blamed Sally. It wasn't Colin's fault. When she got drunk, she would refer to Sally in not very flattering tones. But Sally was so not a femme fatale.'

'I once said that I rather liked Sally,' recalls another of her inner circle, Kate Kagan, 'and it was almost like World War Three going off. It was awful. My husband Michael had to come in and be the referee.'

'She would never blame Colin,' agrees Verity's close friend, Sheila Savory. 'He was carrying on with that woman for quite some time and she was very hurt by him.'

'I think that she really was heartbroken,' says Jenne Casarotto, who was Bucksey's agent at the time.

'She was shattered, absolutely shattered,' sighs her Euston Films colleague and great friend, Linda Agran. 'She'd come around and drink and light a lot of fags and cry and then get on with the job.'

'She was devastated by the end of their marriage,' says another friend, Viv Phillips. 'I think it had a huge effect on her but she also had quite a lot of pride so she wouldn't have put it in those words. Although the shock penetrated very deep, she wasn't prepared to admit her vulnerability in herself; she wasn't prepared to say, "I don't know what I'm going to do without him." She would never had said things like that. She just soldiered on and put on a brave face and got on with her work. But she was terribly affected and always was. I don't think she ever stopped loving Colin.'

Those of Verity's friends and associates who met Sally Yapp were taken aback at how much she resembled a younger Verity. 'He obviously had a type,' sniffs Sheila Savory. 'It's the oldest story in time; a man trading in a woman for a younger model.'

A decade later, Verity was invited to appear on Eve Pollard's Radio 2 show. This was a kind of *Desert Island Discs*-lite, with Verity choosing music from various stages of her life that meant something to her.[5] One of the tracks she selected was *Jolene* by Dolly Parton. 'I love it because it's really very sad,' she told Pollard. 'It's about a woman whose husband leaves her for another woman. I just think there's something terribly tragic about a woman begging another woman to leave her husband alone and yet you know that it

---

[5] Her full choices were Nat King Cole's *Too Young*, Elvis Presley's *Heartbreak Hotel*, the theme to *Doctor Who* ('I was really thrilled the way it turned out'), The Everly Brothers' *All I Have to Do Is Dream* ('My theme tune almost. It's one of my favourite, favourite songs. Every time I hear it, it just makes me feel really good'), Randy Newman's *You Can Leave Your Hat On*, Maria Muldaur's *Midnight at the Oasis*, Ethel Merman's *You Can't Get a Man with a Gun* ('I'd love to be able to sing that song but I'm tone deaf'), The Rolling Stones' *Brown Sugar* ('I dance with myself in the mirror sometimes'), the *Rock Follies* cast singing *Glenn Miller Is Missing*, Dolly Parton's *Jolene*, Dory Previn's *Cold Water Canyon* and The Kinks' *Waterloo Sunset*

happens all the time and most women don't want to say that. There's something very touching about the song. I feel that women should stick together and quite often they do but sometimes they don't.'

'I think the only person she really spoke to about it was Andrew,' says Kate Kagan. 'She was very private and she would confide to the extent of saying how she felt emotionally and then she would suddenly clam up – she didn't like this thing of exposing herself and suddenly feeling vulnerable. When the marriage was splitting up, she went a bit funny. I know myself when things like that go wrong in life, you can go a bit funny. Andrew was a wonderful friend because he was always very protective, to the point that I couldn't get hold of her and she wouldn't return my calls. I thought, "What the hell?" I didn't even know what was going on at the time between her and Colin. And I called Andrew and he got all funny and I suddenly thought it was me – "Have I done something?" Then finally Andrew told me – not Verity – and he said to let her be and she'll come round and, thankfully, she did.'

Schuman was able to remain friends with both parties. 'She didn't put me in a position of having to choose,' he says, gratefully.

'I think that she that did hope that they might get back together,' believes producer Barry Hanson. 'She was always in love with him.'

Her hopes were to be disappointed and the inevitable divorce was finalised in 1987. 'She handled the divorce with incredible clarity,' according to writer Lynda La Plante. 'She said, "It's just…over."'

'I think the thing that Verity would have hated most was that she had failed at something,' says her then PA, Sharon Bloom.

Verity later told Suzie Mackenzie of *The Guardian*, 'I think that he needed someone to make him feel better than I could make him feel. Perhaps I was just too resilient and didn't make Colin realise how much I need him.'[6]

She admitted, too, that when a woman spends the best part of her day telling people what to do, it is tougher then to adapt to not being in sole charge at home. 'I think that's probably emasculating for men,' she commented. In 1989 she spoke to the writer Sophia Watson and expanded on the same theme, echoing Bucksey's own opinion about what fatally damaged their marriage. 'It is hard if the woman is a great deal more successful than the man but I think what's harder and almost more difficult is that when you've got a very high-powered job, you do work very hard – you have to – and that leaves you with less opportunity to do things together and spend time together because you're tired and

---

[6] *The Guardian* (31.10.90)

that accounts for quite a lot of problems. You both get involved with your own things and you cease to communicate with each other.'[7]

'I do remember once,' says Sharon Bloom, 'Verity had just come back from LA or somewhere, and Colin had come back from somewhere else and I heard her on the phone to him saying, "There's something in the freezer." I thought, "God, she's not going to go home and see him tonight," and I think she could have done – I don't think there were any work commitments that night. I wasn't critical of it; I just thought that's an odd way to run a relationship.'

Colin Bucksey went on to marry Sally Yapp and, in time, they had two sons, Alfie and Theo. It can be imagined how this further hurt Verity but, true to form, she did not indulge in the expression of pointless regrets. The Buckseys are still together at the time of writing. 'He ended up having a traditional family life which is, underneath it all, what he wanted,' says Marilyn Gross.

The year before his divorce from Verity, Bucksey got his first break in America, directing episodes of the hit detective show *Miami Vice*. His Stateside career prospered and he has been based in Los Angeles for many years, working with distinction on many series, from *NCIS* to *Breaking Bad*, confounding those who had regarded his early achievements with disfavour and proving what Verity had always believed, that he was a director of considerable talent. In 2014, at the age of 68, he won the ultimate international television award, an Emmy, for his work on the series *Fargo*.[8]

Verity never lost touch with him and, in later years, would lunch or dine with her ex-husband whenever he was in London or she was in LA. 'There were long periods after we split when I didn't see her,' he says, 'but we maintained contact and we always cared about each other. That was mutual. She was a very talented person. She had this tremendous ability to analyse a script. That was her strong point. When I sit down now to read a script I still subconsciously channel a lot of the things I learnt from her.'

'I think she always loved him,' says Kate Kagan. 'They had wonderful times and were terrific together. He was really the love of her life.'

---

[7] Quoted in *Winning Women* (see bibliography)

[8] *Fargo* (FX 2014–) Based on the celebrated Coen brothers film of the same name. Bucksey directed two episodes in the first season

CHAPTER ELEVEN
LEADING LADY
1983–1988

'I learned the difference between television and feature films. I made mistakes. I learned that contracts can't protect you. I learned how to handle difficult situations. Unfortunately, I still didn't know how to make a successful feature film. If I did, I would be a very rich woman.'

Verity to Ginny Dougary, *The Executive Tart*, 1994

When she looked back, Verity would variously brand the years she spent working in the film industry as 'extremely difficult', 'terribly tough' and the 'unhappiest of my life'.

'It was miserable, miserable, miserable,' confirms her close friend and Euston Films colleague, Linda Agran. 'She was tied hand and foot in a way she'd never been before – she was dealing with wankers. All these nonsensical casting suggestions. When she did go out on a limb, it failed. She was used to taking the top creative decisions herself. She hated it.'

Yet for many of her colleagues within this industry, from the outside looking in, Verity's position as director of production at Thorn EMI Screen Entertainment seemed an enviable one. In sharp contrast to the permanent insecurity of independent producers, Verity was heading a fully funded in-house operation with a budget of £30 million a year, backed by an established infrastructure for every key component in a film's life, from marketing to distribution. This is not to say that EMI were immune from the general malaise of the home-grown movie market. Far from it. The company's recent attempts to break into the potentially lucrative but notoriously insular American market had been an unmitigated disaster. Embarrassingly high-profile turkeys like *Can't Stop the Music* and *Honky Tonk Freeway* had been compounded by their wayward budgets.

Brought in on a three-year contract by Thorn EMI executive John Sibley, Verity knew that in return for her annual salary of £100,000, she would be expected to stop the rot and raise both standards and, most importantly, takings. 'Just about the most influential person in the British film industry' was how Barry Norman introduced her on his *Film '83* programme for the BBC, punningly referring to her as 'the original cinema Verity'.[1]

'I don't see myself going in for projects that cost megabucks,' she told Norman. 'I'd like to concentrate on what I call medium-budget pictures, where you have a chance of controlling the budget – it doesn't start to run you and where nobody is too frightened because of the money of operating in a creative manner. I think there's something terribly frightening about $40 million budgets. I would like to make British films with subjects that are universally appealing.'

She gave as recent examples of the kind of British film she had in mind *Gandhi*, *Chariots of Fire* and *The Missionary*, neatly overlooking the fact that the first two of these were almost entirely financed abroad.

Away from the hype, the timing of her arrival was not auspicious. Cinema attendance was in steep decline and, even within Thorn EMI itself, which had major interests in both film and video, the burgeoning home-video market was regarded as an aggressor rather than a companion. But Verity was always energised by a challenge and took on her new responsibilities with all the confidence gained from her staggeringly successful television career.

She was given carte blanche to redecorate the fourth floor of Thorn EMI's base at Golden Square, right in the heart of London's Soho and home to most of the film companies based in the UK. Her office had suede-effect walls, squashy sofas, a well-stocked drinks cabinet and was dominated by a huge desk of smoky black glass. This being the 1980s, Verity effortlessly assumed the power-dressed look of the time, inspired by glossy American soaps like *Dallas* and *Dynasty*, all shoulder pads, high heels and skirts cut to make the most of her showgirl legs. 'We used to love watching *Dynasty*,' says her close friend Kate Kagan. 'We had this running gag that I was Krystle, because I had long blonde hair, and she was Alexis, as she had short dark hair. And I said, "I don't think that's fair because Alexis is always such a bitch to Krystle," and she'd say, "Yes, so you'd better watch out!"'[2]

---

[1] Transmitted 02.05.83

[2] Watching television was inevitably something of a busman's holiday for Verity and her hectic social life restricted the time she had to view. But there were exceptions, many of them comedies. She was a fan of the cult American sitcom *Soap*. ('We played at that one too,' laughs Kate Kagan. 'I was Mary Campbell and she, of course, was Jessica Tate.') She adored the silliness of the BBC's *'Allo, 'Allo* (much to the disgust of her close friend, Andrew Brown) and later she was a huge fan of *Absolutely Fabulous*. She was also a devotee of *Strictly Come Dancing*

Verity usually drove herself to work in her company car, a sleek Mercedes. Once she arrived, she had the support of a small but dedicated team with Bob Mercer as head of development, looking for suitable properties to film, Graham Easton as production executive, overseeing the finances, and Frances Heasman, whom Verity brought over from Euston Films to run her script department.[3] Sharon Bloom, her personal assistant at Thames and Euston Films, came with her, too.

Bloom, whom Verity would later make a producer and who became a good friend, was young, highly efficient and capable. She needed to be. 'The day started the minute she rolled up,' says Bloom. 'She had a parking space outside Golden Square and unbelievably I used to hang out the window to see when she arrived. I'd get her a cup of tea and wait for her by the lift, the lift doors would open, I'd give her the tea, then she'd carry on up to watch rushes for the day. The diary was absolutely packed. I always thought of her as "woman on the run". She had a huge amount of energy and she never really went home much. The thing I liked about her was that she didn't stop and philosophise and she didn't say, "Do it like this." But she told me two things that I've never forgotten. One was "Assume nothing." Someone had come to see her and she was very late back from lunch. He had stormed off in the end and I said to her, "Well, I assumed that you would be back in time." "Assume nothing," she replied and I thought, "That's a good one, I'll remember that." The other was, "Don't argue with yes," and I often think of that still. When people say OK, don't argue with it, just go with it.'

After the spending excesses of the previous regime at Thorn EMI, and notwithstanding the views she'd shared with Barry Norman, there was never any possibility that Verity was going to be green-lighting blockbusters. 'She was looking to have a balanced portfolio of films,' explains Graham Easton. 'We weren't a studio making big action films or thrillers, we were a production department making feature films reflecting Verity's wishes and tastes. If you're making feature films, you don't make very many and I suspect that was intensely frustrating for her. Every film that we made was a flagship film and it can't be like that – you've got to have honourable failures, ones that nearly work that didn't quite. You've got to be allowed to fail from time to time.'

From the start, Verity had to battle with EMI's own internal issues. Gary Dartnall, who was in charge of the entire operation, seemed more interested in the American side of the business than in attempting to revive the fortunes of the domestic market. Not for the first time in her career, she found herself the lone woman at the top in an aggressively male-dominated environment.

'The British film industry at that particular time was very old-fashioned,' says director Christopher Morahan. 'There was something patronising about their approach to women and I think she just found it a rather bleak atmosphere.'

---

[3] Heasman did not remain there for long, however

The business affairs department was 'woefully inadequate', in the words of Kath Williams, who, at the age of just 26, was its head. 'The company was set up like a can of beans factory, very much feeding a video machine,' explains Williams, who rapidly became one of Verity's most trusted colleagues. 'Verity was in charge of British production which was a slow process. There was not a lot of money and not a great deal of support. It didn't work terribly well for her. I think the bureaucracy drove her completely insane. Piles of paper would arrive on a daily basis – we drowned in memos. Unfortunately, she did commission some whoppingly awful things. She wasn't a film person and it isn't easy – if it were, then lots and lots of people would do it.'

Despite the many problems faced by her team, their morale was boosted by Verity's sure leadership and natural exuberance. 'Every day was fun,' believes Graham Easton. 'Every day you couldn't wait to get to work. It was such creative energy; it just buzzed. Anybody could say, "Don't you think this would make a great film?" She just knew how to get everybody contributing. She was inspirational, decisive and knew what she wanted. Once you'd agreed what you were doing, she'd support you more than one hundred per cent.'

Sharon Bloom remembers one summer Sunday when a group of the younger Thorn EMI staff arranged to meet up and play a game of rounders in Hyde Park. 'We invited Verity too, thinking, of course, that she'd never show. There we were, playing away, and suddenly the Mercedes cruises by in the background. Verity had arrived, ready to take part. Was she any good? Of course she was; she was naturally competitive!'

Back in the office, Verity spent her first six months wading through a deluge of scripts, most of which she found either to be too literary or just plain hopeless. More often than not, she would bring her surviving Great Dane, Misty, to the office, where this enormous dog would lounge about the place during the procession of meetings that punctuated the day. Graham Easton remembers one afternoon when Misty was suffering from some kind of minor stomach ailment. During the course of a long and important meeting, everyone became aware of an increasingly unpleasant odour permeating the room. Verity continued regardless.

Her involvement in some of the films for which she was initially responsible was nominal rather than hands-on. These included Bill Douglas' *Comfort and Joy* and Paul Bartel's *Not for Publication*. She inherited some responsibility for David Lean's epic adaptation of E. M. Forster's *A Passage to India*, which started shooting in the spring of 1983. Even with a budget of £17 million, money was a problem and Verity was required to discuss the situation with the veteran director. 'She questioned his figures and he went ape,' recalls her friend, Sheila Savory. 'He tore everything up and threw it all around the office. She'd been so terrified before meeting him but she stood her ground.'

'David was entirely hopeless with women,' says producer David Puttnam. 'He wasn't a very nice man – vain and deeply misogynist. Verity represented everything he was prejudiced about. He would have hated to have been accountable to her.'

Presumably, she was not able to tell Lean that his 1946 version of *Great Expectations* had been her favourite film as a child.

The first film that really 'belonged' to Verity was a hard-hitting crime thriller called *Slayground*, which she commissioned despite her own reservations that it wouldn't work. 'I wasn't very keen,' she later admitted in a 1990 interview with *Options* magazine, 'but I thought, "Well, I'm starting off and this is definitely different to television and maybe I have to go by someone else's judgement." That film lost me a lot of ground, so I could have kicked myself for not sticking out for what I basically felt.'[4]

'It was a very tough and hectic time,' says Sharon Bloom. 'Verity found the pressure from sales and marketing to get it right before you even made the film difficult. It was alien to how she was used to working, much more corporate and less creative. We'd get to the script stage and the script would go, maybe with a bit of casting, to the sales people and you'd get a sales forecast back based on how well they thought the project would do. A lot of store was put on them and that was very depressing. Then Verity would have to fight.'

Given that film-making is necessarily a time-consuming business, *Slayground* wasn't released until the run-up to Christmas 1983, when it confirmed her own lack of faith by failing to make any impact whatsoever. It had been a troubled production from the start. She had commissioned one of her favourite television writers, Trevor Preston, the man behind *Out* and *Fox*, to deliver the screenplay, which was based on Donald Westlake's novel. She asked Barry Hanson, another trusted colleague from both Thames and Euston, to produce. After reading Preston's script, Hanson turned her down. 'It wasn't really a script that you would put on television, let alone film,' he explains. 'She was a bit battered by the movies – the buyers or distributors would come to her and say, "We need a thriller," and she'd try to deliver. But this wasn't going to.'

In place of Hanson, she turned to John Dark, an acquaintance with long experience as a features producer, whom she had first met when he had tried to sell her the idea for a historical action series about the 'peelers', the very first London police force, while she was at Euston. She didn't like the idea but she warmed to Dark, who was old-school and full of fruity anecdotes, as well as offering a strongly pragmatic approach to the business which appealed to her own outspoken nature. Dark agreed to produce *Slayground*, although, like Hanson, he had serious reservations. 'I thought the script was a pile of shit,' he says. 'During the various script meetings, my fears were in no way allayed. The writer was in another world. Later Verity told me that she wished she had taken more notice of the fact that I had fallen asleep in one of these meetings. You can take just so much crap.'

---

[4] *Options*, June 1989

Verity teamed Dark with Terry Bedford, a commercials director making his feature film debut with *Slayground*. She was giving Bedford the biggest break of his career and he had ambitious plans. 'On our recce looking for locations,' continues John Dark, 'we discussed the use of a fairground. I said, "The best fairground will be the one we will build in the grounds of Pinewood studios. There we will have the choice of whatever attraction you want but also the use of all the studio facilities." "Oh no," he said. "I must have the smell of the sea." I didn't know that we were making a "smelly". Actually, we were making a stinker.'

Dark counselled Verity to abandon the film but she was understandably reluctant to concede defeat at such an early stage, feeling that in any case they were already too far down the line. The film was shot on schedule and on budget but that was its only achievement.

Link was another oddity, a horror film about a chimpanzee that turns against the humans in charge of him. This had been turned down by John Dark. 'I thought the script was truly pathetic,' he says. 'But my main worry was what would happen if the chimp stopped co-operating. The animal was in practically every scene. My question to Verity was, "Who do we sue if the monkey stops working?" Although the chimp behaved beautifully, it was a desperately unhappy film and a complete disaster at the box office. It would have been better to let the chimp direct the film.'

Verity fell out with the director, Richard Franklin, and didn't have a good word to say about the film herself, in private at least. She fell out, too, with Barry Hanson, who, having refused *Slayground*, unwisely accepted her offer to produce the vapid comedy *Illegal Aliens*, which was eventually retitled *Morons from Outer Space*. Designed as a vehicle for British comic writer-performers Mel Smith and Griff Rhys Jones, this film, too, was quickly in trouble. 'She got rid of me, though she paid me and wanted my name to stay on it,' says Hanson. 'She said it wasn't funny enough. Humour is spontaneous and individual and what she was actually saying is that I didn't have her sense of humour. She explained, "I need a special effects producer," and she went to John Dark. I knew that John Dark wasn't going to rescue *Morons*. He was too old-fashioned.'

'The film was in a bloody mess,' says Dark himself. 'There was little that one could do. The script had been accepted, the cast established, the director and crew in place. All you can do in these cases is pull the reins in, install some discipline and make sure no more bad decisions are made that delay the finishing of the film.'

Verity's first choice as director was Jack Gold, who had done such fine work on *The Naked Civil Servant*. 'I started reading it,' he recalls, 'and it was awful so I said, "No, thank you, Verity." She didn't try to talk me into it. I think she knew what was required to achieve big audiences for television but the feature film market is a different genre.'

Mike Hodges, the director who accepted the job in Gold's place, brought with him a reputation based on the lasting impact of his cult film *Get Carter*.[5] He had also worked in the very early pre-Verity days of Euston Films. But Hodges was unable to invest *Morons from Outer Space* with any notable flair and the results were distinctly laboured. At least in the UK the writers and stars, Mel Smith and Griff Rhys Jones, had a following. But when it came to the American previews, Smith and Jones were total unknowns and the audience was bemused by them and their lacklustre film. Typical of the comments scrawled on the audience reaction cards were the damning words 'This film sucks.' The film lost EMI several million pounds.

'She always said she had a soft spot for *Morons*,' says Kath Williams, 'but I went to the audience screenings and it was not a happy night.'

Verity gave the go-ahead to another comedy, *Restless Natives*, a lyrical Scottish tale in which two young men become modern-day highwaymen, holding up tourist coaches. At £1.2 million, this was more modestly budgeted than *Morons from Outer Space* but, although it performed well in its native Scotland, it took only £300,000 in overall admissions and so, despite its curious charm, it was judged another failure.

'It was not a happy time for her,' says Ted Kotcheff, who had been the first real love of her life and had subsequently established a successful career in features. Just as Verity took up her position at Thorn-EMI, Kotcheff scored a hit with the first Rambo movie, *First Blood*. She was keen to collaborate with him again in her new capacity. 'I was very interested but it never happened,' he explains. 'It was difficult for her. Raising money for films is such a draining experience. No matter how successful you are, you're always looking for money.'

As well as the continuing struggle to secure budgets, for the first time in Verity's career, the material for which she was responsible was failing to deliver on any level. It was a deeply uncomfortable experience and it is not difficult to imagine the cumulative frustration and misery this caused her. Yet she persevered. 'You have to remember,' points out film executive and friend David Puttnam, 'she was probably earning on a monthly basis a sum larger than any she'd ever received. I would be surprised if she wasn't earning double what she'd got at Euston and that's a reason to stick around. There's a moment in your life when you've done all those things and someone comes along and offers you something that sounds attractive. Verity was extremely credible but she came from a totally different world, where writers were king, so she would have found the process far more stressful than I did, with my background in commercials. It would have been like being a dentist and then wanting to be a doctor. I do remember her saying, "This business is mad!"'

'In television you can get a lot closer to the product,' says agent Anthony Jones. 'In the

---

[5] *Get Carter* (1971) Gritty gangster film starring Michael Caine in the title role

film industry you're at the mercy of forces far greater than yourself – and you have much less control over what happens. You can produce the most perfect film but if it's distributed badly, at the wrong time, at the wrong weekend, it can disappear. And she wasn't hands-on – she was an executive. In television she could twist a button here and there very quickly and easily, which you can't do in the film business.'

'I think that it was too much business and not enough production for her' is the view of veteran agent and producer Beryl Vertue. 'She was the boss in a big company and the bigger it is, the more uncreative you become because you can't get anywhere near it.'

'The film industry is so slow getting something set up,' points out television executive Michael Grade. 'In TV she was used to saying, "Yes, I'll do that, no I don't want that – I want 13 episodes of that" – it's very, very fast. It's the difference between being a buyer and a seller.'

'It was a big thing to be offered and a huge leap forward,' continues Vertue, 'but when she actually came to do it she couldn't be nearly as creative as she had been at Euston Films.'

There were, as Puttnam points out, obvious material compensations. As well as her hefty salary, which enabled her to indulge her passion for clothes, shoes and shopping in general, she could lunch and dine in the hottest restaurants in town. 'I think she quickly got used to those trappings,' says her close friend, producer Graham Benson. 'You get comfortable with all the back-up of a good office. "Get me a car to go to so and so, book me a table..." I'll never forget when a friend was coming over from Canada. I told Verity, "I was going to suggest the Ivy for dinner but I can't get a bloody table." She said, "Leave it to me." Five minutes later, it was booked.'

With her marriage at an end, holidays were spent with friends, sometimes in her flat in Antibes, sometimes as far away as Australia, a country she first visited in 1979. There were Christmases in the Caribbean and shopping trips to New York. Travel had always been a passion, notwithstanding her abiding fear of flying, and the higher she climbed in the industry, the more it became a requirement of the job. Flights were invariably first class, with plenty of champagne to soothe her nerves. She stayed in the finest and most expensive hotels, usually occupying a suite. A natural networker, she became a vibrant fixture at the various international sales conferences, award ceremonies, film festivals and industry shindigs that peppered the annual calendar. 'There was a group of friends all linked by the film and television industry,' explains top Australian publicist Rea Francis. 'Because it was so centred on sales and marketing, we used to travel the world and meet up in various places.'

Francis became one of Verity's increasingly international circle of friends. 'She was a pixie,' she says. 'Such charm! When she was amused or making a wicked or witty comment, she'd just throw her head sideways and she always looked like a little girl being wicked. She was just wonderful – she had such a fun spirit. She was a very loyal friend. One night I was at the Cannes Film Festival and Verity was at her place in Antibes and she had a couple of mutual friends, Val and Rod Hardy, with her. I had a boyfriend who was supposed to visit me and he rang up and said he wasn't coming. Verity and Val called me and I burst into tears. They got in a car with a soft top and drove all the way from Antibes to Cannes to cheer me up.'

'The three of us had been out to lunch and dinner,' confesses Val Hardy, 'and we weren't in any position to drive but we put the roof down and off we went at about midnight. Outrageous stuff and we got away with it all. It started to rain and we got soaked.'

'They all came in laughing,' continues Francis, 'in great spirits, determined to make me laugh too. When Verity laughed, it was a joy to be near her.'

'She'd have a fearful amount of wine and still drive,' admits Kath Williams. But her casual attitude to drinking and driving, not untypical at the time, came to an abrupt end when, in January 1984, Verity found herself in court. She had been driving herself back from a long and liquid lunch with the stars of *Minder*, George Cole and Dennis Waterman, when her car was flagged down by the police. 'She became extremely aggressive and abusive,' PC Mark Horsley told the court at Horseferry Road when the case came up. 'She was objectionable and had been striking out at a WPC assisting to search her.'

'Oh yes, Verity smacked her,' laughs her close friend, Sheila Savory. 'She had been driving down Beauchamp Place and a friend of mine was just behind her in a taxi. He saw what was happening and told me that he was hiding on the floor of the cab, terrified she'd recognise him and he'd be dragged into it. Anyway, she was arrested and had to spend the night in jail.'

Fined, and banned from driving for a year for failing to provide a blood sample, Verity appealed and was acquitted. 'I must admit the publicity was really quite horrible,' she told journalist Anne Cabourn. 'All I can say is I made page three of *The Sun* without taking my clothes off.'[6]

The self-deprecating joke concealed the fact that she was at a particularly low ebb at this time, with her marriage in ruins and the unceasing pressure of day-to-day expectations at EMI. She had also just been forced to acknowledge that it was no longer practical to shuttle back and forth between Euston and EMI and so, with regret, she relinquished her position as Euston's chief executive. There was plenty to occupy her back in her office in Golden Square.

---

[6] *Options*, June 1989

'We were very, very productive at a time when the British film industry wasn't,' says Graham Easton. 'But to try and create from scratch a whole outfit of a film company is an extraordinary undertaking. You can't do that with three films a year – you need a volume. That's why every film was a flagship. Verity had her own vision of how she wanted these films to be made and what she wanted to do with them.'

Much of her time and considerable energy were devoted to the all-too-elusive search for the right material. Given the prominence of her position, she didn't have to do all the running, and plenty attempted to woo her. Director Piers Haggard offered her a package of three projects. 'She hated one, thought one was too expensive and thought the other just too difficult,' he smiles. 'I'd always wanted to make a film about the Satanist Aleister Crowley. I had a lot of material. She said, "Given the nature of the subject, you'll never be able to make the film you'd like to make because of the commercial pressure. You'll only get it anywhere by highlighting the salacious, titillating side and then you'd no longer be able to make the film that would be worth making." It was very intelligent of her, actually – with hindsight, she was quite right.'

'She was the best person with a script that I have ever, ever encountered,' says Graham Easton. 'She had great respect for writers. She would absorb so much – she was dealing all the time with such high octane talent. I can remember somebody being very rude and angry and Verity just smiling sweetly and saying, "But that's what I think." She could fly back if she wanted to. You might be trying to convince her of something and you would suddenly see the eyes go and then you'd think, "Right, I'll finish the sentence and come back tomorrow."'

With the money at their disposal, the big American studios had a virtual monopoly on acquiring the rights to the most exciting and commercially promising novels on the market so Verity had to be more imaginative in her hunt for scripts, making the most of her existing relationships with writers. Howard Schuman had interested the BBC in a potential six-part series called *Fast Food*. 'It was set in Manhattan,' Schuman explains, 'in the booming early 80s when the city had just recovered from near bankruptcy. It was about three British guys setting up a restaurant in a sleazy but perhaps soon-to-be-trendy area of lower NYC.'

Schuman researched the realities of such a venture with the help of top London restaurateurs Jeremy King and Chris Corbin and produced a short outline when Verity persuaded him that rather than pursuing the option of a BBC series, an EMI feature film would be more exciting. 'The first draft had good stuff,' he says, 'and Bob Spiers [who directed *Fawlty Towers* and, later, *Absolutely Fabulous*] wanted to direct. We had an illuminating read at my flat but before I could get stuck into rewriting, Verity left EMI. One saw what happened when you lose Verity – they immediately got rid of it.'

Time and again, projects would stall either because she could not persuade the EMI board to fully fund them or she was unable to attract potential investment from elsewhere. She commissioned Fay Weldon to write a big-screen version of Joan Aiken's magical children's book *The Wolves of Willoughby Chase*, but, although Weldon delivered the goods, this fell by the wayside for want of funds. Another company, Zenith, later backed an unrelated film of the book, which was released in 1989.

Verity was keen to press ahead with director John Carpenter's plans for a Western, *El Diablo*, only to discover at the critical moment that the rights had lapsed and no longer belonged to EMI. *El Diablo* eventually surfaced some years later as a television movie.

Having admired the 1977 comedy *Slap Shot*, about the violent tactics undertaken by an American hockey team to revive their fortunes, Verity was intrigued to discover that the screenplay had been written by a woman, Nancy Dowd. Dowd had also won an Oscar for Best Screenplay with her work on the 1979 movie *Coming Home*. Verity contacted Dowd's agent to arrange a breakfast meeting in New York. It was the catalyst for another collaboration and the beginning of a deep and lasting friendship.

'I knew nothing about Verity,' says Dowd. 'She wanted to know if we could work together. I had been used to working in Hollywood. In those days there were very few women working in the business and I really wasn't used to meeting smart women in that context. The women that I met in Hollywood didn't really have any personal imprint. They were corporate people, scared, and the level of quality wasn't very high. When I met Verity, in some ways, it was like going back to my college days – being with a woman who had a brain and who didn't think it odd that I did too. She had worked for David Susskind and, after *Slap Shot* came out, Susskind had interviewed me on his show. He said to me, "I'm going to pay you the greatest compliment I can – you write like a man." With Verity I didn't have to go through all that shit. Right from the get-go, she seemed to understand my writing, what I wanted to do, and we just got on like a house on fire. From that meeting, I knew she was my kind of person. I liked her a lot. I liked her style.'

Dowd offered Verity the script for *R and R* (short for 'rest and relaxation'), a film she had originally written for Paramount and for which she had bought back the rights when the studio passed on putting it into production. The story was set in Tokyo and based on Dowd's experiences of teaching English in a language college there. 'I bought an apartment right near hers in Holland Park,' explains Dowd. 'We worked on the script together and it was really something wonderful – I'll never have that again. She knew what a screenplay was about. She wasn't coming at me with platitudes. Most people work out of fear: "Oh, this won't work because people don't like such and such." I've seen a lot of that type and she wasn't that type. By that point I'd had enough experience in the business to know that, in her, I'd met something quite unusual and I was determined to profit from it.'

Verity funded a recce to Tokyo and asked John Dark, whom she wanted to produce the movie, to accompany Dowd. The trip was not a success. The various meetings and initial negotiations were a cultural minefield and even with the services of a local 'fixer' and interpreter, it was a nightmare in unknown etiquette. 'We had completed our task,' says Dark, 'and, armed with photos, pages of costs and details of locations, we flew back. All was well till we changed planes at Singapore. Nancy lost her bracelet. She was flapping around, screaming at all and sundry, and I could not see how I could help. This pissed her off and she refused to speak to me, although we were sitting next to each other on the long flight to London. As soon as we landed, she was on the phone to Verity, who very wisely pointed out that people in the middle of the night on a long flight do not always behave as they should.'

'I said, "This guy is a problem person,"' recalls Dowd. 'I know you like him a lot but he goes off on tangents. She was very critical of me and said that I really would just have to put up with it. She actually wrote me a letter. So I did. Later on when he betrayed her totally I reminded her – "Remember that?" She was a loyal woman in a world that isn't very loyal. This quality did Verity a lot of harm. She was very loyal to people right up until the time they fucked her and even after sometimes.'

According to Dark, 'Nancy took an instant dislike to Stephen Frears, whom Verity introduced to her as a possible director and accused Verity of trying to push a television director onto her eminent feature.'

In the event, this objection proved immaterial. Despite Verity's best efforts, *R and R* was another project that slipped through her grasp. 'It was a really big disappointment,' sighs Dowd, 'because I loved that script and she would have done a great job with it. Both she and I knew that it's not easy to be a woman and achieve something – achieve something you want to achieve. When it works it's fabulous, when it doesn't it's an absolute mess.'

'I imagine EMI was an absolute nightmare for her,' says Stephen Frears, the director Verity had in mind for *R and R*. 'They were in it for the money so wanted a certain kind of film that would get a certain kind of audience. Presumably they thought she had the common touch but Verity's values weren't the same values. It wouldn't have helped that she was a woman. If you make feature films, it's horrific – it's just very bruising – and the early 80s was a grim time in British cinema.'

Throughout her three years in charge, Verity's faltering EMI output produced only two moderate successes, *Dreamchild* and *Clockwise*. The former was brought to her as a talent package with producers Kenith Trodd (whom Verity knew from her BBC days), Rick McCallum, director Gavin Millar and writer Dennis Potter. 'I don't think we went anywhere else for it but Verity,' recalls Trodd. 'Dennis had taken *Pennies from Heaven* to Hollywood disastrously but although this was hideously budgeted so that we had to do America at Elstree, the making of it was relatively pain-free. We had frequent meetings and there was pressure to get it right, but Dennis and Verity liked each other, which helped.'

In a spurt of furious creativity, Potter wrote the screenplay for *Dreamchild* in four and a half days.[7] Or so he claimed. 'He was always saying things like that,' smiles Trodd. 'In his eyes, if something came quickly, it was an argument that it was somehow definitive and didn't need rewrites!'

The story centred on an aged Alice Liddell, who, as a pre-pubescent girl, had been Lewis Carroll's muse for *Alice's Adventures in Wonderland.* Potter had chanced to read how, as an old woman, Liddell had visited New York and this fuelled his imagination. The film dramatises Liddell's 1932 trip to receive an honorary degree from Columbia University, in the company of her niece, with flashbacks to her childhood experiences and her nightmares in which Carroll's creations (realised for the film by Jim Henson's Creature Shop) are brought vividly to life.

Verity agreed to using a first-time features director, former film critic Gavin Millar, whom Potter and Trodd sold to her on the basis of Millar's Prix Italia-winning version of Potter's LWT screenplay *Cream in My Coffee.* Starring as the 82-year-old Alice was Coral Browne, an elegant and supremely witty actress with whom Verity struck up an immediate and lasting friendship[8]. But tensions rapidly emerged over another of the leading actors. Verity, still nursing her grievance from the *Rock Follies* court case, strongly opposed Millar's choice of Nigel Hawthorne as Alice's father. Millar insisted and Hawthorne was cast in what was originally a fairly substantial part. But when it came to cutting the film, Verity returned to the fray. 'Every scene with Nigel in it, she was down on it like a ton of bricks,' Millar told *Sight and Sound* magazine in 2014. '"That's frightful, what's he doing?" And she gradually cut him out and out and out of every scene. In the end I said, "Well, I'd rather have him not there at all than insult him by putting him in, holding the scenery up." She said, "All right." So he was cut out.'

Despite his understandable bitterness about this, Millar acknowledged that 'if it hadn't been for Verity, there wouldn't have been a film. She really fought for it, I'll give her that.'

'This is, quite simply, a brilliant British film,' raved *The Sunday Times*' Iain Johnstone, eulogising the fine acting, directing, camerawork and editing. 'And while the plaudits are flying,' he continued, 'why not one for Verity Lambert, who judiciously got Thorn EMI to back one of their finest films?'[9]

But, despite rave reviews on both sides of the Atlantic, *Dreamchild* suffered from poor distribution and inadequate, underfunded publicity. It remains something of a forgotten film.[10]

---

[7] Elements of the screenplay were recycled from his 1965 *Wednesday Play* offering, *Alice* (BBC1, 13.10.66)

[8] When the actress died in 1991, she left Verity a sable coat

[9] *The Sunday Times* (26.01.86)

[10] It was finally released on DVD in the UK in January, 2015

Clockwise, in contrast, did rather better, helped by the broader appeal of its subject matter – a manic farce – and the pulling power of its star, John Cleese. Cleese played Brian Stimpson, the headmaster of a comprehensive school, who has a towering OCD for punctuality and time-keeping. Stimpson is invited to deliver a speech at a headmasters' conference but first he has to get there. After he misses his train, the film wrings excruciating comedy from his increasingly desperate attempts to do so. The screenplay was written on spec by playwright Michael Frayn, and Verity took some risks to realise it. The distinguished theatre producer Michael Codron, who had worked closely with Frayn, brought the script to EMI's veteran executive Nat Cohen, who then took it to Verity. She suggested that Codron produce it, despite his total lack of experience in film, and she took a further risk by inviting her old friend Christopher Morahan to switch disciplines too and direct. 'This was a very, very sophisticated idea,' believes Morahan. 'Codron was an absolutely magnificent theatre producer but it wasn't certain he would translate to film. My track record was in theatre and television. But it was a very good experience – highly enjoyable. Verity was splendid and very supportive. John Cleese was at the height of his powers then. He was very ambitious and wanted hugely to be an international success. He worked incredibly hard and was a delightful man to work with. *Clockwise* was one of the better films of that year but not as utterly successful as John wanted.'

Nonetheless, it made a pleasant change for one of Verity's films to be greeted with enthusiastic reviews. 'A mega-sized tonic,' was *The Daily Express*' Adella Lithman's approving verdict, 'with no sex, no gore, and all British-made...It gave me a critical case of stomach ache from laughter, to say nothing of the tears causing my mascara to run.'[11]

By the time both *Clockwise* and *Dreamchild* reached cinemas, Verity's brief reign at EMI was already over. In the summer of 1986, the company was taken over by the Cannon Group, and it was rapidly decided to cease in-house production and close down Verity's department. Her grand job ceased to be. 'It was the end of a glorious but clearly failed experiment,' shrugs Graham Easton.

'It was all a mess,' says Kath Williams. 'She wasn't a film person, she was a television person and it's always the same problem – anybody really successful goes to America.'

'I did everything I possibly could to protect myself and the brief that I had,' Verity told Sophia Watson in 1989. 'Films are completely different from television. Thames drama had been very successful and consequently they trusted my judgement. They didn't try to second-guess me after a time. In film there was a whole committee. I found I couldn't use my instincts. I had to try and persuade people and therefore I would have to take on board whether they would think they could sell it. And so the most powerful thing I had in my favour, which is my nose, my instinct, was difficult to use. And therefore the films that we made were uneven and I was only entirely happy with two of them – *Dreamchild* and *Clockwise*. But I learned a tremendous amount, as you often do when things aren't

---

[11] *Daily Express* (14.03.86)

going your way.'[12]

Cannon brought over executive Michael Kagan from Los Angeles to act as the new head of production. At first, this was an awkward situation because Kagan was married to one of Verity's best friends. 'It was a bit unpleasant because Cannon were getting rid of her,' explains Kate Kagan. 'But Michael loved Verity. When he and I had been together for a while, he had actually asked Verity for permission to marry me! She said indignantly, "I'm her best friend, not her bloody mother!"'

Kagan did his best for her now, in the face of the hostility of Cannon's Israeli bosses Menahem Golan and Yoram Globus. Neither of them had taken kindly to Verity's attempts to fight their ruthless reorganisation. 'They couldn't stand her and she couldn't stand them,' says Kate Kagan. As a measure to save everyone's face, she was allowed to see out the time remaining on her contract and was offered a deal to develop her own films as an independent producer, with Cannon being offered first refusal. Naming her company Cinema Verity, the obvious but neat pun coined by Barry Norman on his television show a couple of years earlier, Verity was on her own again, albeit with development money to get her new venture going.

There was already a thriller in the works, *American Roulette*, but this humble effort was quickly eclipsed by another project that became a passion, almost an obsession. *Evil Angels* was a book by an Australian lawyer called John Bryson, documenting the notorious 'dingo baby' case, which had become a raging talking-point throughout Australia in the early 1980s. It was Rea Francis who first gave her a galley copy while they were both attending the 1985 Cannes Film Festival. The deeply tragic story immediately captured Verity's imagination. Bryson related how the nine-week-old Azaria Chamberlain vanished from the tent in which her family were camping in Ayers Rock in 1980. Lindy Chamberlain was subsequently convicted of murdering her own child while her husband, Michael, was found guilty of being an accessory after the fact. Lindy was given a life sentence, while her husband received an 18-month suspended sentence. Bryson's book re-examined the evidence and was highly critical of the treatment of the Chamberlains. 'The story divided the nation,' says Rea Francis. 'Half thought Lindy was guilty and the same would say, "Don't be ridiculous." People with a normally high intellect would snap glass stems over dinner over whether she was guilty or not. Those kind of arguments went on all over Australia.'

When she read Bryson's account, Verity became convinced of their innocence and that this miscarriage of justice would make a moving, compelling film. 'What interested me were not the implications of a bizarre murder with no motive and no body,' she told *The Guardian*'s Caroline Baum, 'but the circumstances which had contributed to the Chamberlains being found guilty and how they had coped with such extraordinary

---

[12] Quoted in *Winning Women* (see bibliography)

suffering and injustice on such a public scale. Lindy was the most hated woman in Australia. Here was a story which perfectly illustrated the kind of pressures ordinary private people live under in today's world. Religious prejudice was a major factor in the public's assessment of Lindy; the fact that she and her husband were Seventh Day Adventists definitely counted against them. No one really knew what their religion involved so they made up rumours about ritualistic human sacrifice.

'And then there was the role of the media. Basically, Lindy was tried by television and the press. When her responses were inappropriate, she was declared guilty before she got to court.'

Evil Angels, rechristened *A Cry in the Dark* outside Australia and New Zealand, entirely absorbed Verity's attention for the next two years. She passed the production of *American Roulette* on to her former EMI colleague Graham Easton, retaining only a token involvement and thereby freeing herself to devote her energies to getting *A Cry in the Dark* into production.[13]

'She was passionate about causes and it definitely spoke to her,' says Rea Francis. 'She saw that it was an international story in that a woman was being condemned for being different.'

During the initial research for the film, Verity based herself in Melbourne, where she rented a big two-storey terraced house in a fashionable area. She flew to Ayers Rock to soak up the atmosphere of this ancient place, finding it 'mystical and not always benign. There is certainly a malevolent side to the place.' In order to film there, she had to seek the permission of the Aborigines to whom the Australian government had recently returned control of this sacred site. 'They were very co-operative,' she recalled, 'but they thought we were absolutely mad. They can't understand the white man's scab-picking mentality of wanting to go over a tragedy again and again. To them, it's more sensible to forget and get on with life.'[14]

Given the sensitivities of the Chamberlain case, Verity realised that she needed an Australian director. 'I didn't want to be seen to be using outsiders to criticise the country,' she reasoned in *The Guardian*. She had in mind Fred Schepisi, someone else she had met through Rea Francis, and whose work on films like *The Chant of Jimmy Blacksmith* and *Plenty* she had seen and admired. Schepisi was doubtful. 'I had been quite amazed at what had happened in Australia because of that case,' he says. 'People were either

---

[13] During the production of *A Cry in the Dark*, Kate Kagan took a course in Hebrew at Tel Aviv University: 'It was difficult with the time difference but we used to speak on the phone every day,' she recalls. 'I was sitting there with my books and I'd say to her, "Here's how to say give me money' in Hebrew – 'ten li kessef'"' Verity tried this phrase on Golan and Globus and, to their credit, they were amused

[14] Quotes from 'Trial and Tribulation', *The Guardian* (07.03.88)

vehemently defending or attacking that family, blaming the husband, the wife or the children for the murders. It was just ludicrous, passionate stuff and everything creepy that you can think of – any time the cause of something is unknown, people can't handle it – they want to come up with their own solutions. Lindy was someone who didn't appear to be emotional, and the Chamberlains' religion was considered peculiar. But I felt that because it was an ongoing case, lives were at stake and if you did the wrong thing or made things up, as sometimes happens in movies, it wouldn't be good.'

Schepisi told her that he didn't want to be involved. Typically, Verity refused to take no for an answer. 'She spent a lot of time ringing me and annoying me about it,' he says. 'She must have tried about ten times and on about the tenth time she said, "I know you didn't want me to ring you any more about this but I've worked out you're not doing this because you don't know how to." And I said, "Right – go away Verity," and I sat down and I worked out the structure for the film. A few days later I rang her back and said, "Here's how you do it – now fuck off."'

Armed with his treatment, Verity temporarily retreated. Acting on a hunch, she had sent an outline of the story to Meryl Streep, the star of Schepisi's recent movie *Plenty*, bypassing Streep's agent and hoping that this direct but unsolicited approach might prove effective. She was right. Streep wrote back to say how much it had disturbed her and that she would be interested to see a script.

'Verity rang me again,' recalls Schepisi, 'and told me, "I have someone for you to talk to." It was Meryl Streep, saying, "We have to do this." At that point I thought, "Apart from Verity, now I have a real creative ally who will keep a weather eye on commerciality and accessibility as well as having the intelligence to avoid all the things that I was worried about." At that point, I gave in and said OK.'

Streep was Verity's tactical masterstroke. Her involvement secured not only Schepisi as director but also the investment she needed to get the film into production with a budget of $15 million. She reunited both director and leading lady with another of their colleagues from *Plenty*, Sam Neill, whose career she had helped to launch by casting him in *Reilly: Ace of Spies*. Neill took the part of Michael Chamberlain. The Chamberlains themselves cautiously agreed to co-operate with the project, meeting the actors who were going to play them and attending some of the filming.

For Verity, making *A Cry in the Dark* was an incredibly stressful experience. Even during the worst lows at Thorn EMI, she had the relative security of her contract and the knowledge that it was the company who stood to lose money if a project collapsed or failed to do well. As an independent producer, Verity found herself absolutely in the front line of the daily battle of making a feature film. During pre-production, she had investigated adopting the cheaper filming methods of Australian television mini-series but what she was trying to achieve with *A Cry in the Dark* was scarcely comparable. There was the need to accommodate a range of diverse locations across the country. She had to charter a plane to fly cast and crew to Ayers Rock. There were union disputes over the payments to the cast, which meant that Verity was forced to cut some actors from certain scenes simply to reduce costs. Temperatures on location sometimes reached over 45 degrees and Verity was furious when she was forced to pay an extra allowance to actors for working in 'severe climactic conditions'. 'I'm sure Puttnam didn't have to do that on *The Mission,*' she sniped to the press. It was a novel and disagreeable experience to know that she was directly responsible for every penny being spent. There was the compensation of working with an Australian crew whose hard-working, friendly and helpful attitude she found invigorating. But the terrifying spectre of the money suddenly running out and filming grinding to a halt remained with her throughout the shoot. Writer Lynda La Plante recalls bumping into her during production and noting how unhappy she thought Verity looked.

'The film industry is a much more vicious environment,' says director Herbert Wise. 'Much more money-lusting; that's all it's really interested in. The only time I have ever seen Verity scared was when she was making the dingo film. I was having a meal with her and the executives in charge of that movie came in and she suddenly rushed over to talk to them in such a way that I realised that they were manipulating her. This was something I was not used to seeing in Verity.'

'The finance got very tight,' says Rea Francis. 'She almost lost the film but she wasn't scared of taking on wolves and she was just brilliant at manoeuvring and she pulled it together.'

'A lot of people would have given up on things a lot earlier than Verity,' says Fred Schepisi. 'Obviously she was trying to control the money as much as possible but she had the good sense to know that sometimes you have to spend money to save money – she wasn't a nickel and dimer. That can often cause more problems than it solves. She understood that the film was the important thing. I did have everybody primed that if she was ever coming anywhere near the set to give me the radio signal. You'd hear the door slam open and Verity stomping in with some bee in her bonnet and because I knew she was coming, I used to turn round and say, "Just the person I've been looking for..."'

Schepisi devised a thoughtful and highly effective way of interpreting the story. 'I instructed every actor to totally believe in the character that they played and that that character was doing the right thing, not to play them with prejudices as so often happens, so that the telling of the story was absolutely unprejudiced. I did the same thing with the composer – he stopped speaking to me afterwards because of it – I didn't want the music to telegraph or create emotions – I wanted it to add a bit of energy, drive or tension but not to influence. I wanted the cumulative effect of that to be for people to go, "Well, it's pretty bloody obvious what the truth is."'

Verity remained in Australia throughout both the shoot and the post-production period. Despite the ceaseless demands the movie made on her life, she continued to nourish her many friendships, as her old friend, the director Waris Hussein, testifies. 'Ian, my partner at the time, was one of the first people in New Zealand to develop HIV/AIDS,' he explains. 'He'd gone back to say goodbye to his family and they didn't know how to cope. He was dying in hospital there from an illness nobody wanted to talk about. Verity was on the way to Australia and she took the time to get off that plane, go to Auckland, and visit him in hospital. When she realised that he wasn't being taken care of by his family, she said, "Ian, you are not dying here – you have people who love you." She brought him food and got him up. Then she contacted me. I flew out and brought him back to Britain for the final year of his life. But she made that happen and if she hadn't, he would have died alone in New Zealand.'

A Cry in the Dark was eventually released in November 1988, less than two months after Australia's Northern Territory Court of Appeals had finally overturned the Chamberlains' convictions. The reviews were generally excellent and it won Best Film in the Australian Film Institute awards, with Streep and Neill winning Best Actor and Actress, Schepisi winning Best Director and another win for Best Adapted Screenplay. Streep also won the Best Actress award from the New York Film Critics Circle. But the returns were disappointing, even in Australia, where it had been confidently predicted that the film would do great business. It was entered into the 1989 Cannes Film Festival, where Streep won Best Actress for her performance. But the prestige of this achievement was undermined by back-room squabbling. 'It was such a shame,' says Kath Williams, who accompanied Verity to the festival. 'We had to deal with these awful Italian money men who looked like Mafia. The two Australian producers had brought their wives along and there was a dinner after the film at the Martinez. These Italians wouldn't give the wives tickets and Verity went ballistic and had the most screaming row with them. I remember thinking that we were going to end up in cement boots in Cannes harbour. I dragged her out but it all left a sour taste. I had the most dreadful week of my life but she dealt with it the way she dealt with everything – when she'd finished shouting at who she thought was responsible, she got on with the next thing.'

For Verity, the lasting legacy of *A Cry in the Dark* was her abiding love affair with Australia, which had become a second home, and its people. She had acquired a community of great friends across the country, most of them in the film and television business, like Val Hardy, who was then head of production for the Ten Network in Sydney. Ten covered the Melbourne Cup, the prime horse racing event in the Australian sporting calendar. 'Verity just absolutely adored it,' says Hardy, 'frocking up and partying. She was so ballsy and she loved a good time. She'd love to sit down and talk and get out a bottle of wine – Australians like that. It's a beautiful country and you can get away from the English weather. She could come here and everyone just opened their arms to her.'

In many respects, Verity became an honorary Australian. 'She liked our freer attitudes,' says Fred Schepisi. 'She found kindred spirits in being direct. We like to eat, drink and have a good time. We have a good sense of humour but when we knuckle down to do things, we knuckle down. I think she just liked that. She was a good, cheery spirit most of the time.'

'She liked that reverse humour Australians have,' says Rea Francis, 'Like when you're in a restaurant and you say, "We hated that," but the plate's empty and it takes the waiter a few minutes to think, "Ah, no they're joking." She used to stay with me and then one year she said she was going to hire a house of her own. It was two blocks from me. She rang me up at two in the morning: "You've got to come up here now. I'm hysterical. There are all these bugs flying around." I said, "Don't be ridiculous – you've had too much to drink. Go back to sleep." But she was right – the most amazing swarm of insects had taken over this house and it all had to be fumigated.'

A crucial requirement for any house or apartment Verity was considering renting was that it had a well-appointed kitchen. It wasn't just that she liked to entertain and eat well herself. For Verity, cooking was a form of relaxation. Armed with her wealth of knowledge about different cuisines, she relished the whole process of deciding menus, shopping for ingredients and preparing the food. Often, she inveigled her close friends into acting as her sous-chefs while she remained firmly in command of operations. It was social as well as practical; the cooking would invariably be accompanied with good conversation, abundant laughter and plenty to drink.

'She was a really good teacher,' says Rea Francis. 'She taught me to cook a good steam pudding and she used to cook salmon in foil in the dishwasher. And I still call white bread "sinful white", which was one of her terms.'

Felicity Marshall, then married to the director of photography on *A Cry in the Dark*, became another of Verity's family down under and someone else who benefited from her culinary skills. '"Would you like me to show you how to make chicken soup?" she asked me,' smiles Marshall. 'It took all day to cook the chicken with the vegetables and separate them, make a special sauce and make Matso balls. I've made it quite a few times since and she told me that because I made it so well, I was an honorary Jew. A lot of what she did was an education. I can remember her coming over and saying, "Darling, I've brought caviar over on the plane and I'm going to make blinis." She made them from scratch with the yeast and the buckwheat flour. She was very precise about preparing the caviar – boiling eggs and chopping them and the white onion very finely. It's quite a process. In the meantime, we had champagne to keep body and soul together. By the time we'd had a few Stollys, we were so pissed we stuffed up cooking the blinis. We ended up in hysterics but it was fabulous and we ate everything anyway.'

As she was finishing work on *A Cry in the Dark*, Verity was thrilled to learn that she had been offered an honorary degree as a Doctor of Laws from the University of Strathclyde. This was at the behest of one of Strathclyde's professors, Colin MacCabe, with whom she had become friends after they'd met on the set of the BBC's television review show *Did You See...?*; 'She kept on saying, "I've only got O Levels," and I got so fed up with it, I thought I'll get her a doctorate and then she won't be able to say that any more.'

The ceremony took place in Glasgow Cathedral on 15 April 1988. Verity travelled there the day before, accompanied by her father and step-mother, her close friends Michael and Kate Kagan and her PA, Sharon Bloom. She made a well-rehearsed and graceful speech in acknowledgement of the honour, bestowed on her by Dr W. Hamish Fraser. 'Everybody was delighted with her,' says MacCabe. It may seem curious for a woman used to taking the stage and receiving awards that such a distinction evidently meant so much. But MacCabe had been astute in reading more deeply than most into her regular lament about the inadequacies of her education. However self-deprecating she made it seem, Verity genuinely minded the lack of a university degree and this ritual did a little to restore the damage its absence had inflicted on her self-esteem.

A Cry in the Dark may have been the first fruit of her enduring relationship with Australia but it was the end of Verity's adventures in the screen trade. Against great odds, she had managed to produce her own film without compromising the quality of the production or the integrity of the storyline. Although she was intensely weary of the constant uncertainties of the film business, its shady characters and creative hypocrisy, neither did she want to return to being someone else's employee. She decided that she would reinvent Cinema Verity as a vehicle for making television. She could not have timed her return to the small screen better. In the years since she had last been a television executive, there had been some dramatic and important changes in the TV landscape. The arrival of Channel 4 and changes in the legislation that governed the running of the BBC had created a thriving new market for small independent producers, making programmes for sale to any interested channel. Verity anticipated that, should she succeed, she would have the choice of subjects in which she was interested with the freedom and control still possible in television but which had so often and so frustratingly eluded her in the maddening world of feature films.

'She was very focused,' says Beryl Vertue, a friend and herself a pioneering independent producer. 'She knew what she was aiming for and that's very good. It's the prospect of standing on your own feet, owning something, being more in charge. You've got to be creative because if you haven't got any subjects to sell, you haven't got a business at all. Having to make ends meet brings all your creativity to the fore. I think she had a good business sense, and you've got to think – "This is a good idea, why do I think this is a good idea? Who is it for? Ah yes, that kind of audience, therefore I will go to that kind of broadcaster." It focuses your mind much more than when you're working for a big organisation where it's all going to happen anyway.'

She based the new Cinema Verity in a rented office at Elstree Studios, employing Sharon Bloom and Caroline Gold as prospective producers, with Kath Williams in charge of legal and business affairs and the support of a secretary. 'It was a very tight-knit group,' says Williams. 'We gave ourselves a year. After I joined in September 1988, I could have snoozed quietly under the desk for the first three months and no one would have noticed. Verity was still dickering around in Australia. Caroline and Sharon were in and out on a fairly irregular basis. It was so small and we had no idea if it would work or not.'

From these tentative, hesitant beginnings, Verity's remodelled company would rapidly instigate a complete renaissance of her creative life. She was right on the verge of a triumphant and lasting return to the world of television.

CHAPTER TWELVE
SHE'S OUT
1989–1992

'I think of it as a change of pace and a chance to be my own boss, to make my own decisions. Of course, you're never completely in a position to make your own decisions, because once you've made your decision, you then have to go and sell it to someone else. I'm aiming at producing quality programmes with wide audience appeal.'

Verity to Angus Towler, *Television Week*, September 1989

From a slow start, the fortunes of Cinema Verity suddenly accelerated and for a golden period of four years, Verity presided over an intensely productive company, responsible for an ever-expanding, impressive and diverse output. Such rapid growth was the more impressive because, even at its busiest, the creative nucleus of Cinema Verity was so small. Verity aside, there were just two key producers, Sharon Bloom and Caroline Gold, although they were eventually supported by bright young talents Alexei de Keyser and Polly Hill, who undertook script reading and development duties.[1] It was a work hard, play hard environment. 'We'd take an idea from anywhere,' says Sharon Bloom, simply.

Another indispensable member of the team was Arthur Daley. Tall and naturally imposing, with his melting eyes and friendly nature, Arthur was a fixture of any meeting with Verity. As devoted to her as she was to him, perhaps his only really reprehensible habit was the occasional theft of any food that was inadvertently left within his reach. If you hadn't already guessed, Arthur was the latest of her beloved dogs, perhaps the most beloved of them all, named after the lead character from one of her biggest hits, *Minder*.

---

[1] Alexei de Keyser (1967–2004) After his stint at Cinema Verity, de Keyser moved first to Carlton TV and then to the BBC, where he was working as an executive producer in drama at the time of his premature death. At the time of writing, Polly Hill (1971–) was the head of independent drama for the BBC

Like his predecessors Max and Misty, Arthur was a Great Dane. When Misty had to be put down in 1986, Verity had been so upset that she had decided to live without a four-legged companion for a time. She was so busy with *A Cry in the Dark* that it was scarcely practical either. But she had missed the gentle affection and constant companionship that Misty had provided, and, as 1988 gave way to 1989, she decided that the time was right to choose another Great Dane with whom to share her life. There exists a photograph in which Arthur, a tiny puppy, nestles in the palm of Verity's hand. It seems almost inconceivable to compare this with later pictures when Arthur had reached his full and towering height. 'It was a bit like having a small pony in the house,' says close friend Felicity Marshall. 'She was always up early to take him for his morning walk in Holland Park and he was a total person magnet, everyone would stop and chat. He was a social lubricator.'

Some friends were surprised with the athletic skill and accuracy that Verity demonstrated when she threw a ball for Arthur, unaware that it was a legacy from her cricket-playing days at Roedean. Arthur went everywhere possible with her. 'To see Verity driving her Mercedes convertible with Arthur beside her in the passenger seat was a vision,' says writer Lynda La Plante. 'I used to look after him sometimes and then I had a Great Dane myself – it was all her fault. They are wonderful. Once you've had a Great Dane, the shadow of them is in the house all the time.'

'He's somebody to cuddle who doesn't answer back,' Verity told journalist Lynda Lee-Potter.[2]

One of Verity's circle of Australian friends, Val Hardy, remembers staying with Verity and her great friend Andrew Brown. It was so warm that they all decided to go swimming. 'Verity worried that Arthur couldn't swim, but I said, "He'll learn," so in we went,' says Hardy. 'She was so excited when, lo and behold, he started to swim.'

'I remember babysitting him for a day,' says another close friend, Sheila Savory. 'All he wanted to do was stand in front of the mirror, gazing at himself. And he absolutely refused to have anything to do with any other dog.'

Verity was delighted to find a good Indian restaurant in Shepherd's Bush, which, unusually, allowed Arthur entry. As she was rarely able to walk him herself during the working day, this duty fell to whoever was handy in the office. A local cab company, SWS Services, enjoyed a lucrative account with Cinema Verity chiefly because they were willing to allow Arthur in their cars. This arrangement only came about after an initial misunderstanding with one of the drivers who, expecting the actor George Cole, was aghast when 'Arthur Daley' turned out to have four legs and a tail. Still failing to grasp the situation, he grumbled that Arthur would only cover Mr Cole's clothes in hairs and threw

---

[2] Quoted in *The Daily Mail* (04.09.92)

the dog out of the car. Once the misunderstanding was explained and resolved, the SWS manager, Ronnie, and her 'boys' apologetically composed a special ode to Arthur, which Verity had framed. This declared:

> Oh George Cole
> My how you've changed
> Our driver thought he was deranged
> Same colour coat, no trilby hat
> Eric was knocked out by that
>
> So apologies to Arthur Daley
> Our driver went a little crazy
> Took one look at those big paws
> And thought at once of 'er indoors
>
> A truly GREAT Dane that's what you are
> And as a client now of SWS
> We have to say
> You're simply the BEST
>
> LOVE YOU ARTHUR

At the start of 1989, Cinema Verity moved into new premises. Hidden down an anonymous-looking road by the side of a church, but just a few metres walk from the noise and bustle of Shepherd's Bush Green, the Mill House was home to the company throughout this exceptionally fertile period of creative and commercial expansion. At Verity's behest, the old building, which owes its name to its original function, was expensively transformed into a stylish and idiosyncratic headquarters. Admiring the use of glass bricks in PR guru Lynne Franks' office, she adopted them for the Mill House simply to hide the photocopier. Carpets and sofas were specially commissioned; kilims, carefully chosen at great expense, added colour and detail and a craftsman used MDF to construct a stylish Art Deco-style sideboard for her office. She brought her huge glass desk from Golden Square, and the framed award and nomination certificates on the walls were an impressive reminder of the glories of her many past productions.

The confidence to establish herself in such style came from the success of Cinema Verity's first big television project, *May to December*, and the promise of several others besides, including potential drama series from the writers Alan Bleasdale, Doug Livingstone, and John Flanagan and Andrew McCulloch.

In some respects, *May to December* was a surprising choice to launch Cinema Verity in television because it was Verity's first ever foray into the very different world of situation comedy. The same was true for its writer, Paul Mendelson, who at the time was a 37-year-old copywriter in commercials. More to amuse himself rather than with any serious professional intentions, Mendelson had written a short comic novel about a house haunted by a Jewish mother. He'd called this *Feh*, a Jewish slang word for disgust or disapproval, and he talked about it with a good friend, the writer and film producer, Alexander Stuart. Stuart suggested that he show the book to the director with whom he was currently working, Nicolas Roeg. Mendelson knew and admired Roeg, who as well as his work as a features director on films like *Walkabout* and *Don't Look Now* had directed some Heinz commercials for which Mendelson had written the scripts.

'I told him about it and he said it sounded interesting,' recalls Mendelson. 'A year later I'd forgotten all about it and I got a phone call – "Nic Roeg here, Paul, how are you? I'm finishing off *Castaway* – Verity Lambert's in the next office, she's finishing off *Cry in the Dark* – and I've told her about *Feh* and she really liked it and wants to meet you – will you come up to Elstree?" It took me about a nanosecond to decide – fortunately in advertising, you could have long lunches so I pissed off to Elstree as fast as I could and had lunch with Verity and Nic. I think the fact that we were both Jewish was an immediate bond and I think she quite liked the idea of doing something that was Jewish.'

Verity asked him to write a 30-minute pilot and teamed him with one of her producers, Caroline Gold. 'Caroline and I worked on it and it was pretty good,' says Mendelson. 'Verity seemed to like it, too. She was very sweet with me and anything she said was like diamonds. She had a tremendous sense of confidence and was so sharp on a script. It was like she was born to do comedy because she was funny herself.'

When the pilot script was completed, Verity swiftly took it to the BBC's then head of comedy, Gareth Gwenlan, whom she knew well from her Television Centre days back in the 1960s. Gwenlan liked the writing but rejected the idea. 'He said, "Oh, you've done everything wrong. You've got suspension of disbelief, ethnic humour, ghosts, children, dogs..."' explains Mendelson. 'He said, "Go away and try again with something else."'

'I wasn't hugely impressed with it, he's absolutely right,' says Gwenlan himself. 'In spite of the evidence of things like *Bewitched*, I've always believed that comedy needs to be based in a certain amount of truth and reality. Perhaps that's my own personal taste coming through. There were areas of it I found difficult to take and I didn't see initially that it was strong enough. And I was fortunate that, at that time, I had an absolutely full slate.'

Mendelson went away and thought about his next move. 'At least I knew my brief,' he says. '"No Jews and no dogs" and I decided to write about what I knew. I'd always had this idea about an older man and a younger woman. I'd been a family lawyer and there was a firm I was working for where I'd seen a relationship like this happen and I thought it would be interesting. I'm half Scottish so I made my lawyer Scottish, too, and I liked that. It made him classless. The girl, who initially came to him to sort out her divorce, is a teacher. My wife is a teacher so I knew about that world, too. I didn't have time to research, you see. It was set in Pinner – where I live. I wanted to write something charming, with emotion, about romance and also set it in a world which people might find accessible.'

This time, Gwenlan's reaction was more positive and he asked for a second script to make sure the first wasn't a fluke. As soon as he read this, he bought a series of six episodes. 'Although it was Verity's first sitcom, it was still scripted work,' points out Gareth Gwenlan. 'When Verity was doing things like *Minder*, there were lots of big, funny moments and she obviously had a great sense of understanding a comedy. I was very pleased, too, that Paul had the guidance of someone with her experience of scripts. When you had a producer as trustworthy as Verity, you needn't worry; you only had to keep a paternalistic eye on it because you knew that it was going to work.'

As part of the package, Verity hired the veteran comedy producer/director Sydney Lotterby, whose impeccable credentials included *Porridge*, *Yes, Minister* and *Open All Hours*. 'Verity came to me and said, "I'm going to make you an offer you can't refuse" – the famous words!' laughs Lotterby. 'And I said, "Oh yes?" and then she offered me the scripts and said, "I'd like you to do them – what do you think?"'

Lotterby was keen and masterminded the first two series. 'Verity let me get on with it, God bless her,' he says. 'I did all the casting with the exception of Anton Rodgers, who was already on board.'

Rodgers was Paul Mendelson's suggestion to play the main character, lawyer Alec Callender. Mendelson was unaware that Rodgers had a similar May to December relationship with his own wife, the actress Elizabeth Garvie, who was many years younger. As he was still committed to his day job in advertising, Mendelson had to write much of the series in the toilets at his office. Verity introduced him to an agent so that he would have professional representation. 'She script-edited tremendously,' says Mendelson. 'It's a wonderful gift. It would take the form of a conversation. She knew fine what she wanted but she wasn't a writer. She obviously had a certain confidence in me. She hadn't done comedy and because of naivety I wrote masses of characters. Normally in comedy when you write lots of characters they're all in the same place – like *Dad's Army* – but here they were all over the place, in the school, in the grocer's shop and the law office. I think she almost didn't realise either. But it made for a lot of different stories.'

The first run of *May to December* was only a modest success but the audience appreciation figures were phenomenal, and this encouraged the BBC to repeat the series. This time the ratings matched the audience appreciation and the BBC immediately ordered more episodes. *May to December* eventually ran for six hugely successful series, surviving a change of leading lady (from Eve Matheson to Lesley Dunlop) and proving a cult hit in America, too. 'It was a particularly enjoyable comedy,' recalls Jonathan Powell, then the controller of BBC1. 'Very appropriate for the channel. It was charming, it had heart and did very well. These were the early days of independent production and we were keen to have access to the best talent, and Verity was the very best of talent.'

'She was challenging because you couldn't get away with anything other than your best,' says Paul Mendelson. 'When people love a series, you can almost get away with less because the audience love the characters. You could coast and have them saying the same things and people would be wetting themselves. But Verity wouldn't let you. She wanted it to be as good as when people didn't know those characters. We covered some really interesting issues in *May to December* – miscarriage, homophobia, possible cancer, and her point of view was that the emotions needed to be real.'

On 26 September 1989, Verity returned to the London Studios on the South Bank to preside over the recording of the pilot for another sitcom, this time for London Weekend Television. It was called *Follow the Yellow Brick Road* and was an attempt to capitalise on the enormous popularity of Cilla Black, whose fortunes had been spectacularly revived by LWT when they had chosen her to front their *Blind Date* series a few years earlier. Back at the peak of her powers, Black was keen to dabble in the world of comedy again, having enjoyed starring in two series of ATV comedy plays in the 1970s. A deal was brokered between Cinema Verity and Black's tough-talking husband and manager, Bobby Willis. The pilot was the work of former actress and experienced comedy writer Jan Butlin[3] and the premise was that Cilla would play a divorced suburban woman, working as a florist and looking for love. She finds her escape in a fantasy world of romantic old movies, in which she is transformed into one of the stars of the classic Hollywood era – among them, Mae West, Ingrid Bergman, Lauren Bacall. 'We shot these sequences in black and white before the studio audience came in,' remembers Sharon Bloom, who produced. 'This took time, obviously. Then they were played in during the main recording. We did go on and develop the series but I think a combination of Cilla's schedule and the script not being funny enough meant that it didn't turn into a series. Cilla was very professional and called everyone "sweetheart" in lieu of knowing our names. It was written into her contract that at the supper break she either had a bottle of Aqua Libra or champagne in her dressing room. Guess what we gave her?'

'There's been a lot of comedy in the drama I've done,' Verity told *Television Week*, 'but doing a half-hour sitcom with a live audience is quite nerve-racking. You can do what I call "middle of the road" drama reasonably well and it won't provoke extreme reactions but if you do a comedy nobody laughs at, everybody will say it's terrible.'[4]

Just as the abortive pilot for *Follow the Yellow Brick Road* was going into the studio, a newcomer arrived at Cinema Verity. Her name was Anna Callaghan and she had been hired for the crucial and challenging post of Verity's personal assistant by Kath Williams, the company lawyer and business manager. 'Every time I hired a PA, I took my life in my hands,' says Williams. 'Verity could be impossible and a pain in the arse. Her PAs had to

---

[3] Jan Butlin (1940–1998) Actress and writer. Sitcom credits included *Life Begins at Forty* (1978–1980) and *No Strings* (1989) – both for Yorkshire Television

[4] *Television Week* (14–20.09.89)

have a good knowledge of the business. She'd demand, "Get me Duncan Heath," and if you didn't know who Duncan Heath was, God help you.[5] You also had to have shorthand, which was getting unusual by then. I tried to teach her how to use a tape machine but she liked things to be done the way she was used to having them done.'

'I wasn't thrilled to discover that the two girls who preceded me spent a lot of the time crying in the loos,' comments Callaghan, drily. 'But I was that much older – I was 40-odd and I knew who she was talking about. If she said, "Get me Duncan Heath," I knew exactly who Duncan Heath was.'

This is not to say that Callaghan didn't have a few near misses herself. 'There was a moment,' recounts Kath Williams, 'when Anna booked Verity on a flight to Australia without realising that she'd booked her on to non-smoking. I thought, "Oh shit, I'm going to have to find another assistant." I was sitting in the office next door listening to this drama unfold and Sharon put her head around the door and said, "Have you booked the Lear jet then, Kath?"'

On a couple of occasions, sick of what she calls the 'general yelling and carrying on', Callaghan actually walked out and went home. She was wooed back by Verity's fervent and heartfelt apologies but vowed that if there was a third time, she would not return. There never was. The two women discovered that they shared several bonds; both were only children, especially close to their fathers, both lived alone with much-loved pets (Callaghan had cats)[6] and both shared high professional standards. A firm friendship developed between them. No one could reach Verity without first going through her PA. They developed an absolute shorthand of their own so that Callaghan could anticipate Verity's needs and wishes without always having to check first. 'Anna became really Verity's alter ego,' explains close friend Reggie Nadelson. 'She knew what she needed, what she liked – she could sign her letters – they became very, very close friends. But Anna didn't want to be Verity – to be a producer – and I think that probably helped because if you had two Veritys in a room, it wouldn't be easy.'

'She was quite demanding,' admits Anna Callaghan herself. 'If I wasn't efficient before, I sure as hell became efficient because she didn't take any prisoners and you couldn't mess about.'

Verity took full advantage of her PA's shorthand skills, rattling out her responses to her considerable correspondence at speed. There was always a sideline of strongly worded

---

[5] Duncan Heath (1947–) is a leading British talent agent

[6] After Callaghan's cat Lucy had to be put down, Verity found her a pair to fill the void: 'She rang me and said, "I was just buying Arthur Daley some food and there are these two cats and they've got your name on them, darling." I went to see the cats that night and came home with them – Charlie and Cleo. I always called her the Godmother.'

letters of complaint to be dealt with. 'She was the best grumpy letter writer,' says Anna Callaghan. 'Those about the dog poo in Addison Avenue would fill volumes, all sent to a man at the Royal Borough of Kensington and Chelsea who rejoiced in the name Mr Tidy. She was always threatening to write to Vanessa Whitburn, the editor of *The Archers*: "Darling, there are two things you can't do on radio – sex and photographs." She was also incensed by the breast cancer story with Ruth Archer, a storyline which dragged on forever, feeling that the character shouldn't have been portrayed as a victim.'

The Mill House had a small garden which Verity decided should be as seductive as the interior, a riot of flowers, shrubs and hanging baskets. Staff took turns with the watering and Verity went with Kath Williams to purchase everything needed for a barbecue with the company chequebook. There were regular impromptu parties and get-togethers in the little garden, with good wine and delicious food. Cinema Verity eventually shared the Mill House with a quartet of top casting directors and so the little building was always busy and frequently full of actors, writers and directors coming in for meetings, interviews and readings. 'She had no problems with people bringing their dogs to the office,' says Anna Callaghan, 'and often it was almost impossible to hear the telephones for barking. She was always great fun and treated the staff wonderfully at birthdays – whoever it was would be taken out for a lovely lunch and there would be presents. She loved her staff and was very conscious of taking care of them.'

Even when it wasn't a special occasion, lunch was rarely just eaten at people's desks, as is the depressing habit in so many offices today. Sometimes Verity would take her team to the nearby Shepherd's Bush Pizza Express. Another time it might be a curry or a vegetarian restaurant. At the end of the working day, out would come the wine or the champagne. 'Shall we have a drop of vino collapso?' Verity would ask rhetorically, and sometimes she would lead an impromptu sing-song. A favourite tune was the Irish ballad *Galway Bay*, although no one, least of all Verity, seemed to know more than the words of the first verse.[7] It was a lively, gossipy, hard-working and intensely creative environment. 'We were just doing it,' points out Sharon Bloom. 'We didn't think, "Oh, we're running one of the first 'indies' in the country." We didn't even think, "We are all girls." It was a bit of a riot, really.'

Despite her venture into situation comedy, Verity remained focused on drama. *The Boys from the Bush* was the product of her continuing love affair with Australia. A major ten-part series, shot entirely on film, it was a joint effort between Cinema Verity and Entertainment Media, the Melbourne-based company of which Fred Schepisi, from *A Cry in the Dark*, was a director.

'Verity was always keen on the Australian TV industry,' explains Jonathan Powell. 'As

---

[7] Says Anna Callaghan: 'No one else cared what followed and I'm sure were radiant with indifference when I got the rest of the lyrics from my Dad and V and would launch into our duet. It was not much of a repertoire, it was all we ever sang! Lot of eye rolling from the others I remember.'

was I. As controller, I bought a number of Australian mini-series like *Bangkok Hilton* [with the young Nicole Kidman] which always played very well on BBC1 and, of course, there was *Neighbours* daily demonstrating that the audience was at ease with an Australian setting for drama. ABC, the Australian public service broadcaster, also took and invested in a considerable amount of the BBC's drama. So, when Verity had the entrepreneurial drive to devise and finance a promising-sounding TV series which worked as a co-production, it seemed logical to commission it.'

The series was billed as a 'dromedy' – or comedy-drama – and was designed to take an anarchic and amusing look at life in contemporary urban Australia. 'I liked the whole freshness and feeling of it,' says the then head of BBC drama series and serials, Peter Cregeen. 'It was at the right price and I thought it would attract a popular audience; a good idea with a good writer.'

This was Verity's old friend, Doug Livingstone. 'With Verity you were allowed to get on with it,' he says, with feeling. 'There was no input from the BBC as far as I was concerned. She had come back from filming the dingo baby and said, "There's a tremendous amount in Australia – why don't you go out and spend some time there and come back with a series?" She persuaded the BBC to pay for two months in Australia (though I actually came back after six weeks), all the expenses and a commission for two scripts. I had no basic idea – nothing. Just think of the boldness of that. The only contact I had was an old lady in our local football club, who had a son in Australia. He lived in a small town halfway up Australia and I went to see him. I'd been in the country for three or four weeks, and I was beginning to worry that I didn't have anything. Two nights with this guy and I'd got the entire series – he'd been in Australia 25 years and he still hated it and spoke with an English accent. I thought, "This is fascinating."'

Livingstone's series centred on the work of Melbourne Confidential, – part marriage bureau, part detective agency and part 'almost anything that makes a few bucks' – and the motley collection of characters who run this outfit. Livingstone used the real-life character he had met as the basis of Reg (played by Tim Healy), who has been living in Australia for over 20 years but is still obsessed about his 'exile' from Shepherd's Bush. Reg's distant relation, Leslie (played by Mark Haddigan), arrives from London at the beginning of the series, starry-eyed and attempting to escape redundancy and a broken marriage back home.

The Boys from the Bush performed well enough for Cregeen and Powell to commission a second season, although it failed to develop beyond this into the kind of potential long-runner that Verity had envisaged and hoped for.

It was during *The Boys from the Bush* that Verity contemplated a rescue attempt for *Doctor Who*, the series that had launched her producing career. In the many years since she had left its fate in the hands of others, she had retained a detached interest in its fortunes. She had disliked the Jon Pertwee take on the character, feeling that his Doctor had become too Establishment. In the spring of 1975, she had grumbled to *Over 21* magazine: 'He's got respectable, which he was never meant to be. I once saw Jon Pertwee's Doctor calling up the Prime Minister. If the original Doctor Who had called up the Prime Minister, he'd have been told to fuck off.'[8]

She'd had more time for Tom Baker's interpretation, appreciating the wild eccentricity and alien intelligence that Baker brought to the part. In August 1981, she consented to appear on stage at a *Doctor Who* convention in London, effortlessly drawling her way through the questions and evidently not feigning her affection for the programme and what she had achieved with it against all the considerable hurdles of time and money. A couple of years later, *Nationwide*, the BBC's early evening news magazine, invited her to take part in an item to celebrate the Doctor's 20th anniversary. *Nationwide* was transmitted live from the Lime Grove studios in which so many of the early *Doctor Who* stories had been recorded. Interviewed by presenter Richard Kershaw and introduced as 'the woman who started it all', Verity told him how the TARDIS was originally meant to change shape to fit into the surroundings of wherever it landed but that 'we couldn't afford to change it so we stopped the mechanism.' She also commented: 'It was a series that was designed initially to appeal to 8-to-14-year-olds. The only way I had of being able to judge that, not having any children of my own, I simply said, "If this pleases me, then perhaps it will please them."'

Sadly, in the years since reaching this landmark birthday, *Doctor Who* had slipped into a steady decline and, in 1989, utterly out of favour with BBC management, it had finally been put on hold. Privately, Verity had been scathing about the direction the show had taken under producer John Nathan-Turner, loathing what she regarded as its overtly silly and camp approach. 'Somehow it had lost its way,' she told *SFX* magazine in 2006. '[It] seemed to be a parody of itself and the audience doesn't like that. You must believe in it and play it for real. If you don't do that, how can you expect anyone else to? *Doctor Who* is *not* a joke and you mustn't make it like that.'

The BBC briefly flirted with the idea of putting the series out to tender to the new indie market, hoping that this might bring a fresh approach and revive the ailing format. Verity talked to Jonathan Powell about her company pitching to make the show. 'We were at the research stage,' recalls Sharon Bloom. 'We did a lot of reading about Time Lords and Verity came in and I think she thought, "Oh that's not it at all." It was quite interesting because I don't know how serious she was about it. I don't know why we didn't get a writer in – maybe that's why I think Verity didn't really take it seriously. We had thought about the casting and Peter Cook was who she was thinking about to play the Doctor.'

Verity herself told *SFX* magazine, 'I was very young when I did *Doctor Who* and I think youngish people need to be involved with it. So as much as I love it, I may not have been

---

[8] *Over 21* (April/May 1975)

the right person to produce it. It needs to borrow from what is going on today, from what young people do, the music they listen to, that is a very important part of it. When I was 27 I did it without thinking because that's how old I was. But now I would think, "Oh gosh, what do you young people do?"'

In the event, nothing came of Cinema Verity's tentative efforts and indeed no other indie was awarded a contract to make a revived *Doctor Who*. 'It wouldn't have gone very far,' comments Jonathan Powell. 'It was too close to the closing down of *Doctor Who*.'

Another reason for Verity's hesitancy may well have been that she was aware of the weight of expectations that would bear down on anyone responsible for attempting to revive a once popular and established programme. If she tried and failed, she would mar her unblemished association with a show from which she still derived a certain amount of kudos. Striking out into new territory was not such a potentially poisoned chalice.

In August 1990, Verity was given the opportunity to address her peers at the annual Edinburgh Television Festival when she was asked to deliver the keynote speech, the James MacTaggart Memorial Lecture[9]. It was a great honour but came with expectations. Traditionally, the gist of each year's speech was widely reported and so the content and thrust were expected to trigger some debate and be worthy of the headlines. Although in most business and social circumstances, Verity was admirably confident and assured, making speeches, which came with the territory of her work, was her Achilles heel. She detested the whole experience and suffered agonies of nerves and angst at the mere prospect. But she realised this was an invitation that she could not possibly refuse. She found her resolve, worked hard on her speech and rehearsed its delivery with studied intensity. Such was the impact of her anxiety on her Cinema Verity colleagues that Anna Callaghan penned a comic ode on the subject, which was then framed and displayed in the office:

> There was a young lass called Vee
> The festival said, 'Let's see'
> She'll moan and she'll sigh
> It's Scotch in my eye
> But we need her for the McTee
>
> But darlings, I can't, I'm frantic, I shan't
> You cannot ask this of me
> If I'm not on a plane
> A boat or a train
> There are always rushes to see

---

[9] Named in honour of the eminent and much admired drama director James MacTaggart (1928–1974), whom Verity had adored. As a favour to her, MacTaggart wrote an episode of *Adam Adamant Lives!*, which turned out to be the only one that she felt truly worked

Sensibly, she took as her theme the role and future of the independent producer in the shifting sands of the British television landscape. She argued that it was essential that indies be allowed to retain some share in the rights to their programmes, in order to ensure their survival and security. The rest of the speech amounted to a passionate plea for the industry to fight to retain the high standards which made British television the envy of the world and yet were now under obvious threat from the remorseless march of commerce. She built to a carefully constructed killer ending, and, by the use of capitals, her script clearly indicated the required emphases: 'If de-regulation and the freer market are going to work while still providing quality and diversity of choice, it will depend on how VIGOROUSLY the ITC are implementing their powers; it will depend on how SCRUPULOUS the new franchise holders will be in keeping the promises they make in their applications; it will depend on the BBC and Channel 4 NOT LOSING THEIR NERVE in the face of falling ratings. And it will depend on us, the programme makers, refusing to compromise or lower our standards and seizing the opportunities that ARE there. What we must not do is allow ourselves to think that everything about the past was perfect. NONE of us can afford to be complacent. So let's be aware of the problems, and confront them. Let's be aware that our responsibility is not only to ourselves but to our audience. Resisting change is one of our more maddening British characteristics – DON'T let's go backwards into the future.'

Despite her misgivings, it was generally held that Verity had acquitted herself well, and with her customary fire and passion. The content of the speech was judged more than a few pages of fine words and neat phrases. In particular, her reasoning for indies to be allowed a fairer share of the rights in their output proved prescient and is now standard practice.

Cinema Verity did not possess such an advantage but, at this stage, business was so brisk that this didn't seem to pose an imminent threat to the company's health. The commissions kept rolling in.

The idea for *Coasting* was brought to Verity by David Reilly and Anthony Bygraves, son of the veteran entertainer Max Bygraves. Their concept was for a light-hearted drama series about two brothers, Eddie and Mike Baker, forced to take refuge in the family fairground business in Blackpool because of Eddie's dodgy business dealings. Reilly and Bygraves were not equipped to realise their idea so Verity bought the rights and put Sharon Bloom and Caroline Gold on to developing it into a compelling pitch. Their work paid off and it was duly commissioned. Writers John Flanagan and Andrew McCulloch were invited to flesh out the format and provide some of the scripts. 'We got credited as creating it,' explains Flanagan, 'but it wasn't our property. She thought there was something about this idea and we were just the hired guns brought in to make it work.'

Peter Howitt, then at the peak of his television popularity, took the lead as Eddie and as his co-star, Verity took a liking to a young actor called James Purefoy. 'We always had Peter Howitt in mind,' explains Andy McCulloch, 'but she insisted on casting James

Purefoy because she thought he was sexy and had star quality. I disagreed with her – there was another actor I thought should have got it. But she was absolutely insistent and the chemistry worked.'

Purefoy, who remembers Verity as 'very tough, charming and clearly very capable', rewarded her faith and has enjoyed a prolific and notable career in the years since his big break. Inspired by its setting in the northwest of England, Verity sold *Coasting* to Granada in the form of their drama doyenne, Sally Head, to whom Verity gave her first break at Thames back in the 1970s. 'We worked very happily together on *Coasting*,' she says. 'It was great – a lovely series.'

Encouraged by its healthy ratings, Head very nearly ordered a second series but when it came down to a choice between continuing with *Coasting* or funding a further series of Granada's in-house *Medics*, she felt she had to support her own company's effort. 'Sally always said it was a great mistake,' says McCulloch. 'We had more life in us. We'd got seven million viewers and Verity always said it would have built from that.'

Like all the early television indies, Verity had her suspicions that they were not competing on a level playing-field. Despite government legislation designed to encourage television companies to allocate a quota of their output to independent commissions, hostility to this external source of competition was scarcely concealed. Verity felt this was especially true of ITV, which is one reason why so few of Cinema Verity's projects were placed with the network.

Coasting may have stalled but Flanagan and McCulloch at least had the consolation of their own series, *Sleepers*. They'd been commissioned to write this by the actor Warren Clarke, who had the original idea and was to star. Verity rescued it from another company, which had gone bankrupt during the process of developing this clever and unusual yarn. It told the story of two Soviet agents, sent to Britain in the mid-1960s, who have been all but forgotten by the Kremlin.[10] Over the years, they have assumed utterly British identities and lives – one working-class, the other upper-class. With the advent of glasnost, the Russian authorities want them back and an agent is sent to track them down. Unwilling to co-operate, they go on the run.

Flanagan and McCulloch had intended to write *Sleepers* as a six-parter but Verity felt that this would be stretching the material too thinly and suggested it would work much better as four episodes. She found it refreshing to work with a pair of writers, joking that she didn't know which was 'Mr Nice' and which was 'Mr Nasty'. Like Lynda La Plante, both McCulloch and Flanagan were actors as well as writers and so were used to being given notes and specific feedback, which removed much of the potential antagonism in their collaboration.

---

[10] The first episode included the neat in-joke of a clip from the opening episode of *Adam Adamant Lives!* to help establish the 'Swinging Sixties' context

'She was incredible for writers,' says Andy McCulloch. 'She had an eagle eye for what was wrong with a script but her whole motivation was how do we make this better?'

'She asked all the right questions,' continues John Flanagan. 'She realised that *Sleepers* had one extraordinary conceit – is it credible that agents could have been planted as sleepers and be undiscovered for a quarter of a century? She asked us this and we said that within espionage nothing is a total fantasy. We can make it credible. So then she went on, "You have to keep everything within that rule," and sometimes she'd point out, "I think you've gone too far with the humour there because it's breaking your own rule." She knew exactly where it should be pitched.'

To get *Sleepers* made, Verity targeted BBC producer Michael Wearing, whose track record included the influential industrial espionage thriller *Edge of Darkness*. 'He was her prime choice because *Sleepers* was, in a way, like the jokey side of *Edge of Darkness*,' says McCulloch. 'He was the filter for the BBC. Verity was really decisive but Michael tried to put off making a decision for as long as he possibly could. There was a hysterical meeting where it was coming to the crunch. We had written three scripts and it was a case of were we going into production or weren't we? He showed us into his office, and then pointed out all the new furniture he had. Then he showed us some videos. He did everything he could to delay. After about an hour, Verity looked at her watch and said, "Look, Michael, the boys have to have a decision – they have to write the final script and I want a decision now." And she made him sign on the dotted line at that meeting.'

The stars of *Sleepers* were its originator Warren Clarke and Nigel Havers. Havers was Verity's second choice. She had wanted to cast one of her favourites, Sam Neill, on the basis of what she regarded as his sex appeal. But John Flanagan protested: 'I said, "Verity, the whole point of this is that Jeremy is more upper-class than the upper-class. Sam Neill is not even English."' Forced to agree, she suggested Havers instead, telling the writers that he was 'the English Sam Neill'. Neither of them were convinced and nor indeed was Clarke, for whom the other lead part was always intended. However, all parties came round to the idea when Havers actually started work and the chemistry between the actors was immediate and obvious.

Sleepers was well enough received for the BBC to toy with a sequel. Caroline Gold, who had produced the first series, set to work to develop this with the writers. But the controller of BBC2, Alan Yentob, was lukewarm and even Verity had her doubts that it was possible to extend the concept and improve on the original. Alas, these doubts led to Gold's abrupt departure from Cinema Verity. 'That was a spectacular day,' says Sharon Bloom. 'I think Verity was unhappy with the direction it was going in. There was a very big row and Caroline said what she thought in such a way that there was no going back, really.'

'Happily, I was travelling up Ecuador at the time,' comments Kath Williams.

A more public row erupted just before Christmas 1990, at a lunchtime gathering of the newly formed Women in Film and Television. Naturally, Verity had been an inaugural member of an organisation designed to promote the activities of women in the industry and it was her idea to invite film-maker David Puttnam, who also happened to be a friend, to make that year's keynote speech. 'She said, "A lot of whingeing and moaning goes on here; I think you should try and be a bit controversial." So I spoke about how, in my view, there was no such thing as the glass ceiling and that it was being used as an excuse to explain why some women didn't get on in the industry. If you are competent enough, you will get on. I think, incidentally, that she believed this too. But I'd wholly misjudged her colleagues and the whole fucking room went into uproar. It wasn't funny; it got nasty. Verity intervened and said, "Look, he's our guest and what's going on here?" It was one of the more memorably unpleasant experiences in my life and I don't think it was a very successful lunch for Verity either.'

There is no question that Verity regarded herself as a feminist. She believed absolutely in the equality of women and, as her career accelerated, she increasingly employed and empowered them. But she was, above all, a pragmatist. Merit came first and such a violent, primal reaction at a lunch designed to stimulate intelligent conversation and debate repelled her. She felt no intrinsic hostility to men for their advantages because she had not suffered from them. Also, as she often pointed out, her own management role-models were men, and men of a different generation and outlook too. Chief among all these was her father, with whom she had always identified, whose example of hard work and good conscience she had followed consistently as she made her own way in the world and whom she loved and revered.

On 6 March 1991, just a few weeks before *Sleepers* began transmission, Stanley Lambert died. He was 82 years old. They had always weathered the various storms in their relationship, from his disappointment in her marriage, and the lack of any grandchildren, to her anger and annoyance when, shortly before his death, he had casually warned her not to expect too much in the way of an inheritance. He had, he explained, been guilty of living too well in his retirement with Verity's stepmother, Betty. 'I can't believe it,' Verity told her close friend, Kate Kagan. 'Since almost as long as I can remember, he's encouraged me to invest in this and save up that and think about my finances – and now this!'

Whatever the occasional tensions, their relationship had been the most constant of Verity's life. The connection was not simply familial and predicated on the father–daughter archetype. They were both ebullient and outgoing, cheerfully social and intrinsically optimistic. There was genuine mutual admiration, too, for their shared work ethic and considerable professional achievements. She had always deferred to him for financial advice and sent him many friends and colleagues as clients, not just out of loyalty but because she knew his skill to be first-class.

The death of a parent invariably evokes a complex array of emotions and Verity was not immune. She mourned her father and missed him keenly, always.

'When her father died, she completely changed her whole attitude to Betty,' says her old friend, Kate Kagan. 'She was like that. Deep down, for all her toughness, she was very protective and generous. She looked after Betty extremely well, both emotionally and financially.'

Work was, as ever, a useful prop and salvation from emotional turmoil. Stanley Lambert had died at a point when his clever and talented daughter was in superb fighting form, driving her company forward with her passion and energy for television unabated by the knock backs, endless petty politics and worrying changes in the industry that threatened to diminish budgets and restrict the freedom and autonomy of producers. She was just about to deliver one of her all-time triumphs, a project whose origins lay in the infancy of her company.

Alan Bleasdale's *GBH* (short for Great British Holiday) started life as an attempt at writing a novel. Verity saw its potential as a drama series instead. The story was a satirical fable of modern Britain, with a strong theme of local political corruption. The central protagonist was clearly based on Derek Hatton, the controversial sometime deputy leader of Liverpool County Council. A few years earlier, Bleasdale had been at the centre of a bruising political row over his BBC serial *The Monocled Mutineer*, which was also, in part, inspired by real characters and events. The BBC had fudged and fumbled their defence of his work and, in consequence, Bleasdale was wary of taking this new project to them. His main supporter at the BBC during *The Monocled Mutineer* crisis had been Michael Grade. Grade had since jumped ship and was now the chief executive of Channel 4.

'Michael came into my office,' recalls Peter Ansorge, then the commissioning executive for drama at Channel 4. 'He said, "Verity Lambert's been on the phone. She's got this project by Alan Bleasdale."'

Ansorge knew and admired Bleasdale from their time at the BBC's Pebble Mill drama department, where they had both cut their teeth on a range of experimental and groundbreaking series and plays. Grade made it clear that it was up to Ansorge whether or not to proceed with Bleasdale's latest idea. 'Michael said, "They'd like to come in the day after tomorrow,"' Ansorge continues. 'I asked if there was any kind of treatment. Half an hour later, Michael's PA, Ros, came in with this unfinished 800-page novel. Obviously I had to read it. By three o'clock in the morning, I'd got to page 500. As the book went on there was less and less prose and it was almost pure dialogue. There was a scene I remember – the hotel scene – which almost stayed in verbatim. I felt very comfortable going in to the meeting, thinking we're going to do this. I said, "We'll commission the scripts." Verity came back with, "If you commission the scripts, we must have a guarantee that it's going to be produced." I said I'd "have to talk to Michael and Liz [Forgan – Channel 4's director of programmes] about this," but that's very hard to do – just suppose the scripts don't work. So Alan was growling. I said "if I like episode one, I could more or less give you that guarantee but not without that."'

Liz Forgan read the existing manuscript and told Ansorge that she thought it was 'terrible' and that the channel should withdraw. Grade, on the other hand, kept faith with his promise that Ansorge could decide and told him to go ahead and give Verity the guarantee she wanted. 'Just put it in writing – we can always get out of it if we have to,' he advised.

Bleasdale got on with the mammoth task of scripting and when he delivered the first drafts, it was evident that they were all far too long for the six episodes that had been commissioned. Verity was only semi-joking when she suggested that they should weigh them first. 'Alan overwrites like mad,' says Michael Grade. 'That's just the way he does it.' Grade indicated that he was prepared to be flexible with the running times of the episodes but still a sizeable amount of editing would need to be accomplished before the scripts could be considered ready for shooting. Verity cleared two weeks to focus on the complex and emotive task. 'I sat in her office in Shepherd's Bush with her from Monday to Friday,' recalled Bleasdale. 'We took out 238 pages and 120 scenes. By the Wednesday night, I did tell Peter Ansorge that I was contemplating murdering her and Peter actually went and told Verity. I think Verity wasn't quite sure whether I was serious or not. She was murdering my babies.'

'Every cut was driving him mad,' says Ansorge. 'It was a monster of a piece. "I want to phone Michael Grade and call the whole thing off," he'd say. Then I noticed that I'd got all my scripts and Alan had all his scripts but Verity didn't have any. I've never, ever, in any other script session with a producer or script editor seen that before. She knew the scripts, and precisely where a scene took place, better than Alan. That's how she got the cuts through. It was astonishing. That also happened in the editing. It was all in her head. Once or twice, it was quite clear that Alan didn't know what scene she was talking about. He had forgotten it. Once it was clear that Verity knew his work so well, somewhere in him he had to acknowledge that professionalism and submit to it.'

Throughout these torturous script sessions, Arthur Daley lounged on his mattress in the corner of Verity's office, unaffected by the angry outbursts that erupted at intervals around him. 'After a morning of cuts, Alan suddenly gets up and says, "Well, I'll take him for the usual walk,"' recalls Peter Ansorge. 'Verity smiled and told me, "Alan takes him for a walk every day, it's so touching, I've never seen that side of him." "Wanna come Pete?" says Alan. So I do and the dog clearly knows where it's going – straight to the Bush pub. The barman says, "How's it going, Al?" "Oh terrible, they're cutting my script, I hate that woman." The barman gets out a bowl, pulls a pint, puts it in the bowl and gives it to the dog. That was Alan's revenge. Getting the dog pissed. Alan insists this didn't happen but it's something you couldn't make up. I never told her because if I did, Alan would have been killed.'

'Her work for me with Alan was masterly,' believes Michael Grade. 'From the script that he had delivered to the time that Verity had finished with it – she was just a genius script editor and she had a magic touch.'

'A year later when we had filmed it,' admitted Bleasdale, 'I didn't miss any of those 238 pages or any of the 120 scenes.'[11]

Such was Bleasdale's strength of character and close involvement with every aspect of his work that several potential directors were scared off. Verity suggested Robert Young, who was experienced and had enjoyed a long career, including a stint on *Minder*. Ansorge was unsure. 'I was a bit nervous because he hadn't done anything that substantial,' he admits. 'In actual fact, he did a fantastic job. I think if a producer says they believe in someone you have to back them and Verity thought he would have the right sensitivity to deal with Alan and get the best out of the actors.'

'I remember reading it on the Underground,' says Young. 'I was going back to Kew and I was so immersed in this marvellous script, I ended up somewhere completely different.'

The series starred Robert Lindsay as Michael Murray (the part inspired by Derek Hatton) and Michael Palin as schoolteacher Jim Nelson. Verity had long wanted to work with Palin, wooing him as far back as 1975 when she was first ensconced as director of drama at Thames. 'Verity was very keen for me to do the Michael Murray part,' recalls Palin. 'At first, Robert Lindsay couldn't do it – he was booked to do a musical in New York – and I think Billy Connolly was going to be Jim. I saw her a lot in the early stages to discuss the project – I remember her huge dog. I was slightly in awe of her and the amount of things she had done. Verity suggested me to Alan. I was quite impressed that he'd be interested in me playing the part because he had all his Liverpool links. I felt rather flattered that someone like Verity and Alan were so determined to get me. I didn't see myself in that rank of actor. Once I was in the frame, they stuck with me tenaciously.'

When Lindsay's availability meant that he was able, after all, to play Murray, Palin took the more conventional, though no less pivotal, part of Jim. 'It was a huge thing to do,' he continues. 'It established me as a serious actor. Jim was very complex and he had to be believable. I couldn't take refuge in a wacky character.'

Palin was full of admiration for Verity's doughty professionalism. 'She rose to a challenge very well,' he says. 'Someone would tell her that something couldn't be done and she would get about a foot taller, her terrific eyes would blaze, she would take a great drag on her cigarette, and she'd go into battle. I wouldn't like to get on the wrong side of her and I don't think I did. But I always thought she had a nice ability to connect with everyone involved on a shoot. She'd not be stiff and aloof, she'd have a drink and a

---

[11] All the Bleasdale quotes taken from his interview for the BBC's *Drama Queen* (2008)

cigarette. There were certain tensions between Verity and Alan. She was this silky, sophisticated, cigarette-smoking, public-school Southerner and he was this growling Liverpudlian. But she liked difficult people and projects and she believed in someone like him. They both saw themselves as something outside the establishment which is odd, because she *seemed* to be part of it. She obviously liked Alan and his toughness and the toughness of his work.'

'I think a lot of the success of *GBH* is Verity's,' says Robert Young, 'because she didn't allow Alan, who's not done anything as good since – to always have his own way. She made him really knuckle down. We were a really good combination and like a lot of things in our industry, the good combinations get destroyed for all sorts of reasons – things fall apart and it's a pity. On *GBH*, it started to fall apart towards the end – it was a power struggle. If only she had kept control of *GBH* to the end but she didn't. She was outmanoeuvred.'

A final jostling for position emerged in the cutting room. Rather than being shot episodically, for essential economies of scale, *GBH* was filmed in one continuous sweep, rather like an epic movie. It was a trick that Verity had learnt when masterminding the similarly ambitious *Reilly: Ace of Spies*. But by the shoot's conclusion, there was so much material a debate emerged about whether the six episodes might be stretched to seven. Verity was opposed to this plan, feeling that it would be a tighter and more effective narrative if it remained confined to the intended duration. 'She always said that *GBH* could have been ten per cent better if she'd been allowed to scissor out more of it,' says Kath Williams. 'Bleasdale wouldn't have it – every single word was a battle.'

One scene that survived was a sly nod to Verity's *Doctor Who* past. Towards the end of episode four, Michael Murray, in the midst of a nervous breakdown and beset by a nervous tick, finds himself in a hotel overrun by drunken *Doctor Who* fans. Here he is confronted with the surreal spectacle of a Dalek partying with two young women and intoning, 'Fornicate! Fornicate!'

Although Verity's view was that less is more, Ansorge backed Bleasdale and *GBH* was granted an additional episode. 'I'd love to know why she lost that battle but she did,' says Young. 'Of course, it was more money for everybody if it went to seven. It was a fatal error, I think. It started to get too long and too rambling.'

Despite her reservations, and those of the director, when it was screened over the summer of 1991, *GBH* was an overnight triumph, with reviewers falling over themselves to eulogise the power and poignancy of its narrative and the perfectly nuanced performances. It was nominated for and won a clutch of awards, with Robert Lindsay winning Best Actor in the Broadcasting Press Guild awards, the Royal Television Society awards and, most prestigious of all, the BAFTA awards. In all, *GBH* was nominated for a staggering nine BAFTAS. Despite Lindsay's win and another for Best Original Television Music, for Verity, this glittering evening became not an occasion for basking in the well-deserved limelight of an enormous success but the start of the bitter final act of her long-running feud with her former friend, Irene Shubik.

Shubik, who was eminently qualified, had been invited to act as the chair for the jury of that year's category for Best Drama series. Those serving on the jury included directors Herbert Wise and Ross Devenish, writer Clive Exton, producer Louis Marks and former head of BBC drama series and serials, David Reid. The procedure was that the jury carefully discussed the merits of each nominated series before a secret ballot was held. Only the chair would see the results of these votes and would then feed the result through to the BAFTA administration. In the event of an even split, the chair would have the casting vote.

'It was all very gentleman-like as far as I recall,' says Herbie Wise. 'Everybody said their piece. Certainly, I got the impression that the result reflected what went on in the jury room.'

Other than *GBH*, also in contention were the BBC's classic serial *Clarissa* and two entries from Granada, their long-running *Coronation Street* and *Prime Suspect*, a bleak and hard-hitting crime series from Lynda La Plante. A perfect marriage of clever writing and charismatic playing from its star, Helen Mirren, this had been enormously popular and well-received, but industry gossip still had *GBH* as the clear favourite in the contest. But when the winner was announced on the night, it was not *GBH* but *Prime Suspect*. No one was more surprised than Lynda La Plante. 'Alan Bleasdale came up and said, "What about my fucking BAFTA?"' she recalls. 'Verity liked me and loved my work but she would have killed for that award. She was in Alan Bleasdale's court that night and, as far as she was concerned, he should have won that BAFTA.'

'Before the ceremony took place,' says Robert Young, 'Verity was the one who said, "We will not win it. She'll get me – she won't allow me to get a BAFTA." Irene Shubik hated her so much. It was still a shock when it happened. It was so obvious that *GBH* deserved it over *Prime Suspect*. It was just a better work. But the moment you start crying out about things, it looks so bad. I felt for Alan. Whatever had happened between him and me, he deserved a huge award. Irene Shubik and BAFTA really had a lot to answer for.'

'It was quite disappointing,' concedes Michael Palin. 'That's the way things go with awards. *Prime Suspect* was terrific but *GBH* seemed to be the more original, exceptional and unusual work. We all felt "Oh" when it was announced. Obviously, for Alan and Verity it meant a great deal. I remember glances being exchanged with Michael Grade. I heard from Alan what was supposed to have happened. We had had four votes and Irene Shubik had used her casting vote to make sure that Verity, with whom she had a long feud, didn't win. No trace of the voting slips could be found. There were all sorts of stories that she'd flushed them down the toilet.'

Regardless of the gossip and the grumbling that greeted the news of the award, this might have been the end of the matter but, shortly after the ceremony, David Reid happened to bump into Ross Devenish in the Hatchards book shop in Piccadilly and recalls 'He said something like, "I'm surprised you voted for *Prime Suspect*." I said, "I didn't." He said that was weird because, chatting perfectly innocently to the others and adding up their votes, this would mean *GBH* should have won. I think he then went home and checked round again on the phone. He called me and said according to what people reported, *GBH* should indeed have won. I agreed to telephone Richard Price, then the Chairman of BAFTA and express concern. The next thing I knew all hell broke loose in the press.'

The BAFTA-gate story was a gift to any jaded hack. Much was made of the simmering enmity between Verity and Irene Shubik and the implication that Shubik had used a position of trust to rig the results and take her revenge on a woman she deeply despised. 'Verity was convinced that Irene manipulated the secret voting,' says Herbert Wise. 'As far as I'm concerned, it's absolutely not true. Irene was dead honest; there was nothing deceitful about her. I knew her very well and I certainly do not think that she would have been capable of behaving so blatantly. I don't think that she would have dared. It was too risky – you could be found out – and she was not a courageous personality.'

'It's *unproven*,' says Michael Grade, with careful emphasis. 'I can't shed any light and people have always got excuses why they didn't win, though it was not difficult to fall out with Irene Shubik.'

'My take on that is that it was probably a miscount,' says producer Ken Trodd, who was then closely associated with BAFTA. 'She just added it up wrong. When they were alerted as to what had happened, I believe someone at the top of BAFTA destroyed the voting slips. I tried to say that we have to take this seriously but, very speedily, right or wrong, BAFTA took the view that they shouldn't rock the boat. I then suggested that *Prime Suspect* and *GBH* should share the award but BAFTA just wanted to draw a line and move on.'

'Verity thought that something smelt horrible,' says Sharon Bloom. 'To this day, I've never joined BAFTA because Verity said, "None of us can join BAFTA now."'

'What amazed me then – as it still does – is that someone from BAFTA did not immediately ring round the jury members and ask them to confirm how they voted – end of story,' says David Reid. 'But it never for one single moment occurred to me that it might be construed as a criticism of Irene. Unfortunately, she immediately took it to be exactly that. I tried several times over the years to explain or even apologise but she would have none of it. For a start I don't think Irene would have done anything underhand as chair of the jury no matter how long-running her feud with Verity might have been. I conclude now, as then, that someone actually made a dreadful mistake and to this day doesn't know it. In their head, they thought *GBH* but they wrote down *Prime Suspect*. That's really the only thing that makes any sense to me.'

BAFTA's handling of the situation cannot be said to have helped matters. They claimed that it was impossible to verify the vote as all the slips had been destroyed. BAFTA director Tony Byrne told *The Guardian* defensively: 'You've only got to have one person whose memory is at fault.' But the Academy's process was revealed as unflatteringly amateur and disorganised. Steps were hurriedly put in place to change the voting system so that the possibility of such damaging confusion might be avoided in the future. This was scant consolation for Irene Shubik, whose reputation necessarily suffered by implication, nor for Verity and her supporters, who would never know for sure whether they had been cheated out of an important award which should rightfully have been theirs. For the declared winner, it dulled the shine of the gilded BAFTA mask, too. 'There was a lot of gossip,' says Lynda La Plante. 'It was horrible and it tarnished the award for me.'

Foolishly, a wounded and ever-defensive Shubik spoke her mind to an *Evening Standard* journalist, who equally foolishly printed her comments without offering any right of reply to those whom Shubik had effectively slandered. 'She compared Verity to Ceauescu,' points out company lawyer Kath Williams, raising an eyebrow. 'He was a mad dictator, for God's sake. It was all such rubbish. I sent it straight to Keith Schilling and said, "Not a word of this is true."'

Both Verity and Alan Bleasdale sued and, in July 1992, were awarded substantial damages. David Reid and Louis Marks followed suit. They, too, won their case. 'It was a very unsettling, emotionally draining time,' says Reid, 'and something none of us wished to be involved in.'

There was an unpleasant coda to the whole messy saga at writer Doug Livingstone's annual Boat Race party, held at his Hammersmith flat, which commands superb views of the River Thames. Livingstone, who had met Verity through Irene Shubik, and who admired and had worked with both women, always invited them to the party and continued to do so even after their feud. They would carefully avoid each other during the party, usually remaining in separate rooms. Livingstone was also friendly with David Reid, and the year after BAFTA-gate Shubik refused to speak to him, too. It was the last time Livingstone and his wife Anne invited her. It was just too awkward to accommodate such simmering resentment in what was supposed to be a convivial atmosphere. Verity and Irene Shubik were never reconciled.

There was one last encounter between the two women at the memorial service for actor Leo McKern in 2002. This was witnessed by the director John Gorrie: 'I went on my own and Verity went on her own. We sat next to each other in the church and went on to the wake at the Theatre Museum together. When we were leaving, we got into the cloakroom to get Verity's coat and Irene was there. It was just the three of us. And Verity said, "Still not speaking to me?" Irene turned to her and said, "I wouldn't speak to you if you were the last woman in the world." I've never seen such hate in somebody's eyes. I said, "Oh Verity, just ignore it," but she was quite upset. This is why in the end you had to sympathise with Verity.'

For Cinema Verity, *GBH* was the pinnacle of a success story, which seemed to show no signs of abating. 1992 was to be their busiest and most productive year yet. Now that

May to December had become a banker for BBC1, Verity revisited writer Paul Mendelson's first idea, for a comedy in which a house is haunted by an archetypal Jewish mother. Verity suggested a new title – *So Haunt Me*. 'So we went back to Gareth Gwenlan with it,' explains Mendelson, 'and he said, "Oh, I really like this." We didn't remind him that he had rejected it a few years earlier. What had happened in the meantime was that Maureen Lipman's BT commercials had become very popular and *Ghost* had come out so suddenly Jewish mothers and ghosts had a currency.'

With veteran Jewish comedy actress Miriam Karlin in the lead as the garrulous but deceased Yetta Feldman, *So Haunt Me* ran for three series and might have continued had it not been for a change of controller. Mendelson had an idea for a third sitcom, based on the domestic life of a superhero. Sharon Bloom thought it had potential but Verity hated it and turned it down. 'So I took it elsewhere,' says Mendelson. '*My Hero* was a huge hit and ran for years. She did say, later on, "I made a mistake there, didn't I?" I think she sort of assumed that if she didn't think it was good, it would go back in a drawer.'

Verity often displayed a possessive streak in her relationships, personal and professional. 'I had this conversation with another company,' continues Mendelson. 'They said, "Well, you've got a first-look deal with Verity." I said, "It's news to me." There was no first-look deal. I think she put that around so nobody approached me. As long as you intimate to other people that there's a first-look deal, you don't have to pay the person for one.'

But Kath Williams refutes this: 'No way would she have said we had a first-look deal if we didn't. That's dishonest and she wasn't. People may have *assumed* we did.'

Two years on from *Coasting*, Verity finally placed another series with ITV. This was *Sam Saturday*, another Jewish-character-led entertainment, a London-based detective show with Ivan Kaye playing the lead.[12] Six episodes were produced by Cinema Verity's Sharon Bloom and veteran producer/director Alvin Rakoff. 'I got this idea for a Jewish detective and took it to Verity,' explains Rakoff. 'She took it to Nick Elliot at London Weekend. I still think it's a good idea. I'm a non-practising Jew and I was trying to exploit the fascination I have for the north London Jewish community. I think it didn't quite work because we weren't ambitious enough.'

'We were too cautious about the Jewish thing,' agrees Bloom. 'If we had been in America we would have just embraced it rather than hide it away a bit. It's what happens when you get three Jews together and they're a bit scared of putting it out there and making it like the Maureen Lipman ads. We thought we can't be like that so we were a little bit north London reserved. It could have been a lot more of a riot and a lot funnier. It wasn't good enough. Also Alvin's wife was dying and his mind wasn't on it.'

---

[12] Verity gave her old friend Viv Phillips' son, Jonathan, his first job as a runner on *Sam Saturday*. Phillips later became a producer himself and, at the time this book was written, was working on the BBC's *Father Brown*

Rakoff's wife, the actress Jackie Hill, had terminal breast cancer. She was an old friend of Verity's and had played Barbara for her in the first two series of *Doctor Who*. Yet again Verity was faced with the scourge of this devastating condition which had taken her close friend Nora Fielding and from which she herself had suffered. Hill eventually succumbed to the disease in February 1993.

Verity was worried about another friend, too, her closest friend of all, the producer Andrew Brown. Since the charmed days of their work together at Thames Television, Brown had continued to prosper. Among his varied achievements were the mini-series *Kennedy*, *Selling Hitler* (another collaboration with *Rock Follies* writer Howard Schuman) and *Prick Up Your Ears*, the caustic film biography of Joe Orton. He had just won his fourth BAFTA, this time for the elegant series *Anglo-Saxon Attitudes*. But Verity was one of the few who were aware that he had also contracted the HIV virus. In these dismal years before the development of any effective drug treatment, diagnosis of the virus was an almost certain death sentence. For Brown, who had retained a lifelong ambivalence about his homosexuality, it was more than a debilitating and occasionally disgusting illness. It was a blow to his privacy and dignity. As his health deteriorated, he fled from the scrutiny and concern of friends, and left England for Sydney, Australia. Verity remained in close contact and did what little she could. It has often been remarked upon that they were more like siblings than friends and, understanding the boredom and depression his failing health caused him, she talked about anything but and tried instead to amuse him, and to carry on as she had always done.

Even for a dedicated workhorse like Verity, it was a serious distraction. For years, she had become used to functioning effectively and efficiently under continual pressure but this was only possible because her emotional life was largely under such tight control. As Andrew Brown began the grim and inevitable slide towards death[13], she can be forgiven for finally faltering in her professional life. But the timing could not have been more unfortunate. Cinema Verity had just been awarded the biggest contract of its existence. It was a golden opportunity to guarantee the long-term future of her company and secure a fortune for herself.

The project with so much at stake was a brand-new BBC1 soap opera, to be transmitted three times a week, tentatively christened *Little Britain*. 'It's going to be my pension,' she confided in friends, Brown included, during the first heady rush of excitement at winning such a huge and confident commission.

The BBC disliked the working title and it was Verity who came up with an alternative – *Eldorado*.

---

[13] He died in Australia on May 16 1994. Verity organised a wake in London. 'He left money is his will for there to be a party,' says Howard Schuman, 'but not a memorial. So there was a party in Kew Gardens and it was forbidden to reminisce about Andrew or for anyone to speak. It was ghastly, distressing. In the air was the desperation of many of us just wanting to say what Andrew had meant.'

CHAPTER THIRTEEN
SUNBURNT
1992–1993

'I believe this programme will work. I believe it. The cast believe it. The BBC does. We all believe. I believe that it will become part of the fabric of television. I also believe it will be a success regardless of whether the press stop trashing it or not.'

Verity to Lesley White, *The Sunday Times*, 1992

'The big blooper of Verity's life,' says Jeremy Isaacs.

'It did her a lot of harm,' believes director Waris Hussein.

'The only real failure that she had,' adds fellow director Herbert Wise. 'And my God, was that a failure...'

'I suppose if I was going to have a failure,' said Verity herself, 'I might as well have had a major one.'

The road to *Eldorado*, the one resounding disaster of Verity's career, began with a crisis for BBC1 and its then controller, Jonathan Powell. Powell had followed Michael Grade into the job and, for his first couple of years in post, had benefited from an inheritance of strong scheduling and established and successful programmes. By the dawn of the 1990s, however, the main competition, ITV, were fighting back, empowered by the dynamic leadership of Greg Dyke. Dyke and his fellow executives chose drama as their principal weapon against the BBC, pouring huge sums of money into extended runs of popular middlebrow titles like *The Bill, London's Burning, Soldier, Soldier, Peak Practice* and *Heartbeat*. 'They forgot about doing posh series like *The Jewel in the Crown*,' explains

Jonathan Powell. 'That all went out the window. There weren't any more mini-series or single films on Sunday night. Setting aside their soap operas, they were running 200 hours of one-hour drama a year – we had much less. It was difficult and there was a limit to what I could do.'

Powell was eventually granted some additional funding from the BBC governors for an expansion of his drama output. However welcome, this was never going to enable him to compete in equal terms with the munificence or aggression of ITV's drama offering. He would need to be more strategic. Back in 1985, Terry Wogan's three-times-a-week chat show had been one of the cornerstones of Michael Grade's revamp of the channel. Five years on, the show had begun to flag. This was an acute headache for Powell as *Wogan*, transmitted at 7 p.m., had been constructed as the gateway to an evening's schedule. But as the amiable Irishman's audience and share steadily declined, the programmes that followed suffered too. Powell considered his options and came up with a plan to replace *Wogan* with a brand-new soap opera and shore up his schedule still further with yet another to run twice weekly at eight o'clock. 'This was going to be *Casualty*, split into two,' he says. 'I thought you could probably find something else for Saturday. In those days, people weren't so adept at thinking of popular formats. The factual department was wonderful but nobody had invented *Dragons' Den*[1] and all that sort of stuff. You were looking at a landscape with very few opportunities. It was a really, really difficult logistical exercise.'

If *Casualty* was reconstructed as a twice-weekly, year-round proposition, it would remain an in-house production. But it was decided that the BBC simply did not have the resources to make the other new soap, which would have to be commissioned from an independent producer instead. This would offer the added advantage of appeasing the government who were putting the Corporation under pressure to open up their markets to external producers. Powell was understandably anxious to make his changes as quickly as possible, so there was a phenomenal amount of work to be accomplished in just a few months. In the meantime, he had the sensitive and difficult task of persuading Terry Wogan to remain where he was, albeit under notice to quit. 'He wasn't happy about it,' comments Powell. 'I don't blame him, really.'

Nonetheless, the star acquiesced. Unexpectedly, another obstacle then presented itself in the form of Powell's senior colleague, John Birt, who was about to become the BBC's Director-General. When he learned of Powell's plans, Birt made it plain that he did not want two additional soap operas launched on a channel which was already home to *EastEnders* and the imported *Neighbours*. Birt's squeamishness was chiefly political. The BBC were under ever-increasing scrutiny and he was nervous of provoking a storm of criticism should they take such an aggressively ratings-chasing approach. Reluctantly, a frustrated Powell had to concede and reconsider.

---

[1] Factual entertainment series in which budding entrepreneurs pitch their ideas to a panel of potential investors. It has run on BBC1 since 2005

A girls' best friend – with her beloved Arthur Daley, 1997

Shooting *Running Late* with Peter Bowles, who worked with Verity as actor and originator of projects, 1992

She's Out reunited Verity with writer Lynda La Plante and director Ian Toynton, 1993

Forced smiles – on the set of the ill-fated *Eldorado* with 'godmother' Julia Smith, 1992

With Andrew Brown, the brother
she never had

Making hay while the sun shines
with Waris Hussein in Lindos, 1974

Photograph Waris Hussein

With Waris in later years – no longer the 'outsiders'

In fine form at her 70th birthday gala, 2005

'An almost exclusive relationship...' with David Renwick

Onwards and sideways with Joanna Lumley on *The Cazalets*, 2001

At the palace – L to R: Kate Kagan, Verity, her stepmother Betty and stalwart PA Anna Callaghan

The Prince and the Showgirl – OBE ceremony, 2002

Television royalty

The first producer of *Doctor Who* with the man who brought it back to life, Russell T Davies: 'When I met her, she said, "All those Daleks flying into Canary Wharf, I wish we could have done that." Oh, but you did, Verity. You made it all.'

The June Mendoza portrait, painted just months before Verity's death

He decided that it was more straightforward to backtrack with *Casualty*, leaving the programme where it was, running as 50-minute instalments on Saturday nights. The three-times-a-week independent project would, however, continue. A score of companies had been invited to pitch for the slots. Two of those which had offered concepts and loose ideas were Witzend (fronted by executive producer Allan McKeown)[2] and Cinema Verity. For Verity, the prospect of winning such a major commission was a potential game-changer. She was well aware that successful soaps can run for years, if not indefinitely. The sheer scale of the potential business was mouth-watering. She wasn't joking when she remarked to friends that, should it come off, this would be her pension. 'For all her incredibly successful career, she was not a millionairess,' says writer Lynda La Plante. 'It was going to be big money. That's why she did it.'

Powell asked both Witzend and Cinema Verity to develop their ideas into fully fledged proposals. Witzend pinned their hopes on *Westbeach*, the story of two feuding families set in a seaside town. Verity's pitch was far more audacious. The seed of what became *Eldorado* was first suggested to her in 1988 by her film producer friend, John Dark. Dark had relocated to Spain during the early 1980s and felt that the thriving life of the British expatriate community throughout the Costa del Sol would form the perfect setting for a glossy drama. He had in mind a kind of European *Dallas* or *Dynasty*. 'There's a story on every pavement in Marbella,' he enthuses. 'I mean, it's got everything – the rich and the poor, the wonderful bikini-clad girls on the beaches – the glamour, that's what people want to see, I think. I envisaged the viewer in England sitting in the cold and the wet watching people frolicking about in the sea. I talked to Verity about it and said, "Well, you're the television queen, what do you think?" She said, "I think it's a great idea, let me talk to the BBC." The BBC had just announced that Terry Wogan was going to leave his programme and they needed a replacement, so she approached them just as the market was desperate for a product.'

'I and everyone else involved were certainly very torn between the two ideas,' explains Jonathan Powell, 'mainly because both were being suggested by particularly talented, experienced and entrepreneurial people. I had real faith in Allan, in his ability to put things together and to deliver talent. So it was a close call between the two projects and neither was given an unfair advantage during the short-listing process which demanded further story, business and talent development.'

As the debate continued, however, Cinema Verity's pitch began to edge ahead of its rival.

'I think Jonathan was very attracted by the thought that Verity was involved,' says Peter Cregeen, who was then the head of drama series, 'and by the idea of it being something set abroad and in the sun, particularly when it was going to be shown in the winter.'

---

[2] Powell enjoyed an excellent relationship with Witzend which dated back to his commissioning of the hit series *Lovejoy*. Further Witzend successes included *Birds of a Feather* and *Love Hurts*

'They made certain stipulations,' says Dark. 'One was that it shouldn't be about the rich; it needed to be a working-class programme – in other words, *EastEnders* in the sun. I'm not really interested in working-class entertainment but it was fair enough.'

Two experts of the soap genre were invited to develop and mastermind this ambitious new flagship. Producer Julia Smith, nicknamed 'The Godmother' within the BBC, would work alongside her close friend and long-time colleague, script editor Tony Holland. On the face of it, hiring the Smith-Holland team was eminently sensible. Between them, they had an impressive track record in delivering popular and well-made serial dramas, from *Z Cars* and *Angels* to *The District Nurse*. Most significantly, they had also created the BBC's *EastEnders*, the last major soap opera successfully launched in the UK and which remained an absolute bedrock of BBC1's identity and output. Smith later confided to the director Henry Foster that she was 'never going to top the success of *EastEnders*'; and that 'she was the last person she would have employed to deliver on *Eldorado*.' But as she made these comments when the eventual production was mired in crisis, this may have had an element of saving face about it. Privately, Verity was not a fan of *EastEnders*. 'I remember when it started,' says her close friend Kate Kagan. 'Janet Street-Porter was saying, "Oh, isn't *EastEnders* terrific, Verity?" and Verity said, "No. It's bollocks!"'

'The idea to attach Julia Smith and Tony Holland to develop the idea came from Verity,' says Jonathan Powell. 'All the conversations regarding this were conducted by Verity. When the decision to award the contract to her had been made, it was probably contingent on the proven participation of Julia and Tony. There is nothing unusual about such a key talent requirement, but it is something which may very well have contributed to Julia and Tony's own sense of importance and the difficulties between them and Verity, although it should always be borne in mind that they were difficult by nature and that their opinion of themselves, some may say justifiably, was extremely high after the success of *EastEnders*.'

'At the first meeting when it was announced we had it,' says Anna Callaghan, 'Jonathan said words to the effect that "We cannot consider going ahead with this project without the input of Julia Smith" (and I think Tony Holland too). This gave Julia carte blanche to do anything.'

While in theory Julia Smith was now working for Verity, in reality Smith regarded herself as her own woman and, what is more, the woman in charge. As was her fashion, she made all this perfectly plain and, whatever Verity's private distaste for Smith and her brusque manner, she was prepared to go along with it – and not just for the sake of the deal. There was more to it than that. Despite her fleeting experience with *The Newcomers* back in the 60s, and her role overseeing Thames' daytime soaps, *Rooms* and *Couples*, Verity was not an expert in this form of drama. Smith was someone everyone felt could and would deliver, in partnership with the capricious but gifted Tony Holland.

'The Queen and Queen of British soaps,' John Dark referred to them disparagingly. As with *EastEnders*, Holland was the creative motor. He claimed that he had a suitable idea already waiting in his 'bottom drawer'. This he now worked up into a serial based around a small community of British expats living and working in a Spanish town on the Costa del Sol. He christened this *Little Britain*.

When Holland delivered his 'bible' for the new soap, Verity was impressed and enthused. 'It was incredible,' says Kath Williams, Cinema Verity's business manager. 'Absolutely fantastic – it's the only fan letter I've ever written anybody. I said, "I think it's a work of genius."'

'It had a real siege mentality to it,' says Tony Jordan, one of the writers who formed the initial scripting team. 'Brits abroad in a British complex. Over there were the Germans and over there were the Spanish and over there were the French and you just knew that a British audience would have an empathy with it and it would be funny and joyful. All of us on the writing team bought into that. Suddenly one day, Tony came in and said, "We're going to have a German character – to make it more of a European project," and the next day he said, "We're going to have some Spanish characters and some Dutch characters too." Gradually, the whole concept was changed because we were told to include all those different nationalities. That's why you couldn't call it *Little England* [sic] anymore.'

For both Verity and Jonathan Powell, expanding the aspiration of the new serial to make it more truly European was an essential part of its appeal and difference. There are some who feel that, in different circumstances, and had it not been derailed by the ineptitude of the casting, this might indeed have worked and played strongly in the programme's favour. Peter Ansorge was the commissioning executive of Channel 4's drama at the time. 'We could have done that European languages thing,' he says. 'Interestingly, we were having problems with our own soap, *Brookside*, back then. Phil Redmond [who was in charge] had taken his eye off the ball. Michael Grade said the way to deal with this is to put out the word that we were looking for a new soap. So I called Verity in and explained this and she said, "I've got this new idea for a soap set in Europe but I've just sold it to the BBC." But yes, I might have commissioned it on the basis of the melting-pot of disparate nationalities – though I guess it would have been very different in treatment.'

'When the programme was conceived,' Verity explained, 'Europe was opening up and it was possible for people to move out into European countries and work there. I thought it would be interesting and informative to develop a soap opera about people who had moved away from their roots and how they'd do it, what would happen to them. That was the original concept.'[3]

Verity came up with a new title – *Eldorado* – the mythical Spanish city of gold – an

---

[3] Kaleidoscope convention interview

oblique reference to many of the characters and their search for a life in the sun. 'I thought the idea was a good one,' says Peter Cregeen. 'Sometimes you get people who present an idea and they sell it so hard that you think, "Let's try and see between the lines here." That wasn't the case with Verity at all. It was very reasoned and she was very charming, very practical and very good. Jonathan was the final arbiter in the same way that he was with any programme.'

On 11 November 1991, on the eve of her flying to Australia to finish the second series of *The Boys from the Bush*, Powell gave Verity the glad news that he had decided to award her the commission. Runners-up Witzend did not walk away completely empty-handed. Their *Westbeach* idea was commissioned as a standard ten-episode series. *Eldorado*, meanwhile, was requested to be ready for transmission from July 1992, timed to coincide with that summer's Olympic Games from Barcelona. It was a daunting deadline to meet but Verity agreed to the challenge, obeying her own mantra of 'Don't argue with yes.'

Cinema Verity's lawyer and business manager, Kath Williams, flew out to Australia with Verity so that the start-up paperwork could be completed while Verity also attended to *The Boys from the Bush*. 'It was a very difficult two weeks,' says Williams. 'I'd spend all night on the phone to the BBC. I remember staggering out one morning and getting into the car and telling her, "The BBC says…" and her going off like a rocket and ranting for ten minutes. Then she'd break off and say, "They're having an auction of jewellery at this place – shall we just pop in and have a look?" So in you'd go and it'd be, "Oh, What do you think of that, darling? I think I'll bid for that." Then we'd get back in the car and she'd pick up right where she left off, ranting about the BBC.'

Once everything was in place, a press conference was arranged to announce the birth of this enticingly ambitious new soap. It was held at Brown's Hotel in central London and here Jonathan Powell presented his credentials and those of his top team; as well as Peter Cregeen, the head of drama series, and Cregeen's deputy, Mervyn Watson, there were Julia Smith, Tony Holland and Verity herself. 'This press launch was the first danger signal,' believes Cregeen. 'Jonathan said what a great idea it was and how lucky he was that he'd been able to get Verity's company to make this and what an amazing amount of talent was involved. There was Verity, who was one of the great names in British television, there was Julia and Tony, who in *EastEnders* had created one of the most successful programmes ever, there was Peter Cregeen, who had been one of the main forces in creating *The Bill*, Mervyn Watson, who had been such a successful producer in this genre in *Coronation Street* and, of course, there was himself, Jonathan Powell, who had the most amazing track record. All of that. We came out of that meeting and Julia went berserk. She said, "How dare you do that to me? This is MY show, I am the person totally in control of this and nobody else has any direct responsibility for it. It is mine and that's how it's going to be." It made it very difficult for Verity.'

There has been much speculation about the true nature of the relationship between Verity and Julia Smith. Both had reputations as formidable women who wanted their own way and both were renowned and respected experts in their craft. 'Julia was a very positive lady,' says Peter Cregeen. 'She was lovely and extremely committed. Her problems on this were that she wanted to do everything. She wanted to know absolutely every element of everything – who was doing every job on the show, every detail about the scripts. I'm not sure that her relationship with Verity was very happy. Julia got so committed she resented what she deemed interference from anybody else.'

'She was a monster,' counters John Dark. 'Rude, aggressive and generally unpleasant.'

'Julia was horrible to work with,' says script editor and producer Betty Willingale. 'I really don't know why she was so nasty. She was always flouncing about, shouting. She knew how a studio worked but she was just so obnoxious all the time. I must say my eyebrows went up when I heard she was going to work with Verity.'

'You were never quite sure which Julia you were going to be speaking to on any one day,' says director Garth Tucker. 'I have a lot to be grateful to her for because I was a cameraman and she plucked me out and gave me *EastEnders* to direct. But once you were there, she spared no quarter. Sometimes she would give you a dressing down which really had nothing to do with you but was actually about how she happened to be feeling at that particular moment.'

'I really, really liked Julia,' says writer Tony Jordan. 'If she thought that you were doing your best, she was funny and she had a twinkle in her eye. But if she thought that you weren't doing what you could do or what she expected you to do, she wouldn't be quietly disappointed in you, she'd say, "You're a cunt." And people didn't like that.'

'Without knowing it, Verity took on someone more than her size in Julia,' believes director Herbert Wise.

'I think she very strongly felt that Julia just took over,' says Verity's journalist friend, Reggie Nadelson. 'I think Julia was able to bully even Verity.'

'I don't remember Verity having much to do with Julia,' says Cinema Verity producer Sharon Bloom. 'I don't remember her sitting and talking with her. What I didn't understand is why someone like Julia didn't look at Verity and think, "My God, she's made some good stuff, let's see what she says."'

'It was a huge mistake to just let Julia get on with it,' says Kath Williams. 'She was unmanageable. She lied and hid information.'

The show was to be made as a partnership between Cinema Verity in Britain and JD y T in Spain, a company which John Dark had established with his Australian business partner there, James Todesco. 'In Spanish,' explains director Henry Foster, 'JD y T is pronounced "hoe-dee-atay". And if you say that to somebody in Spain, you're basically saying, "Fuck you."'

'Does it?' says Dark himself, innocently. 'I've never heard that before.'

'Dark was a strange man,' continues Foster. 'There was a rather sinister and cynical aura surrounding him and there was no creative input from him. I think he was just taking the BBC for a monumental ride.'

Dark claims that he strongly counselled against a specially built set, suggesting instead that the production be shot in real locations until the show established itself. Only then, with the prospect of a sustained run, might the investment of purpose-building be worthwhile. Julia Smith completely disagreed. She felt, with some justification, that it simply wouldn't be practical to shoot everything in real locations. There would be countless issues with scheduling, continuity and security.

EastEnders had hugely benefited from having all its key facilities – from the studio interiors, the exterior lot and the rehearsal rooms to production offices, edit suites, costume and make-up – all in one controllable space. The difference was that for *EastEnders*, the BBC had merely customised an existing studio, the former ATV Elstree. There was obviously nothing comparable to house *Eldorado* in southern Spain. Everything would have to be created from scratch, at enormous expense. Smith lobbied aggressively for all the advantages this would bring, and Verity supported her ambition. Her own experience of amortising costs over a projected long run went way back to *Doctor Who*, which had nearly been derailed over the expense of designing the TARDIS interior, until Verity pointed out that it would pay for itself over the course of the first series. Applying the same logic again, the BBC consented to the plan and agreed to a budget of £2 million to build the *Eldorado* complex.

John Dark's business partner, James Todesco, arranged a deal to locate this on 25 acres of forest land owned by the town hall of Coin, a municipality in Malaga. There was high unemployment in the area and, after much stalling and politicking, the Spanish authorities were persuaded that this new television behemoth promised to bring generations of work to the local people. Julia Smith brought in Keith Harris, the gifted designer who had given life to *EastEnders* and, working at extreme speed, Harris devised a complete 'urbanisation' incorporating a Spanish market square, a supermarket and shops, a petrol station, swimming pool and theatre. As well as these 'front of house' buildings, there was a phalanx of offices and technical facilities, dressing rooms and a canteen (nicknamed 'Auntie') to feed the sizeable cast and crew. 'Verity had trust in Julia to make it work,' says Guy Gilks, who was the BBC's series department manager at the time. 'Julia wanted to replicate what she had done at Elstree but I don't think there was enough discussion about the complication of working abroad and the budget, which was tight. We were expected to train a Spanish labour force alongside the crew, too, and there wasn't enough time to do everything.'

Work on the site began in January 1992. Constructed at lightning speed, the jerry-built set was to cause innumerable teething problems, from the appalling acoustics within the villas to the imminent threat of flooding whenever it rained. Back in Britain, Julia Smith temporarily established herself in some nondescript offices in Chiswick, West London. Here, Tony Holland's writing team concentrated on the scripts, while Smith battled with the interminable practical problems. 'I think she was a woman doing quite a tough job,' says Emma Rolf, whom Smith employed as office manager. 'Most people were really scared of her but she appreciated honesty and straightforwardness. I think what she found difficult was having had all the support and infrastructure of the BBC – things were there and just happened. You could tell your PA to sort something out and it would get sorted. Verity didn't give her that support. It was all very stressful and the atmosphere was strained.'

Much has subsequently been made of the unreasonable pressure to get such a mammoth undertaking ready for the July start date. Several of those involved insist that the original intention was to launch the programme in the autumn season of 1992 and that Jonathan Powell made a strategic scheduling decision to move this forward to July. During the many postmortems in the wake of *Eldorado*, Verity publicly blamed herself for not having dug in her heels and refused to deliver to such an unrealistic deadline.

'It was complete madness,' says Kath Williams. 'We spent all this money building a set and we did nothing by way of a practice run. We should have taken a year. All of it was a real cock-up.'

'As an independent, we should have said we can't get it on the air that quickly,' agrees Sharon Bloom. 'The way to put it would have been, "I can deliver but I need another two months."'

'It was a case of the Emperor's New Clothes,' says writer Tony Jordan. 'Somebody should have said, "Let's not do it in July – let's do it next July." But the BBC couldn't have done that because then they would have lost face and it would be seen as a shambles. It was a corporate thing.'

But Powell himself vehemently contests the point: 'The launch was *always* envisaged to be in July and for very good reasons,' he says. '*EastEnders* had launched in the autumn[4] and had taken several months to find its feet. There had been a lot of discussions about its tone, in particular. Inevitably, with projects like *EastEnders* and *Eldorado*, there were going to be teething problems as it found its place on the screen.[5] For *Eldorado*, I had always envisaged a summer launch out of the fire of the autumn schedules in the hope that the relative security of the summer would allow the audience to get used to it and

---

[4] It actually launched in February, 1985. But Powell's point holds true as this was also peak viewing season

[5] David Reid, who commissioned *EastEnders*, comments: 'I take slight issue with Jonathan Powell. It is not my memory that *EastEnders* took several months to settle down. I think everyone (including Jonathan) was amazed how successful it was and how quickly.'

for adjustments, whatever they might be, to be made. It may be that the producers were expecting an autumn transmission or that they were told of the transmission date rather late in the day, but there is a strong sense that the makers have inflated this as an excuse for the show's lack of readiness.[6] It is also important to stress the point that at no time did anyone come forward – the drama department, who were responsible for looking after it, Verity or Julia Smith – and say that they simply did not have enough time. Had they done so, in clear enough terms, we would have been able to delay it somehow. The lines of communication were always open for this kind of conversation.'[7]

In the absence of such a conversation, the production juggernaut simply accelerated. Julia Smith appointed a hugely experienced BBC cameraman and director, Geoff Feld[8] to recruit all the technical staff, most of whom were, like him, long-term staff members fed up with the rapidly changing culture of the BBC and only too willing to go freelance with the promise of a year's contract. This turned out to be an uncharacteristic case of good timing for the programme and, in the trying months which followed, it was the importing of so much collective craft expertise that prevented many of the practical problems being even more acute and damaging. 'It's one thing setting up a show in London,' comments Feld, 'but when you're in an area with very few facilities, it is extremely difficult. Everything had to be brought over. It made it very expensive. It was a hell of a job but very exciting.'

Recording was scheduled to begin in May. 'It was cast in three minutes,' continues Tony Jordan, shrugging his shoulders at the implied idiocy. Anna Callaghan remembers Verity commenting in disbelief, 'With her track record, I never thought that she could get it so wrong.'

To find her regular actors, 31 of them in all, Julia Smith did enlist the help of a casting director but otherwise undertook this daunting, complex and artistically critical process entirely on her own, refusing to let anyone else, neither the BBC nor Verity, have any input. One problem was that the financial package on offer wasn't sufficiently attractive to secure the interest of more experienced and well-established actors. There were some credible actors among the producer's choices, including Hilary Crane, William Lucas and Jesse Birdsall (as the obligatory heartthrob 'bad boy' Marcus Tandy), but there was a whole clutch of improbable wild cards too, including a young German lad called Kai Maurer, whom Smith apparently spotted on a beach in Spain and, thinking he had the right look, promptly offered him an audition and then a contract. 'They were trying for

---

[6] Contemporary press indicates that until as late as May 1992, their expectation was for the serial to launch in the autumn

[7] 'Jonathan can say what he likes,' says Kath Williams. 'The opening episode started with the Olympic flag coming down on the village at the end of August.'

[8] Feld's reward was the chance to further his directing career

the teenage market,' sighs director Garth Tucker, 'but no parents back home were prepared to let their kids go out to act in this untested soap during their A Levels. That made the casting of the young characters a real problem.'

Throughout her career, casting had always been one of Verity's strengths and it seems utterly out of character for her to have allowed herself to be sidelined in such a peremptory fashion. 'I was quite surprised she let that happen,' agrees Sharon Bloom. 'She didn't run it as she might have run other things, but remember Jonathan gave Julia and Tony the power. Verity was excluded from a lot of the decisions. There were a number of times when I wondered, "Why aren't you saying, 'Fuck this'?" But there *were* some people that she didn't blow up at, depending on who they were and if there was some mystery about what they did – people whose job she couldn't do herself.'

'She had trust in Julia,' says the BBC's Guy Gilks, simply.

'She thought, as we all thought, that Julia knew what she was talking about,' agrees John Dark, who, despite being credited as a fellow executive producer, had minimal involvement. 'Actually, I think her time was out. When I said, "But this is crap," Verity said, "If we don't agree to it, they won't give us the money to make the show." I thought they are obviously getting on very well without me, I'll go and try and set up something in the States and that's exactly what I did.'

Verity did have one safe pair of hands on the ground in the form of line producer David Shanks, who had worked for her on *Minder* and *Coasting*. Troubled by Julia Smith's despotic and controlling approach to the work, Shanks fed his concerns back to Verity. But she was seriously distracted by the terminal illness of her closest confidant, Andrew Brown, who had fled to Australia to die away from the scrutiny of friends. 'There was this huge gap in the diary,' recalls Sharon Bloom. 'Right at the start of *Eldorado*.[9] I remember saying, "What, she's going on a trip and not going to be there?" She went out to see him and took a while doing it. That was her goodbye to him. He was a gorgeous man and it was very sad. But it took her away from the job.'

'Julia was difficult – we couldn't fire her because the BBC said so,' shrugs Kath Williams. 'Verity was difficult – and she wasn't bloody there.'

'I don't remember seeing Verity much at all,' says writer Tony Jordan. 'I can recall maybe two or three meetings where the whole team sat round a table. But they were very generic.'

'Verity wasn't hugely hands-on whereas Julia certainly was,' says director Henry Foster. 'A kind of mother figure and boss figure with a massive amount of energy. She had a

---

[9] Verity was in Australia from early January to the end of March, 1992

reputation but she did do the best that she could. She was not an easy person to work with but most of us that did held her in a great deal of affection. Verity had no concept of the genre – I think soap was outside her life's experience.'

Towards the end of April 1992, rehearsals began without a fully complete cast in place. One of the more experienced actors was Patricia Brake, who played Gwen Lockhead, and whom Tony Holland, an old friend, had suggested for the part. 'I knew at the first read-through that we would probably be in trouble,' she says. 'So many of the young people had never done it before and when you're working as fast as we were having to, that was a big problem. It made me angry because Britain is a wonderful country for theatrical talent and people were virtually brought in off the street. Of course, they weren't really up to it and weren't professional enough.'

'We had scripts that were singing on the page,' says Tony Jordan. 'I remember Tony booked this table in a restaurant for the writers – and we all brought our scripts to this lunch. The idea was that we passed them along and read each other's cliffhanger. We were pumped up. I was doing episode one and my first cliffhanger was Bunny coming back with Fizz. The Fizz that we talked about was like Miley Cyrus – she had this Mohican. Then, when you saw who they went with, you thought, "That's wrong – that is not understanding the text." It had to be down to time. When I look at that again, the storyline is all right and the dialogue's not bad but that casting...'

From the first day of shooting, there were unceasing problems. This was just before the dawn of the modern media era and so it was a production without the benefit of technology we now take for granted – mobile phones, email and digital production methods. Julia Smith, obsessed with the need to keep everything top secret, insisted that all scripts be delivered in person from the UK to Spain. Flights would have to be booked at the last minute, which was an impossibly frustrating business before the advent of the internet. Customs were frequently obstructive and vital equipment would often vanish in transit, presumed stolen. Once edited on site in Spain, tapes would have to be couriered back to the UK for transmission.

'I joined very soon after they started recording,' says director Henry Foster. 'From day one, it was fire-fighting. It was thrown together with indecent haste. Scripts just hit the screen and having to make three episodes a week was a hard target. They hadn't factored in what shooting in Spain was going to be like with the heat at midday and the resonant sets caused huge problems.'

'The set hadn't been finished,' points out fellow director Garth Tucker. 'We were shooting with building work going on around us, which added to the pressure. One of the problems technically was that Julia was very much bound to multi-cameras and thought that we ought to be using at least three cameras on every scene but some of the flats were so small, you could hardly get one camera in there in the first place. I was on the sharp end of that on several occasions: "Why have you only got one camera here?" You'd look around and say, "Well, where are the other two going to go?"'

'I remember going to watch the first episode shot,' says writer Tony Jordan. 'There was a monitor there and lots of very important people gathered round it. I watched that first scene and I remember going and phoning [fellow writer] Tony McHale and saying, "We're fucked. It's like fucking *Thunderbirds*." We were screwed by the casting, the awful acting and the technical limitations.'

Script editor Tony Holland presented his own difficulties. No one doubted the man's genius for serial storytelling and the creation of characters but under the remorseless pressure, he had become increasingly unpredictable. 'Tony was a pretty difficult person to manage,' says Guy Gilks. 'He'd been given his head too much in *EastEnders* and he had a huge ego and an inflated opinion of his own importance.'

Whenever he was crossed, or if he was unhappy or frustrated, Holland would disappear for days at a time on a frenzy of drinking. 'Most of my job when I was in Spain was to go and find Tony,' smiles Tony Jordan. 'Julia would call me in and say, "He's gone again." I used to trawl along from bar to bar. He used to resign on a regular basis because he got so frustrated. He'd just walk out. You've got to remember that at the time this was a big show for Tony – it was going to cement his place in soap history. He had this weird relationship with Julia – it was completely dysfunctional – they'd be screaming at each other, he'd tell her to fuck off, and that they'd never work with each other again, that he carried her or she carried him. I think that he loved her.'

'He adored Julia but he hated her at the same time and vice versa,' continues Emma Rolf. 'She was his keeper but also his gaoler and vice versa. Tony was a bitchy gay man – very talented and tortured. They loved each other dearly and made a good team but they had no life outside of their work. In theory, *Eldorado* was a good idea and could have worked really well. But everybody panicked. Having said, "Let me do it my way," Julia was backed into a corner.'

Inexorably, the transmission date loomed closer. Anxious for the maximum fanfare, the BBC arranged to fly a horde of journalists and photographers over to the set to meet the cast and crew and preview the first episode. Series department manager Guy Gilks sought the advice of the BBC's head of press and publicity, Keith Samuel. 'I said, "If we throw some money at it and pour booze down them, will it help?"' Gilks recalls. '"Well, it might," he said. I asked Jonathan, "What are you going to do? Show the first three episodes?" and he said, "Yes." "Have you seen them?" I asked. We had a look at them and they weren't awfully good. Jonathan wasn't very happy – there were quite a lot of technical problems. We sent BBC technicians over to work on them to get them into shape. Julia and Tony weren't talking to each other and we had to get them on to the same table for the press to meet them. Tony had locked himself in his hotel room. I eventually managed to persuade them to sit on opposite ends of the table. We got all the so-called stars there and filled the press full of alcohol. They were pretty kind, I have to say. I thought they were going to savage us but that happened later on.'

'Are you ready for *Eldorado*?' was the unintentionally ironic line adopted for the advertising campaign designed to promote the start of the show. 'It was overhyped,' says Peter Cregeen, bluntly. 'BBC Bank on Sun, Sea, Sand and Sex to win the ratings war' was a typical headline.

Determined to do their best to spoil the party, ITV scheduled an hour-long edition of its perennial *Coronation Street* in direct competition with the first episode, which went out on 6 July 1992. 'We went round to Verity's flat for the transmission,' recalls Sharon Bloom. 'Verity got some food in and we watched it and I can remember thinking, "God, I don't really know what to say." If I had criticised it, she would have been bullish and loyal. When something wasn't working, her argument would always be, "Well, *Minder* didn't work at the beginning…"'

'It was a mess,' says Michael Ferguson, who had started his directing career on *Compact* and had been an executive producer on both *EastEnders* and *The Bill*. 'I can't understand how it happened. In my experience, one of the key things about soap is that you need extremely accomplished actors to be able to do it very quickly; you need to cast well. On *Eldorado* they cast a lot of people who'd never been near a camera before – absolute foolishness. You can do that when everything has settled down and everything's working well. There are plenty of young actors who have experience. And I think the scripts were poor – they didn't take advantage of the situation, there was no sense of tension, there was no sense of relationships, which are the two things that sort of drama depends on. I don't see why it shouldn't have worked with good writers, actors and directors.'

Over the years, some of Verity's work had occasionally been found wanting in the pages of the press. *Eldorado*, however, received an entirely different and most unwelcome level of criticism. 'This is television for the naff at heart,' sneered veteran television critic Margaret Forwood in the *Daily Express*. 'Costa del Cobblers,' offered *The Sun*'s Garry Bushell. 'A turkey – a hunk of junk,' added *The Observer*'s Russell Twisk. Lynne Truss in *The Times* spoke for many when she commented: 'Will the youngsters (particularly the foreign ones) learn to open their mouths when speaking, or will the scriptwriters just concede defeat?'

'*Eldorado* is really nothing more than *Crossroads*-on-Sea,' was the damning verdict of Craig Brown in *The Sunday Times*.

The decision to include some characters speaking in their own language and without subtitles was widely derided and condemned as alienating for the mainstream soap audience. 'Tony Holland was so passionate about it, he sold it to everyone,' explains Tony Jordan. 'I thought, "That is fucking genius and has a real integrity to it." That sailed through, past the writers like me, and Julia and Verity. But actually it was a terrible decision.'

A more serious issue emerged in which *Eldorado* became the focal point of the debate about whether the BBC should be investing in such nakedly audience-pleasing enterprises. Not a week seemed to pass without catty references to the beleaguered show, its amateurish production and floundering cast. 'El-boreado' was one of many punning headlines. Newspaper cartoonists regularly satirised the situation. Verity acquired the originals of several of these and had them framed for display in the Mill House, testimony to her robust sense of humour. But there was nothing amusing about the relentless barrage of criticism which the serial attracted.

'It became a curious *cause-célèbre*,' says Jonathan Powell. 'More than just a programme that didn't work. It goes back to the incredibly difficult relationship of the BBC and populism. When the BBC gets populism right it somehow makes it its own. I think that's one of the triumphs of the new *Doctor Who* – that it's a populist programme but absolutely of the BBC. But when the BBC steps over the line and its populist attempts become not of the BBC, they very quickly blow up into a huge political row, which is what happened to *Eldorado*.'

Poor ratings didn't help, though these owed something to launching in an early evening slot in the summer months, always the leanest time for television audiences.

'It was very demoralising,' says Emma Rolf, 'and that's when Verity started becoming more interested. Unfortunately, in a crisis Verity just wanted to blame and scapegoat and she scapegoated Julia and it wasn't entirely Julia's fault. Julia could be difficult and wanted to be independent but it was Cinema Verity's production and it was up to them to make sure that things were running properly. I think Julia was quite isolated. Verity and Julia didn't work as a team and there wasn't enough openness. I think everybody was scared of everybody else and they dealt with it by endeavouring to be assertive but actually being arrogant and passive aggressive.'

'We were aware that things were not going well with Julia,' says Guy Gilks. 'We were getting reports back that she was being more and more secretive and wearing herself into the ground.'

Perhaps inevitably, the belligerent and embattled Smith was the first casualty of the barrage of criticism and complaints aimed at *Eldorado*. Her sudden departure made headlines on 1 August 1992. 'She left in the middle of a writers' meeting and never came back,' says Emma Rolf.

'Julia literally disappeared overnight,' says Henry Foster. 'I don't think there was huge surprise, though it was mildly traumatic. We all felt like a colony of bees whose queen has been taken away.'

'The rumours had been going on for so long and Julia had seemed so distracted that it didn't come as a surprise,' says Patricia Brake. 'But it was very unsettling.'

'The decent thing would have been for everyone to sit down and find a way of resolving everything,' believes Emma Rolf. 'And it could have been resolved. Instead, Julia was marginalised. Tony was part of the undermining and I think that probably broke Julia's heart. He didn't mean to, he was just desperate to keep his job. It was to do with reputation and ego; writing was his life and his identity. They made it so difficult for her, she had no choice but to walk out. *Eldorado* was a very elegant example of the BBC going from an organisation where you were safe and looked after and could blossom and grow and everybody was looking out for you to the world we now live in, which is much more ruthless and driven by the need for success.'

The press relished the sudden and total downfall of the 'Godmother' with some hacks settling old scores with a woman whose iron control of the publicity on all her shows had earned her few allies in the street of shame. The official story was that an overworked Smith was taking an extended break to recover from exhaustion. 'She definitely was ill,' says Peter Cregeen. 'But why was she ill? She was ill as a result of the show.'

Smith never worked again. 'She was a broken woman,' says Emma Rolf. 'I saw her several times after she left and she was completely different – very quiet and not flamboyant in the way she had been. She felt betrayed – that the BBC had let her down.'

Tony Holland remained. 'He stayed out of pride,' says Tony Jordan. 'He really cared about his characters. He had that sense that they became his family. There was also maybe an element of, "If I turn this round, I did it without Julia." It was his moment to prove that he was the real genius in the partnership.'

Verity now cleared her desk to prioritise the attempts to rescue *Eldorado*. 'Verity will move into Hell-dorado' was how one newspaper announced it. 'I see very clearly the team needs a leader,' she told *The Sunday Times*[10] and she swiftly found one in the steely form of new producer Corinne Hollingworth. It must be said that there wasn't much competition for the job as the ailing infant soap had already acquired a toxic reputation within the industry. But Hollingworth was bright enough to see that at this stage of her career, it presented an opportunity. She had worked her way up the ranks of the BBC's drama department, and had already attracted attention as an efficient and ambitious producer on *EastEnders*. She had both the necessary experience and the obvious hunger to prove herself a player. Once her position was confirmed, she wasted neither time nor sentiment in getting to grips with the wayward soap.

'I was probably more scared of Corinne than Julia,' laughs writer Tony Jordan. 'She went at it and it was brutal on all sides. Everything was different and the scripts had to be right. The sense that I got from her was, "You've been making shit." Scripts were written and rewritten and as writers we earned a fortune because the brief kept changing. I was

---

[10] *The Sunday Times* (09.08.92)

writing stuff that was changed literally every five minutes. But she was respectful of Tony and his talent and she understood writers.'

'The main problem was the scripts, which weren't as good as they could be because the writers were allowed to write them in London,' said Verity. 'They were able to visit Spain, then go back and write the scripts. I think that that was a big, big mistake. They were like visitors and consequently you didn't get a feeling that the characters even lived in this place. Corinne came in to produce it and she very firmly made all the writers and script editors live in Spain. I think she started to get more realistic scripts and acting.'[11]

With Verity's backing, Hollingworth began her reign with a flurry of tabloid-pleasing blood-letting, rapidly dispatching several lacklustre members of the cast and reducing the number of regulars to a more manageable 24. 'It was terribly sad for some of them who were sacked,' says Patricia Brake. 'Like Kathy [Pitkin – who played child bride Fizz]. She wasn't an actress and she tried so hard. It's not as if we didn't like the kids – it wasn't their fault that they had been cast. But things began to change when Corinne came in and it gave us a new confidence. It just seemed to be more streamlined.'

Verity, for months kept determinedly at arm's length by Julia Smith, or absent for her own reasons, finally began to become more of a presence in Spain, spending around two weeks a month at the *Eldorado* complex . 'One worked with directors who regarded her with awe,' says Henry Foster, 'so I was really quite scared but when I met her I found her totally charming and very easy to talk to. She cared passionately about programme-making and there was not an element of cynicism in her about *Eldorado*. When Julia got shafted, Verity was very much more an executive producer, leaning on Corinne. There was always a very positive aura surrounding Verity. She'd give us a load of energy to carry on and hold drink-dos where she'd talk to people and ask, "What do you think is going wrong?" When you spoke one-to-one with her she would actually be genuinely interested in your opinion of what would make it better. She really did want it to improve. I think the culture of the BBC frustrated her massively.'

As well as long hours spent behind the scenes, Verity went on her own charm offensive, granting interviews to broadsheet newspapers and trying to encourage some positive publicity. But the scale of the ridicule and hostility bemused and depressed her. 'The press went for Verity,' says director Herbert Wise. 'They love somebody who is at the top that they can shoot down. They enjoy doing it and once one of them starts it, they all join in, like dogs. That public castigation she got was disgusting and most unfair. I mean, it wasn't very good but it did get better. No doubt because of the long line of successes, she had this belief that if she only worked hard enough, she could make it work.'

'It was tough for Verity,' agrees her PA, Anna Callaghan. 'But she didn't really let it show.

---

[11] Kaleidoscope convention interview

I remember going with her somewhere in Soho and all these journalists appeared and started firing questions. She handled herself very well. One journalist said to me, "We all think she's marvellous, we're all rooting for her, actually." And I thought, "Well, it doesn't show." But I think the hostility was really being thrown at the BBC, not her. It was flat-out crazy. I used to crawl home sometimes. But she never shrank from it, that's for sure.'

Slowly, improvements began to be made. A dialogue coach was brought in to help some of the less experienced members of the cast and circumvent some of the problems that came from having practically no rehearsal time. 'On any disastrous programme you get an aura of solidarity,' observes director Henry Foster. 'The crews worked their butts off and the cast were totally delightful. We were all out there determined to make the best product we could and it did certainly get better.'

'Turning a soap round is like turning an ocean liner round,' says Sharon Bloom. 'You need time to do it.'

Jonathan Powell publicly pledged his support but in December 1992, it was suddenly announced that he was leaving the BBC to become head of drama at the new ITV company, Carlton. Invariably, the press made much of the coolness between Powell and incoming Director-General John Birt – and implied that Powell's departure was not unconnected to the epic disappointment of *Eldorado*. Certainly, Powell was weary of working in the teeth of the gale. 'At that time,' he says, 'it seemed that every day there was a new story attacking the BBC. For those of us on the sixth floor of Television Centre, it really did feel like being in a constant state of siege.' The Carlton job was a step back towards his first love: active drama production. He told *The Independent* that he hoped the BBC would continue with *Eldorado*: '[It] has cracked eight million viewers. It has improved. The look of the show has improved. The acting and storytelling have improved. People are watching. I think having stuck with *Eldorado* so far that it would be a pity not to stick with it for at least a year and a bit' [12]

Verity could not but regard Powell's departure as a body blow to her expectations for her soap's long-term future. There was still hope, however. The new man, Alan Yentob, moving over from running BBC2, was someone she liked and got on well with. Yentob was in an unenviable position. No one disputed that by the New Year of 1993, *Eldorado* was showing definite signs of improvement, both in terms of its content and its viewing and audience appreciation figures, which had risen dramatically. But Yentob was equally well aware of the concerns of those above him in the BBC hierarchy. The renewal of the Corporation's charter was just months away and Birt and his supporters felt that *Eldorado* represented a millstone around their necks in the continuing argument for the BBC's future.

---

[12] *The Independent* (11.03.93)

A decision could only be delayed for a matter of weeks. The deadline for taking up the options on the cast contracts was imminent and there were a host of practical and logistical reasons why everyone involved needed to know as soon as possible whether or not *Eldorado* was going to continue into a second year. Yentob prevaricated for as long as he could. This was in character but it also enabled him to get a sense of everything at stake should he cancel or renew. Neither option was without risk. If he cancelled, there would certainly be a fresh round of adverse publicity focused on the millions of pounds that the BBC would be compelled to write off. Overnight, the set alone would become an embarrassing albatross. Yentob floated the possibility of a compromise, hedging his bets by extending the show for six months rather than a full year. Verity, never one for a compromise, was unwilling. She felt that this would send a dangerously mixed message to the audience – that this still wasn't a programme worth the investment of their time and emotions – and that for the production, there would remain the uneasy sense of working under the sword of Damocles. Instead, she held out forcefully for a second year, using all her powers of persuasion to argue the futility of cancellation just when the worst of the crisis had been averted and everything was beginning to point towards success and renewal.

'Alan felt that there was a strong case for keeping it going,' says Peter Cregeen. 'The research people told him that if he kept it for the next year, the audience figures would double at least. But he also had a brief from above to revitalise the channel. He had meetings with Verity and Corinne. He hummed and hawed and found it an incredibly difficult decision to make. We came to the very last couple of days when it was possible to make a decision.'

On 12 March 1993, a final summit meeting was held at Television Centre, chaired by managing director Will Wyatt, with Mark Shivas, the overall head of drama, Yentob and Cregeen, who recalls that: 'Alan told us, "I haven't yet decided – I've got to have further discussion today." Will said, "Well, somebody has got to go out there today to be ready to tell everybody one way or the other by the end of the day." So I said, "I suppose I'd better go. How do I get a ticket at this stage?" Will said, "This is the BBC. When you get to the airport there will be a ticket for you." So I got the plane and found myself sitting next to Corinne. Neither of us knew what decision had been taken. I was told that when I got to the other end there would be a message for me. I was met by Dusty Simons, who was a BBC representative out there, and he handed me a fax from Alan saying he'd decided not to go ahead. I told Verity and she was very impassive. She was always a realist and was probably resigned to it by that stage. We then drove straight to a hotel where the entire cast and crew were assembled and I said, "I'm afraid that it's going to be all over."'

'We had been hoping for a reprieve,' says actress Patricia Brake, 'but I'd worked with Peter Cregeen in the theatre and you could tell by his body language. When he walked in, we just knew. It was very sad and the saddest thing of all was the local people – they were in bits because there was no other work up that mountain. We actors all knew that we'd go home and life would go on as usual but for them it was so awful.'

'I think with Yentob it was a case of, "I'm going to show somebody that I've got big bollocks and cancel *Eldorado*,"' says writer Tony Jordan. 'Whereas the bigger bollocks would have been to say, "I'm the man who turned *Eldorado* around."'

But Verity reserved her ire not for Alan Yentob but for John Birt, whom she always held as ultimately responsible for the execution. 'Alan was put into a very difficult situation in that he wasn't going to win either way,' she later explained. 'He wouldn't win if he kept it going and it didn't work, and he wouldn't get anywhere by cancelling it because it wouldn't make its money back. So Alan decided that he could get rid of it and it would never be his fault. Which was true. If he'd kept it and made the wrong decision, he could be blamed instead of Jonathan Powell. If somebody at the BBC had been there to champion it, it would've succeeded eventually. The problem with *Eldorado*, in terms of BBC politics, was that John Birt didn't want *Eldorado*. He never wanted it. He wouldn't have wanted it even if it had won a Pulitzer Prize. He was very unsupportive in the press as well as in the BBC and the press were gunning for the BBC. They were against the amount it had cost to build the set, and we became the whipping boy.'[13]

During the remaining weeks of their contracts, cast and crew displayed admirable professionalism, working with a will so that the show might end on some kind of high. Recording came to an end in May 1993.

'When they had a party to celebrate the finish,' says John Dark, 'I was really upset and I refused to go and I said to her that I was not very happy that the Spanish technicians we had been training suddenly had no future. It wasn't something to celebrate.'

Despite the *fait accompli* of the cancellation, Verity accepted an invitation to appear on the BBC2 arts and culture magazine programme *The Late Show*,[14] to argue her firm view that the programme was, at least in part, a victim of an unfair witch-hunt by critics and reviewers. It was perhaps unwise. In marked contrast to her usually confident and relaxed television manner, from the start, she necessarily appeared defensive and slightly needy in the face of the mild scepticism of the other contributors, Craig Brown from *The Sunday Times* and Marcus Berkmann of the *Daily Mail*. Branding television critics 'irresponsible' for not allowing a soap time to find its way could only make her seem schoolmistressy and patronising. 'We're not health visitors,' Craig Brown responded robustly. 'We're not there to save ailing programmes...we're there to give our honest reactions.' Berkmann, too, was unapologetic: 'I've been watching it quite a lot over the last year and I still think that the fundamental idea turned out to be misconceived.'

Glaring over her glasses, and whipping out a couple of Berkmann's reviews as though they were inadequate pieces of homework, Verity scolded him. 'I don't see any evidence

---

[13] Kaleidoscope convention interview

[14] Transmitted live on 17.05.93

in this writing that you've actually seen the show at all. You even use the same quote: "This notorious soap now watched only by an elderly couple in Lincolnshire whose remote control is broken." That's used in both – I don't know if you thought that was a terrifically funny joke and therefore needed to be repeated?'

When it was his turn, Brown faced her out with casual aplomb. 'Why did it become fair game? Because it's jolly bad!' he said, before confronting her directly. 'If you were a bad TV producer or even a not particularly good one I'd believe completely that you're earnest in what you're saying. But you're one of the top five, you're very, very good and you shouldn't be excusing yourself.'

'I'm very sorry if I appear to be excusing myself,' Verity replied, clearly incensed. 'I have to tell you that I totally believe what I'm saying.'

Presenter and referee for this spat, Sarah Dunant, courteously allowed her the last word. 'I think what I'd like to say is that I don't think that any television series or very few television series could survive the kind of scrutiny that *Eldorado* has been put under and I absolutely still stand by the fact that it's a good idea, an idea for the 90s and I'm very sorry that I'm not going to have the chance to prove that I'm right.'

Extricating herself and her company from *Eldorado* was complex, messy and unpleasant. Following various newspaper revelations, serious questions were being asked about John Dark's business partner in Spain, James Todesco. 'At the end of the show,' says Kath Williams, 'we were having all these problems with the BBC. They crawled all over us for a year and tried to prove some kind of financial impropriety. John Dark had said to us, "When you come to Spain, you've got to be really careful who you deal with. Don't deal with any crooks. I've got just the man." He got us into bed with this James Todesco character, who was a crook and a complete nightmare and when it all turned nasty, he was nowhere to be seen. Both Verity and I are as honest as the day is long and were entirely straight and now our reputation was shit. It was a terrible time. There were these BBC meetings and you'd get a sick note from John to say that he wasn't coming. He ran away, basically.'

'They were right about James,' says Dark himself. 'It's one of those things. It was my decision to involve him and my fault but he had a wonderful personality, he spoke fluent Spanish, and he got us the town hall's OK to have the land for practically nothing. All the setting up was done by him. Poor chap died quite soon afterwards. It was all very upsetting.'

Meanwhile, the Spanish authorities, furious at the impending desertion, indicated that the BBC's fleet of mobile outside broadcast trucks would be impounded if anyone attempted to remove them. In the end, most of the expensive technical equipment was simply abandoned. There were protracted arguments about contracts with some disgruntled members of the cast. The actors' union Equity became embroiled in the dispute and once it leaked into the pages of the press, this only provided more unwelcome innuendo about the working practices of Cinema Verity and the BBC. John Dark gave *The Independent* a characteristically outspoken interview, which Verity interpreted as a final betrayal from a man she had been fond of and to whom she had been consistently loyal over many years.[15] 'I was in London at the time that article came out,' says Verity's friend, screenwriter Nancy Dowd. 'I thought, "You've got to be fucking kidding me." That little worm ought to have been down on his knees thanking Verity for the chances she gave him. He was a predator and that article did her a lot of harm.'

'She never forgave him,' says Kath Williams. 'He wrote to her and she never replied. She felt he had just dumped us.'

'It's a great sadness to me still,' says John Dark. 'I went to see her and she just didn't want to know me. I wrote her a letter saying "This is bloody stupid – so we've got a failed show, big deal" – and she never replied. I was quite glad the show collapsed because it wasn't doing any good for me. She was a nice person, Verity, and I was upset that she didn't want to make friends again. Very upset. When I was in hospital recovering from my heart attack, I wrote her another letter and said, "I'm lying in hospital. All I can think about to cheer me up is to see you coming in through the door," and she never did. A dear friend of mine, Lewis Gilbert's wife, was a friend of Verity's too and she said, "Why don't you make friends with John again?" and Verity said, "If he says he's sorry, I'll make friends," but I'd done nothing to be sorry about. I think she had people around her who knew how to stoke the fire. I wouldn't say anything against her ever. I think she was a wonderful woman in television and we all make mistakes in life.'

Verity walked away from the wreckage, determined to pick up the pieces and devote her energies to a host of projects simmering within Cinema Verity's Mill House home. But nothing would be quite the same again. Although there were further successes to come, *Eldorado* represented the end of her expansionist period, when commissions seemed assured. 'I think *Eldorado* damaged her reputation,' says Kath Williams. 'We never recovered from it or truly got over it. I think we suffered from it enormously.'

'I suppose it did damage her,' says writer and friend Doug Livingstone. 'The idea in so many ways was good.'

'Verity went for everything,' says another close friend, Graham Benson. 'She was excited by it and it didn't sound as if it was going to be so disastrous.'

'It's a wonderful idea to do a soap that's set somewhere else,' says Linda Agran, Verity's Euston Films partner. 'I wasn't surprised she wanted to do it because we'd often discussed

---

[15] *The Independent* (24.10.93)

doing a soap and how brilliant that would be and so I was actually rather thrilled when I heard that she was going to get the chance to do it. I think that it should have been given time.'

'I think Verity got off very lightly over *Eldorado*,' says writer and producer Robert Banks Stewart. 'On a lot of counts, I think Verity was guilty. It wasn't her cup of tea. She didn't know about the real atmosphere of the plebs in the south of Spain. I remember the press weekend to introduce the series. I had a house nearby and I went out and saw a bit of what they were doing. All these people were flown out and Verity was the main figure. I knew it was going to be a no-no. Verity got some blame but it was Julia Smith and Tony Holland who got the most.'

'I think *Eldorado* was a huge disappointment and embarrassment for her,' says Patricia Brake, 'because she had done so well before.'

'It was a stain on her CV,' agrees writer Tony Jordan. 'I think the damage to Verity was that she epitomised everything that was quality television and she crossed over to the dark side and started to talk about her pension. I'm sure that the world of soap was not one she was comfortable with. It was a huge lesson for me not to get sucked into the mentality of the Emperor's New Clothes or to think that just because someone is a genius, they must know what they are doing.'

'I thought it was an astonishingly bad decision right from the off,' concludes writer Howard Schuman. 'Soap opera is a craft and a treadmill and I didn't think it was her strength. It's not the most awful thing that's ever been done – it just wasn't worthy of her.'

'It took a lot out of her,' says writer Andy McCulloch, 'and I think it caused her considerable damage. She was very bitter that they didn't give it longer. It was probably an unfair and bad decision. Why did she do it? She told me that she felt the big future for television was going to be in soaps.'

Two decades on and this premonitory instinct has been vindicated. BBC1 now runs *EastEnders* four times a week, while *Casualty* and its sister show, *Holby City*, run all year round. On ITV, *Coronation Street* and *Emmerdale* are stripped across the early evening schedule while over on Channel 4, *Hollyoaks* also runs remorselessly throughout the week. But *Eldorado*, appropriately enough, has evidently cast a long shadow; since its demise, no one has attempted to launch a new soap with comparable scale and ambition.

On 28 February 2002, BBC2 transmitted *Fool's Gold*, an edition of their documentary series *Trouble at the Top*. Ten years on, it attempted to piece together the story of exactly what went so wrong with *Eldorado*. John Dark, John Birt and Jonathan Powell all declined to appear, although Powell was represented in the form of archive material and was mentioned at various points in the narrative.[16] Verity, by contrast, was conspicuous by her total absence. She received not one mention throughout. Instead, the film focused the narrative through the perspective of Tony Holland with the result that it was a good story but not quite the whole story.

Producer Daniel Barry had tried hard to persuade Verity to appear. 'I eventually managed to set up a meeting,' he recalls. 'By having a face-to-face you are much more likely to convince someone to do something that perhaps they are reluctant to do. We met in a café in Holland Park. Verity was very cool and not particularly responsive. It was obvious that *Eldorado* was a very painful experience, and while a decent amount of time had passed, a bitter taste still lingered. There was definitely still anger there and it was directed primarily at Julia Smith and especially Tony Holland. She felt that Tony was too intent on having a good time out in Spain and as a result the project suffered and contributed to the breakdown in Julia and Tony's relationship. During our meeting, Verity was definitely questioning me as much as I was questioning her. She was very interested to know who I was talking with, who had agreed to take part and what story I was trying to tell. At the end of the meeting, she declined to get involved.'

When Barry interviewed Holland, he did ask the former script editor about Verity. Holland's answers were elusive. 'Whenever I tried to go there he would just repeat the same story about meeting her years previously when she was draped across a desk wearing Yves Saint Laurent. There was something oddly bitchy about the way he told the story but it wasn't anything I could really use or take anywhere within the *Eldorado* narrative. If I had been able to get any of the people contributing to talk about Verity then I would have included her. As it was, she never really figured in any of the contributions and therefore her involvement was never mentioned.'

Still, Barry did not entirely give up. Well into production on the film, another meeting was arranged, again in a café in Holland Park. 'I thought that the best tactic was to tell her the story that was emerging from the research and interviews, especially as she was not coming out of it badly at all,' he says. 'In retrospect, this was a fatal mistake as what I showed her was that I was making a film about what was undoubtedly her biggest failure and she didn't even get a mention. I now think that was probably why she wanted to meet me again. She wanted to find out whether she would need to get involved or not. And I gave her the answer. Touché, Verity.'

---

[16] 'I made it quite clear that I was not interested in appearing,' says Powell. 'I couldn't see how it would advantage me at ten years distance from the event. I didn't particularly object to the use of the archive footage and whatever voice over they may have used in the final programme, but it was not done with any collaboration from me.'

At a distance of over two decades, there are few who now dispute that *Eldorado* was no better and no worse than many other comparable soap operas or the notion that, had the BBC kept faith with it and with Verity's conviction, it would probably still be running today. The line between great ambition and utter recklessness has always been thin and, had the programme endured, no doubt this chapter would have been a eulogy to the risks taken and the rewards that resulted. In the final analysis, *Eldorado* was a casualty of a vicious combination of dysfunctional personal relationships, bitter power struggles and political grandstanding both inside the BBC and among its many critics and enemies beyond. Verity, caught in the crossfire, and wounded in the process, now wanted only to return to the business of making television drama for which she had some feeling and truly understood.

CHAPTER FOURTEEN
ONWARDS AND SIDEWAYS
1993–1997

'Independent producers live from hand to mouth, however successful we might appear. You sit there wondering, "What next?" I won't do anything I don't believe in. I want to hold up my head and say, "I'm not ashamed." It's wonderful to entertain, sometimes illuminate and make people laugh or cry.'

Verity to *The Sunday Express*, 1994

Despite the voracious demands of *Eldorado*, Cinema Verity had not become a one-show wonder. Given the dismal outcome of Verity's Spanish dream, this was just as well. It was not in her nature to sit still or reflect, to moan and waste time on bitterness and regrets. Instead, she looked resolutely forward and devoted her energy to what the future might bring. There were always other projects and partnerships to focus on and these were both a welcome and necessary distraction from the death throes of her doomed soap.

However successful an independent producer may be, the programmes they actually hustle to the screen will always represent the tip of a development iceberg, outnumbered by the massed ranks of the 'might have beens', those projects which, for all their merits, ultimately don't find a buyer.

The layman might be surprised at the considerable sums of money spent by television companies on development; paying for options on books and outlines, funding the writing of formats and scripts, along with all the sundry but far from inconsequential costs of staff, recces and research. It is an utterly unpredictable game of chance, hope, opportunity and timing. Only sometimes do all these elements come together to ignite an enterprise and turn it into a reality. Every indie will also tell you that the chances of these ideas reaching fruition are vastly enhanced when a company has other projects in active production. It is a case of 'speculate to accumulate'.

Accordingly, inside their chic surroundings at the Mill House, the small Cinema Verity team were always harbouring a diverse range of concepts and proposals, hopeful that any one of them might catch the eye and win the backing of someone with the money to pay for them. Most started with Verity's enthusiasm to work with a particular writer or to bring a certain book to the screen. But it wasn't all a question of hunch and instinct. She knew many of those with the commissioning power at the main channels and used her natural business acumen to anticipate what they might be looking for. She was aware of the importance of a channel's identity and that a good fit for BBC1 would not necessarily translate to ITV or Channel 4.

It was increasingly difficult to sell single films to any channel. The costs involved were usually regarded as too high for the chancy return of one night's transmission. Nonetheless, Verity continued to try. She had first refusal on Alan Bleasdale's follow-up to *GBH*. This was initially planned as a feature film, to be partly financed by a major American film company and ultimately televised by Channel 4, who were also keen to invest. 'She was in Australia when the script arrived,' says Cinema Verity's business manager, Kath Williams. 'I had to ring her up and report, "I don't know what to say to you, Verity, but this ain't going to be a movie – it's way, way too long." She went mad as only Verity could and that was the beginning of the end of her and Bleasdale.'

It wasn't just the length of the screenplay. Bleasdale had second thoughts about an American movie venture, as he explained to television critic Sean Day-Lewis: 'I said to Verity, with the best will in the world, some dentist from Oklahoma with money in the thing would fuck it up. Also the story was a big one and I knew it had to have nine hours if it was going to have breadth and not be sensationalised.'[1]

'She had more commercial ambition for it,' says Peter Ansorge, the commissioning editor for drama at Channel 4. 'She still wanted to do it as an American film. I think she was wrong about that. I had lunch with her and offered her the eventual series, *Jake's Progress*, but she didn't want to take on Alan again.'

During the early 1990s, with Michael Grade as chief executive and Peter Ansorge in charge of drama, Channel 4 was Verity's first port of call for many of her putative projects. Ansorge agreed some development funding to pursue *Tamara*, a biographical mini-series about the turbulent life of the 1920s Art Deco painter Tamara de Lempicka.[2] The idea had been brought to Verity by Tina Jamieson, who had been working as a production manager in television and as a commercials producer. 'I think that she loved the story,' says Jamieson. 'It was quite glamorous and I knew she liked that period. Her only caveat was to make sure we got the real drama out of it.'

---

[1] Quoted in *Talk of Drama* (see bibliography)

[2] There was also development funding for the project from the European script fund

Lynda La Plante showed some interest in writing *Tamara* as a 90-minute screenplay but withdrew when Verity and Jamieson expressed their view that the story would sustain twice this length. They flew to Paris, where Lempicka had enjoyed her heyday, in an attempt to seek co-funding from French producers. Meanwhile, the novelist Malcolm Bradbury took charge of the scripts, but this intriguing collaboration eventually petered out with disagreement over tone and approach. They abandoned the allure of a 'name' writer, and instead commissioned the promising Greg Snow to draft a first script. 'It all went on for about three years,' explains Tina Jamieson. 'We had a window of rights to the biography of Tamara, written by her daughter, on which we were basing our story and it just went on too long. Channel 4 got fed up. There's a momentum to these things – the natural state of all film-making is not to get made. What was lovely was that, throughout, Verity treated me absolutely equally. She was very inspirational.'

'I think the rest of us within Cinema Verity didn't know how that was ever going to get made, really,' says producer Sharon Bloom. 'It seemed too exotic really, and not something that someone in the UK would fully invest in.'

Verity's tastes were as eclectic as ever. She set her sights on *Two Weeks with the Queen*, a novel, ostensibly for children, by Australian, Morris Gleitzman. On its publication in 1990, the book had been critically well-received and caused a degree of controversy because a key element of the plot involved the leading character, a 12-year-old boy, making friends with a homosexual man and his boyfriend, who is terminally ill with AIDS. Verity read it and loved it. It was a story that combined her favourite ingredients of humour, conflict and compassion, with a contemporary issue right at the heart of the narrative. To bring it to the screen she joined forces with her friend Val Hardy, who was then running the South Australian Film Corporation. 'I had called Morris Gleitzman,' recalls Hardy, 'and said, "I've read this book – will you give me the rights?" and he replied, "Oh bugger, Verity Lambert rang me yesterday and I've given them to her." But when I spoke to her, she said, "Well, let's do it together." It was very generous of her to do that. It's a wonderful story but we couldn't get it off the ground because the central character was a child and people, especially the Americans, couldn't get that this story would also be enjoyed by adults. They kept saying, "But it's a children's film." There comes a time when you have to say, "That's it for that one," and it's a pity because I do believe it would have been fabulous.'

Another casualty of interminable development was *Aunts on the Cross*, a slim volume of memoir by leading literary agent and film producer Robin Dalton, with whom Verity was on good terms. In the book, Dalton had written charmingly of her upper-class childhood in a vanished Australia. It had become a minor cult, enthusiastically promoted by the likes of Clive James, and David Aukin, who was head of film at Channel 4, initially funded some development for a possible feature. This came to nothing, principally because Dalton herself felt it was more suited to television. Aukin introduced her to his colleague, Peter Ansorge. Dalton recalls: 'He said, "Can you think of anybody you would like to produce it?" and I suddenly remembered that Verity had read the book and was a terrific fan. She was thrilled and said she'd love to produce it.'

Various prestigious writers were discussed to provide the screenplay, among them Arnold Wesker and John Mortimer. The book was episodic, anecdotal and incidental, and capturing its humour and eccentricity proved elusive for most of those who attempted the task. Verity suggested her old chum Doug Livingstone but Dalton was unconvinced. Morris Gleitzman was another possibility and he was interested but simply too busy. The considerable demands of *Eldorado* then intervened to distract Verity and eventually, the development money from Channel 4 and ABC in Australia ran out. *Aunts on the Cross* remains a hidden gem, ready for someone with the skill and stamina to bring it to life on screen.

Another project that caught Verity's imagination was *Into the Heart of Borneo*. As the title implies, this was the colourful account of explorer Redmond O'Hanlon's 1983 expedition to travel to the centre of an exotic and inaccessible country with his good friend, the poet James Fenton. It was brought to Verity by Nancy Dowd, the American writer who, during the course of various abortive projects in the past, had become a good and valued friend. 'I'd convinced Paramount to option *Borneo* for me to do the screenplay,' explains Dowd. 'When I'd written a first draft, I sought a producer and I went to Verity.'

There were the usual creative and collaborative meetings. 'I remember Verity and I going to Redmond's house in Oxford for dinner,' Dowd continues. 'As we left, he gave Verity a wooden trunk filled with something mysterious to put in the boot of her car. Redmond said, somewhat ominously, that this had been given to him years before. For all we knew, we were headed to London with a trunk filled with anything from hash to porn to body parts! Verity said, "What are we going to do with it?" We even contemplated pulling over to the side of the highway and dumping it. After all that, I think it turned out to be candles!'

Like so many before him, Redmond O'Hanlon fell under Verity's spell. He nicknamed her 'Legs Lambert', and this was how he addressed all his subsequent correspondence to her, greatly to Verity's amusement. Seeking a box-office name to help sell the screenplay, she travelled to Paris for discussions with Gerard Depardieu's agent. The Canadian actor and comedian John Candy, soon to die prematurely young, was another star on whom she set her sights. The frustrations of trying to put together a credible and commercial deal continued for some months. 'Of course, a few creeps and villains entered the picture,' comments Nancy Dowd. 'A well-known producer wanted me to dump Verity so that he could produce at Paramount instead. I declined and I don't think I ever told her about that because she would have said, "Oh, go ahead."'

Verity sent the screenplay to John Lloyd, who had made his name as the producer of enormously successful comedy series including *Not the Nine O'Clock News*, *Blackadder* and *Spitting Image*, but was now at the peak of a highly successful career as a commercials director and looking to make the break into features. Lloyd was one of Verity's many fans within the business and they knew each other from the usual circuit of awards shows and industry events. 'There was something about everything that Verity did that had Verity all over it,' he says. 'They always had some sort of Verity spine to them. She was absolutely not a one-trick pony. I looked up to her, of course. I can remember watching the very first *Doctor Who* as a prep schoolboy and being completely knocked out by it and all the other stuff over the years which followed. She was extraordinary the way she kept reinventing herself.'

Keen to work with her, Lloyd read the script Verity had sent him. 'Redmond goes to Borneo with his friend to look for something called the dwarf rhino,' he explains. 'The script was flawless, a tremendously funny picaresque of these two slightly eccentric, slightly hopeless people and their adventures, getting into pickles all over the place. It was very entertaining with an interesting subject matter, interesting locations, great characters and very good jokes. It just rolled off the page, although I didn't think the last few pages delivered the ending it needed and deserved.'

'The difficulty with the ending was the rhinoceros,' says Nancy Dowd. 'Were they to finally see the rhino or not? In the book, and real life, they did not. But Verity wanted them to find it. "Call the prop department. Make us a rhino. Anna, get the zoo on the phone."'

Ambitious, unusual, and bound to be expensive, *Into the Heart of Borneo* stalled and finally collapsed, joining Verity's intriguing catalogue of projects which, despite their great dramatic and imaginative potential, never got made.

For Cinema Verity, it was series which remained the bread and butter. The presenter-turned-writer, Kieran Prendeville was responsible for *Lawless Men*, which revolved around the migrant Irish labour force that flooded into London in the 1960s. 'I think it would have been very good,' says Sharon Bloom, who worked on its development. 'We got quite close to selling it to BBC Northern Ireland but in the end they didn't like it enough to go ahead with it.'

Drama was not a prerequisite. Attempting to board the early-90s bandwagon of panel shows, Verity mined her own love of cookery to devise *A Question of Taste*, a culinary quiz game intended for Channel 4, which paid for a pilot. She asked her friend Nigella Lawson to appear as one of the intended regulars, alongside celebrated London chef Alastair Little. Among the guests was the comic actor Mike McShane, then a staple of Channel 4's *Whose Line Is It Anyway?* To Verity's disappointment, the pilot failed to sell a series.

Neither was she successful in getting off the ground a word game fronted by lexicographer and slang expert Jonathon Green. The idea for this had originated with her friend Colin MacCabe. 'I must admit to feeling almost wholly out of my depth,' comments Green, who had to devise the questions as well as chair the game. 'I think the underlying fantasy was a words-based variation on *Have I Got News for You*. I had no experience and probably no skill in creating game shows. As a lexicographer, my interest has always been in the history of words rather than in playing games with them. The premise of the games escapes me. I imagine there would have been a round of "odd one out" based on lists of synonyms for a single item, questions based on etymology, and similar things. One would have had to have enjoyed the idea of words and their origins and meanings to have enjoyed the format. It was not especially populist. We performed in front of a senior Channel 4 figure in the hope of interesting him sufficiently to obtain funding that would push things further.'

A belt-and-braces pilot was recorded on location at Dr Johnson's house in Gough Square, London, with contributors including Nigella Lawson (again), firebrand writer Christopher Hitchens and Verity's American journalist friend, Reggie Nadelson. 'Although the answers were spontaneous,' Jonathon Green continues, 'as were the bulk of my links, it was reminiscent of a theatrical read-through. I had very little confidence in my TV persona and felt that the show and its questions would have vastly benefited from a skilled and professional creator of such things, and feared very much that I might let down those who were involved. I would have loved for the show to have taken off; I did not really believe that it would. I did my best. Some years later, in 2005, when the second edition of my Cassell Dictionary of Slang appeared, the Channel 4 panjandrum before whom the show was performed had me on Dara O'Briain's show in Dublin. He assured me that he had been impressed, but felt that the format was not worthy of taking to the next step, which would have involved putting in money.'

Attempting the adventurous in scripted comedy, Verity developed a series based on the topical humour and observation of the cartoon strip *Alex*, which had started life in the pages of the *London Daily News* in 1987, eventually finding a permanent home in the *Daily Telegraph*. From his first appearance in print, Alex, an investment banker, was the embodiment of 'yuppie' values and the challenge was to capture the strip's sharply satirical edge and ability to subvert expectations. Creators Charles Peattie and Russell Taylor worked on a script but it was another no-sale. Verity remained upbeat and philosophical in the face of such disappointments. 'Onwards and sideways,' she would say, having done everything she possibly could to get a project away.

Unlike *Alex*, *Where the Country Lies* started life as a more traditional situation comedy. It came to Verity from her old friend, the actor Peter Bowles. 'I brought her some ideas which she loved,' he says. 'The premise of this one was that dream which everybody has of going to live in the country. You arrive in your little idyll and then you find they do night farming. I had lived in quite a remote cottage, you see, and some extraordinary things had happened to me there.'

Peter Ansorge at Channel 4 liked the premise enough to order six hour-long episodes but by the time writer Stephen Fagan began to deliver the scripts, Ansorge had had a change of heart: 'It was very funny in places,' he says, 'but I didn't go ahead as it read a bit too BBC1 for Channel 4. I recall that Michael Wearing [another executive] then read it at the BBC and also took it quite seriously. Perhaps it was too close to being a kind of UK-based *Year in Provence*, which hadn't performed as well as hoped for the BBC.'

Another series which Bowles developed with Verity was a drama, *First Loves Found*, about a father and daughter who set up an agency to find other people's first loves. 'My very first love was a girl who I lived with for three years,' says Bowles. 'She was extraordinary but suffered from schizophrenia and I always wondered what happened to her. That's what gave me the idea. You want to find out what's happened to an ex-girlfriend or a car you once loved – whatever was your first love – and so you employ a man who will find whatever it is that you want. As a result, you walk into incredible situations.'

Jonathan Powell commissioned scripts for ten episodes while he was still controller of BBC1 but, following his departure from the Corporation, the series was abruptly shelved. When Powell re-emerged as the head of drama at the newly formed Carlton Television, Bowles again went to see him to pitch the idea. He recalls: 'Jonathan said, "My God, this is wonderful," and I told him, "You had it at the BBC," but he explained he hadn't actually seen the scripts. He now said he'd like to commission a script for a Carlton version, which was duly written. Then it had to go to an ITV controllers' board which was headed by a man called Vernon Lawrence. This board decided what was going out across ITV and had the final say. I went with Verity and pitched this idea with her. Vernon had been the producer of *Only When I Laugh* [a popular sitcom in which Bowles had starred] and let's just say that I don't think he was mad about me. He said, "We've already commissioned something about missing people," so *First Loves Found* was never done. It just disappeared.'

Bowles had better luck with the third idea he took to Verity. This was for a single play, the hardest sell of all. 'It was called *The Backward Glance*,' he says. 'Based on some of my own real-life experiences. A very strange and haunting story of child murder. I went over to Verity, told her the idea and she said, "Great timing – the BBC are doing a series of films and they're looking for scripts." She made a phone call and we literally walked from her office in Shepherd's Bush, across the green, to visit Richard Broke, the man in charge of these films, in his office. We pitched the idea and Richard said, "I love it, I'll give you the budget but you need a writer." I remember walking back across that green and Verity and I were so happy. It felt like the beginning of all sorts of things and it really was very exciting. Verity suggested Simon Gray as a writer. I wouldn't have dreamt of going that high.'

Gray, whom Verity liked as much as she admired, accepted the job but at the eventual lunch to hand over his script, the distinguished writer commented: 'Before I hand it over, you must know I have completely changed the storyline so I don't want Peter's name attached to it. Also, I never do rewrites, so this is it.'

Bowles was understandably aghast and upset. He made his way home, where he immediately composed an angry letter to Gray. Before posting it, he decided to call Verity and read it out to her. Once he had finished, she told him: 'I think you have every right to say what you say but if you send that letter, Simon will withdraw his script and there will be no film. By the way, have you read his script?'

Bowles admitted that he had not. Verity counselled him to do so before making a decision. 'I read the script,' he says. 'It was the best script I had ever read. The words and scenes were delivered and written like bullets or shells from a powerful gun. Such passion, such bitter humour. I rang Verity again – and I still have the stamped, sealed addressed and unopened letter to Simon Gray in my files.'

The film, retitled *Running Late* and transmitted as part of the BBC's *Screen One* strand, was a darkly comic thriller about an obnoxious TV presenter, George Grant, whose life suddenly begins to unravel. It won excellent reviews as well as the Best Television Drama award at the 1993 San Francisco International Film Festival. The experience of making the film only cemented Peter Bowles' deep admiration for Verity. 'You were always aware that you were with an attractive, highly intelligent woman who understood irony and jokes,' he says. 'People get me wrong quite a lot because of my sense of humour. I say things and they take it literally. She always knew when I was joking. I'm so very glad that I met her. She was an important part of my life and development. I learnt determination from her. If you believe in something, convince the other people and don't doubt yourself.'

Since their first collaboration on *Widows*, Lynda La Plante had become one of the most bankable and talked-about British television writers. When ITV drama executive Nick Elliott turned down her mini-series *Comics*, a furious La Plante took it to Verity instead. 'I told her a little bit about it,' she says. 'Verity said, "Well, let's do it. I'll go and talk to Channel 4" and within hours she's on the phone – "Right, on we go." Every show was her baby. If you worked with Verity, she gave you one hundred per cent. I remember on *Comics*, they'd been filming for quite a few days when she took an actor out and said, "I want you to dye your hair black, you look too old." Now that's a very big decision because of the reshooting but she didn't care. It had to be right.'

A bigger crisis emerged over the central casting, which required an American actor to play the lead role of Johnny Lazar, a stand-up comedian at the heart of the story. The original choice quickly began to deviate from the script, improvising his words and delivering them in a way that made them almost impossible to understand. It was decided that he would have to be replaced even though this would mean that shooting would have to be suspended for a few weeks while a replacement was sought. Verity flew out for a weekend in New York with Lynda La Plante and Peter Ansorge in search of their new star. 'We went out club class,' recalls Ansorge, 'and they gave us an American Express expenses account. The plane had an engine problem and Verity said, "We're going to crash. Oh well, we'll have some champagne and you're not a bad person to be the last person to be alive with." She was very funny. She wanted to stay in the Philippe Stark hotel, the Paramount, which had just opened. Lynda hated it because she likes a bottle of champagne and the Paramount didn't have a licence. It was all open-plan but very dark and she kept falling over in the gloom. She hated the place. "I can't see the bathroom!" she'd complain. "Don't be ridiculous," said Verity, "It's state of the art!" Basically, in between the casting sessions with Bonnie Timmerman, Lynda and Verity mostly went shopping.'

They returned to London loaded with purchases and happy with their new lead, actor Tim Guinee.

Having renewed her connection with La Plante, Verity next suggested that the writer return to the characters she had created in *Widows*. 'She just called up and said, "Do you want to go again with Dolly Rawlins? Come up with something..."' says La Plante. It was a decade since the sequel, *Widows 2*, with which Verity had not been involved. This had been a very unhappy experience for La Plante. 'It was a completely different journey,' she says. 'The director [Paul Annett] was obnoxious. There was some terrible casting. I didn't like the producer on it. It was dreadful.'

This latest sequel represented an opportunity to heal some of the lingering wounds from the second *Widows*. When she'd had some time to think about the story she wanted to tell, the writer invited Verity to lunch to talk her through it. 'I said, "They're going to rob a train,"' explains La Plante. 'There was a pause. Verity just said, "Uh huh?" "And the train careers off a bridge" "Uh huh" again. "They also do the robbery on horseback." At that point, she burst out with, "Oh my God, are you taking the piss?" And I replied, "No, I'm absolutely serious." Then she started to think it through and I can remember her standing by the fire with the script in her hand, saying, "I know where we can get that train going over the bridge." She was on it.'

Verity engaged Ian Toynton, who had directed the original *Widows*, to mastermind the new six-episode story, *She's Out*. The critical negotiations for the return of actress Ann Mitchell as Dolly were so intense that, once they were finally concluded, Mitchell's agent, Marina Martin, had to retire to her bed for an entire weekend. 'Because of course I was asking for an increase in salary,' laughs Ann Mitchell, 'I was told that Verity had referred to me as Joan Crawford and Bette Davis rolled into one!'

This time, as well as being the writer, Lynda La Plante was also associate producer, which gave her the chance to learn yet more from Verity's experienced lead. 'She taught me to watch the edit,' says La Plante. 'She said, "Don't go on the floor, there's enough people faffing about there. Learn how to edit." Numerous people I've worked with since are astonished with the knowledge I have in the edit suite. The edit suite is still an area where you get more discrimination if you're a woman. You have to handle it and stay persistent. That's what she did. She told me, "You will never get a 'Sorry, you were right' from the edit suite when your notes make something better." She wasn't exaggerating. I have felt the venom from directors and editors. But I learnt how to cope with all that from watching her.'

She's Out was commissioned by Verity's old ally from the BBC, Jonathan Powell, now firmly ensconced in his role as head of drama at Carlton Television. Powell had also given his blessing to *Class Act*, a fast-moving comedy-drama starring Joanna Lumley as Kate Swift, a rich bitch whose gilt-edged world suddenly collapses from under her when her husband disappears, leaving her embroiled in trouble and debt. Kate forms an unlikely alliance with a young Australian burglar, Gloria, and Jack Booker, a cowardly tabloid journalist. Each episode follows their attempts to stay out of prison and find enough money to keep going. Writer Michael Aitkens was then a hot property on the strength of his hit BBC sitcom *Waiting for God*, and when Verity asked him if he had any ideas for her, he had offered a script he had written on spec. This became the basis of *Class Act*. For Aitkens, it was 'an anti-recession programme. I was a bit tired of all those gritty, realistic series – the *Taggart*s and the *Spender*s. We tend to make depressingly real television in this country, full of grubby streets and people being serious about life and I thought, "I want to go back to pretty people in beautiful surroundings who have no social conscience and are totally politically incorrect and whose attitude is, 'Forget everyone else, I'm having a good time.'" I enjoyed the idea of three very different people forced together by circumstance, who all come under the banner of "fairly awful people". Kate is that sort of relentless Englishwoman. I come from a family of strident, matriarchal, loony women and when you look at someone like Kate, you can see why we had an Empire.'

Although Aitkens was used to strong women, he took time to get used to working with Verity. 'She used to frighten me a bit to start with,' he explains, 'because when you went to a script conference, she had a habit of turning over any page she wanted to talk about. Not just a little bit, but half the page. If you went and sat opposite her and your script looked like a damned great Japanese fan, you knew the meeting was going to last forever. But she was an awfully good editor and kept you well on your toes. She'd write "CDB" on things meaning, "could do better". She was pretty demanding and expected you to keep going until it was right. I was writing by the seat of my pants. I would just start and see where it was going. She found this approach somewhat alarming and would say, "Can we have a treatment first?" and I would counter with, "I don't know what it's going to be about until I get the characters right."

'I had lots of children and vast debts,' continues Aitkens, 'and I remember thinking that [writers] Laurence Marks and Maurice Gran make an awful lot more money than I do because they hang on to the rights so I said to Verity, "I'd like to be co-producer on this." She just looked up and said, "No." "All right," I answered and then she said, "You can have an Executive Producer credit." I asked her, "What does that mean?" and she told me, "Not much. There's no more money in it but it does stop the actors asking you to get coffee for them."'

Joanna Lumley was offered the star part because of her huge success as the outrageous Patsy, foil to the equally OTT Edina (played by Jennifer Saunders), in the BBC's decade-defining sitcom *Absolutely Fabulous*. 'She really loved that series,' says Kath Williams. 'Verity was just like Edina in many, many, many respects. She would be ringing you from the car going, "I'm five minutes away from the office, darling."'

'Verity sent me a script,' recalls Joanna Lumley, 'and I just thought it was divine. It was an odd arrangement but it absolutely worked. The stories were rocketing, I thought they were fabulous and we got some cracking actors in.'

Alongside Lumley, Verity cast John Bowe as Jack and Nadine Garner, who had been a regular in *The Boys from the Bush*, as Grace. The veteran character actor Richard Vernon played Lumley's father in the series, with Verity's beloved Arthur Daley playing his faithful dog. 'Arthur was completely disobedient,' smiles Lumley. 'He would be in any scene that he wanted or not, depending on what he felt like.'

The first series did very good business and Jonathan Powell ordered a second.

'It was the chance to do something funny and entertaining but at the same time a little different for ITV,' he explains. 'They were funny, off-the-wall, original and rather wonderful scripts with a great star attached. I loved the humour.'

For the second series, Verity handed over the demands of day-to-day production to Sharon Bloom, although she continued to work with Aitkens on the scripts and to visit the set on a regular basis. 'It was like the headmistress coming,' says Joanna Lumley. 'We would all look sharp and be on board, ready to explain what we were doing. There was a sense of wanting to be seen doing her work well. I always think it is a great sign when a producer or executive is respected by the crew, which she was. We had a director who became very unhappy in her personal life and so for a couple of days, Verity stepped in. She adored it and was completely on fire, and knew exactly what she wanted, which was just as well because we were filming under a flight path so everything had to be done in the 30-second gap between planes.'

Alas, series two suffered a budget cut and a change of time slot, so that neither writer nor star was as happy with the show. 'I thought we were on a hiding to nothing,' says Joanna Lumley. 'Everything had started out fabulously and then money was taken out of it and it got bled to death. The audience know when confidence is going out of something.'

'I was irritated that they changed the time slot,' admits Michael Aitkens. 'This meant that we dipped below the magic ten million viewers and that's why we didn't do a third series. It would have been fun to do more.'

Budget woes are a perennial source of stress within the television industry. During 1995, Verity worked at both ends of the spectrum. She persuaded BBC1 controller Alan Yentob to commission a lavish one-off film version of P. G. Wodehouse's *Heavy Weather*, for Christmas transmission, with the prospect of further Wodehouse films to follow should this prove a success. She engaged Doug Livingstone to provide the screenplay and another favourite, Jack Gold, to direct. The cast list groaned with distinguished names from Peter O'Toole and Richard Briers to one of Verity's all-time favourite character actresses, Judy Parfitt. 'P. G. Wodehouse is tough to do on television,' says Jack Gold. 'They are wonderful stories and it's all in the casting. You need to do it as straight as possible. I thought Dickie Briers was already a Wodehouse character in his own life and Peter O'Toole was naturally dotty and eccentric, too. Some people thought he was over the top but I thought everybody played it well. It had a decent budget and was handsomely produced. But it didn't take off.'

Right at the other extreme was a project which began shooting the day after Verity wrapped on *Heavy Weather*. This was a series of five half-hour screenplays which had the lowest budgets she had worked with since her days on *Doctor Who*. They were part of an ongoing Carlton TV project called *Capital Lives*, a laudable attempt to showcase the potential of writers new to television. As well as the restrictions of the peppercorn sums involved, it was a regional project which meant London-only transmission with accordingly minimal audiences and publicity. But it appealed directly to Verity's principles. She could see only too clearly how television drama was beginning to polarise, so that increasingly opportunities for new writing talent were confined to the nursery slopes of soap operas. Her entire career had been based on an understanding of the critical importance of the writer, and her own instinctive ability to nurture, guide, cajole and shape their work. While *Capital Lives* was not going to add any lustre to Cinema Verity's end-of-year returns, it was absolutely a project in which Verity herself was keenly invested. 'What attracted me to it was the idea of working on scripts with writers new to television,' she explained in the series press release. 'They were able to write outside a format which is quite unusual these days. Unless you're writing a *Screen One* or a *Film on Four*, there is very little opportunity for any writers, let alone new ones, to write completely outside someone else's format.'

The first series of *Capital Lives* had been shot on the same set, and the second in a warehouse where different sets were built. For this third series, Verity decided that each would be recorded in one specific location, so that the feel of the plays could be less contained and claustrophobic. The writers were restricted to three characters which, as Verity acknowledged, 'was quite onerous for them because there couldn't be any action, so it all had to do with relationships and interaction of character. That really sorts out the men from the boys and the women from the girls.' As another exercise in economy, the five plays were shot back-to-back over a gruelling five-week schedule. 'Filming under such constraints requires an extraordinary amount of ingenuity, organisation and chutzpah,' said Verity. 'It's a wonderful thing to do once in a while; people are really working together and they know they can't snap their fingers and have five cats arrive!'

It is noteworthy that all of the writers involved, Moira Buffini, Kate O'Riordan, Jonathan Coe, Stef Penney and Pete Lawson, have fashioned diverse and successful careers in the years since. This would certainly have pleased Verity.

In November 1995, though her appearance belied her years, Verity turned 60 and became a pensioner. She pronounced herself thrilled with her free bus pass and was determined to make use of it. 'I was single at the time,' says Michael Aitkens. 'So Verity adopted me as her sort of "walker" – she used to say come to this function or that function. I used to think it was terrific. Writers don't get out much so she would make me dress up and escort her to some awards or other at wonderful hotels. On the way there, we'd get into cabs and she'd always tell the driver which way to go. He might have done five years of "the Knowledge" but she knew far better routes to anywhere. But when she got her bus pass, and we'd been at some bash, I'd say, "Come on Verity, time to go home" and she'd say, "No, no, no. We have to take the bus," and we'd be standing there in Piccadilly at midnight with her insisting that she use her pass. It was handy for her to have a bloke as a walker who wouldn't try and jump her at the end of the evening.'

There were no more serious relationships, although Verity always claimed to remain open-minded about the possibility. She sometimes joked that her ideal man was David Attenborough and that she 'would definitely go there' but, by this stage of her life, it is difficult to imagine her genuinely wanting the intrusion and compromise of sharing her life with anyone. Some of her friends suspect that, increasingly, she was lonely. 'I always sensed that,' says producer Paul Knight. 'I used to do escort duty sometimes and I sensed the loneliness. Men were slightly overawed by her.'

'There was a sadness about her,' believes agent and producer Robin Dalton. 'One felt that she had never had a happy, fulfilled personal life. I always felt sorry for her. I think she concentrated on her professional life because her personal life was so unrewarding. Probably she was too powerful and too ambitious for men.'

'I think it was a case of once bitten, twice shy,' says publicist and friend Rea Francis. 'She stayed away from that kind of emotional involvement again.'

'She was pretty much single,' agrees Felicity Marshall, another close friend from Australia. 'There were lovers. I think she probably would have liked to have met someone to spend more time with but it just didn't work out that way.'

'She made out that she didn't care,' says her friend, Viv Phillips. 'She said to me, "I would never live with anybody ever again. I'm very happy on my own." I think she meant it in a certain way but there was something lacking in her life. That sort of intimacy – being comfortable with somebody who knows you really well. I think she would have loved to have kept her own special man.'

'She wasn't a lonely woman,' insists writer and good friend, Nancy Dowd. 'That's caricatural. Her life is easy to pigeonhole but hard to understand. She had already done, "I am Mrs Norman Maine," and that had not worked out. No, she loved being Verity Lambert and she had a great life.'

In her later years, Verity worked increasingly closely with women and this, coupled with her many close female friendships, have led some to speculate that her sexuality may have had a lesbian aspect. 'She was *sympatico* but she didn't actually become a lesbian,' asserts her friend, producer Graham Benson, 'though in moments of insecurity and loneliness I suspect she craved some affection and friendship.'

'As a lesbian, I can assure you she wasn't,' says Kath Williams, shortly.

'Nothing could be further from the truth,' adds Anna Callaghan. 'The speculation about her sexuality is nonsense. Verity would have giggled about it.'

If it is true that she was sometimes lonely, Verity kept these feelings to herself and allowed little time to dwell on them. 'She didn't welcome you diving into her psyche,' says Rea Francis, emphatically.

'She never talked about her feelings,' agrees Kath Williams. 'She was very self-sufficient. She wasn't married and had no children and no one to go home to.'

'She told me that she was quite happy being on her own,' says Reggie Nadelson, 'though she liked somebody to travel with. But she was just as happy if that was a companionable woman. I don't think she was weeping tears for the lack of a man.'

When quizzed about her solitude by *Options* journalist Anne Cabourn in 1989, Verity herself commented: 'In the end, it's a choice. I believe that if I wanted to get married again, I could find someone who would marry me but obviously, I don't want to enough. From time to time you think, "Oh, it would be nice to have a relationship," because you share things with someone and that's fun. But equally, I enjoy being on my own. Maybe it's partly pressure of work and partly that I travel and am not always in one place for very long. Then perhaps some of it's laziness or selfishness.'

Her many friendships filled the gaps and her life remained intensely busy, with a diary which might daunt a woman half her age. The demands on her time were many and various, from parties and professional functions to first nights and dinner with friends. She adored eating well in good restaurants and relished the buzz of trying somewhere new as much as she enjoyed returning to an old favourite like the classic French establishment L'Escargot or the humbler Patio, which specialised in Polish cuisine, on the Goldhawk Road. Whatever the engagement, Verity was rarely at home in the evenings. 'I don't think she allowed herself to be lonely,' says Sharon Bloom. 'I used to think, "I wonder what goes through her head when she gets home at half past ten at night?" She surrounded herself with people and she was always out. Every invitation that came in she would take seriously. I don't know if Verity saw networking as networking – it was her part of her life, her social life, and that was what she wanted to do. She wasn't a snob either. At my wedding one of my friends got rather drunk and invited Verity to a boxing match. I genuinely think that if she had been free that night, she would have gone.'

'She had such a full life,' says Michael Aitkens. 'The drive was phenomenal. I wonder if that was something to do with having had cancer when she was younger? That might have given her a certain impetus because it was a dreadful smoking gun. It was always, "What's happening next? What we have to go and see – what restaurants are worth trying out?" She was just one of those great life forces.'

'She was not shy in any way,' says Paul Knight. 'I remember we'd gone to Linda Agran's and we'd all had a few drinks and Verity proceeded to do this full Isadora Duncan dance that she'd learnt at Roedean, using scarves, and ever-so-slightly ungraceful. It was typical of her. She laughed a lot and was tremendously sociable.'

'Everything was an event with her,' says her PA, Anna Callaghan. 'Going for a pizza would be an event.'

'She loved student-y eating,' explains actress Joanna Lumley, 'and she liked being with a girlfriend. She had a barrister's brain, an intellectual woman's brain and although she got on famously with men, I think she preferred women.'

As well as food, shopping was another pleasure to be shared with friends. As Verity got older, her interest in contemporary art developed and her knowledge of it deepened. She began to amass an interesting collection and, because her eye was good, many of these represented an investment. 'She was interested in all aspects of art,' says Felicity Marshall, a friend from Australia. 'I remember she bought this self-portrait with a cow by an artist called William Robinson. She just said, "I kind of like that, it's a bit mad – I think I might buy it."'

'Verity adored paintings,' agrees Joanna Lumley. 'She had an interesting eye – she had these Aboriginal paintings which she liked. They were good. She adored beautiful jewellery, not tittle-tattle from Accessorize. She wouldn't just wear lashings of old bangles, she'd buy a really fine necklace or a really beautiful ring, which she loved to wear – she didn't just keep them in the drawer for best. She liked good clothes, good things and was aristocratic in her choices – not fancy but grand. She always looked marvellous, like a Russian noblewoman with those dark eyes.'

Verity herself always claimed that she was naturally idle and could waste time just lying around day-dreaming. If this was so, she only indulged the habit rarely, although she generally she kept her Sunday mornings free so that she could lie in and listen to the omnibus edition of *The Archers*, to which she was an addict. 'God forbid if you made a mistake and called her on Sunday morning before 11.15,' laughs her close friend, Kate Kagan. 'You got hell!'

Once she had rallied herself, she would generally begin preparing a huge Sunday lunch from scratch. These lunches were a ritual and a regular posse of close friends would assemble to enjoy her excellent cooking and share a long afternoon of lively conversation and laughter. 'Her kitchen was a great place to be on a Sunday,' enthuses Michael Aitkens. 'She'd invite everybody. There were always a lot of people passing through from Australia. She had her little gang of people she could rely on to turn up at the last minute. She had a lot of high-powered friends, too. We'd talk about everything and she'd coax the best from everyone round the table. It was almost a political skill.'

'As people who live on their own for a long time do, she had a huge range of friends in different boxes,' agrees Kate Kagan. 'We used to cook together. We once spent a whole weekend making this Indian meal absolutely from scratch. Although professionally she could be very impatient, when she was cooking, she would take infinite care over every last detail. She had this wonderful old oval table – it easily seated 12 and could be extended and we invited all these people.'

'Her friends were her family,' says Kath Williams. 'When she was interested in you and what you were saying, you were like the centre of the universe.'

'She had this ability to make everybody relax and enjoy themselves and feel important,' says another friend, Val Hardy.

'She had a fabulous intelligence,' adds Felicity Marshall, who often stayed with Verity when she was over from her native Australia. 'You can always learn something from being around someone that sophisticated. She had a radar for phonies and she wasn't afraid of anything. She was quite feisty but expressed it all with unbelievable charm.'

'She certainly was curious about everything,' says Reggie Nadelson. 'If you got her on to a subject and she had an obsessive opinion about it, that was it. There was no point talking about anything else.'

When a friend was in trouble, unhappy, perhaps bereaved or going through a painful divorce, Verity would be staunchly loyal and ever-practical. She had the ability, rare in someone so gregarious, to listen as much as talk, concentrating on what she was told, advising without commanding and providing solidarity and distraction. It is telling that several friends asked her advice before making a proposal of marriage.

'If ever I wanted to talk to her about something or if I was having marital problems or whatever, she would drop everything to talk,' says Viv Phillips. 'She had a very sensible approach to everything – she was very clear-sighted and could cut through all sorts of diversions that one was going down. She always stressed the positive.'

'She was very caring in a lot of ways,' says Paul Knight. 'She was very good to me when I lost my first wife, taking me and my son out a few times for lunch and dinner.'

Another who shares Knight's view is the actress Sheila Brennan, whose friendship with Verity dated back to the 1960s when Brennan married Verity's then boss, BBC head of plays, Gerald Savory. 'Her friends mattered a lot to her and she liked to help them,' explains Brennan. 'I remember once I hadn't been well at all and she said, "I think you're looking a bit peaky – you've got to come and stay with me in the south of France." She would suddenly do things like that.'

Verity's generosity, impulsive, heartfelt, was another characteristic common to all her true friendships. 'She was hugely kind and generous,' says Michael Aitkens. 'She used to make a lot of money and she'd just spread it around her friends.'

'She knew I had a crappy car,' says Sharon Bloom, 'so she said, "We'll get you a company car." What company? It was only her! Anyway, we went to the showroom. It was always an adventure going out with her because you never knew what way it was going to go. We were left waiting five minutes so she was already in a bad mood. She had a go at the guy for keeping us waiting and stomped off to have a look at the cars, but she was still in earshot and then the guy said to me, "Have I upset your mother?" As you can imagine, that didn't go down very well either!'

All her life, and even when married or in a relationship, Verity enjoyed including friends in her holidays and trips. 'We had a lot of hilarious times together,' says Verity's journalist friend, Reggie Nadelson. 'One year I was working for *The Independent* and I was going to do a piece about renting a dacha in the Moscow countryside. Verity came too and she was screamingly funny. We got there and the people who owned it hadn't left. They had this terrible child. She said, "If that child is staying, he's going to have to be chained up..."'

'I went to a health farm with her one year,' says Linda Agran, Verity's Euston Films script executive. 'We shared a room and they put a little card under your door to tell you what your treatments were for the day. This card slid under the door and the next thing I hear is a click and a puff of smoke. Seven o'clock in the morning and she's lit up her fag so she can see what her treatments are going to be at this health farm! Oh dear...'

Verity's maniacal smoking came to an abrupt end at the behest of another close friend, American screenwriter Nancy Dowd. 'One day, she was visiting my house in Hollywood,' she explains, 'when I noticed that, as she stood smoking outside on the terrace, and I was inside in the kitchen, the smoke appeared to be coming out of her blouse. I said, "Verity, you look like Beelzebub!"'

Dowd had a holiday home in the Caribbean island of Saint Lucia and invited Verity to spend the first of several Christmases there. 'The house is old and made of wood,' Dowd continues. 'I told her, "You've got to stop smoking or you can't come." She had a lot of willpower and so she stopped, and I was very glad about that because it wasn't doing her any good.'

In 1995, Cinema Verity reached the milestone of its tenth birthday and to celebrate Verity decided to take the whole team on the Eurostar to Paris for a memorably lavish lunch at a restaurant called Benoit, where she had organised a delicious chocolate mousse cake as the *pièce-de-résistance* at the end of the meal. Assisted as ever by Anna Callaghan, Verity smuggled champagne and plastic glasses onto the train to produce at the moment they entered the tunnel. The party was Verity at her most joyful and a fitting celebration of all that she and her Cinema Verity team had achieved over the previous decade. But the sad truth was that her company was now in slow but serious decline. All its returnable series had come to an end and, despite everyone's best efforts, there was little to fill the void.

Television may by this stage have been markedly less sexist but it was increasingly ageist and so another invisible battle emerged for Verity to engage with: trying to be taken seriously by much younger commissioners not especially interested in and, even put off, by her dauntingly long heritage. The work that now came her way was from a dwindling group of executives usually with shared history and some degree of personal loyalty. One of these was the BBC's bright and personable head of comedy, Geoffrey Perkins. He commissioned the final Cinema Verity project to be made from the Mill House, a situation comedy by Michael Aitkens called *A Perfect State*. This was a variation on the theme of the classic Ealing film *Passport to Pimlico* and had been inspired by an article which Aitkens had read about a new EU regulation on fishing quotas. 'They were trying to pull the ships off the sea, basically,' explains Aitkens. 'You only got your subsidy if your boat was smashed up. There were these dreadful people overseeing the smashing of beautiful old fishing boats. I thought, "Why don't the fishermen break away and rebel?"'

Aitkens created the fictional coastal town of Flatby with its feisty deputy mayor, Laura, a relentless crusader for every cause that attracts her interest. Outraged by the EU's destructive treatment of Flatby's fishing industry (one man and his old boat), Laura rallies the whole town to declare itself an independent state. This farcical situation also owed something to another classic comedy series, *Clochemerle*, which the BBC had screened in 1972 and repeated in the early 1990s. 'It wasn't a very original idea,' Aitkens concedes. *Clochemerle* had been filmed entirely on location, and this was an approach that Aitkens was also keen to emulate. Geoffrey Perkins agreed so the writer devised an hour-long comedy-drama series with ten principal characters. At this point, the BBC decided that the single-camera approach was going to cost too much money and asked Cinema Verity to rethink the series so that it could be recorded mainly in a multi-camera studio, in a more conventional half-hour format. 'Of course, being an independent you roll over and say yes,' shrugs Sharon Bloom, who produced. 'None of us were happy about it. We should have said no but you want the commission. The first day when I walked into the studio I just thought, "God, this all looks very brown."'

'As far as I was concerned, doing it in the studio like that was a disaster,' says Aitkens. 'They just shot the script that I'd written for film to be done in the studio. It didn't work. You can't suddenly introduce ten characters to an audience like that. I was in a panic. I could see that the audience weren't laughing because they didn't know these people or the set-up, so then we'd go into rehearsal and I'd start adding lines and visual humour. It was not one of my proudest moments. Verity was ever enthusiastic. She hoped to get a second series out of it.'

It was not to be. Fatally wounded by its switch to the studio, *A Perfect State* failed to connect with the mainstream BBC1 audience.

Verity's last great hope to save the fortunes of her ailing company was a typically ambitious project that had been in development for Channel 4 since Christmas 1994. This was an adaptation of Vikram Seth's sprawling novel, *A Suitable Boy*, which had been published the previous year. The rights to the book had been swiftly obtained by film producer David Puttnam, who was getting nowhere with his attempts to interest backers in a movie version. 'Then Verity approached me and said, "What about a TV series?"' he explains. 'I said yes, we'll do it together and we made a deal with Peter Ansorge at Channel 4 to develop the scripts and everything else.'

'I hadn't read it,' admits Ansorge. 'David Puttnam said that we wouldn't have to fully finance because he had secured all this money in India. I then read most of the book but unlike *GBH*, I thought it was going to be tricky because it's a sort of Indian Jane Austen. I found it a bit unengaging but I did commission the scripts.'

Set in the months following Indian independence, the book presented many challenges, not only with its length and sheer number of characters, but in capturing the particular quality of Seth's narrative style. Verity decided to engage three writers to take on the enormous job of translating the book into a filmable entity of 13 hour-long instalments. She chose her old friend Doug Livingstone as lead writer and teamed him with the established Indian screenwriter Sooni Taporeleva and a gifted new talent called Tanika Gupta, who was then at the very beginning of her career.

'I knew about her,' she explains. 'I had watched *Doctor Who* as a child and I had seen *GBH*. But when I first went to meet her, I was terrified. She had this huge dog which had just had some kind of operation on his testicles. He sat there all the way through the interview licking his balls and making these horrible slurpy noises. I had read the book, so I was able to talk about it and she gave me the job on the spot. '

The plan was for Livingstone and Taporeleva to script five episodes each, with Gupta supplying the rest. 'This was very complicated as far as continuity was concerned,' points out Livingstone. 'But we had a good meeting with the author and it seemed to be going swimmingly.'

'We all loved the book,' says Gupta. 'It was very enjoyable going through and dividing it all up. It's a very easy book to read. Basically, it's about a girl who is looking for a husband and is torn between two men. A classic situation, really. The added issue of Muslim versus Hindu was very topical and remains so. A lot of it was Sooni and I giving our expertise as Asians, as well as writers. Verity was very concerned that it should translate for a British audience. At the beginning, I kept thinking, "What am I doing in this room? I've not even done anything." But there was never a moment when she made me feel junior. I grew really fond of her. She was very clear about what she did and she didn't want and what she felt worked, yet she was very open to what I had to say too. The fact that Verity took me seriously gave me a lot of confidence. I was a community worker for Islington council at the time and I remember telling Verity that I'd given up my job to become a writer. She pulled a face and said, "You're always going to need money so look for other things to do as well as writing." And I said, "Yeah, but I was a community worker." "Oh, GOD! Yes, give *that* up." Within about a year, I'd had my first play on at the National.'

As well as David Puttnam, and his associate producer, Steve Norris, Verity asked her close friend, film producer Michael Kagan, to become a partner in the epic venture. He was an old hand at the complex demands of filming in India, having shot sections of his 1994 live-action version of *The Jungle Book* on various locations in the sub-continent. Kagan accompanied Verity on a recce, the highlight of which was an early morning boat trip to witness hundreds of Indians from around the world scattering the ashes of their loved ones into the sacred waters of the river Ganges in Varanasi. They were both deeply moved by the spectacular sight.

In search of a director with the right credentials and a cinematic vision, Verity turned to the man who had taken charge of her very first production, Waris Hussein. Hussein was also an old acquaintance of Puttnam's, having directed Puttnam's first movie, *Melody*, in 1970. Hussein readily accompanied Verity on a further trip to India. 'It would have been ahead of its time,' he comments. 'But I think Channel 4 decided who wants to spend all this time and money on a bunch of Indians talking in English?'

'I don't know if I knew about Waris,' says Peter Ansorge. 'Because I would have responded to that and it would have been attractive. I would have got him in to look at the scripts.'

Instead, having worked on the proposed series for nearly two years, Verity was told that Channel 4 no longer had the money to make *A Suitable Boy* and that the whole project was off.

'I couldn't believe it,' says Kath Williams. 'We'd done so much work on it and we'd spent a fucking fortune of Channel 4's money and then they turned it down.'

'Was it lack of financial backing?' asks Doug Livingstone. 'Quality of the scripts? A feeling somewhere that it was not commercial? I never really knew.'

'If I'm really honest, I wasn't that keen,' explains Peter Ansorge. 'Doug is a good writer, a jobbing writer, but I don't know what his sense of India was and in some ways when I read the scripts, I thought that the story then became even cruder. I had been expecting the opposite. The other thing is that Puttnam didn't have the additional money from India. He knows that I know this. In order to avoid Verity's fierceness, I was a bit political and blamed it on budget problems, which was partly true. If I had committed to it, it would have been a huge spend, half my budget for the year. So when I told her, I was trying to the sugar the pill a bit, which was probably a mistake. I was aware that it was her last chance as Cinema Verity.'

'It was a very big deal for her,' continues David Puttnam. 'She was bitterly disappointed and very, very upset, which is probably why I went for Michael Grade. I think it's the only row I ever had with him. I challenged him and told him that I knew that he had got trapped into a bidding war for *Friends* and had spent the money. I was doing something at Warners [who distributed *Friends*] and that's where the intelligence came from. It was as simple as that. I said, "I know what's happened, you've spent the money on *Friends*, and now you've scuppered a UK-made series." He absolutely flared up and said, "That's not the case!" He was ridiculously defensive. I'd never seen that side of Michael, before or since. I'd touched a nerve because it was true.'

'I genuinely don't remember that,' says Grade himself. 'But I don't believe that it was anything to do with *Friends*. We had been keen to do *A Suitable Boy* but there's a limit to what you can spend on any drama.'

'It was gutting,' concludes Puttnam. 'My impression was that, for Verity, it felt like the end of her career.'

Verity tried to muster her usual optimism and spirit but she could not ignore the impact of losing such an essential commission. Kath Williams, who was in charge of Cinema Verity's finances, spelt out the death warrant in figures, but the end of Cinema Verity was more than financial. There was still the lingering damage to Verity's reputation left by the abject failure of *Eldorado*. This was brought home to her shortly after the cancellation of *A Suitable Boy*, when Waris Hussein asked Verity to read *These Foolish Things*, a novel by Deborah Moggach which he was keen to film. 'I said to Verity, "You love India and it didn't happen for us on *Suitable Boy* – what about this book?" She read it and said, "Let's meet Deborah Moggach and see what we could do." We had lunch at the Wolseley with Deborah Moggach's agent and guess what the agent said? "Verity, do you really think you could finance this *on your name*?" I will never forget Verity looking at me and saying, "Well, I think I'm going to have to discuss this between Waris and me. Do you mind?" We walked out of there and she said, "Not a chance." It was over before it began.'[3]

With nothing else on the books, Verity took her team to lunch at the Shepherd's Bush Pizza Express to break the news, which was scarcely a surprise to anyone, that she was going to have to leave the Mill House and drastically downsize the company. 'When *A Suitable Boy* didn't happen, everybody had to go,' says Sharon Bloom. 'We had been relying on that and we were all devastated. She was very upset. We were sitting in Pizza Express talking about the end of Cinema Verity and she had tears in her eyes.'

Verity could not bear to contemplate making a totally clean break and winding up the company. Neither did she for a moment consider retirement or seeking a return to the corporate world as an executive. 'The terrible thing about Verity is that she should have

---

[3] *These Foolish Things* was eventually filmed as *The Best Exotic Marigold Hotel*, released in 2011

been controller of BBC2 or managing director of the BBC or whatever,' says Linda Agran. 'She should have taken all her expertise, all her incredible knowledge and experience, and been allowed to use them in another area. I think she probably would have loved it. Verity was ten times better than John Birt and Greg Dyke and all those people. LWT sent Greg Dyke to the Harvard Business School to polish him up professionally. Just think what they could they have done with Verity. But the men at the top of these organisations never saw her as anything but a producer who had success – and made them millions, let me tell you. Yes, she loved being at the coal face but she never had the chance to do anything else. It's outrageous. I can feel the tears in my eyes when I think about it.'

'Linda's right in theory,' says writer and presenter Melvyn Bragg, 'but maybe Verity didn't want to be a chief executive. If she'd been a chief exec, who would she be talking to? Other executives in meetings. Who is running her life? As an executive, you are under the control of a lot of other people. Whereas she called the meetings and she called the shots in her life. She was a truly independent person. Would she be a good channel controller? Well, maybe. Was she a good drama producer? Yes, definitely, she was a brilliant drama producer. So she could wake up every morning and think, "I'm really good at what I do, and I want to do it again today," instead of "Christ, I wish I'd never taken this BBC2 job, I've got to meet sport this afternoon."'

Michael Grade, who has spent much of his long career as a senior executive in top television companies, takes a similar view. 'I think if she had wanted to go down that route, she could have achieved it.[4] But she loved scripted drama, that was her thing. I don't think she had much interest in news, current affairs, documentaries, light entertainment. Narrative drama is where she really enjoyed herself.'

Having moved out of the Mill House, Verity's plan was to continue her efforts to find new projects but on a vastly reduced scale. She found a new office in Ravenscourt Park and her faithful PA, Anna Callaghan, readily agreed to continue to work for her, albeit now on a part-time basis. But hardly had they started working within this slimline Cinema Verity when chance intervened and changed everything. 'We were sitting there one day and the phone rang,' recalls Callaghan. 'It was Geoff Perkins saying, "We need a producer very quickly, would you consider doing *Jonathan Creek*?" The scripts were sent over by courier there and then.'

'I'd watched the first series and thought it was good fun and quite unusual,' Verity explained. 'It wasn't like anything else I'd seen. All my life I tried to make programmes that had some kind of originality.'[5]

---

[4] Industry rumours had it that in 1983 the BBC flirted with inviting Verity to become head of their drama group. In 1986, *Television Today* reported that she had been offered the job of director of programmes for Thames Television over lunch with its then managing director, Richard Dunn – but that she had turned the opportunity down

[5] Kaleidoscope convention interview

What Verity had yet to discover was that this interesting, if sudden, opportunity had arisen from a crisis behind the scenes.

A series of hour-long comedy-thrillers, often with a dark edge, *Jonathan Creek* was the creation of the idiosyncratic comedy writer David Renwick. Celebrated for his witty dialogue and precise visual humour, Renwick was then at the absolute peak of his career, with another standout hit, *One Foot in the Grave*[6], running alongside *Jonathan Creek*. Although both series shared certain elements of Renwick's distinctive style and tone, *Jonathan Creek* was conceived on a grander, occasionally operatic, scale. The eponymous hero was a sardonic professional illusionist and magician who, in a haphazard fashion, teams up with an impulsive investigative reporter, Maddy Magellan, and uses his skills to decode and solve apparently impossible crimes and mysteries. The role of Magellan was written especially for Caroline Quentin and, originally, Renwick had in mind either Nicholas Lyndhurst or Hugh Laurie to play Creek. Alan Davies, the 30-year-old stand-up comedian eventually cast, was discovered by *Jonathan Creek*'s initial producer, Susie Belbin. The first series had been an enormous success and won BAFTA's Best Drama award, which was ironic as it was actually produced by the BBC's comedy department. 'That's where my history was,' explains David Renwick. 'I just felt that although it was a hybrid notion, the comedy was harder to get right and that it was easier for comedy practitioners to get the drama right than it was for drama people to make things funny.'

Controller of BBC1 Alan Yentob confidently ordered a second series while the first was still in production but at this point, Susie Belbin, Renwick's long-term collaborator, decided to take early retirement. 'They needed to find somebody who could work with David Renwick,' says Esta Charkham, who replaced Belbin. 'They saw me and Susie said, "That's the person," and David said, "Esta is the person," and so they hired me and I started work. I knew Caroline really, really well. It was all going beautifully when Geoff Perkins called me into his office and said, "I need to talk to you. It's Caroline – she won't work with you." I said, "Why? I don't understand."'

It transpired that Quentin was unhappy with her new producer because of a connection between Charkham and Quentin's former agent, who had defrauded her of a considerable sum of money. 'It was nothing to do with me,' continues Charkham. 'Geoff said, "Caroline told me that you were her agent's best friend and you probably know where the money is!" I replied, "I shared a flat with her 18 years ago. As a matter of fact I got rid of her because she didn't pay her rent on time." But Geoff was adamant and said, "I have to send you home – you can't work on this show." I called my agent who called in lawyers. It was just awful. Geoff said to my agent, "If Esta does anything else about this or goes public, life could be very difficult for her at the BBC." So I didn't. David said he still wanted to work with me, so they moved me onto a Christmas special of *One Foot in the Grave* but I never, ever worked at the BBC again after that. It took them four weeks to

---

[6] Verity was a fan

find another producer for *Jonathan Creek* and it was Verity. I said at the time, "Well, I'm very flattered that it's Verity who has replaced me."'

When she discovered the bitter history behind Geoff Perkins' offer, Verity momentarily hesitated, as she later explained: 'I said, "This sounds like a poisoned chalice. Who do I have to impress?" And he said, "Well, you have to meet David Renwick."'

'I'm notoriously nervous about working with new people,' says David Renwick. 'I was just getting bedded in with Esta and that had all been going along quite nicely. I'd met Verity at a BAFTA awards five or six years earlier. I was on Jonathan Powell's table and she was also there – there was a lot of red wine, which she was very partial to and she got terrifically drunk as I recall! Of course, Verity was absolutely legendary and she'd done *May to December* and *So Haunt Me* so on the basis of that and obviously her vast drama experience, Geoff thought that she would be a good candidate but so much of it is to do with personalities. I was called in to meet her. There was a certain formality to that session. She'd had to mug up on the scripts. My greatest concern – which she obviously detected – was whether she would understand the comedy, particularly in the area of casting. Some drama people will say, "This person was a brilliant Lear at the National" and you'd respond, "Yes, they might be a very good actor but they're not funny." So all these worries were swilling round in my head.'

'I think at that point David felt that this woman's going to come in and want to change everything,' recalled Verity herself. 'He said, "What do you think about the show?" And I said I really liked it, and a few things I thought could improve the show. They weren't major changes, just refinements really. So I started working on it. For the first three months I think I was there under sufferance. David is a quiet and shy man and he doesn't really tell you very much. Writers can be like that. I just felt he hated everything I was doing. Then finally one day he said, "I really like working with you." After that, it was all good.'[7]

The sudden offer to produce *Jonathan Creek* rescued Verity from the doldrums of development and placed her back in active production. The compromise was that to do so she had to put her own company on ice indefinitely, surrendering the autonomy she had fought so hard and so long to retain and becoming an employee once again. She was not blind to the strange symmetry of the situation. She was returning under contract to the BBC, the very place in which she had started producing 34 years earlier, to make another popular Saturday night fantasy-adventure series. For Verity, at first, it was one more case of 'onwards and sideways', but, in the years that followed, *Jonathan Creek* richly rewarded her with some of the most satisfying work of her career, as well as one last, great creative partnership with David Renwick, which was to keep her fully active in the industry she loved until the very last weeks of her life.

---

[7] Kaleidoscope convention interview

CHAPTER FIFTEEN
PLENTYSOMETHING
1997–2007

'Now the controller wants to read all the scripts. That isn't what they should be doing – they shouldn't even have the time. Controllers should trust the people they've hired to bring them stuff of a certain quality. If they make a huge cock-up, you fire them and get someone else. But if you don't trust them, then why employ them? Power now rests with two or three people and if they're not up to it, there's going to be a problem.'

Verity to David Benedictus, *The Guardian*, 2001

Few of Verity's friends were mystified by her decision to return to the coal-face as a jobbing producer. She was well past retirement ('plentysomething' was her stock answer to those impertinent enough to ask her age) and could certainly have afforded to give up the daily grind and just enjoy herself. But she never seriously considered this. She still enjoyed working and the challenges it presented. She was excited by talent and the thrill of the chase, ever optimistic that she might realise some of the projects she nursed in development. The prospect of having nothing to do except shop, travel and plan her social life would have robbed these activities of their enjoyment. They were facets of her full life but, by themselves, not enough.

Returning to the BBC to produce *Jonathan Creek* offered Verity a break in the remorseless pressure of responsibility for her own company and affairs. There was a degree of freedom in being a contracted employee, with only the requirement to deliver one programme within the specified period. Unlike a small indie, the BBC could still offer an unprecedented level of back-up to its producers. But the BBC of the late 1990s bore scant resemblance to the organisation Verity had first joined in 1963. Director-General John Birt, whose implacable distaste for *Eldorado* had been a significant factor in its demise, unleashed an aggressive free-market approach to the BBC's finances which, as he intended, wreaked havoc on its long-established internal systems. Laughably christened 'Producer choice', its arrival rapidly eroded both the morale and many of the assets unique to the BBC. Valuable resources such as the design department, the costume and wig store, the vast repository of small props, the research libraries and the purpose-built rehearsal rooms were rapidly priced out of existence. The assets of these were sold off at rock-bottom prices, destroyed or otherwise dispersed. Thousands of skilled craft jobs were discarded in the process. An unwieldy new culture of jargon-loving middle management thrived and programme budgets were battered as funds were diverted to pay for the Birtist regime, and for follies like the hideous and impractical White City building he sponsored. Birt was openly despised by many of his staff.[1] Some wag coined the phrase 'Birt is a four-letter word.' 'Just a Dalek in a grey suit' was another jibe, the irony of which would not have escaped Verity. BBC insiders joked wearily that good programmes were now made despite the system rather than because of it. There was the strange psychology that with each subsequent series, successful programmes were invariably required to reduce their budgets. The skewed logic of this approach, which still persists, is that it must be cheaper to continue an established formula than to devise a series from scratch. Verity produced 20 episodes of *Jonathan Creek* over an eight-year period, and much of her energy and ingenuity was spent on wringing the best from a budget often at odds with the ambition of the scripts.

Here at least she had the advantage of a writer whose work was delivered in such finished form that there was no need of long script sessions. David Renwick was surprised at the speed and strength of the bond that developed between them. 'Our backgrounds were very different,' he explains. 'I was immediately rather suspicious of her because she had been to Roedean and she had that voice and everything that, as a working-class man, I wouldn't initially feel very comfortable with. Which made it even more remarkable that we just gelled so amazingly well. I think you can't overstate the way that our personalities connected – we became such great friends and then you get to a stage where you can just say whatever you want to each other. "Well, I think you're talking bollocks there, actually." You're not treading on eggshells any more, you just feel really, really comfortable with each other. I didn't row with her. One of the things I respected her so much for was her honesty. Traditionally, it's almost the role of the producer to be a bullshitter – telling people what they think they want to hear in order to keep everybody happy. There are so many people I've really enjoyed working with, who I like and admire, but who tell you stuff which I still have to take with a pinch of salt. It's been fashioned for your ears on this occasion and for someone else it will be adjusted. But Verity was always very direct and very honest. When the news wasn't particularly great, she just told you exactly what it was. "You're going over budget again; the design budget is too high; you can't afford this sum of money for this actor; I'm afraid you're going to have to look at that again." Moments like that.'

---

[1] Verity took a pretty dim view of him as well. In 1993 she told the Broadcasting Press Guild: 'I do not know what John Birt's vision of the BBC is because I don't think he's told anybody.'

Verity became the curator and protector of David Renwick's vision, screening him as much as she possibly could from the increasingly tangled and contradictory bureaucracy of the BBC. 'She was on David's team and that was important,' says Alan Davies, who played Creek. Renwick admired her instinct and knowledge of casting, her imaginative approach to solving creative problems and her ceaseless attention to detail.

'She was perfect,' says Sandy Johnson, one of lead directors on the show. 'She knew how to give David the space that he wanted and also to make things happen for him but she could also do the moves in the background that were needed and make everything right with the BBC. David's scripts were so particular and specific but he needed a strong producer to say, "Well, David I don't think this is going to be right." He works best if he's got a person like that who can be realistic about things. I think he really respected her judgement. She was a great producer with a creative eye who had seen it all before and knew when things were right and things were wrong. She could be so seductively persuasive and wonderful on the one hand and absolutely demolish someone on the other, if she felt they weren't doing the job properly. But she used her powers at the right time and the right place.'

'People respected her, that's the key to it all,' continues Alan Davies. 'She had honesty, intelligence and good manners. They are the three best things you can be armed with as you go through life. She was also cursed with terrible impatience and couldn't bear it if things didn't go to plan because of what she saw as simple errors. If you weren't doing your job properly, she'd come and give you a bollocking. It didn't matter if you were the director or the caterers, everybody was the same, everybody knew where they stood and everybody was very fond of her.'

'There was a kind of beautiful girlish quality about Verity,' continues Sandy Johnson. 'She was obviously older than most of us but there were times when she suddenly looked like a 30-year-old and she would have very vivacious, beautiful qualities when she was enjoying something or was pleased with something. But when she was putting the boot in or tearing a strip off somebody, she would become Zelda from *Terrahawks*.'

'She was just utterly practical and realistic about everything one encountered,' points out Renwick. 'Here was someone who had been head of Euston Films having to deal with these semi-moronic characters in promotion and on-air trails and the sort of resistance and ineptitude you come up with a lot of the time. Promotion and trails were areas that were particularly fraught with frustration because it was so hard to get people to promote your show. Whether it is already a hit show or whether it's a fledgling show that needs careful nurturing, you still need to treat it with exactly the right approach. People didn't always appreciate this. They'd say, "It's a comedy drama – we'll lift a few jokes out and put them in the trailer," but everything relies upon context and a lightness of touch. It was much better to try to trail *Jonathan Creek* with the mystery element. You would go through all these drafts of trails and there were a lot of times where I felt, "Verity's bigger than this" – she shouldn't have to be wasting her time on this kind of minutiae and trivia, yet she did and that was one of the most amazingly tenacious aspects of her – one minute she was dealing with the magnitude of budgets but at the same time really piddling little queries about things that weren't right. If she didn't do it, nobody would take care of it. She'd be going through contact sheets of photographs to pick the right one out and be on the phone to me about this and that. She really spanned the whole process.'

There were constant petty frustrations. BBC regulations forbade staff to bring dogs (or any other kind of pet for that matter) to work. Verity charmed the security guards to turn a blind eye to Arthur Daley, and his eventual successor, Bon Bon, so that they could lounge in the office while she worked. The quality of the production offices was another bone of contention, as director Chris Gernon remembers: 'She was on the phone saying, "I want the architect who's designed these offices to come here and explain to me exactly why they've done this…" She didn't have any fear and she had an opinion and she didn't really worry about upsetting people. Now people worry about who they are going to upset and nobody has an opinion until they know what other people's opinions are. She was terrible at taking no for an answer if she wanted the answer to be yes. If she believed in something, she would fight for it till the last possible moment.'

Verity had never been a deskbound producer. She relished being at the heart of the action on location and enjoyed the company of casts and crews. As sole writer, Renwick was under intense pressure and once a series was in production, shooting and editing dates would often clash. Forced to choose, Renwick would base himself in the edit but with the reassurance that the shoot remained under Verity's care and scrutiny. At every stage, her inherent optimism and positivity acted as a rigorous antidote to Renwick's natural pessimism and doubt. 'She would always joke that her glass was half-full and mine was completely empty,' says Renwick. 'I'd be at my lowest ebb, saying, "What's the point of going on when so many things are conspiring against you? It isn't worth it." She'd kind of haul you up by the bootlaces and give you the spirit to go on. "I believe in what you're doing." That's why she was so good for me.'

For the star of the series, Alan Davies, Verity's reputation preceded her. *Minder* had been one of his favourite television programmes and his veteran producer became a mentor and friend. 'She was a very important confidante for me,' he says. 'Someone you could look up to, someone I could talk to about my private life, decisions I was making about agents, moving house or my girlfriend – she didn't mind. She took me to lunch at the Wolseley in Piccadilly. It's a fancy place and a treat and a couple of tables away, there was Lord Puttnam and Lord Attenborough. She goes to me, "Do you know David Puttnam and Dickie Attenborough?" "Er…no." "I'll introduce you." She could do that. They leapt up. "Verity, how absolutely marvellous. How wonderful to see you!" and they obviously loved her. She said, "This is Alan Davies, who plays Jonathan Creek in the show that I produce," and Dickie Attenborough looked at me and said, "Have we met before?" and when I said, "No," he replied, "Well, that's disgraceful." I'm suddenly in a world of old-school good manners, with everyone behaving like grown-up people.

'Another time, we went to Stamford Bridge together to watch Chelsea play Arsenal because she was a big Arsenal fan. Afterwards we walked all the way back to her house in Holland Park and she listened to me waffling on and gave me all kinds of sage advice. She said to me, "You've got to have an agent." I argued about it. "Verity, sometimes these people talk such nonsense and I get people saying to me, "I rang your office and I was told you weren't available," when I was available. I can't understand why they feel the need to filter everything." It irritated me and I'd end up not trusting the person who's handling my career. Why do I need one? She said, "You really do need to have an agent, for contracts, for when things go wrong. They are the ones who have to deal with it when the shit hits the fan." But she wouldn't tell you what to do. It was more that you could say, "If in doubt, what would Verity do?"'

With its deft hybrid of suspense and humour, and its charismatic leading players, *Jonathan Creek* appealed to children exactly in the same way as *Doctor Who* had done all those years before. When the BBC children's department live Saturday morning magazine programme *Live and Kicking*[2] decided to invite Verity to take part, game for anything, she agreed and made her entrance via a prop police box, billed as the woman who 'helped create the Daleks' and 'what you might call the first Spice Girl of broadcasting'[3]. Looking chic in black top, trousers and patent shoes, with a scarf adding a dash of colour, Verity was only slightly bemused by the high-energy quick-fire style of the show. When presenter Zoë Ball asked her about being a pioneering woman producer, Verity told her, 'In some ways it was an advantage because I was such an oddity; no one knew quite how to deal with me so I usually got my own way.'

Later, she fielded further questions from children in the studio and over the phone lines. One girl wanted to know what Verity liked about producing drama. Verity explained, 'I like it because you can reflect what's going on today and sometimes it's funny and sometimes it's sad but there's a whole variety of things you can do with it.' Asked for her opinion about the dormant *Doctor Who*, she said: 'I think there could be a new series. It has an audience that is always replenishing itself.' She explained that a six-episode season of *Jonathan Creek* took about nine months to produce and, like a true pro, plugged a repeat run starting that same evening.

The viewing figures were so strong that the BBC would have been perfectly content to screen a new series of *Jonathan Creek* every year but David Renwick was reluctant to allow other writers to contribute and this meant that the BBC were limited to when he was able to find the time and inspiration to conjure up new stories. Nevertheless, *Creek* fully occupied Verity for a couple of years and so she closed her Ravenscourt Park office and downsized her company to an office at the top of her new house in Addison Avenue.

---

[2] Transmitted 10.04.99

[3] Verity was, perhaps unsurprisingly, enthusiastic about the Spice Girls. 'She loved them!' says her friend, Kate Kagan

She had finally settled here after months of staying with friends. Her original plan had been to buy another flat and she located one that she liked in her favourite neighbourhood of Holland Park. She was in the process of having this extensively remodelled when she discovered that the other residents of the building had objections to Arthur Daley, the Great Dane. 'She was up in arms about it,' says Kate Kagan. 'You did not tell Verity what to do.'

Despite the considerable sums she had already spent on the new flat, the brouhaha changed Verity's mind and she put it back on the market. She decided a house would free her from having to consider other people and their canine prejudices. She found the one she liked close by, number 11 Addison Avenue, and she set about having this altered to her exacting specifications. The decor was bright and contemporary, and one wall of the well-equipped kitchen featured a brightly coloured canvas by Verity's Australian artist friend, Felicity Marshall. Verity called it 'My murial'.[4] Upstairs, she installed a roof-terrace garden, useful for entertaining.

She had not completely surrendered her hopes of reviving Cinema Verity and, during the lapses between series and specials of *Jonathan Creek*, she continued to search for projects that might act as the necessary catalyst. In June 1998, she had a meeting with actress-turned-writer Maureen O'Brien, whose television career she had launched in 1964 when she'd cast her as a regular in the second series of *Doctor Who*. O'Brien was the author of an ongoing series of crime novels and one of these, *Mask of Betrayal*, featured a supporting character whom she felt might work as the focus of a television series. 'She was a young police constable and based on a real person,' explains O'Brien. 'I called her Edgely. An Oxford graduate, the daughter of left-wing intellectuals, with very high principles. I also made her a lesbian, which you don't know till very late on in the book. My editor wanted me to put her in the next book but I'd finished with her as far as books were concerned. I did feel she was a good character though and I started to think of plots about her. I realised they were television series plots and I thought, "Maybe it's time?" Verity had done *Widows* and this was the time of *Prime Suspect*, so I wrote to Verity. She wrote back and told me that she'd enjoyed the book and said, "I think PC Edgely is an interesting character – do you want to have a chat about where it might go?" So I went to see her and we had a really good talk about it. She was very interested. Curiously, I still felt this sense of nervousness, shyness and fear which I'd felt all those years before. At the same time, we got on very well. The conversation was absolutely positive but it never got any further.'

The same was true of the treatment for a film script that *May to December* writer Paul Mendelson brought to Verity. This was based on a custody case he had been involved

---

[4] This was a reference to Hilda Ogden, a character in the ITV soap, *Coronation Street*, who was intensely proud of a vulgar picture wall in her living room, always referred to as 'my murial'. Verity left her 'murial' to Felicity Marshall, who shipped it back to Australia

with during his earlier career as a lawyer.[5] 'We had lovely meetings and she was very keen on it but she just couldn't get it off the ground,' he says, with a shrug.

Verity was irritated and concerned by the steady encroachment of television schedules favouring reality and lifestyle programmes over drama, which was more expensive. She told David Benedict of *The Guardian*[6]: 'When you felt something was truly boring, you used to say it was like watching grass grow or paint dry. Now that's all we see.'

She was talking to Benedict to promote her latest venture. In 1999, she had acquired the rights to a quartet of books by the distinguished novelist Elizabeth Jane Howard. *The Cazalet Chronicles*, as they became known, were a fictionalised account of Howard's own upper-middle-class family in the period between the two wars and the immediate aftermath. Verity recognised that this was more than a compelling historical family saga and that Howard's writing, shrewd and observant, beautifully illuminated the manners and mores of life for many British people during times of great change and upheaval. 'I knew that they would make wonderful TV,' she told *Homes and Antiques* magazine.[7] 'The characterisation was so rich, full of wit, warmth and observation, and it was such an accurate evocation of the time.'

The author, who was in her late seventies, took to Verity from the first time they met. The feeling was mutual and Jane Howard became another fast friend. They shared a keen intellect and love of good food and would spend hours happily engaged in making and bottling jams and marmalade, and talking about their shared love of the arts. Howard encouraged Verity in her new hobby of painting, something that she was curiously shy about, perhaps fearing that she wasn't very skilled with her brush. It was pleasant to feel that they would be partners on a long-term project. Verity proposed that Howard's quartet of books would provide enough material for three series and went in search of someone bold enough to commit to such a commission. Jonathan Powell, her old ally from the BBC and Carlton, resisted her overtures. She had better luck with Jane Tranter, who had worked under Powell at Carlton and for whom Verity had produced the new writer showcase, *Capital Lives*. Tranter was now at the BBC, as head of drama serials, and, with Pippa Harris, the head of drama commissioning, took Verity's ambitious proposal for *The Cazalets* to the controller of BBC1, Peter Salmon, who saw the potential for a high-quality, glossy returnable Sunday night costume drama and so decided to give it his backing. The timing was perfect for Verity as David Renwick was embroiled in another series of his *One Foot in the Grave*, so that *Jonathan Creek* was temporarily in abeyance.

---

[5] Mendelson was representing a mother in the custody case. 'I got on very well with her and realised she deserved the child. The husband's father had a friend who was a dentist take out all the child's milk teeth and certify that the child had been neglected to such an extent that the child's teeth were rotten.'

[6] *The Guardian* (21.06.01)

[7] *Homes and Antiques*, July 2001

The press made much of the fact that Verity's co-producer on *The Cazalets* was Joanna Lumley, for whom this was a first time behind the lens. Their collaboration came about quite by chance, as Lumley remembers: 'A friend of mine, with whom I was always swapping books, just said, "*Cazalet Chronicles*, I'm putting them through the letterbox. You will read them straight through." I looked at them – four fat books – and thought, "This looks a bit women's lit. I wonder if they're Aga saga drama?" I started to read them and got completely enchanted.'

Lumley was filming a one-off BBC drama, *A Rather English Marriage*, at the time and so engrossed was she that every spare moment, she would return to the books. The costume designer, Janey Fothergill, suggested that if Lumley was so keen on them, she should acquire the rights and produce them herself. 'I said, "Are you ill? I'm an actress!"' laughs Lumley. 'But she said, "No, that's how you do it if you love something and want to see it done, otherwise other people will adapt and film it." So I raced to the publishers and said, "I wonder if you would think of selling me the film rights?" and they said, "Alas and alack, we have already sold them." Blub, blub, blub.'

Lumley's disappointment was slightly assuaged when she learnt that it was Verity who had purchased them. They had enjoyed a very happy working relationship on the *Class Act* series a few years earlier and Lumley sensed that the books she had loved so much would be in safe hands. She wasn't expecting the phone call which followed. 'It came suddenly, out of the blue,' she explains. '"Hello – *Cazalet Chronicles*?" "Yes?" "Let's do it together!" With Verity Lambert, who's one of the greatest producers of all time. It was an extraordinarily generous thing to do.'

Verity took her new partner to meet Jane Howard at the author's Sussex home. 'Verity drove us down in her green Mercedes,' smiles Joanna Lumley. 'She had marvellous cars, which she adored, but she had literally no idea about them. She'd say, "Damn the car" and you'd point out, "Verity, it's run out of petrol." On this trip, she said, "The only thing about this car is that it gets steamed up," and I said, "No, look there," and showed her how to unsteam the car. She had no idea. And she had an interesting way of driving. She'd push the car along and then coast, so being a passenger was green-faced stuff. We drove to Jane's house and were met with vases of champagne which we drank immediately, not having had tea at all.'

'What a combination I thought,' wrote Howard in her autobiography, *Slipstream*. 'They came down to stay for a night that was heady with champagne and all the lovely dream-like plans that occur at this stage of most dramatic enterprises. We had a marvellous time, casting and recasting, discussing what would have to be left out and what was essential.'

Verity, ever the pragmatist, had the good sense to realise that Lumley's name added a certain amount of cachet to the project and she tried hard to persuade her co-producer to take the part of a femme fatale in the series. Lumley, however, was unconvinced. 'We haggled and haggled and haggled,' she explains. 'I said, "If I'm going to play anything, I want to play Sid." She said, "But Sid's half-Jewish." So we had this wonderful row. I said, "I could be Jewish, how do you know I'm not? And she's only half-Jewish, anyway. I could easily be Jewish." Verity said "No, you can't. I'm Jewish, I can tell if you're Jewish or not."'

Finally, Verity relented and Lumley was off the hook. Doug Livingstone was invited to adapt the scripts covering the events of the first two books in seven episodes. Late in the day, the BBC, nervous of the mounting expense of such a lavish all-film production, cut this back to six and, despite her spirited grumbles, Verity had to submit. She did so on the proviso that there would be six episodes in each of the subsequent series, which would cover the events of one book each. With so much to cram into the first series, the script conferences were often heated. 'She'd fly off the handle with Doug,' says Joanna Lumley. 'The rows were loathsome, terrifying, head-on. Verity could go from 0-100 in about ten seconds. And Dougie gave as good as he got. I think she loved it, I think it made her juices run and she was fine with it. I couldn't bear it because I remembered what was said even if they couldn't and also I had no input. I was the indulged child who had come down in the dressing-gown, if you know what I mean. So I said to Verity, "I don't think I'm going to come to any of these any more, I can't bear it," and she said, "What, what? Why?" and I said, "I cannot stand those screaming rows you have. I find it absolutely heartbreaking – I can't bear it, it gets us nowhere and it makes me shake, it's no good talking to either of you." She was amazed. "Dougie and I always talk like this, this is how we do it." and I thought, "Bloody hell, I'm really out of my depth here."'

This remained a constant feeling for the actress-turned-producer. Production was based at Twickenham Studios and Verity installed a desk for Lumley in her own office. 'It was chastening because she knew what she was doing and she'd be on the phone a million times to everybody. I couldn't get on the phone to anybody – I didn't know what to ask them. She knew all that stuff like how much it cost to hire a ladder for half a day. It was mother's milk to her – she'd done it so long, it was in her DNA. I learnt a lot. She was like the senior prefect; I walked around behind her watching how she did things.'

In booking Suri Krishnamma to direct, Verity was repeating the approach she had taken with *Edward and Mrs Simpson*, placing an apparent 'outsider' in charge of interpreting and bringing back to life this vanished world of manners and class, privilege and repression. 'One of the aspects of Verity's intellect was her ability to see through the surface of everything,' says Krishnamma. 'That whole Elizabeth Jane Howard territory doesn't appear to be on my CV. The film I had just made beforehand was about a suicide pact between two teenage boys.[8] I think that she saw through my work and me and realised how suitable and appropriate I'd be for *The Cazalets*. I grew up in a house on the Isle of Wight which was very similar in a way to Home Place, where the Cazalets lived. I had quite a large family and the interrelationships were very similar. Verity couldn't know that but she knew my agent, Tim Corrie, very well and I suspect they'd talked about me.

---

[8] *New Year's Day* (released June 2001).

I think she wanted someone slightly younger and slightly less establishment. She also wanted someone well in with the higher echelons of the BBC, which I was – I had done *A Respectable Trade*[9] on which Alan Yentob was one of the execs, as was Michael Wearing. On a practical level it made sense.'

The budget presented the usual challenges. The original plan had been for Krishnamma to shoot the first three episodes, followed by a two-week hiatus in production, before another director took over for the second trio. 'There was a big squeeze on money,' explains Krishnamma. 'I went to Verity's office and said, "I can solve this in one stroke – I'll direct the entire series." We took out the two-week hiatus. She said, "OK, that works". She questioned constantly the decisions you made as a director but, if you were proved right, she had the humility to go out on a limb and say how right you were. Meetings could become quite stormy because Verity would always say what she thought. But I respected her for being comfortable and honest enough to be direct with everyone above us at the BBC.'

There was a large cast to find. The task was complicated by the need for many of them to seem credibly related and because the parts encompassed every age range. 'The most ghastly thing I've ever done in my life,' pronounces Joanna Lumley, with certainty. 'Like judging a bathing competition.'

The three Cazalet sons were played by Hugh Bonneville, Stephen Dillane and Paul Rhys. There were notable performances from Lesley Manville, Patsy Rowlands, Ursula Howells and Anna Chancellor (in the part Verity had originally earmarked for Lumley), and Joanna Page impressed with the maturity of her performance as a selfish young wife who gradually matures as experience changes her perspective. Jacqueline Tong played the cook, and was delighted to be working once more with Verity, who had been responsible for her first break in television back in the 1973 LWT play *Voyage in the Dark*. 'She had been a significant part of my career,' says Tong, 'and she was always very elegant, friendly and good fun as well as carrying her terrific intelligence and ability lightly.'

'She was a phenomenon as a producer and a human being,' says Suri Krishnamma. 'One of her really smart skills and beliefs about how you get a team together to pursue a single purpose was that you have to be a family. Filming is a collective and collaborative art. To actually achieve it in a way that seems natural and effortless is unusual. With *The Cazalets* we had both the family making the film and the family in the film. Verity would always turn up just after we started and lurk in the background almost like a predatory animal, looking at what we were doing, with her Mona Lisa smile. You were not quite sure if she was smiling or grimacing. I adored her but I couldn't read her – you didn't know whether she loved or hated what she was seeing. But it was one of the most

---

[9] *A Respectable Trade* – dramatised in four episodes for BBC1 from the novel by Philippa Gregory and transmitted in 1998. The narrative revolved around the British slave trade

wonderful experiences of my career because the whole thing was inclusive. Working with her at any level – whether you were the director, the first assistant, the clapper loader, whatever your job, you couldn't work with her without being in some way part of her family.'

Just as production was about to start, Verity wrote a note for her co-producer, which Lumley keeps to this day as a treasured bookmark: 'Here we are at last – the train is about to leave the station. I just want to say how very, very good it is working with you. It's been wonderful for me to have another voice, someone who loves the books as much as I do, someone to have a laugh with in the dark days. So onwards and sideways, the sun is shining, much love, Verity.'

'Verity made very clever use of Joanna's personality to coax people to do things where she wasn't able to,' says Suri Krishnamma. 'Coaxing wasn't her style.'

Filming for *The Cazalets* took place throughout the summer and autumn of 2000. For Krishnamma, there was the added challenge that he and his wife were expecting their first child. 'She was several weeks late,' he explains. 'We knew the baby would have to be induced and I said to Verity, "I have to be in London at the birth," and she never questioned it. It fell on a day where we had to shoot a scene on board a train. "What do we do?" she asked me. I said, "Why don't you direct that day?" I think she was unbelievably flattered and I know relished that day. I think the actors were utterly terrified!' [10]

Shooting coincided with a national petrol strike. Cast and crew were briefly but expensively marooned on location in Sussex, and the filming schedule was knocked off course. 'We were pleading for a bit more support but the BBC just said, "There's no more money,"' recalls Joanna Lumley. 'Verity was insulted because she was, and I think remains, one of the most skilful and experienced television producers of all time, and to be treated by these children as though she had got it wrong…'

There was a further financial tussle over the soundtrack for the series. 'It became a big issue,' sighs Suri Krishnamma. 'I had a composer that I wanted to do the score but the BBC didn't think they could afford an original score because that meant hiring musicians and so on. The editor had put on some temporary library music and Pippa [Harris – head of drama commissioning] had heard this and said, "I quite like it," and I told her that I did too. When Verity heard it, she went through the roof and Joanna almost had to pull us apart. She was fuming. "This is eight months' hard work for all of us. How could you even think about putting on some cheap library music?" She was absolutely right, of course, but I was trying to manage a situation. I told Pippa I thought Verity was right and, finally, the money was found.'

---

[10] Krishnamma's son Ollie was born 17 October 2000. 'The very first present we got from anyone outside the family was from Verity,' says the director. 'A pair of woolly boots.'

More serious than the various issues with the budget was a sudden shift in the balance of power back at Television Centre. Peter Salmon's undistinguished period as controller of BBC1 came to a sudden end when he was shifted sideways to make room for the first woman to be appointed to the role, Lorraine Heggessey. She was hungry to succeed and determined to deliver. A populist, she took a dim view of anything she felt too esoteric or out of touch for her vision of a contemporary mass-audience channel. *The Cazalets* belonged to Salmon's era, and it was an expensive leftover. Verity had been lobbying for a prime slot in the autumn or winter schedule, preferably on a Sunday night. Heggessey demurred, delayed and eventually scheduled the series on a Friday night the following summer, when audiences are always at their lowest. It was a move calculated to kill *The Cazalets* at birth and although the reviews were laudatory and the figures, considering the obstacles, were respectable, Heggessey was able to claim that the audience had failed to find the programme. She declared herself unable to honour Salmon's commitment to any further series, despite the first concluding with a number of significant cliffhangers which would now remain forever unresolved. 'I was disappointed,' comments Doug Livingstone. 'Verity was *furious*.'

'She was devastated it didn't go on,' says Suri Krishnamma. 'The plan was to continue filming later that year. The sets had been paid for. It would have been more economic. I was told by Pippa Harris that Lorraine wanted to move away from what she perceived to be that traditional Sunday night costume drama.'

On 7 September 2001, Verity went to see Heggessey, with Joanna Lumley, to plead their case for a stay of execution. 'It was hopeless,' says Lumley. 'Lorraine Heggessey had a very bright, chirpy face and manner which made it even more irritating. I think we fell over ourselves in our kind of plea-bargaining. Maybe only to do six more and have it rewritten as another six instead of twelve. We kept saying, "We've set the story up, now we're not even following it through, how can we do that?" Little bright face. "I'm so sorry." It was quite obvious that she hadn't seen it, didn't get it, wasn't going to have it. There was nothing to be said. Verity was fuming because we were treated like amateurs who couldn't quite get it right. We were turning in this sensational show and suddenly we got this smack in the face. We were both unbelievably depressed.'

Lumley returned to acting, and her experience of *The Cazalets* did not tempt her to try producing again. Verity had a Christmas special of *Jonathan Creek* to occupy her but the disappointment she felt at the curtailment of *The Cazalets* was harder to shake off than the various setbacks of the past. This had represented a real chance to revive her credibility as a player among the independents. There was nothing lined up to take its place and in the months to come, when asked 'How's Cinema Verity?' she would sometimes shrug and answer, 'It's a lot of files in the attic.'

'She wasn't quite the Verity of old,' says agent Jenne Casarotto. 'I couldn't believe that this woman wasn't being begged to do stuff. Instead, she had to listen to people who are mainly idiots – and they *are* idiots. I can remember asking her, "How can you even listen to them when you know so much more than they do?" She just said, "That's the way it is."'

But perhaps the biggest sadness for Verity at the start of the millennium was in her private rather than professional life. Arthur Daley, the personable Great Dane who had become almost synonymous with Verity, finally faltered and had to be put down. He was 12 years old, which is unusually long-lived for the breed, but this was no consolation. He had provided a much needed source of unconditional love throughout some challenging years and Verity was genuinely distraught. 'I remember meeting her in the Groucho Club just after Arthur had died,' says film executive and academic Colin MacCabe. 'She went to the loo and there were black and white floor tiles. They had made her think of him and she came back in tears. It had been a very deep emotional relationship for her.'

'He doesn't do stairs,' she would explain as she lugged Arthur up from one floor to another. Now, aware that she was getting older, friends begged Verity to think twice before buying another high-maintenance animal. She decided that she could not bear to live without a dog but that as Arthur was irreplaceable, there would be no more Great Danes. She would try a different breed instead. The writer Michael Aitkens had a miniature Schnauzer called Digby. Aitken's partner at the time was Australian screenwriter Judy Morris, and she often took Digby for walks with Verity and Arthur. 'She decided she'd have a small dog this time,' explains Morris. 'We started going to dog shows to meet people who were there with puppies. Once we got there we would just go crazy and buy gourmet dog foods and eclectic collars. It was a great joy and laugh for us. We found these shows so wonderful and hilarious, especially the dancing dogs. The dogs were just too extraordinary for words and so talented.'

Verity eventually chose her own miniature Schnauzer, whom she initially christened Bonnesville. She soon thought better of this name and tried a string of others, including Lola. 'Sounds like a lesbian,' remarked Verity's Parisian friend Miriam Worms, which put paid to that. Finally, Verity settled on Bon Bon. She loved the little dog, nicknamed 'the princess' but never in quite the same way as Arthur, whose ashes she kept in a small wooden casket.

On 9 November 2001, a letter arrived for Verity from William Chapman, the secretary for appointments at Number 10 Downing Street. He wrote: 'The Prime Minister has asked me to inform you, in strict confidence, that he has it in mind, on the occasion of the forthcoming list of New Year Honours, to submit your name to the Queen with a recommendation that Her Majesty may be graciously pleased to approve that you be appointed an Officer of the Order of the British Empire. Before doing so, the Prime Minister would be glad to know that this would be agreeable to you.'

Verity was thrilled and signalled her immediate acceptance of the honour, which was made for services to film and television production. She had to keep it strictly confidential until it was formally announced at the end of 2001 but she couldn't resist telling a few of her friends, among them the director Suri Krishnamma. 'She rang me and said, "Suri, it's Verity, can you come over to my house a week on Saturday?" And I said, "Yeah, sure." "But you mustn't tell anyone." "Right – why?" and she said, "I'm being given an OBE." "Where are you?" I said. "I'm at home." "Who's with you?" "No one." "Then why are you whispering?!"'

Krishnamma joined Doug Livingstone, Joanna Lumley, Lynda La Plante, Janet Street-Porter and others in Verity's close circle for a small buffet to celebrate the news. When it was finally made public, Verity was deluged with messages of congratulation.

'I was thrilled and delighted to hear about your OBE,' wrote television executive Greg Dyke. 'It is a great recognition of all you've done for the industry and richly deserved.'

Gavyn Davies, then the chairman of the BBC, echoed these sentiments in his letter, although Verity must have rolled her eyes at his tactless mention of *The Cazalets* as an example of her 'immense' contribution. 'You have been an inspiration to a whole generation,' Davies added, 'both as a producer and as a businesswoman.'

A fax arrived from the agent Jenne Casarotto: 'YOU made me believe that television really could be bold, innovative, about something and really, really good. I wish I could say I still believed it in the year 2002.'

There were letters from Tessa Jowell, then Secretary of State in the Department of Culture, Media and Sports, Iain Duncan Smith (then the Leader of the Opposition in the House of Commons), the Board of Deputies of British Jews, and the Doctor Who Appreciation Society.

'Dearest Verity,' wrote the actress Jean Marsh. 'How fantastic, and just, that you should be awarded the Order of Beautiful Executives or is it Order of Brilliant Epicureans…'

'It couldn't have happened to a nicer person,' enthused Jack Andrews, her old friend and ally from Thames Television. 'But why did it take them so long? By the same gazelle, I was given an MBE. Does this mean that when we get to heaven I can sit at your feet? I do hope so.'

'I think that when we get to heaven we should sit side by side,' replied Verity, with neat charm.

Verity was punctilious in answering all her correspondence and stressed how rewarding she had found her career. Hot on the heels of her OBE came the news that BAFTA were to present her with the Alan Clarke Award for outstanding creative contribution to television. Verity hadn't forgiven BAFTA for the *GBH* debacle a decade earlier but neither was she going to turn down industry recognition she knew she deserved. 'Great that BAFTA have acknowledged your creativity,' actor Russell Enoch wrote to her after they had shared one of their periodic lunches, '[and] lovely to know that you haven't lost your mischievous twinkle!'

On the morning of 27 June 2002, accompanied by her guests, her stepmother Betty, her PA and friend Anna Callaghan and another close friend, Kate Kagan, she travelled to Buckingham Palace where the honour was duly bestowed on her by Prince Charles. A celebratory lunch at Locatelli's[11] followed, attended by more old friends including Michael Kagan, Reggie Nadelson, Michael Aitkens and Judy Morris, and Mike and Viviane Phillips, who gave Verity a costume jewellery tiara to wear to commemorate her brush with royalty. It was a happy day of congratulation shared with people she loved. Afterwards, Viv Phillips wrote to her: 'I was thinking how proud your parents would have been, and Andrew.'

Despite the awards, and because of the loss of *The Cazalets*, 2002 was Verity's quietest working year yet. There were only three episodes of *Jonathan Creek* for her to produce, although she never completely gave up the quest for different material. For some time, there was talk of an American movie version of her television series *Sleepers*. As well as this, she optioned *At Risk*, an engaging thriller written by the former head of MI5, Stella Rimington. 'Whenever Verity got a new contact, she'd say, "This is my new best friend,"' says writer Andy McCulloch. 'When we were going to do the film of *Sleepers*, she took me and John [Flanagan – McCulloch's writing partner] to lunch with Stella Rimington. They'd just been on a research trip to Prague. "You got pulled in by the police at the border didn't you, Stella?" said Verity. "It's because you've got a suspicious face!"'

Verity again turned to Doug Livingstone to write a three-episode adaptation of *At Risk*, which Channel 4 paid for. 'It was a good spy story,' says Livingstone, 'but the BBC had *Spooks* by then and it was a bit too similar.'

As these various projects burnt brightly then ebbed away, David Renwick provided the consistency in what was left of her career. 'With the exception of *The Cazalets*, she spent the last ten years of her life working exclusively with me,' he says. 'I felt incredibly blessed and more than flattered about that. You get so familiar and comfortable with someone and you'd have to stop and pinch yourself, "This is Verity Lambert." By 2003, there wasn't any question that I would contemplate working with anyone else except Verity.'

Feeling increasingly burnt out with *Jonathan Creek*, Renwick turned his attention elsewhere. He was interested in devising a series to star Tamsin Greig, an actress he much admired. Greig had guest-starred in the 2003 *Jonathan Creek* episode *Angel Hair*. 'The first time that I met Verity was in a café,' says Greig. 'We were filming a scene on Primrose Hill and it was very bad weather so we kept having to go and sit in this café. Verity wasn't interested in talking about the piece we were doing. She was much more interested in talking about *The Archers*. She knew that I was in it [Greig plays Debbie Aldridge, on an intermittent basis]. She thought I'd have insider information!'

---

[11] Verity knew the proprietors of the restaurant well and was greeted with enthusiasm

Renwick came up with *Love Soup*, another comedy-drama premise, based on the old romantic notion that everyone has someone out there who is perfect for them if only they can find each other. 'The whole premise of the series was based on my life, really,' he explains. 'Tamsin's character [Alice] was based very largely on my wife.'

Renwick wrote a first episode and showed it to Verity, who loved the idea of the two main characters leading parallel lives but never meeting. Encouraged by her reaction, he then offered the script to the BBC's head of comedy, Sophie Clarke-Jervoise. 'She took it to Jane Tranter, who was head of drama,' recalls Renwick, 'and within the space of a couple of weeks we were talking about dates. All just inconceivable now.'

Early in 2004, a lunch was arranged with David Renwick, Tamsin Greig and Verity. 'It was enormously flattering to have a writer of David's stature and a producer like Verity saying, "Listen, we want to do this with you and for you,"' says Greig. 'I was very excited by it but also confused as well because I was heavily pregnant with my third child and I couldn't quite see how it was going to happen. That's when Verity really came into her own. Rather than making it a difficulty, she worked around trying to understand how I was going to manage. It was very unusual. I started filming when my daughter was three months old and she built the filming schedule around my need to breast-feed at eleven o'clock in the morning and three o'clock in the afternoon. There was an extra trailer on set for the baby and our nanny. She set that up and was always concerned that the way that I worked as an actor and a human being were in harmony. She's the only woman I know in show business who made breast-feeding a contractual obligation!'

As Greig's co-star, Renwick and Verity had an American actor in mind. Matt Rippy had appeared in the 2001 *Jonathan Creek* Christmas special, *Satan's Chimney*, and both writer and producer felt he had the necessary charisma and good looks to play Gil in *Love Soup*. 'We did some tests with him,' explains Renwick, 'but it didn't quite work out in the end. But by that stage I'd committed to Gil being an American and I quite enjoyed writing in that American idiom. There were a couple of eyebrows raised upstairs about this but I dug my heels in. After we decided not to go ahead with Matt, it meant that we had to cast around for another American.'

They found him in Michael Landes, familiar to British audiences from his short-lived role as Jimmy in the popular *New Adventures of Superman*.[12] As well as the stars, there was strong comic support from a young Sheridan Smith. The directors were Chris Gernon and Sandy Johnson. It was Gernon's first experience of Verity. 'She was a complete one-off,' she smiles. 'I've never met anyone like her before or since. She was such a fantastic raconteur and every time we finished a show we would go and have lunch at the Wolseley – invariably we would still be there at dinner. *Love Soup* was pretty hard work. David writes brilliantly and expansively and you were trying to do it on a budget. She loved just

---

[12] This made its debut on BBC1 in January, 1994

being a producer and she was so motivational and inspirational. When you were knackered or things weren't going right, she'd just go in and talk to you for ten minutes and you'd be all fired up again. She was just a bundle of brilliance.'

'God, I think of her all the time,' adds Sandy Johnson. 'She was such a strong influence on me personally. I'm always looking for a good producer to work with and nobody matches up to her. It's a creative eye on things; there was a kind of dogged enthusiasm about getting it right and how you must serve the script and tell the story.'

Her habitual impatience remained the only fly in the ointment. 'She had the most fearsome temper,' says Chris Gernon. 'I've never been shouted at before or since by anyone quite so much. When we were doing *Love Soup*, we had one of those days with a big stunt to film. We had a car going into a ditch, wind machines, rain machines. We needed a really terrible storm and the sun was shining brightly. Verity hauled me, Geoff, the director of photography and Lee, the first assistant director over. "What the hell's going on, why aren't we shooting?" "But Verity, it's bright sunshine – we can't do it in bright sunshine." She went off on this rant and I turned round to see that Geoff and Lee had vanished. I said, "Verity, I can't control the sun." You would carry on and it was almost like it had never happened. She just had to get these things out. Two minutes later she'd bring you a cup of tea and you would be laughing uproariously.'

'I remember going for a script meeting in her house,' says Sandy Johnson, 'and her grilling me, "Well, how are you possibly going to shoot this?" She would make me come up with the answer. I wanted to give her the answer. I wanted to impress her and please her.'

When Johnson was felled by a virus that kept him confined to his sickbed for several days, Verity again took over, as she had done in similar circumstances on *Class Act* and on *The Cazalets*. 'She was very proud of the scenes that she did,' says Johnson. 'When we got to the edit, she'd say, "Now look at my scenes – aren't they good?"'

Throughout *Jonathan Creek* and now *Love Soup*, Verity often volunteered to direct 'second unit' sequences. Typically, these might be driving shots or perhaps an action scene in which a car comes off the road. 'Second unit' sequences are filmed at the same time as the main action to ensure everything can be achieved within the schedule. Ever mindful of the strictures of the budget, Verity lent the services of her miniature schnauzer Bon Bon whenever the action required a dog.

The first series of *Love Soup*, broadcast in the autumn of 2005, was quietly successful and appreciated for its poignant wit and engaging performances but, like everything else the BBC made that year, its impact paled in comparison with the juggernaut of the relaunched *Doctor Who*. The revival had been commissioned by the hated Lorraine Heggessey but its fate rested principally in the hands of writer Russell T Davies. Whatever Verity's view of Heggessey, she instinctively approved of putting such a talented writer in charge of the new *Doctor Who*. 'When we were setting up, Verity was never far from the forefront of our minds,' says Davies. 'I'm not just saying that to be nice. It was a proper legacy – like being handed the family china. I remember having a debate with myself, saying I must go to London, take her out for lunch, ask her advice, I must get her blessing and then, you know what it's like, problems come along, the budget's a nightmare and suddenly it's nine months later and you haven't got time to make a piece of toast, never mind trying to meet someone who you've never met. But I did hear that she approved of what we had done, which was immensely moving and gratifying. I was so pleased. If that's not a vote of confidence, I don't know what is.'

SFX magazine arranged a combined interview with Verity and the man who had brought her creation back to life in the twenty-first century. It was a joyous, gossipy encounter. Verity enthused about the casting of David Tennant ('I just think he's so winning') and Billie Piper ('The real revelation for me; she always plays it for real, which is just wonderful') and admitted that 'I do feel proud that, years ago, knowing very little, I started something that is still running.'

Against all expectations, *Doctor Who* had made a triumphant and lasting return to television and its renaissance triggered a fresh interest in the show's heritage and the architects of its genius. Verity was one of the last survivors from its genesis – both her script editors, David Whitaker and Dennis Spooner, were dead. So, too, were her associate producer, Mervyn Pinfield, the first writer, Tony Coburn, the creator of the Daleks, Terry Nation, and actors Jackie Hill and William Hartnell. Sydney Newman, the man to whom she owed so much, had died in 1997. Verity was an important witness to the launch of a programme that had become a defining part of the British cultural tradition. With more time on her hands, she was happy to embrace the role *Doctor Who* now returned to play in her life. She was regularly asked to take part in commentary recordings for the spruced-up DVDs of her stories and to tape interviews for assorted *Doctor Who*-related documentaries. She was even persuaded to take part in a Caribbean cruise with a boatload of fans. This was at the behest of actress Carole Ann Ford: 'I'd done one of these *Doctor Who* cruises before. So I asked her and she said, "I was warned it probably wouldn't be a good idea," and I told her it was actually a huge amount of fun, not at all as one had anticipated. I had thought it was going to be a whole cruise ship of *Doctor Who* fans all absolutely swarming over you all the time. It was not like that at all; it's a perfectly normal cruise ship except that there's a party of around 30 fans and a few celebrities. The only things you have to do are have dinner every night with the fans and if they should pass you on the boat somewhere, you just smile nicely at them and be prepared to have a little chat. That's all. The rest of the time, just enjoy yourself. She really, really enjoyed it. She introduced me to margaritas and I've not been the same woman since! We had to get the cruise from Miami and my husband has relations in Miami – wonderful but totally off-the-wall people. We were going to visit them and I have a feeling she thought, "Oh dear, rellies," but she came too and she completely loved them. We had a wonderful, wonderful time.'

The nostalgia of the baby boomers who had grown up with *Doctor Who* and many of Verity's other signature shows created a demand for clip-heavy retrospectives and documentaries wallowing in what was now lauded as the golden age of British television. Verity, an assured and eloquent interviewee, was always in demand to contribute to these and, with the increased space in her diary, she rarely turned them down.

In November 2005, Verity celebrated her 70th birthday with a huge party in a rented mansion in Holland Park and, for the first and only time, scores of her friends from every aspect and period of her life gathered in these elegant surroundings to raise their glasses to her. Someone challenged her, 'Verity, you can't really have all these people in your life?' to which she replied, 'You have to understand, all these people are here for a reason and I have a bond with them all.'

'You just felt so proud to be included among her friends,' says actress Sheila Hancock. 'I remember sitting with a group of amazing women there, people like Stella Rimington and Helena Kennedy.'

Hancock had known Verity on and off for years but they became closer when Hancock invited her to join the book club to which she herself belonged. This was an activity Verity embraced with gusto. 'We all went to one another's houses in turn,' explains Hancock. 'Verity was a very valuable member of the group, very knowledgeable and with strong opinions. Everyone respected these because she read scripts and books continuously. She was a cultured woman. I loved her company and I admired her elegance and culture hugely, having neither myself. She was a girlfriend, in the true sense of the word. It's a very special relationship. A close confidante whom you are able to be frank with and ask genuine advice from. She was very wise. She didn't exactly give advice but she'd question you in such a way that helped you to reach a conclusion.'

Verity also belonged to an organisation called Links, a group of high-achieving women who met for erudite dinners and went on cultural trips together. Another member, the eminent journalist Katherine Whitehorn, recalls: 'We would take ourselves off for long weekends to places like Rome and Prague. She was never a sheep following other people. When she was with the group, she was inclined to do her own thing. I think she thought she might find something more fun. She was always buying something really exotic and marvellous like a wonderful fur or some really good amber. She was sort of dashing. She jolly well did what she wanted to do and nobody was going to stop her.'

Most of all, she wanted still to work. Although its impact was somewhat less spectacular than the dramatic rebirth of *Doctor Who*, *Love Soup* had been successful enough for the BBC to request a second run. This time, Renwick was asked to provide both a series and a concluding special, in which Alice and Gil would finally meet, neatly tying up the whole story. Renwick had finished the series and was about halfway through writing the special finale when Michael Landes' agent informed Verity that he was no longer available. Landes had been offered a part in *The Wedding Bells*, a major new drama on the ABC network in America. 'This was a fairly massive blow,' says Renwick. 'The whole premise was that these were the only two people in the world suitable for each other and we'd lost one. People said why didn't you just recast? You couldn't. The American show was an offer he couldn't refuse but it totally clashed with our dates. Our scripts were all written and we were into pre-production. All the legalities were being pored over and Verity was constantly on the phone to Los Angeles, trying to find out what was happening. Then he said he was going to do the other series and not ours. Christmas was approaching and Verity was just preparing to call all the crew in and say, "We're going to have to stand the production down. We can't do it – we've lost the leading actor."'[13]

Instead, Renwick suggested a radical rethink of the whole show. He offered to restructure everything he'd written and turn the six hour-long episodes into twelve half-hours, which would focus entirely on Tamsin Greig's character, Alice. Gil would be killed off in the background and quickly forgotten. 'The Alice and Gil stories were pretty much autonomous and independent,' Renwick explains, 'so it meant that I could take all of the six Alice stories out of the existing episodes. We could film those straightaway, which gave us a bit of breathing space and the time for me to rewrite the Gil strand into something which involved Alice. So that's how we went ahead and we actually managed to stick to our original filming schedule. I think Verity was quite surprised by my resilience – that's what she said to me. But in large part, I'd learnt that from her. It was the kind of practicality and realism which she brought to any situation. Just realising that this is the hand we've been dealt and we've just got to get on with it. She was like that about everything in life and that was so, so admirable.'

This quality sustained Verity, not only through the demands of her work, but through the gradual but inexorable deterioration of her health. In 2003, she developed lymphedema, which manifested itself as a swelling of her arm. Then there was a persistent and itchy rash. No longer working for her full time, Anna Callaghan had trained as an aromatherapist and concocted a variety of soothing lotions to try to help. But this holistic approach had little effect and, in 2005, tests confirmed that the cancer she had vanquished back in the 1970s had returned. Still, there was hope. During the early months of her treatment, she was advised to keep busy – which was preaching to the converted. She continued to work throughout her illness and it was some time before there was any serious cause for concern.

There was a course of oral chemotherapy and as this took effect, Verity began to lose her hair so she travelled to Paris to visit her old friend Miriam Worms – and buy the first of a succession of wigs. Some of these were more successful than others. At first, Verity refused to spend too much money on them, reluctant to consider them as anything other than a temporary inconvenience. Some friends failed to notice and many even complimented her on her new, shorter hairstyle and different colour. Those that did

---

[13] It was small consolation that *The Wedding Bells* was cancelled after only five episodes

recognise the significance sensed that it wasn't a topic for enquiry or conversation. 'Suddenly, she was wearing a fright wig at the Sunday lunches,' says writer Michael Aitkens. 'You knew but you didn't bring it up.'

'I was appallingly obtuse about how ill she was,' says Jeremy Isaacs. 'There was an event at the British Film Institute and Verity came to that. She was wearing a wig. Wake up, Isaacs. I didn't realise how heroic she was being.'

'They say that illness is a manifestation of what's going on inside,' says Verity's close friend, Viv Phillips. 'I'm sure it was an inner thing that had to get out. I once said that to Verity and she absolutely exploded, "No, that's rubbish!" She was not having it. It would have been like an admission of weakness. She got very angry with me for even suggesting it.'

During a period of respite, Verity agreed to sit for a portrait by the artist June Mendoza. The canvas is reproduced in this book and brilliantly captures Verity at this stage of her life, with the shorter hairstyle she had adopted, sitting side on with a somewhat pensive expression. The pose was Mendoza's response to her reading of Verity's personality and character. 'She was not a flamboyant, in-your-face, lady of the theatre,' she explains. 'She seemed to me to be quietly secure and at ease with her talents and achievements, with no need to assert or trumpet them abroad, so I didn't feel any need to have the face confronting, straight-on, the viewer. The painting was built up of the colour contrasts, the rich, positive colours of Verity and the shapes and cool colours of her furniture, which, with the side view, gave balance and movement and conveyed that private, contemplative aspect of her.'

The portrait shows a woman of authority, dignity and style. There is something inscrutable about it, too, and whether by accident or design, this was astute interpretation by the artist. Verity had never been one to shout about her private thoughts and feelings and this didn't change now. She dreaded pity and worried that if people thought she was ill, they might not consider her fit to work. It was business as usual. When she went to stay with her old friend Jenny King, she even refused the offer of a cup of tea in bed, insisting she rouse herself and come downstairs for breakfast. Kate Kagan drove her to the hospital as the chemotherapy was stepped up and became more intensive.

As the cancer renewed its insidious attack upon her system, Verity complied with everything the doctors asked of her but found the whole relentless business boring and depressing. 'Oh, Anna, it's so time-consuming being ill,' she told her old friend and sometime PA, who says: 'She dealt with her cancer with a courage I know I will never again witness. During all the indignities heaped upon her by this curse of a disease, there was not one word of self-pity, never "poor me" or "why me?"'

'When the news from the doctors wasn't good, we would go out,' recalls Judy Morris.

'Later that night I'd think, "She's just told me this terrible news and within a very short period of time, she would be giggling away at something we both found funny." I remember one day we were walking arm-in-arm from her house to her favourite Indian restaurant. There was a girl on the side of the road, having a fight with this guy. Verity just turned like a virago on this man and she told him where to get off. She insisted that the girl stay with us and she looked after her until we knew that she was safe. She was so brilliant. That story always sticks in my mind because it was so typical of Verity – she had an innate sense of fairness and was very protective. She wasn't feeling great that night but that went completely out the window and she came to that girl's rescue without a second thought. I was just in awe of her when she was like that. She was fabulous and feisty, yet so tender and kind.'

The second series of *Love Soup* went into production in 2007 and Verity, whose prognosis was no longer hopeful, willed herself to see it through to the end. 'She was on set every day except Wednesdays,' recalls Tamsin Greig. 'I never questioned it. It was only afterwards that I clicked that she was having her treatment on a Wednesday. She never talked about it. She found that kind of revelation almost abhorrent, I think. I don't think she wanted people to treat her any differently. She just wanted to be able to do the job that she did so brilliantly without people's view of her changing. There was a part of me that wished she had told me but then I'm sure that would have changed an element of my behaviour towards her. In a way, it was an act of generosity on her part so we could just continue to be ourselves around her, because people don't know what to do with that sort of news.'

'When she told me that she had cancer, I burst into tears,' says Chris Gernon. 'I felt awful because she was the one who had this terrible disease but she said, "I'm actually incredibly moved." It's making me cry now thinking about it. She was tough as old boots, really. None of the actors and most of the crew didn't know and it was really difficult to keep the secret. There were times when she would come from her chemo onto the set and I'd say, "Verity, please just go and lie down" – sometimes she would be forced to.'

David Renwick told Alan Davies: 'I've just had a call from Verity and I could hear all this rattling going on in the background. I asked her, "Where are you?" and she said, "Oh, I'm at the Marsden. I'm having a transfusion, darling." But her attention wasn't on that, it was focused on talking about scripts.'

'The trouble is that when it's someone like Verity who just seems to be able to cope with anything, there's almost a kind of denial,' sighs Renwick. 'You say, "It's Verity." It was really only in the later stages, when we were in post-production, she just wasn't able to come along. I don't think she could get up the stairs.'

By now, Verity knew that she was dying. 'Are you scared?' a nurse asked her. 'Yes,' she replied, 'but not as scared as I was the first time, 33 years ago.'[14]

---

[14] According to Anna Callaghan

She continued to guard her privacy and keep the true extent of her illness to her closest friends. 'She didn't want everyone to know,' says Viv Phillips, 'and it was very difficult to get close to her. I think when you have a serious illness and you're battling with it and you feel like absolute shit, you have to narrow your life down to the absolute minimum, cut away everything that isn't absolutely necessary and it becomes very difficult to see people – you don't want to be seen in the state you are in.'

'It was all kept very secret,' nods Anna Callaghan. 'The thought of that many people ringing up every five minutes and saying, "How are you?" would have driven her mad.'

But for some of Verity's wider circle, all this secrecy proved painful. 'I was on the South Bank, about to go to a matinée at the National,' recalls writer Howard Schuman, 'and someone called out, "Howard," and I turned around. "It's Verity," and she was so diminished. I didn't know, I hadn't heard. It was such a shock, I don't know what my expression looked like. I wanted to do something – I wanted to be useful. But she didn't want lots of people around her, helping. She didn't want the look of pity, which I wouldn't have given her. She had been an important part of my life, emotionally and professionally, and I felt I wasn't able to be there for her in any sense.'

'I hated not knowing how ill she was,' says Joanna Lumley. 'It knocked me sideways. I thought, "Did I say everything I always wanted to say to her? Had I rounded off anything?" I had nothing but admiration for her. I loved her. She knew I loved her.'

Part of the dilemma was her sheer number of friends and close acquaintances. All of them mattered to her. She did her best to marshal her declining energies and see as many as she could, without telling that them that this was her own way of saying goodbye.

'She took me to a little restaurant for lunch,' says actor Russell Enoch. 'We sat outside and talked. She was telling me how much she loved Australia. I had no idea that she was ill. It was ten days before she died and she never mentioned it.'

'I went round for a coffee and a chat,' says writer Doug Livingstone. 'We didn't talk about it – we talked about everything else, really.'

'She dragged herself out for a meal,' says Michael Aitkens. 'I hadn't seen her for quite some time and she was obviously very tired.'

'I was away on a recce for *Gavin & Stacey*,' says director Chris Gernon. 'Anna rang me and said, "You should go and see Verity quite soon." So I rang Verity and said, "I'll pop in on the way back from Wales." I went in with a bottle of champagne – I think we drank two bottles. It was a brilliant night. I left her thinking "news of her demise has been greatly exaggerated" and that was about two weeks before she died.'

When the director Waris Hussein found out on the grapevine that Verity was terminally ill, he called her up and said: '"Verity, how much of a friend am I to you?" "Why are you asking?" "Because you haven't told me and there are other people who have been told and it really is very upsetting to me. I don't understand where my link with you stops or goes." And she said, "Waris, I'm sorry I didn't tell you but I'm so conscious of not wanting people to go through what I've gone through." I said, "I'm coming to see you." At that point, she was very weak. She'd made herself some soup and my partner, Jean-Louis, and I watched her have this and I thought, "Shit, this is awful." As we were leaving the house, she said, "Did you see my new car?" It was a Mini. I was joking, "I must get one," but in my heart, I was so sad because I knew I was never going to see her again.'

When she did manage to go out, it was never too far from home. Fortunately, there were plenty of favourite restaurants and cafés nearby. 'We went off to see *La Vie en Rose* at the Electric Cinema in Portobello,' says Judy Morris. 'We sat up near the back, put our feet up and had champagne and then, at the end, we had dinner together. She started playing with ideas of music she would like to have played at her funeral. She had a very wide range of songs that she loved and we just sat there and sang them all, very softly and very gently. We did a rather smashing version of *Non, je ne regrette rien*. It was my perfect time with Verity – it was just so beautiful. She had come to grips with it in her mind – she really knew she was going to die and there was a sort of acceptance.'

Verity made an enormous effort of will to attend the director Jack Gold's 75th birthday lunch on a floating Chinese restaurant in Regent's Park. 'We picked her up from her home,' says her old friend, the producer Graham Benson. 'She was on fantastic form. If you didn't know she was so unwell, you wouldn't have known. She talked to everybody, drank a bit and then she said, "I'm tired now," but still went on to drinks in Chelsea. But that was the last time she went out.'

Verity was invited to attend a Women in Film and Television lunch, scheduled to take place on 7 December 2007. The intention was to bestow a lifetime achievement award on her[15]. It was welcome more as a distraction than for the distinction. Weak though she now was, Verity began to draft a speech and asked her old friend and mentor Jeremy Isaacs to deliver the citation at the gathering. She would not live to hear it.

As November arrived, Verity began rapidly to fade. There were daily phone calls from the small group of friends Anna Callaghan nicknamed 'Verity's Vestals': Miriam Worms in Paris, Nancy Dowd, Judy Morris, Felicity Marshall, Reggie Nadelson and Marilyn Gross. Callaghan christened herself 'Nurse Ratchet', while Dowd was referred to as 'Sister Mary Hershey Bar' and Gross was 'Sister Sadie'. Felicity Marshall, who lived nearby and would often visit first thing in the morning, was 'Sister Early Shift'. Another stalwart was Verity's close friend, Kate Kagan, with whom she had shared so much history. 'Anna would be there during the day and I used to go and visit in the evening,' she explains. 'Verity and

---

[15] The organisers asked Russell T Davies to present the award

I would have supper with her and, if she was strong enough, we'd take Bon Bon for a walk.'

Verity's first great love, Ted Kotcheff, travelled from America to say his own goodbye. 'She was confined to her bed,' he says. 'She told me all about her latest production and we just talked and laughed and reminisced as we always did.'

When he left, Anna Callaghan asked Verity: 'How did you let him slip through your fingers? He's gorgeous!' She replied, 'I think we let each other slip through our fingers, really.'

Another long-term friend, Sheila Savory, came to see Verity for the last time too. 'I hadn't seen her for a few months,' she says. 'Anna had warned me, "You're going to be terribly shocked," and I was because she had gone down to nothing. She would not talk about her health at all. The last thing she ever said to me was, "Sheila, I promise you, I never had an affair with Sydney Newman." She kept saying that and I wondered why. But it seemed to be important to her that I should know that she had got her first job as a producer on her own merits.'

Warned by Callaghan that time was running out, 'Sister Sadie', aka Marilyn Gross, arrived from her New York home to stay at Verity's house for the weekend of 17 and 18 November. 'Anna had said, "I'd like the weekend off," so I went and it was very, very tough,' says Gross. 'Her little dog normally slept on the bed but she wouldn't any more. For the two nights I was there, she sat with her nose in the corner away from her. It was weird. The dog somehow realised. They have a sense. She was in so much pain and was so drugged that in a way she didn't care that much. She said, "I don't know what's the matter, look, she won't come onto the bed." But I knew.'

'I phoned her on the Saturday afternoon,' continues Kate Kagan. 'That evening, Verity was supposed to be having supper with [writer] Simon Gray and his wife, Tory. But Verity said, "I feel so bad I think I want to go to the hospital – I'm going to phone for a taxi." And I said, "No, you're not, I'll come over," so I went over and Marilyn and I took her into hospital for the last time.'

After being admitted to a ward, Verity was eventually taken to a private room in the Royal Marsden Hospital. There was nothing to be done except to make her as comfortable as possible. 'Even then, she was joking about what we were going to do for Christmas,' smiles Kagan. 'We had spent so many Christmases together – Verity, me and my husband Michael. Just before Christmas he was due to go into hospital himself. We joked that we were going to have to take the goose there. We had this whole fantasy of planning it. We were going put on our rubber gloves and clean the kitchen thoroughly before we cooked our goose. We laughed about it so much. Michael and Verity adored one another. He had been very ill and she said, "I can't believe it – I really thought he'd go before me!" And I said "Verity! Neither of you are going anywhere." But that was very Verity – being rather indignant. She was herself on the Monday, giving everybody hell.'

It was the week of Thanksgiving in America and Marilyn Gross had to return home as she was expecting her entire family for the occasion. 'I was booked to go back on the Monday flight,' she says. 'I told her, "I will come back on Friday." I actually couldn't face going back to that empty house again, so I just turned on my heels and went straight to the airport.'

Verity asked Anna Callaghan to bring her shorthand pad with her to the hospital. 'I knew what was coming,' says Callaghan. 'She told me about the gifts she wanted made to friends after her death and her wishes for her funeral. I tried, not very successfully, to hide my tears. She said softly, "I'm really sorry to have to ask you to do this, Anna."'

For the first half of that final week, Verity remained lucid and in good spirits. Kate Kagan spoke to Colin Bucksey in America and he decided to fly over to see his ex-wife one last time. A car was sent so that Verity's stepmother Betty could visit the hospital daily from her Brighton home. The doctors advised that visitors should be strictly limited and between them, Anna Callaghan, Kath Williams and Kate Kagan acted as the gatekeepers. Close friend Viv Phillips was one of those allowed to approach the bedside. 'I whispered in her ear,' she says. 'I just said that I loved her and I thanked her for her friendship.'

David Renwick visited and told Alan Davies that Verity was not going to survive much longer.[16] Davies immediately went to the hospital himself, as he recalls: 'Anna said to me, "She's just too frail and I don't want you to see her like this. So many people are coming and the doctors are saying she's too tired and can't possibly see everyone. I'm really sorry." And I said, "It's OK, I understand, you're in a difficult position." I wrote a note and asked her to read it to Verity and to give her my love and say that I had been there – I wanted her to know that I had come. It was absolutely heartbreaking. Verity was so full of vigour and mentally absolutely as sharp as a tack – and this thing had got her. It seemed so unjust and so harsh.'

Anna Callaghan, Kath Williams or Kate Kagan were always present, keeping Verity company and watching over the woman they loved so much. Gradually, inevitably, she slipped out of consciousness.

'I told her that I loved her,' says Kagan. 'I stroked her hair and held her hand. Her oncologist encouraged me to carry on talking to her because he said that, even though it doesn't look like it, she would still be able to hear me.'

At exactly 9 p.m. on the evening of Thursday, 22 November 2007, just days before her 72nd birthday, Verity's long struggle came to an end.

The news of her death reached her ex-husband Colin Bucksey just as he was about to board a flight to London to say his own last goodbye.

---

[16] You can read an extract from Renwick's diary which describes this visit as an appendix in this book, page 373

EPILOGUE

'I believe to a large extent you get from life what you expect from it. If you look at it optimistically, you find the good things. In the same way, you can believe it is all bad. Even when I've been in the blackest tunnels, and there have been some, I've always known there would be an end to them.'

Verity to Janice Morley, *The Daily Express*, 1980

'Dying is a very un-Verity thing to do,' said writer Howard Schuman at her funeral, and the laughter that greeted his words came from a gathering of friends and colleagues who recognised the truth in them.

The day after Verity's death, Friday, 23 November, was the anniversary of the first transmission of the programme that had launched her producing career, *Doctor Who*. On that day, the cast and crew of the 2007 version were meeting in a London church hall for a read-through of two forthcoming episodes[1]. 'It was really moving because so many people around that table had worked with her,' says showrunner Russell T Davies. 'I announced, "Welcome to the read-through, everyone. This is the 23 November and I have to tell you the very sad news that Verity Lambert has died." There was an incredibly charged atmosphere. After the read-through, everyone relaxed and told stories about her.'

Davies took the decision to dedicate that year's Christmas special to Verity's memory. It was not the first time he had honoured her inestimable contribution to a programme that had now become a global brand. In *Human Nature*, an episode of the series screened

---

[1] For the episodes *Midnight* and *Turn Left*

shortly before her death, the Doctor has assumed human form in a pre-First World War boarding school. At one point, he explains that his father was called Sydney and his mother Verity. 'I put that line in on a whim really,' says Davies. 'It was quite an emotional story about his past and his childhood. And his past and his childhood was our past and our childhood. So I added that and thought it was a nice touch and would give a shiver to fans.'

Back in the real world, all the broadsheet newspapers marked Verity's death by devoting entire pages to detailed obituaries that paid tribute to a career of extraordinary achievements.

Verity had left characteristically precise instructions about the exact nature of her farewell. She was adamant that she wanted no grand memorial service (perhaps she had endured too many of these herself) and that a straightforward funeral would suffice. It was to be a strictly non-religious, humanist service and the coffin she chose was environmentally friendly and made of wicker. The service took place at Golders Green Crematorium on 4 December 2007 and was packed to the rafters with the great and the good of show business. 'It was standing room only,' says director Moira Armstrong. 'Everybody was there.'

There were executives like Paul Fox, Jeremy Isaacs, Michael Grade, Jonathan Powell and Jane Tranter. Johnny Goodman and Chris Burt were present from her Euston Films days. Eminent producers included Ken Trodd, Paul Knight, Graham Benson and Barry Hanson. Among the notable women were Helena Kennedy, Judy Morris, Janet Street-Porter and Beryl Vertue. Many of the writers Verity had championed gathered to pay their respects: John Mortimer, Simon Gray, Keith Waterhouse, Alan Ayckbourn, Doug Livingstone, Michael Aitkens, Paul Mendelson and Andy McCulloch. There were directors from throughout her career: Alvin Rakoff, Herbie Wise, Waris Hussein, James Cellan Jones, Jack Gold, Sandy Johnson, Chris Gernon, Suri Krishnamma and Chris Morahan with his wife, the actress Anna Carteret. Other actors included Peter Bowles, Judy Parfitt, Patricia Quinn, Joanna Lumley, Sheila Hancock, Sheridan Smith and Ann Mitchell, the star of *Widows*. Verity's last dog, Bon Bon, was among the crowd, resplendent in a pink Swarovski collar and escorted by casting director Susie Bruffin, who had often looked after her[2]. The Cinema Verity cabal were out in force, too. 'It was wonderful,' says presenter Joan Bakewell. 'So full of dazzling ladies who all adored her. They were all very glamorous and full of fun and had loved Verity and rejoiced with her. It was a celebration – there was no doubt.'

Verity's ex-husband Colin Bucksey had travelled from Los Angeles to be there. He was in floods of tears. 'I was very, very sad,' he says, quietly. 'There was a tremendous sense of some large part of my life having gone for good.'

---

[2] When the dog died on 26 November 2012 (the day before what would have been Verity's 77th birthday), she was buried in Kath William's garden, with the toys Verity had bought her

Lifelong friend Marilyn Gross had rushed back from America too but her plane was delayed. 'When I got there, there were so many people that they'd closed the doors. I had to stand outside with my little wheelie case. There were several others there too and we heard the service from there. I was very moved to see tears streaming down the faces of all these people I didn't know but who obviously loved Verity.'

Jill Satin, a celebrant from the British Humanist Association, led the ceremony. There were five key speakers.[3] Tamsin Greig paid fulsome tribute to the way Verity had made it possible for her to continue filming as a working mother. Linda Agran told the story of her riotous Concorde trip with Verity, while Alan Davies addressed the crowd with a degree of trepidation. 'It was a big thing to be asked to do,' he says. 'I'd never spoken at a funeral before or since and I found it very difficult. Her coffin was just a few feet away, so it almost felt like she was there, right in front of you. I told the story about the time we had a Jack Russell on the set of *Jonathan Creek*. The Jack Russell was supposed to attack Jonathan, and Verity had been told that this dog would bark and growl on command. It was the meekest animal you've ever seen in your life. Verity tore into this dog handler. We were joking about it, saying, "Can't we just get Verity in a dog outfit?" All her friends laughed and laughed.'

But not everyone was amused. 'I got very upset at her funeral,' admits writer Lynda La Plante, 'because I thought that it wasn't serious enough. Verity was one of the most talented women we have ever had in television. She had her hand on the pulse and she fought for it. She was never ever afraid to fight for something, rightly or wrongly. She was my mentor and even to talk about her now makes me emotional because I just loved her strength. She was a tigress. It saddened me greatly that there wasn't someone there who could stand up with authority and say, "We've just lost a very important person." To add some weight to the funny, silly stories.'

The actress Eileen Atkins read a farewell note from her friend Miriam Worms and another from a group of Verity's many Australian friends, saying: 'Verity's second home was Australia. She was a woman of intelligence, creativity, passion and extraordinary kindness. She loved sunshine and laughter and provided both. She became one of us. We just loved her. You remain in our hearts forever, Verity. You are a star in our Southern Cross.'

Howard Schuman was the last to speak and he was finally able to articulate how much she had meant to him over the years, albeit not to Verity herself. 'But she had asked that I speak,' he says. 'I found that incredibly powerful and moving. She was one of the most vivid people I've ever met – I miss that atmosphere of passion, vitality and ebullience.'

The music played included some of the themes from Verity's most successful

---

[3] In addition, Lynda La Plante and Joanna Lumley were invited to speak. Both declined on the grounds that they feared that they would simply be too upset

programmes, including *Doctor Who*, but when the coffin slid out of view, it did so to the defiantly cheerful strains of the signature tune from her beloved *The Archers*. Most of the congregation left with smiles as well as tears, although veteran television executive Paul Fox was heard to remark, 'If Verity had been in charge, it would have been half an hour shorter.'

'Fair enough,' says Kath Williams, 'but Verity loved to laugh and would have enjoyed that people both cried and laughed at her funeral.'

'She had organised the whole thing right up to the last minute,' comments actress Carole Ann Ford. 'Typical Verity, really. It was beautiful, uplifting. People said, "It sounds totally incongruous but I've had a wonderful time." A couple of years later when my mother died, I had to organise her funeral and I based it on Verity's.'

Over in Australia, a small group of friends timed their own gathering to coincide with the day of the funeral, among them director Fred Schepisi and his wife Mary, Jill Bilcock, the film editor on *A Cry in the Dark*, and the actress Nadine Garner from *Boys from the Bush* and *Class Act*. 'We all went out for lunch,' says Felicity Marshall. 'We put some roses on the table with a beautiful photo of Verity and we toasted her and talked about her. We gave her a send-off as best we could.'

'She was a very dear friend of ours,' adds Schepisi. 'I just liked her spirit. She got good things done, sometimes groundbreaking things, and that's important. I miss her energy, I miss the humour and the encouragement. I wish she was around now.'

Back in London, the wake was held at the Groucho Club, a private members' establishment beloved of London's media types in which Verity had shrewdly invested. Director Chris Gernon was among the crowd who gathered to drink the night away. 'I was filming in Wales but I said, "I've got to be there." The company were brilliant and let me have the day off. I was supposed to be on the eight o'clock train back that evening but I was still in the Groucho Club at half past eleven. They just sent a car for me. Verity would have approved enormously.'

The next day, the *Daily Mail* carried an unusual story claiming that, on leaving the club, Alan Davies had become embroiled in an altercation with a tramp, culminating in him biting the man's ear. It was farcical and odd but more than anything, humiliating for the actor. 'That day was so emotional,' he says. 'I came out and there was someone shouting abuse at me and calling me Jonathan all the time. I told him that if he didn't shut up I'd bite his ear. He didn't, so I did. The fact that this guy then went straight to the tabloids and not to the police tells you all you need to know. But I was very ashamed about doing what I did because I was conscious that it would become associated with her funeral and she was so dignified and classy. In fact, she was one of the few people that, had she been alive, I could have spoken to about it. I could have called her up and said, "Oh God, I've really fucked up this time, I don't know what I've done. I lost my temper with someone." And she'd have found the right way to tell me, "Not to worry. Don't read the papers. You're a good person and you were provoked and I understand. You've got to be careful if you've had a lot to drink in London; people are going to get in touch with the tabloids. You've got to watch out for these people." She would have been protective of me. Now, if I recall her, then I behave better.'[4]

'That biting of the ear,' laughs Kate Kagan. 'Verity would have been in heaven. When I next saw Alan, I told him, "You've no idea how Verity that was – if she'd been with you, she'd have gone for the other ear!" She would have loved it.'

Journalist Reggie Nadelson, who had known Verity for 20 years, arrived from her native New York just too late to see her before she died[5]. But she was able to attend the funeral and, a few days later, pay her own tribute at the Women in Film and Television event at which Verity had been due to receive her lifetime achievement award. Nadelson told the audience: 'Verity said, in her inimitable way, that she was lousy at making speeches and didn't want to bore anybody. One of the things a lot of people don't know about her is how modest she was, diffident almost, and shy. You think of her as tenacious, fierce, powerful, assertive, and she was, a woman who defended her own work and those of people she believed in. But she would have been astonished at the outpouring of attention and admiration and love. I wish she was here for it.'

Nadelson then introduced Jeremy Isaacs, who delivered a summary of Verity's glittering career before returning to read the words Verity herself had written during her last weeks: 'I feel very fortunate to have worked with some of the best actors, writers, directors and crew throughout my career. I was so lucky when I was a young woman to work with Sydney Newman and Ted Kotcheff on *Armchair Theatre*. I learnt a great deal from watching Sydney produce and Ted direct. But the two most important things I learnt were never to be afraid to say what you think and you never have to take no for an answer. I have had a wonderful time working. I've had loads of fun and I have been happy 95 per cent of the time, which I think is pretty damned good.'

For some of Verity's wider circle, her death was undoubtedly a shock although one from which they soon recovered. But for those with a deeper emotional engagement, the sense of loss continues. During the writing of this book, it was evident to me that Verity has left an enormous and lasting void in the lives of those who truly loved her.

'She was more of a sister than a friend,' says Marilyn Gross. 'She was a true individual with a strong sense of herself and what is right. I'll always miss her.'

Unsurprisingly, the 'sister' analogy recurs among several of the women closest to Verity; another who shared the same sentiment, Viv Phillips, says: 'She was a big sister to me

---

[4] David Renwick included a sly nod to the incident in the 2014 *Jonathan Creek* episode, *The Letters of Septimus Noone*

[5] She was busy with a newspaper writing assignment

and a bossy one at that. People often commented that they didn't know how or why I put up with the way she spoke to me at times, but that's what sisters do and I knew it was a sign of affection. Her friendship was a delight to me. She had this reputation for being as hard as nails and volatile, but I was terribly privileged to see the other side of her: the sweet, shy and gentle side. When she died, she left a huge empty space in my life.'

'She was my big sister,' smiles Kate Kagan. 'She used to call me her "kid sister". She was a very positive, optimistic person. If I ever got down or distressed about anything, she was wonderful. She was a huge part of my life. I loved her very much.'

'Damn it, I miss her, I really do,' says writer Nancy Dowd. 'She was a groovy older sister. I've just finished writing a play. I used to pass everything I wrote past Verity and knew I was going to get an intelligent response, one that would be valuable to me. Now I realise there's no one to show it to – nobody. I sincerely hope my friendship meant to her even a fraction of what hers meant to me. Ever since Verity died, I just feel totally alone.'

'I was devastated when she died,' says writer Doug Livingstone, who keeps Verity's photograph on his kitchen wall. 'I haven't worked in television since. I miss the way that we worked and the relationship that we had. I don't remember a single serious row with her about scripts. Certainly, she was never cruel and she was always such wonderful company. I really do miss her every single day.'

'I think I have a problem with really processing it,' says her screenwriter friend Judy Morris. 'I will see someone in the street and I will definitely think, for maybe a split second, "Oh, there's Verity." Afterwards, maybe for three or four seconds, I have to go through it in my head and think, "No, it can't be her." Things remind you. I miss her terribly but, on the other hand, Verity is a joy to me. When I think of her, and I do so all the time, I find myself with a smile on my face.'

'I was just heartbroken because she was one of my best friends,' says Australian publicist Rea Francis. 'And I'm sure 20 or 30 people would call themselves that. She was special. When she laughed, it was a joy to be near her.'

'The first thing that comes into my head is her smiling and laughing,' says actress Sheila Hancock. 'I've still got her picture on my desk. She was an inspirational figure for women, breaking through at a time when it was very unusual. She taught the guys that they needn't be frightened of women in that position. She had a vision and she went for it.'

'It was like losing a relative,' says the writer David Renwick. 'I just miss her presence as a person. After that, work comes a poor second because in the scheme of things, it is so incidental. One does wonder what she'd have made of the way the industry has gone. She was getting frustrated, as we all were, by the way things were going anyway. But I can't believe that she would ever have opted for retirement.'

'If you were to ask me if I had any regrets in my career,' says director Suri Krishnamma, 'it would be that I never worked with Verity again, because she had every single possible

EPILOGUE

characteristic and quality – intelligence, style and sensibility – that you'd want in a producer and also a friend. I don't think there is anybody else like her and I don't think there ever will be.'

'She was a wonderful enabler,' says Sharon Bloom, who started as Verity's PA and is now a leading drama producer herself. 'I'm here because of her. No one will ever have a career like her because now with television you just can't. But we were all her kids, in one way or another.'

'I'm going to be outrageously sexist here,' says producer John Lloyd. 'There is a class of woman you see now who are power-dressed, supposedly ball-busting and tougher than the men. They are sort of pretend-men. Verity was able to be really, really good and hold down proper, serious, responsible jobs and yet never not be feminine. She could be tough and nice at the same time, and was always herself, whether she was in a board meeting, or running a programme, or at a party. There weren't a set of Veritys that would apply to different people. She would be exactly the same to an office cleaner or a member of the royal family.'

'My view is that she was profoundly content with what she did,' says writer and presenter Melvyn Bragg. 'That's because she knew she was really good at it and she knew she was good at it because good people told her and audiences told her. She was a serious star.'

'Her legacy is that she was an important part of a very creative moment in our history,' believes director Alvin Rakoff. 'We were working in the most profound theatre of our time. Television was everyman's theatre. We knew we were communicating and setting new boundaries, vistas of entertainment, in every aspect. It will never happen again.'

For the principal executors of Verity's will, Anna Callaghan and Kath Williams, her death was just the beginning of a colossal and complex dispersal of her estate. Verity was a wealthy woman and, as well as the sizeable sums left to the principal beneficiaries, Kate Kagan and Anna Callaghan, there were various generous cash bequests besides, including provision for Verity's stepmother Betty, as well as to her godson, Finn MacCabe. Money was also left to the Royal Marsden hospital, the International Fund for Animal Welfare and Crusaid, an HIV/AIDS charity. In addition, there were a range of specially chosen gifts for friends far and wide. Marilyn Gross was bequeathed jewellery that had belonged to Verity's mother. Viv Phillips treasures an exquisite gold bracelet. Verity's South Sea pearls went to Miriam Worms. Sheila Savory received a beautiful Victorian lorgnette. Reggie Nadelson still wears one of Verity's watches. Sharon Bloom was given a charm bracelet[6]. For Kate Kagan, there were precious pieces of Art Deco and Art Nouveau

---

[6] Sharon Bloom recalls: 'Years before, at Thorn EMI, there was somebody who had been left downstairs for too long and was about to leave. I told her this and she was angry with me and said, "Well, go and use your fucking charm and get him to stay." She did think I was quite charming so I wonder if that was why she gave me the charm bracelet?'

pewter and glass. Others were given scarves, paintings, *objets d'art*, pieces of glass and some were grateful for a selection of Verity's extensive collection of cookery books. Even the last jars of jam she had made were distributed among friends. At Verity's request, Kath Williams took care of the little dog, Bon Bon. Williams also took possession of the striking June Mendoza portrait of Verity, which she gave pride of place in her home.[7]

'There was a lot of stuff to do,' says Williams. 'Verity was a woman who never threw anything away. She even filed her electricity bills. Any present which anybody had given her over the last 50 years was kept even if it was crap. She had these underground vaults – two of them – and when you opened them, it was like Aladdin's Cave, floor to ceiling, but filled with rubbish. Things like salt and pepper shakers shaped like a banana and an apple.'

'You've never seen so much stuff,' continues Anna Callaghan. 'Every time we opened another cupboard, another tonne of luggage would fall out. Her clothes were kept beautifully. There were long cupboards full of evening dresses and some for jackets – it was practically colour-coded, with shoes kept mainly in their boxes. She had the most enormous amount of storage space. There was a spare room at the top of the house next to the office with more storage space. Those two rooms alone were groaning with stuff. I remember having lunch with Marilyn Gross. It was only a week or so after the funeral and we were all fairly raw. She said to me, "You know this is going to take two years of your life," and I thought, "I can't believe that," but it was actually almost exactly two years until we sold the Antibes flat. It was onerous because you have a responsibility and it is very emotional besides.'

Eventually, there was an auction of some of the finest pieces of furniture, art, glass and ceramics from Verity's homes. Boxes of cuttings, photographs, awards and other ephemera were sent for posterity to the University of Strathclyde. Bundles of the more personal photographs were claimed by friends and family.

Although she had never seriously contemplated retirement, Verity had hoped to spend more time in her bijou apartment in Antibes. It was not be. But it was here that she wanted her ashes to be scattered. Accordingly, around midday on 29 June 2008, a small group of Verity's inner circle gathered in Antibes to follow her final wishes and carry out this farewell ritual. It was a brilliant summer's day with scarcely a breeze. A boat, poetically named Paradise, was arranged to take the mourners – Anna Callaghan, Kath Williams and her partner Kate Dunn, Peggy Taylor, who had found the Antibes apartment for Verity, and Kate and Michael Kagan[8] – out into the startling aquamarine waters of the bay which had made the view from Verity's apartment such a delight to her. The Kagans had written some words which Michael now read out, his voice thick with emotion: 'We

---

[7] Her intention is to leave the portrait to the University of Strathclyde

[8] Also present was the lady who had cleaned Verity's Antibes flat

spent many happy years together. We shared a lot of happy and sad memories. You going away leaves an enormous vacuum in our lives. Farewell, our dearest friend. We love you and will never forget you.'

He then took Verity's ashes from their container and, with Anna Callaghan's help, tipped them gently over the side of the boat. Verity had asked that her beloved Arthur's ashes be scattered with hers but the little casket in which they had been kept was so well sealed that it had to be dropped into the water unopened.

Soon, the last of the ashes vanished into the depths and there was nothing left to see.

But Verity has not entirely vanished from view, nor will she. Such was the vivid force of her personality that she has left the echo of herself everywhere, not just in the hearts and minds of those who knew and loved her, but in the many interviews she gave, her frank and good-humoured contributions to documentaries and commentaries, in the scores of anecdotes told about her on screen and in print, and with the breathtaking legacy of five decades' work, which will ensure that she continues to fascinate and enthral in generations to come.

A reassuring thread of consistency runs throughout the timeline of Verity's life. Whenever you stop the clock, she emerges recognisably the same – bright, demanding, tenacious, full of humour and vitality, quick-tempered and impatient, loyal and generous, frequently strident, sometimes curiously shy. It is not difficult to close your eyes and conjure her up again; as the apple of her father's eye, sensing that, for her, there was more to life than suburban Jewish respectability; as ABC's live-wire PA, ambitious, quick-witted, chain-smoking, sexy and capable; as the young producer at the BBC, beautifully dressed, smiling with delight at the viewing figures of her first great success; as the dynamic head of department, short of time but full of purpose, ready to let her temper blaze at the first sign of incompetence or idleness; as friend and lover, beguiling with those pitch-black eyes, ready to drink and dance and party, enjoying herself without inhibition; someone with the intoxicating power to make those on whom she fixed her attention feel at the absolute centre of things; and then, finally, there is the older woman both enriched and scarred by experience, dying by degrees and facing the cruel havoc of a terrible disease with dignity and no rancour for the random injustice of it all.

All of these women were remarkable and interesting and worthy of celebration.

All of these women were Verity Lambert.

APPENDIX

DAVID RENWICK DIARY ENTRIES

These extracts from David Renwick's diaries are reproduced with his kind permission and they are presented as originally written.

Still some daylight about when I left the house at three, but by the time I rolled up in the Fulham Road the roads were black and damp and the atmosphere decidedly uninviting. I had no trouble locating the Horder Ward on the fifth floor of Granard House, the palliative care wing to which Verity had now been transferred. I had a short wait by the unmanned desk before someone appeared and directed me to Room Eleven, and when I tapped on the door and opened it there were a couple of doctors inside, and Anna hastily stepped out to welcome me. I gave her a huge hug and told her how magnificent she had been through all this, and she immediately collapsed into a mass of tears, and as we sat in the nearby day room she poured out her emotions, how astonishing Verity had been – 'Never a word of self-pity, of 'Why me?', she just says 'Well, you just have to get on with it don't you'.'

And the tragedy of this Women in Film lunch on the 7th December where she was about to receive a lifetime achievement award: she and Anna had made arrangements to go to Selfridges tomorrow and have a personal shopper help with a new outfit for the occasion. Even the fact that her 72nd birthday is looming, a week today ... and only ten days ago she had been to a friend's party, looking so nicely turned out and had such a great time, drank some champagne and stayed rather later than planned - and now it had all accelerated so alarmingly. 'Today has been the worst so far,' Anna said, as she clutched all the paperwork for Verity's will, and various codicils which she was having to deal with, having struggled with all the complicated business of signatories – the fact that the nurse wasn't entitled to witness because she was caring for the patient, and so on. And then the doctors left and we went in, and Verity greeted me with a big smile and thanked me for coming, and I gave her big kisses and embraced her and said 'How could I not?' And just said how pleased I was she wanted to see me. Because in truth she's not seeing many people at all – Anna had arranged for her stepmother, 92, to be driven up from Brighton today, and she'd now left, but is due to return tomorrow. Verity hadn't seen her for a year or more, and hadn't even told her she was sick, so it must have been quite a shock. The room was small and sterile in that rather institutional way, not remotely modern, and with little feel of creature comforts about it: you couldn't call it cosy. A tiny TV slung on a bracket in the far corner, a couple of chairs, in which Anna and Verity's friend Kate sat while I opted to perch on the bed and clasp her hand as we talked.

Anna had warned me how ill she looked, saying she was much more yellow today, as the liver just continued to shut down. But the colour of her skin didn't strike me that much, more the weight she'd lost since I last saw her a few weeks ago. And for the most part she remained pretty bright in her personality, though without the energy and strength to behave the way she would have liked to. She was propped up in the bed, with no wig, but enough grey curls on her head to look more than presentable, with oxygen tubes disappearing up her nose and various other tubes connected into the chest. And her voice, still utterly recognisably her own, was weakened and faltering, but her hearing seemed absolutely fine and mentally she was as alert as ever. Which helped enormously, because her brightness and evident acceptance, now, of the inevitable meant we could talk with the subtext of complete understanding, with no need to bring it directly to the surface. The closest she got was to say 'The news isn't very good I'm afraid …'

And then we began reflecting upon our ten-year collaboration, she said how very fond of me she was, and how inauspicious it had all been when she first went into Geoffrey Perkins' office and said 'Who do I have to impress?' and he said 'David Renwick', and Verity thought 'This sounds like a poisoned chalice.' But, I said, it wasn't long was it, before everything settled down and we built up a mutual respect and trust that was to last throughout our relationship. One of the many things I had always admired about her was her honesty (how her name couldn't have been more appropriate!), and her ability to confront problems and deal with them, whereas I had always had this head in the sand attitude. 'Yes I'm sorry,' she said, 'that I've very often had to be such a nag.' She quoted some bits of advice she'd always remembered from Sydney Newman and Ted Kotcheff that she'd been planning to feature in her speech at this lunch – 'which I'm not sure if I'll get to now' … and this, along with her confession that she was missing her beloved Bon Bon, was one of the most upsetting moments of all. At one point Emma Strain popped in briefly to drop off a disc for me from the office, and a bunch of well-wishing cards for Verity, her face wreathed in a big grin – 'Can I have a kiss?'

A tray was brought in with some tea – a plate bearing a tiny sliver of plaice with two slices of lemon on top, and a little jug of parsley sauce which I poured beside the fish for her. She struggled with her knife and fork to detach a morsel or two, but the effort of actually chewing and swallowing seemed to defeat her, and after a while she had to give up: 'This is such a bore.' I said one of the worst things was to have to stare at food you couldn't manage, so I covered it up again and put the tray down on the floor, while she had a valiant go at a little pot of red jelly with a spoon, and managed about half of it. Then Anna brought in a carton of Fruits of the Forest flavoured nutritional drink, which she had better luck with, sucking through a straw. But it was at these moments that the raw sapping of all physical power became sadly evident. She even struggled to get through a long message Jane Tranter had written in her card, saying she'd leave it till tomorrow. She was half way through a spy book, but I got the feeling her appetite for reading was receding dramatically now. They had just started her on morphine today, to head off any prospect of pain, which was presumably making her drowsy.

When I looked at my watch and found it was seven o'clock I was quite surprised. Anna was now preparing to leave and said she looked a bit tired, so it was a natural point to say our goodbyes. All of which you just try and make as casual as possible, with references to talking again if she's up to it, and religiously steering off the dreadful realisation that this is probably the last time I will ever see her. And she thanked me again for coming and sent her love to Ellie and we kissed on the lips, and then Anna and I closed the door upon her and walked away, and once again Anna's brave front was wiped away as if with a duster, as her voice crumbled and outside on the pavement she told me that Verity had made all her wishes known now – she wanted a wicker coffin, no religious ceremony, and no memorial service, just a big party. Goodness alone knows how Anna's managed to cope with all this – only yesterday she was talking to Lynda La Plante and Jeremy Isaacs about coming to this big lunch - and there's another friend who's supposed to be coming over from America on Saturday but she doesn't know how best to advise her now. 'When I started working with her 20 years ago, someone asked me, "What's Verity Lambert like?" and I said, "Oh she's very nice, very nice to work for, but she'll never be a friend."' And how wrong could she have been. Now she would just go home and have a very large gin. And I left her and returned to my car full of haunting thoughts and images, and drove home through the dismal autumn rain, relaying it all to Ellie for much of the way, then rang off, and was left alone with my memories. So hard for the enormity of it all to really sink in, but as I said to Ellie, it's astonishing how those tiny, final shreds of life are still so, so important, marking the utter, infinite distinction between existence and non-existence. For all her frailty and reduced circumstances, sitting there in the bed with her life ebbing away, it was still Verity, in the flesh, communicating with me, her essence intact. And I shall be forever grateful for this experience. Anna said she had definitely perked up while I was there, but I worry now, whether I may have stayed on too long and tired her too much.

DRAMA AND DELIGHT

Verity's funeral, Golders Green Crematorium – 4th December 2007

Outside the West Chapel the crowd was building, as instructions were barked out for everyone to make way for the hearse, which pulled up just past the entrance, with Verity's strangely attractive wicker coffin visible inches away from us through the glass, covered with flowers. By now you were noticing so many familiar faces it was impossible to keep track or catch their eye and acknowledge them all. On the other side of the vehicle opposite us were Tamsin Greig and her husband Rick, and Sandy Johnson, and then Jonathan Powell, Paul Fox, Jeremy Isaacs, Will Wyatt and Rebecca Front. And seemingly everyone from our own crews on *Creek* and *Love Soup*, past and present. John Mortimer, looking grave and fragile, was pushed in, in his wheelchair, and as the coffin was borne off Anna followed with Verity's closest friends, and her surprisingly fit looking stepmother. The chapel was already filling up as we entered – the front rows already fully occupied. John Asbridge, our designer, was distributing programmes bearing moving photographs of Verity at various stages of her life, and I gave him a hug and we took our seats in a long pew near the back. Film editor John MacDonnell to my right, Sheridan Smith on Ellie's left – the latter sobbing sporadically through the service, while Ellie passed her some tissues. From then on the mourners seem to increase exponentially, to the point where you just didn't imagine any more people could be accommodated in the old wooden vaulted building. The likes of Michael Grade and Joanna Lumley were all standing with the best of them, and it proved to be a long, slightly rambling affair, which you can't help but feel Verity would have taken the scissors to, with some fairly brutal script editing. The sentiment was unquestioned though – everyone desperate to pay tribute to this remarkable individual, who the celebrant Jane Satin declared had touched all our lives.

Tamsin was the first to step up, although through the sea of heads we could see nothing of any of the speakers. But at least their words were amplified. She spoke with steady, unhurried confidence, semi-improvising as she recounted the details of her first meeting with Verity at the Russian Tea Room in Primrose Hill during a guest appearance on *Jonathan Creek*, and elicited chuckles along the way as she moved on to her time spent working on *Love Soup*, how accommodating Verity had been about her need to breast-feed on the set, and finally cracking just before she came to read out the letter she'd written that last day in the hospital.

Linda Agran gave a highly eloquent address that painted an interesting picture of the Verity we barely knew, in her earlier, headier days, and said of one thing she was certain, that Verity had absolutely no fear of death, and had regarded the breast cancer she fought in the seventies as a rather stimulating challenge.

Howard Schuman spoke of her support when he did *Rock Follies* and how close they had grown in the ensuing years, working on a batch of projects which ultimately never saw the light of day. All interspersed with more remarks and other tributes read out by Ms Satin. So much so that I think we were sorely (literally) in need of the more cathartic, effortless laughs that Alan Davies delivered when he stepped up towards the end. With all the skill you would expect of a practised stand-up comedian he elicited genuine amusement describing the incident with the uncooperative Jack Russell on *Creek*, when Verity had completely lost her rag with the handler and demonstrated all the canine fury that was lacking in the performer. And a similar doggy story describing the antics of her Great Dane Arthur Daley at the unit base at lunchtimes.

Eileen Atkins concluded the proceedings with some messages from Verity's friends in Australia, and then the familiar music from *The Archers* struck up, followed by a succession of theme tunes from Verity's massive output of programmes, as we all slowly filed out through the door at the other end. Passing Bon Bon, on the lap of her friend Suzy, was too much for Ellie and me – and for Terry Elms our sound recordist, who emerged weeping – and once again we broke down as the harsh reality of it all sank in. Most people present were going on to the Groucho Club for the 'party', but with our sick cat Walter to worry about we proffered our apologies and drove home, leaving them all to their scheduled revels in town.

BIBLIOGRAPHY

Alvarado, Manuel and Buscombe, Edward: *Hazell: The Making of a TV Series* (BFI/Latimer, 1978)

Alvarado, Manuel and Stewart, John: *Made for Television: Euston Films Limited* (British Film Institute, 1985)

Battaglio, Stephen: *David Susskind: A Televised Life* (St Martin's Press, 2010)

Bowles, Peter: *Ask Me if I'm Happy: An Actor's Life* (Simon & Schuster, 2011)

Carney, Jessica: *Who's There?: The Life and Career of William Hartnell* (Virgin, 1996)

Cowgill, Bryan: *Mr Action Replay* (Sports Masters International, 2006)

Dark, John: *Dark at the Top of the Stairs* (Arima Publishing, 2007)

Davies, Russell T and Cook, Benjamin: *The Writer's Tale: The Final Chapter* (BBC Books, 2010)

Day-Lewis, Sean: *Talk of Drama: Views of the Television Dramatist Now and Then* (University of Luton Press, 1998)

De Bono, Edward: *Tactics: The Art and Science of Success* (Collins, 1985)

Dougary, Ginny: *The Executive Tart and other myths* (Virago Press, 1994)

Franklin, Bob (Editor): *Television Policy: The MacTaggart Lectures* (Edinburgh University Press, 2005)

Graham Scott, Peter: *British Television: An Insider's History* (McFarland and Co, 2000)

Grove, Valerie: *A Voyage round John Mortimer* (Viking, 2007)

Haining, Peter (Editor): *Doctor Who: A Celebration* (W H Allen, 1983)

Howard, Elizabeth Jane: *Slipstream* (Macmillan, 2002)

Isaacs, Jeremy: *Look Me in the Eye: A Life in Television* (Little Brown, 2006)

Kelly, Richard (Editor): *Alan Clarke* (Faber and Faber, 1998)

Naggar, Jean: *Sipping from the Nile* (Amazon Encore, 2008)

Neame, Christopher: *A Take on British TV Drama* (Scarecrow Press, 2004)

Norden, Denis (Narrated by): *Coming to You Live!* (Methuen, 1985)

Pike, Frank (Editor): *Ah! Mischief: The Writer and Television* (Faber and Faber, 1982)

Shubik, Irene: *Play for Today: The Evolution of Television Drama* - second edition (Manchester University Press, 2000)

Sturman, Robert: *Eldorado: The Definitive Guide to a Year in the Sun* (The Gilded Man Publishing, 2001)

Various: *The Armchair Theatre: How to write, design, direct, act, enjoy television plays* (Weidenfeld and Nicolson, 1959)

Vinnicombe, Susan and Bank, John: *Women with Attitude: Lessons for Career Management* (Routledge, 2003)

Walker, Alexander: *Icons in the Fire: The Rise and Fall of Practically Everyone in the British Film Industry 1984–2000* (Orion, 2005)

Walker, Stephen James (Editor): *Talkback: The Unofficial and Unauthorised Doctor Who Interview Book: Volume One* (Telos, 2006)

Ward, Mark: *Out of the Unknown: A guide to the legendary BBC series* (Kaleidoscope, 2004)

White, Leonard: *Armchair Theatre: The Lost Years* (Kelly Publications, 2003)

FROM THE SAME AUTHOR

THE LIFE & SCANDALOUS TIMES OF

by Richard Marson

For more than a decade, John Nathan-Turner, or 'JN-T' as he was often known, was in charge of every major artistic and practical decision affecting the world's longest-running science fiction programme, **Doctor Who**. Richard Marson brings his dramatic, farcical, sometimes scandalous and often moving story to life with the benefit of his own inside knowledge and the fruits of over 100 revealing interviews with key friends and colleagues, those John loved and those from whom he became estranged. The author has also had access to all of Nathan-Turner's surviving archive of paperwork and photos, many of which appear here for the very first time.

"Extraordinary. A great piece of work. I read it in two days' flat, I couldn't stop. I've never seen a biographer enter the story like that, it was brilliant and invigorating. It really is a major piece of **Doctor Who** history and the history of an entire industry. An entire age, really. In the end, I think the book is clear - we have to forgive JN-T. That ending - he didn't deserve that. And I think by writing about it, you have made something elegant and even beautiful out of such a wretched mess. And I think that's very kind of you indeed. This book says a lot about JN-T but it says a lot about your good and kind heart too."

Russell T. Davies (Writer/Producer)

ISBN 978-1-908630-13-1

ALSO AVAILABLE FROM MIWK PUBLISHING

THE QUEST FOR PEDLER

THE LIFE AND IDEAS OF DR KIT PEDLER

by Michael Seely

For many people, Kit Pedler is best remembered as the man who created the Cybermen for **Doctor Who**, a real life scientist who was brought in to act as an advisor and bring some science to the fiction. The Cybermen were his ultimate scientific horror: where the very nature of a man was altered by himself, by his own genius for survival, creating a monster. Pedler was that rare animal, a scientist with an imagination. He liked to think 'What if...?'

Together with his friend and writing partner Gerry Davis, he created the hugely successful and controversial BBC1 drama series **Doomwatch**, which captured this fear and frightened the adults as much as the Cybermen scared the children.

Resigning from the Institute, Pedler turned his back on the world he had spent his adult life working in, and spent the rest of it campaigning for a real Doomwatch, to stop the unnecessary and cruel animal experiments in the laboratory (which he himself had seen in his earlier academic days), experiment in what we would now call eco-friendly housing, alternative technology and began to change his own relationship to the world. This lead to his book *The Quest For Gaia*, published in 1979 where he envisaged how a Gaian life-style would work in the post-industrial age. He also designed and built a nuclear bomb in rural Kent.

Before his premature death in 1981, he had just finished a documentary series for ITV called **Mind Over Matter**, which was the first serious look at the world of the paranormal through the eyes of his enquiring and rational, but imaginative mind.

With contributions from his family, friends, colleagues and critics, this book tells the story behind a fascinating, charismatic, complicated, and demanding human being; a natural teacher who didn't just want to pontificate about the problems facing the world in a television or radio studio, but actually do something practical about them..

ISBN 978-1-908630-12-4

COMING SOON FROM **MIWK PUBLISHING**

ELSIE HARRIS
PICTURE PALACE

A GRAPHIC NOVEL FROM JESSICA MARTIN

Elsie Harris may be serving tea now, but in the next few years she'll be one of the most powerful women in Hollywood.

Sometimes single, seemingly catastrophic events in a person's life can be the most serendipitous. Sacked from her job at Lyons Corner House, Elsie's life is only just beginning.

ISBN 978-1-908630-38-4

COMING SOON FROM **MIWK PUBLISHING**

MAC

THE LIFE AND WORK OF MALCOLM HULKE

by John Williams

Malcolm Hulke wrote some of the best-loved **Doctor Who** stories and novelizations and his work continues to be influential long after his premature death in 1979. All the various manifestations of **Doctor Who** since then, including the New Adventure novels, the Big Finish audio adventures and the 2005 series have returned regularly to his creations, particularly the Silurians and Sea Devils, but also to his abiding ideas and themes.

Despite this enduring influence, little is known about the man himself aside from his background as a member of the Communist Party of Great Britain and the bare facts of his career as a writer. That career involved writing for some landmark television series including **Armchair Theatre**, **Pathfinders in Space**, **The Avengers**, **Crossroads** and, of course, **Doctor Who**. Hulke also had a flourishing career in non-fiction writing, most notably when he used his many years of experience to produce Writing for Television in the 1970s which became the standard text in its field.

Hulke was the writers' writer. He was always professional, never missed a deadline and would take pride in turning his hand to anything. Although engaged in an intensely solitary profession he constantly forged alliances either with other writers such as Eric Paice and Terrance Dicks, or enthusiastically engaged with socially significant group endeavours such as Unity Theatre or the Writers' Guild. All these aspects of his life will be explored in depth and add to the picture of a complex and paradoxical individual.

ISBN 978-1-908630-09-4

www.miwk.com/

www.facebook.com/MiwkPublishingLtd

www.twitter.com/#!/MiwkPublishing